The
American
Scene

The American Scene

BY HENRY JAMES

Introduction and Notes by *LEON EDEL*

Indiana University Press
Bloomington and London

JUN 8 1978

Contents

INTRODUCTION

Henry James's book about his own land and his own people was written after a twenty-years' absence from the United States. He had sailed from New York in 1883 in his forty-first year, leaving behind a modest bustling city–modest by comparison with London and Paris–of small buildings huddled together on the lower part of Manhattan Island. He returned in 1904, in his sixty-first year, to find sunlight catching the tops of the early skyscrapers and a skyline that looked like a "broken hair-comb turned up." He had known a provincial city of commerce; he found "a vast crude democracy of trade."

He came back with a confusion of feeling: a desire to re-assess his personal past; to put himself into touch with the homeland to which he had always remained loyal in spite of his constituted cosmopolitanism. Moreover he wanted to write a book of impressions, a kind of *Return of the Native*–only, as he remarked, Thomas Hardy had used that title long before. He found, in the end, a happier one for this particular book, *The American Scene*.

James did not regard himself as a Tocqueville or a Bryce, examining the New World through the measured values of the Old, through the lens of history, economics, or political science. Nor was he like the novelist-travelers in America, Dickens or Trollope, foreign voyagers with an eye for the bizarre and the idiosyncratic. He was simply an American who had skipped twenty years of his nation's life–twenty crucial years, as he knew; and if he could not altogether catch up with this past that had been *his* future, he could at least take an honest look at the present "with much of the freshness of eye, outward and inward." His eye had become almost as fresh as that of inquiring strangers; and yet he had the advantage of not being a stranger. He had been, all the years of his writing life, a conscientious trav-

eler, in England, France, Italy; his travel writings, ultimately embodied in *English Hours, Italian Hours, A Little
Tour in France*, had been shrewd and good-natured observations of people, life, customs, manners, art. He had called
himself, on the Continent, "the sentimental traveller," in
England, "the observant stranger." In his own land he now
thought of himself as "the restless analyst." *The American
Scene* contains an exuberance of observation, a depth of
historical feeling, and a personal involvement not to be
found in his other travel writings. The others had been
written mainly to bring home to Americans—then still distant from Europe—a sense of the picturesque, the quaint, the
beautiful, in foreign lands; and always as a sensitive American might see them. *The American Scene* contains a more
personal fund of emotion, and the stance of an elderly seer.
His book, James explained, would have to be "absolutely
personal to myself and proper to my situation." This situation was that the country he had left had been still the
land of the Founding Fathers; now it was a land in the full
tide of expansion and exploitation, with the gates of immigration wide open, bringing into the eastern cities strange
languages and accents and faces alien to his own time.
James told himself that he could not be vague or speculative; he could write best that which he saw, and he insisted
on seeing all that he could. He asked himself subtle questions, such as whether his impressions represented "the
extinction of old sensibilities" or "only new forms of them."
He was careful not to allow nostalgia or the elegiac to
becloud the immediate. Of his earnest search we can judge
by the "hard" traveling he did, southward and westward,
into parts of the United States that had barely existed two
decades before; and by the packed pages of his book, filled,
as he said, "with the romance of elderly and belated discovery"—but also with an active despair. He did not have
the frustrated melancholy of Henry Adams; his tour of
America shows us a vigorous sense of intellectual adventure, a faculty for using his eyes beyond that of his fellow
writers of the time, and an endless quest for metaphor to

reflect the teeming, exploding, materialistic, unhistorical, here-and-now continent that America had become.

His stance is indeed prophetic, a touch of Tiresias with eyes unsealed. "I would take my stand on my gathered impressions," he wrote in his preface, with an air of decision and finality. "I would in fact go to the stake for them." When feeling runs as deep and as militant as this, we do well to listen.

I

His first hours, after landing in Hoboken on 30 August, 1904, comprised a glance at Gramercy Park and at Washington Square, landmarks of his childhood, before he was whisked away to the Jersey side again, to the suburbs of Wall Street (as Van Wyck Brooks would later call them), where for twenty-four hours he was the guest of his publisher, Colonel George Harvey of Harper's, at Deal Beach. A fellow guest that night, let it be recorded, was Mark Twain. James could not more promptly have been put into touch with the essential America. After that he took a train for New England, for Chocorua in New Hampshire, his brother William's summer place. He was in no hurry; he remained at Chocorua for several weeks, watching the leaves turn to russet and gold and recovering the glories of American autumns of his youth. Then, still unhurried, and with a close look at everything, he began his inspections. He rewalked the streets of Boston and Cambridge; he visited Concord and Salem, asking his way to the House of the Seven Gables, as he tells us, of a youth who turned out to be a newly-arrived Italian immigrant. Then he went to the metropolis, his birthplace, and restlessly tramped the streets of the Village and the 14th Street neighborhood where he had lived as a boy. By the same stages he proceeded to Philadelphia to visit the daughter of Fanny Kemble; long ago, in Germantown, he had visited Fanny herself, during her later American time. In Washington, a city he had never known intimately, he stayed with Henry Adams, grown old and contemplating an American past that seemed to him less real than the Middle Ages. Chester Arthur had been in the White House when James had visited Washington in 1882. In 1905 he found the first Roosevelt presiding as a kind of athletic *roi soleil*. James attended a great dinner at the White House and was amazed and amused by the ostentation. The presidency had been a modest office in the old time; the first citizen used to circulate in the streets and visit in private houses. A few years earlier, in the darkness of Washington's muddy streets, one might stumble against errant cows. In his own New York there had been chickens in the streets and pigs rooting in the gutters; Central Park had been farmland. All this had changed within a single generation.

To escape the northern winter, James went to the South (Virginia, Richmond, Charleston, Florida)—to what had been in his youth the Confederacy. This journey, together with his New England and eastern seaboard impressions, are fully told in *The American Scene*. There was another journey intended for a second volume: but this was never written. It would have contained an account of the lecture tour James made in the spring of 1905 westward, to Indianapolis, Chicago, St. Louis, and on to California. By this time the restless traveler was exhausted and surfeited. He fell back into New England with a sigh of relief, spending a series of tranquil days with Edith Wharton and her circle at Lenox. In the early summer of 1905 he sailed back to England. There he began to assemble his crowded memories of his ten months' journey—the grandeur and confusion of polyglot America, his close and intense study of "the living and breathing and feeling and moving great monster"—a continent striving to be a nation. The sound of the train, as he had covered thousands of miles, had seemed to say to him "See what I'm making of all this—see what I'm making, what I'm making!" He had seen; and his response was a book-length protest. If he had had a quarrel with the United States of old, this had been on simple ground: he was an artist and his nation was then too busy for art. He had wanted to study men and manners, tradition and change, and he had gone to the old civilizations to do this. His quarrel now ran much deeper. More than the Atlantic separated him from his ancient American roots. History had carved a deep chasm–and all within twenty years.

The American continent was still being opened up when he had gone abroad. It was now well on its way to being plundered. In the intervening period there had arisen the tycoon and the "robber baron," as they would later be called–commerce and industry, the railroad and the corporation; these had bred a new kind of aristocracy based wholly on wealth, and it was still raw with its pioneering, its rapacity, its exploitation. These Americans–he had seen them around the tables in Theodore Roosevelt's White House–were like the *parvenu* of the Napoleonic era. Some few had begun to have a kind of Medici-vision, and had built museums, libraries, concert halls; but art and commerce flourished in America as incongruous siblings in the glare of a new invention called "advertising," of which James had had sinister premonitions in *The Ambassadors*. The leap America had taken was demonstrated in James's own fiction. His Christopher Newman had made a "pile" that was counted in thousands in the 1870s. Adam Verver, in the novel James completed just before his journey home, counts–if he counts at all–in millions. Abroad "business" and "trade" were functional parts of life; they enjoyed no status save as instruments of civilization. In his homeland James began to discover the meaning of "the crudity of wealth"–everything existed to nourish bigger and bigger business; and business existed in everything. If he could not foresee the "commercials" of the electronic age, he was nevertheless aware of such possibilities. A civilization had been produced in which apparently everyone might be convinced of–and sold–almost anything. A great new mythology of deception was being set into force; and the danger was that Americans presently would persuade themselves of the truth of their own fictions. This James saw, and much besides.

II

What were the impressions and opinions for which Henry James was prepared to go to the stake? The first—it meets us from page to page—was his horror at America's cult of impermanence. The country—too large, too large for any "human convenience"—incessantly obliterated the past to create an ephemeral present. This "perpetual repudiation of the past, so far as there had been a past to repudiate" confronted him not only in the disappearance of old landmarks, but in the "expensively provisional" character of the new ones. "It takes an endless amount of history to make even a little tradition," he wrote, "and an endless amount of tradition to make even a little taste, and an endless amount of taste, by the same token, to make even a little tranquillity." James could find no tranquillity in America. He had had his suspicions twenty years before, on his fortieth birthday. Sitting in a New York club, he had then written to a friend: "I have seen many persons—but no personages, have heard much talk—but no conversation. Nevertheless the sense one gets here of the increase of the various acts of life is—almost oppressive; especially as one is so often reminded of it. The arts of life flourish—but the art of living, simply, isn't among them." The art of living required stability, unity, a sense of place, a sense of attachment; and yet the absence of this, the sense of impermanence, was actually a matter of pride—economic pride: that of a society serenely plundering in order to re-invest, and re-investing in order to plunder. This seemed to James a way of life dedicated not to preservation but to a kind of constant upheaval. The word *tradition* in such a society became meaningless; and it made for an absence of tranquillity since the humans, bereft of a sense of place—with "place" always changing—felt transient, dissociated, ephemeral.

The note of impermanence is sounded from page to page:

and most particularly in Henry James's account of his going to 14th Street in search of the house of his boyhood. The dwelling was gone; that was to be expected. He looked then for a church that stood opposite the parental home. He had watched it being built, when he was a boy, watched each stone go into its place, until the completed and sanctified house of worship had welcomed its worshipers. He had felt certain that this House of God would still be there. There was no trace of it. It had vanished "as utterly as the Assyrian Empire." Commerce had replaced it with a row of nondescript stores.

Not only was the familiar church gone, but others, which survived in Manhattan, and in particular Trinity, at the head of Wall Street, were "mercilessly deprived of their visibility," surrounded by high buildings of a "cliff-like sublimity." What astonished James was that, in the case of Trinity, the superseding skyscrapers had been built by the churchwardens themselves, the trustees of the church property. This was "the heaped industrial battlefield"– and the image into which James translated it is eloquent– "a southface as high and wide as the mountain wall that drops the Alpine avalanche, from time to time, upon the village and the village spire, at its foot."

The impression of a magic-lantern shift of old landmarks, symptoms for James of an absent past and an absent future, was renewed when he sought out his birthplace in Washington Place, just off the Square. On its site stood a loft building, harboring a shirtwaist factory (later a disastrous fire would kill many young women as they worked, and stimulate legislation against the sweatshop). The note of supersession and annihilation was repeated for James in Ashburton Place in Boston, where he found the house in which he had written some of his early stories. Here at least he could record survival. But he spoke too soon. Returning a few weeks later for a second look, he found the building gone; it had been as transitory as the rest.

The skyscrapers, symbol of American daring and prosperity, became thus for James usurpers of the past; in all their assertive newness, they were questioned by him as sharply as if they were witnesses in a court room. What was their function? their meaningless arrangement?—this crowding of the sky in a single spot in a land stretching for three thousand miles to the Pacific? He saw at once—as an artist might—the composed picture: the city held in the embrace of its two rivers, the skyscrapers set with extemporized effect, without regard for river-scene and river-vista, the linear streets, the chaotic waterfront, a concealing instead of a revealing of view. "We are only instalments," he could hear the skyscrapers saying, "symbols, stopgaps; expensive as we are, we have nothing to do with continuity, responsibility, transmission, and don't in the least care what becomes of us after we have served our present purpose." The skyscrapers are resolved into a passage of prose describing "the thousand glassy eyes of these giants of the mere market"—

> Crowned not only with no history, but with no credible possibility of time for history, and consecrated by no uses save the commercial at any cost, they are simply the most piercing notes in that concert of the expensively provisional into which your supreme sense of New York resolves itself. They never begin to speak to you, in the manner of the builded majesties of the world as we have heretofore known such—towers or temples or fortresses or palaces—with the authority of things of permanence or even of things of long duration. One story is good only till another is told, and skyscrapers are the last word of economic ingenuity only till another word is written.

Products of the "economic ingenuity" in upper Manhattan were the new stately mansions which offered a view of domestic manners. Henry James studied both their exteriors and their interiors and pronounced their "costly demonstration" to be "a record in the last analysis of individual loneliness." They seemed to him "waste," as homes, as architecture, as the center of life, since they gave him no feeling that the existence of the family was any more permanent than the buildings themselves. The new generations would create their own mansions and yield these in turn to the wreckers. The family units, in the "so flagrantly tentative residences" could not be considered part of an organic, moulded, and coherent society.

In this light, the luxury hotels of America became great islands of alienation and impermanence; and no passage in this book is better known than James's description of the old Waldorf-Astoria, fulfilling all the needs of the people –offering an "immense promiscuity"–"it walked and talked, and ate and drank, and listened and danced to music, and otherwise revelled and roamed, and bought and sold, and came and went there, all on its own splendid terms." Here perhaps was "a social order in positively stable equilibrium" a "conception of publicity *as* the vital medium organized with the authority with which the American genius for organization, put on its mettle, alone could organize it." The age of the ubiquitous and standardizing Hilton is foreseen.

Surveying Manhattan, skyscrapers, mansions, hotels, James found a highly contemporaneous word for his vision. He speaks of "blight," foresees as early as 1905 the erosion of the proud cities. Human decay would go hand in hand with city decay. The corruption would be civic and personal. The poor would feel the weight of "the new remorseless monopolies"–and the children of the immigrants would enjoy the new-found freedom in America, but not necessarily as America had planned–"there is such a thing, in the United States, it is hence to be inferred, as freedom to grow up to be blighted, and it may be the only freedom in store for the smaller fry of future generations."

> Here, strikingly then, was an American *case* . . . the way in which sane Society and pestilent City, in the United States, successfully cohabit, each keeping it up with so little fear or flutter from the other. The thing presents itself, in its prime unlikelihood, as a thorough good neighbouring of the Happy Family and the Infernal Machine–the machine so rooted as to continue to defy removal, and the family still so indifferent, while it carries on the family business

of buying and selling, of chattering and dancing, to the danger of being blown up.

James was hardly forecasting the "blow-up" of our time, the bomb or the race riots. He saw simply, half a century ago, with the vision of genius, the ambiguities and anomalies of a world founded wholly on buccaneering and gain, the canker within a society "dancing, all consciously, on the thin crust of a volcano."

III

There are no pages in *The American Scene* packed with closer analysis and humane feeling than those James devoted to the aliens. What has put some readers off, doubtless, has been James's air of Grand Seigneur, his essentially aristocratic way of looking at the newcomers. Thus he has been thought of as both snobbish and narrow in his account of his wanderings in the Italian and Jewish neighborhoods of New York, and some critics have mistakenly characterized his picture of the immigrant Jews as "anti-Semitic." Indeed, F. O. Matthiessen says that James "drifted dangerously close to a doctrine of racism" in *The American Scene*. The book provides no warrant for so strange a conclusion. That James should have visited the crowded tenements of the aliens shows an active interest; and that he should dwell at some length on what he saw is understandable in one who had devoted his life and art to social citicism and the study of racial traits and national characteristics. He looked closely because he was curious and interested, and puzzled by what the "melting pot" would yield. In the two decades of his absence millions had poured into the United States from all corners of the world through the Ellis Island gateway. James took the trouble to visit this now-discarded human corral and express his horror at America's strange way of extending Brotherhood to the world. By the same token he sought talk with encountered Italians; in Italy he had always found them responsive. In America they seemed to have suffered a sea-change; and if James found them taciturn, or squirmed at the smell in the Yiddish theatre, or pondered the fractured English in the old Café Royal (whither he was conducted by the Jewish playwright Jacob Gordin), he indulged neither in snobbery nor in condescension; he expressed rather the bewilderment of an enlightened inquirer who asked himself what kind of America would emerge from these grafts upon the land he once knew. He is fully aware that the Italians have come to a country where they have more to eat, wear shoes, and have dental care—if they can afford it—but on this ground he felt they should be even more spontaneous than in their own land, where he had always found in them a heart-warming *bonhomie*. "What has become of that element of agreeable address in *them*, which has, from far back, so enhanced for the stranger the interest and pleasure of a visit to their beautiful country." He could only observe that "they shed it utterly."

It astonishes him to discover this "coldness" in the aliens and "in the land of universal brotherhood," as if immigration had stripped them of part of their being. He believes that the children of the immigrants "will fully profit, rise to the occasion and enter into the privilege." They should be "the stuff of whom brothers and sisters are made." Yet he wonders how soon Old World habits can be transformed, how quickly ethnic change can be brought about; and whether this will be to the good. Might there not be "a hotch-potch of racial ingredients" and in the end "a tolerably neutral and colourless image." Riding down Broadway to the Bowery in the streetcars, he searches the faces of the new New Yorkers and gasps "with the sense of isolation" they convey. Despoiled of their character and habitat, they have undergone a "varnish of consecration" and he adds "out of a bottomless receptacle, by a huge whitewashing brush."

Although James devotes many pages to the Jews he has only one or two references to the Irish. They were not, perhaps, aliens in the same sense; they spoke English; and then James's grandfather had been an Irish immigrant. The novelist nevertheless had reservations: he speaks of an earlier

Boston "exempt as yet from the Irish yoke." The Irish apparently did not interest him as ingredients of the melting pot. The Jews offered a startling contrast with the Anglo-Saxons or Celts, a deeper problem in assimilation; they had the barrier of language and an old religion, and they had to free themselves from their long ghetto servitude. James accordingly paid a long and searching visit to the East Side. Looking at the tenements, with their external fire escapes, in which the human spectacle, with display of laundry and bedding, resembles for him a scrambling of squirrels and monkeys in a zoo, he speaks of "the whole hard glitter of Israel" and asks himself whether this is the awaited "New Jerusalem." To be anti-Semitic, however, he would have had to be a bigot; and a bigot would not have seen the immigrant Jew as having an "intensity of aspect" and "the unsurpassed strength of his race." He adds, "This I think, makes the individual Jew more of a concentrated person, savingly possessed of everything that is in him, than any other human noted at random." And he images the Jews he sees swarming in the ghetto as a race which has been divided, fragmented, and has yet maintained a diffused intensity so that any array of Jews resembled "some long nocturnal street where every window in every house shows a maintained light." He speaks of this vision after being guided by Jewish friends and admirers (he had dined in a Jewish home in the heart of the tenement district in the area of Rutgers Street) through the streets, restaurants, and cafes. His final observation of the East Side is to take note of the great "overtowering School" dominating the neighborhood. It is almost as if he foresaw the role it would play in the self-betterment of the American Jews.

Above all, however, his view of the uprooted immigrant population in New York—since the ethnic question then had no predictable answer—was that it reinforced the feeling of impermanence and alienation in the city. A society in flux, with no settled customs and manners, confused about the old, uneasy about the new, seemed to him extemporized and unstable. The promise of affluence, of good shoes and good dentistry, spoke for material, physical things. But it did not make for a constituted, comfortable community; it represented improverishment of values, or no values at all. We find James circling again and again in this book to the observation that in the American cities, with their heterogeneous populations and dissociated humanity, there was no society "in a composed sense." And if we ask what he meant by "society" we find the answer—"the number of organic social relations it represents," man living with man in an organized and harmonious social unit or units. The aliens had uprooted themselves from their social units abroad, where it had taken long ages of history to produce them and to bind them together. Racial strains could not be extinguished or transformed in an hour and what James recurrently asked was—the melting-pot, the conversion—into what? He saw nothing sufficiently coherent in America to give him the answer.

IV

Finally, in the rediscovered country, Henry James found a corrosive materialism, a vulgarity of affluence, as if the very plumbing, in which the nation took such excessive pride, had to be made of gold. He comes back to phenomena of this order nearly always in the language of gilt and of gilding—"the human note in the huge American rattle of gold," the refusal to allow "*any* planted object to gather in a history where it stands, forbids in fact any accumulation that may not be recorded in the mere bank-book." He adds "this last became long ago *the* historic page."

Or again:

> To make so much money that you won't, that you don't "mind," don't mind anything—that is absolutely, I think, the main American formula. . . . This basis is that of active pecuniary gain and of active pecuniary gain only—that of one's making the conditions so triumphantly pay that the prices, the manners, the other conveniences, take their place as a friction it is comparatively easy to salve, wounds directly treatable with the wash of gold.

The "gold-dust in the air" haunted James; the sky-scrapers were "triumphant payers of dividends;" at the Metropolitan Museum there was "ever so much money" for exquisite things "except creation, which was to be off the scene altogether." Or there was gold in other forms—the "white elephants" at Newport, great houses with their affront to proportion and discretion. Every section of the book leads James back to a national acquisitiveness, to the gouging out of fortunes without the creation of a true civilization: it was as he had found it long ago—a flourishing of the arts of life without the art of living. He had said as much in his tales of rich Americans uncomfortably traveling abroad. He repeated this now again, in a new form, in the tales he derived from his American journey. These express, with uncommon directness, the deepest feelings within the poetry of *The American Scene*. They are among James's angriest and saddest tales. We have only to glance at a single paragraph in the story of "Crapy Cornelia" to see in it the vivid and uncompromising stance of the returned American traveler:

> This was clearly going to be the music of the future—that if people were but rich enough and furnished enough and fed enough, exercised and sanitated and manicured and generally advertised and made "knowing" enough . . . all they had to do for civility was to take the amused ironic view of those who might be less initiated. In *his* time, when he was young or even when he was only but a little less middle-aged, the best manners had been the best kindness, and the best kindness had mostly been some art of not insisting on one's luxurious differences, of concealing rather, for common humanity, if not for common decency, a part at least of the intensity or the ferocity with which one might be "in the know."

James had long planned to write a short story about a young man carrying a secret sorrow and seeking to ease himself of the burden. He was able now to give it form: New York offered him the setting. His young American returns from a decade abroad to discover that his best friend, his college mate, whom he had placed in charge of his properties, had absconded with everything. Mark Monteith feels a deep, sore, inward ache; he leaves the alien hotel and its baroque splendors in search of faith again in humankind; he feels not so much robbed as betrayed. The lonely city offers him its cold indifference; and the drawing-rooms are filled with fatuous ugly matrons "with extraordinarily gemmed and manicured hands" who know nothing of the gift of sympathy. One does not need to be told the resolution of the tale to read its personal statement: James felt robbed of his old patrimony; worse still he feels "sold." An old faith has been shaken, and the world shrugged its shoulders. So, in another tale, the returned American, in the mansion of his childhood, stalks the ghost of himself—as he might have been. The face he finds is terrifying; and the apparition's hand is maimed. If he had stayed at home he would have not had the fingers with which to hold his pen.

V

James's visit to the South fills the last pages of *The American Scene*. It is a haunted, spectral visit. The South looms for him as vivid and painful—

> a figure somehow blighted or stricken, discomfortably, impossibly seated in an invalid-chair, and yet fixing one with strange eyes that were half a defiance and half a deprecation of one's noticing, and much more of referring to, any abnormal sign. The deprecation, in the Southern eyes, is much greater today, I think, than in the old lurid challenge; but my haunting similitude was an image of the keeping-up of appearances, and above all of the maintenance of a tone, the historic "high" tone in an excruciating posture.

"Had the *only* focus of life then been Slavery?" James asked himself; for he found that with the extinction of that interest "none other of any sort was left," save the hate and cruelty which James saw in the eyes of a smiling Virginian toward a Negro: "It came to me that, though he wouldn't have hurt a Northern fly, there were things (ah, we had touched on some of these!) that all fair, engaging, smiling, as he stood there, he would have done to a Southern negro."

The Negroes scarcely figure in this book; they were not, like the Jews or Italians, to be observed as yet in their Northern slums and had but reached an intermediate stage between slavery and their present militancy. However James's first glimpse of the Southern Negroes, lounging and sunning themselves at a railway station, led him to perceive the central issue of their emancipation. He imaged it as resembling "some beast that had sprung from the jungle" using the metaphor from his remarkable tale about a man and his unlived life. In the "ragged and rudimentary" types—and their unlived lives—he recognized the tragic irony that the Negro was supposed to be "in possession of his rights as a man." The discrepancy between history and actuality led him to say that "sweet reasonableness" on the part of a Northerner in the South "would never pour oil upon the waters." James had been reading W.E.B. Du Bois's *Souls of Black Folk*; he called it "the only Southern book of distinction in many a year," thereby testifying to the Negro's capacity for literacy and literature. But otherwise he encountered the facts of his day—the Negro as porter or waiter; and he found in these descendants of slaves an "apparently deep-seated inaptitude for any alertness of personal service" that is a persistence of the mentality of slavery. The waiters were apt to put sugar in his tea or coffee without asking him whether he wanted it; and a Southern porter obviously disturbed him by setting his bag into the mud of a street just before James boarded a crowded trolley, where he had to place the same bag on his knees.

With the visit to the South the book ends; and as the train takes him North from Florida James has his great disturbing reverie: it is written as an eloquent oratorical summing up of the America he has seen, a land plundered but showing no sign of replacing ravage by civilization. The passage was omitted from the American edition of

1907–whether through editorial carelessness or design we do not know. Perhaps Harper's felt that the book ended on too great a note of despair for the national optimism. The peroration appeared, however, in the English edition, and was read by that part of James's audience for which it was least intended. The pages are re-included here; they offer "the eloquence of [James's] exasperation," his vision of "the triumph of the superficial, the apotheosis of the raw."

> You touch the great lonely land–as one feels it still to be–only to plant upon it some ugliness. . . . You convert the large and noble sanities that I see around me, you convert them one after the other to crudities, to invalidities, hideous and unashamed; and you so leave them to add to the number of the myriad aspects you simply spoil, of the myriad unanswerable questions you scatter about as some monstrous unnatural mother might leave a family of unfathered infants on doorsteps or in waiting rooms.

These pages speak before the era of polluted air and polluted rivers, before the audio-visual saturation, before the landscape laced with asphalt ribbons. If he were, James said, "one of the painted savages you have dispossessed" he might have been impressed by what America was making–since he would not expect the despoilers to supply beauty or charm. "Beauty and charm would be for me in the solitude you have ravaged and I should owe you my grudge for every disfigurement and every violence, for every wound with which you have caused the face of the land to bleed."

The American Scene has been almost wholly neglected in a country at present busy with self-examination and self-evaluation. Only one other edition has appeared since the original truncated edition of 1907; it was edited by W. H. Auden in 1946 and included the missing peroration. In his essay, Auden called the book "a prose poem of the first order"; and subsequently Wright Morris added a novelist's tribute out of his intimate knowledge of the American land, in an essay included in *The Territory Ahead*. Edmund Wilson had, before this, called *The American Scene* "one of the best books about modern America." For the rest, there have been only minor academic papers and deprecation by writers who found the book anti-alien, anti-American, anti-Semitic, or simply, as Matthiessen did, "a curiosity of literature." Auden's essay takes its place as a large corollary statement, a poet's postscript. Speaking as a transplanted European who had reversed James's expatriation by coming to live in America, Auden searchingly describes the tyranny of the majority, the compromises of an egalitarian society proclaiming the importance of liberty over virtue and constantly forging defeating compromises. As one instance of this Auden speaks of the egalitarian refusal to recognize "the unequal distribution of intellectual gifts," so that "the institutions of the Higher Learning in America cannot decide whether they are to be Liberal Arts Colleges for the exceptional few or vocational schools for the average many, and so fail to do their duty by either."

Now, almost a quarter of a century since Auden's essay, and more than half a century since James's book, we can see that in fundamental matters there has been little change in America, only an accentuation of the confusion, distortion, and fragmentation James discerned. He could not foresee that the mass media would diffuse with ever greater speed the superficialities and the chatter of which he took note; or that the motor car would make faster work of the remaining trees and remaining green in its demand for more and wider highways. But even if we set aside the question of technology, we can see in the humanism of James's book an abiding patriotism: that of a man writing out of a deep love of country and a concern for its future. His is the voice of the outraged citizen as well as that of the prophet and poet, speaking with a sense of history, a belief in civilization.

LEON EDEL

PREFACE

THE following pages duly explain themselves, I judge, as to the Author's point of view and his relation to his subject; but I prefix this word on the chance of any suspected or perceived failure of such references. My visit to America had been the first possible to me for nearly a quarter of a century, and I had before my last previous one, brief and distant to memory, spent other years in continuous absence; so that I was to return with much of the freshness of eye, outward and inward, which, with the further contribution of a state of desire, is commonly held a precious agent of perception. I felt no doubt, I confess, of my great advantage on that score; since if I had had time to become almost as "fresh" as an inquiring stranger, I had not on the other hand had enough to cease to be, or at least to feel, as acute as an initiated native. I made no scruple of my conviction that I should understand and should care better and more than the most earnest of visitors, and yet that I should vibrate with more curiosity—on the extent of ground, that is, on which I might aspire to intimate intelligence at all—than the pilgrim with the longest list of questions, the sharpest appetite for explanations and the largest exposure to mistakes.

I felt myself then, all serenely, not exposed to grave mistakes—though there were also doubtless explanations which would find me, and quite as contentedly, impenetrable. I would take my stand on my gathered impressions, since it was all for them, for them only, that I returned; I would in fact go to the stake for them— which is a sign of the value that I both in particular and in general attach to them and that I have endeavoured

Preface

to preserve for them in this transcription. My cultivated sense of aspects and prospects affected me absolutely as an enrichment of my subject, and I was prepared to abide by the law of that sense—the appearance that it would react promptly in some presences only to remain imperturbably inert in others. There would be a thousand matters—matters already the theme of prodigious reports and statistics—as to which I should have no sense whatever, and as to information about which my record would accordingly stand naked and unashamed. It should unfailingly be proved against me that my opportunity had found me incapable of information, incapable alike of receiving and of imparting it; for then, and then only, would it be clearly enough attested that I *had* cared and understood.

There are features of the human scene, there are properties of the social air, that the newspapers, reports, surveys and blue-books would seem to confess themselves powerless to "handle," and that yet represented to me a greater array of items, a heavier expression of character, than my own pair of scales would ever weigh, keep them as clear for it as I might. I became aware soon enough, on the spot, that these elements of the human subject, the results of these attempted appreciations of life itself, would prove much too numerous even for a capacity all given to them for some ten months; but at least therefore, artistically concerned as I had been all my days with the human subject, with the appreciation of life itself, and with the consequent question of literary representation, I should not find such matters scant or simple. I was not in fact to do so, and they but led me on and on. How far this might have been my several chapters show; and yet even here I fall short. I shall have to take a few others for the rest of my story.

H. J.

1

New England

AN AUTUMN IMPRESSION

Conscious that the impressions of the very first hours have always the value of their intensity, I shrink from wasting those that attended my arrival, my return after long years, even though they be out of order with the others that were promptly to follow and that I here gather in, as best I may, under a single head. They referred partly, these instant vibrations, to a past recalled from very far back ; fell into a train of association that receded, for its beginning, to the dimness of extreme youth. One's extremest youth had been full of New York, and one was absurdly finding it again, meeting it at every turn, in sights, sounds, smells, even in the chaos of confusion and change ; a process under which, verily, recognition became more interesting and more amusing in proportion as it became more difficult, like the spelling-out of foreign sentences of which one knows but half the words. It was not, indeed, at Hoboken, on emerging from the comparatively assured order of the great berth of the ship, that recognition *was* difficult : there, only too confoundingly familiar and too serenely exempt from change, the waterside squalor of the great city put forth

again its most inimitable notes, showed so true to the
barbarisms it had not outlived that one could only fall to
wondering what obscure inward virtue had preserved it.
There was virtue evident enough in the crossing of the
water, that brave sense of the big, bright, breezy bay ;
of light and space and multitudinous movement ; of the
serried, bristling city, held in the easy embrace of its
great good-natured rivers very much as a battered and
accommodating beauty may sometimes be "distinguished"
by a gallant less fastidious, with his open arms, than his
type would seem to imply.   But what was it that was
still holding together, for observation, on the hither
shore, the same old sordid facts, all the ugly items
that had seemed destined so long ago to fall apart from
their very cynicism ?—the rude cavities, the loose cobbles,
the dislodged supports, the unreclaimed pools, of the
roadway ; the unregulated traffic, as of innumerable
desperate drays charging upon each other with tragic
long-necked, sharp-ribbed horses (a length and a sharpness all emphasized by the anguish of effort) ; the
corpulent constables, with helmets askew, swinging their
legs, in high detachment, from coigns of contemplation ;
the huddled houses of the other time, red-faced, off their
balance, almost prone, as from too conscious an affinity
with "saloon" civilization.

It was, doubtless, open to the repentant absentee to
feel these things sweetened by some shy principle of
picturesqueness ; and I admit that I asked myself, while
I considered and bumped, why what was "sauce for the
goose" should *not* be in this case sauce for the gander ;
and why antique shabbiness shouldn't plead on this
particular waterside the cause it more or less successfully pleads on so many others.   The light of the
September day was lovely, and the sun of New York
rests mostly, with a laziness all its own, on that dull glaze
of crimson paint, as thick as on the cheek of the cruder

coquetry, which is, in general, beneath its range, the sign of the old-fashioned. Yes; I could remind myself, as I went, that Naples, that Tangiers or Constantinople has probably nothing braver to flaunt, and mingle with excited recognition the still finer throb of seeing in advance, seeing even to alarm, many of the responsibilities lying in wait for the habit of headlong critical or fanciful reaction, many of the inconsistencies in which it would probably have, at the best, more or less defiantly to drape itself. Such meditations, at all events, bridged over alike the weak places of criticism and some of the rougher ones of my material passage. Nothing was left, for the rest of the episode, but a kind of fluidity of appreciation—a mild, warm wave that broke over the succession of aspects and objects according to some odd inward rhythm, and often, no doubt, with a violence that there was little in the phenomena themselves flagrantly to justify. It floated me, my wave, all that day and the next; so that I still think tenderly—for the short backward view is already a distance with "tone"—of the service it rendered me and of the various perceptive penetrations, charming coves of still blue water, that carried me up into the subject, so to speak, and enabled me to step ashore. The subject was everywhere—that was the beauty, that the advantage: it was thrilling, really, to find one's self in presence of a theme to which everything directly contributed, leaving no touch of experience irrelevant. That, at any rate, so far as feeling it went; treating it, evidently, was going to be a matter of prodigious difficulty and selection—in consequence of which, indeed, there might even be a certain recklessness in the largest surrender to impressions. Clearly, however, these were not for the present—and such as they were—to be kept at bay; the hour of reckoning, obviously, would come, with more of them heaped up than would prove usable, a greater quantity of vision, possibly, than might fit into decent form: whereby, assuredly, the part of wisdom was to put in as much as possible of one's recklessness while it was fresh.

It was fairly droll, for instance, the quantity of vision that began to press during a wayside rest in a house of genial but discriminating hospitality that opened its doors just where the fiddle-string of association could most intensely vibrate, just where the sense of "old New York," of the earlier stages of the picture now so violently overpainted, found most of its occasions— found them, to extravagance, within and without. The good easy Square, known in childhood, and as if the light were yellower there from that small accident, bristled with reminders as vague as they were sweet; within, especially, the place was a cool backwater, for time as well as for space; out of the slightly dim depths of which, at the turn of staircases and from the walls of communicating rooms, portraits and relics and records, faintly, quaintly æsthetic, in intention at least, and discreetly—yet bravely, too, and all so archaically and pathetically — Bohemian, laid traps, of a pleasantly primitive order, for memory, for sentiment, for relenting irony; gross little devices, on the part of the circumscribed past, which appealed with scarce more emphasis than so many tail-pieces of closed chapters. The whole impression had fairly a rococo tone; and it was in this perceptibly golden air, the air of old empty New York afternoons of the waning summer-time, when the long, the perpendicular rattle, as of buckets, forever thirsty, in the bottomless well of fortune, almost dies out in the merciful cross-streets, that the ample rearward loggia of the Club seemed serenely to hang; the glazed, disglazed, gallery dedicated to the array of small spread tables for which blank "backs," right and left and opposite, made a privacy; backs blank with the bold crimson of the New York house-painter, and playing upon the chord of remembrance, all so absurdly, with the scarcely less simplified green of their great cascades of Virginia creeper, as yet unturned : an admonition, this, for piety, as well as a reminder—since one had somehow failed to treasure it up—that the rather pettifogging plan of the city, the fruit, on the spot, of an artless age, happened to leave even so much margin as that for consoling chances. There were plenty of these—which I perhaps seem unduly to patronize in speaking of them as only "consoling"—for many hours to come and while the easy wave that I have mentioned continued to float me : so abysmal are the resources of the foredoomed student of manners, or so helpless, at least, his case when once adrift in that tide.

If in Gramercy Park already, three hours after his arrival, he had felt himself, this victim, up to his neck in what I have called his "subject," the matter was quite beyond calculation by the time he had tumbled, in such a glorified "four-wheeler," and with such an odd consciousness of roughness superimposed upon smoothness, far down-town again, and, on the deck of a shining steamer bound for the Jersey shore, was taking all the breeze of the Bay. The note of manners, the note that begins to sound, everywhere, for the spirit newly disembarked, with the first word exchanged, seemed, on the great clean deck, fairly to vociferate in the breeze— and not at all, so far, as was pleasant to remark, to the harshening of that element. Nothing could have been more to the spectator's purpose, moreover, than the fact he was ready to hail as the most characteristic in the world, the fact that what surrounded him was a rare collection of young men of business returning, as the phrase is, and in the pride of their youth and their might, to their "homes," and that, if treasures of "type" were not here to be disengaged, the fault would be all his own.

It was perhaps this simple sense of treasure to be gathered in, it was doubtless this very confidence in the objective reality of impressions, so that they could deliciously be left to ripen, like golden apples, on the tree—it was all this that gave a charm to one's sitting in the orchard, gave a strange and inordinate charm both to the prospect of the Jersey shore and to every inch of the entertainment, so divinely inexpensive, by the way. The immense liberality of the Bay, the noble amplitude of the boat, the great unlocked and tumbled-out city on one hand, and the low, accessible mystery of the opposite State on the other, watching any approach, to all appearance, with so gentle and patient an eye; the gaiety of the light, the gladness of the air, and, above all (for it most came back to that), the unconscious affluence, the variety in identity, of the young men of business: these things somehow left speculation, left curiosity exciting, yet kept it beguilingly safe. And what shall I say more of all that presently followed than that it sharpened to the last pleasantness —quite draining it of fears of fatuity—that consciousness of strolling in the orchard that was all one's own to pluck, and counting, overhead, the apples of gold? I figure, I repeat, under this name those thick-growing items of the characteristic that were surely going to drop into one's hand, for vivid illustration, as soon as one could begin to hold it out.

Heavy with fruit, in particular, was the whole spreading bough that rustled above me during an afternoon, a very wonderful afternoon, that I spent in being ever so wisely driven, driven further and further, into the large lucidity of—well, of what else shall I call it but a New Jersey condition? That, no doubt, is a loose label for the picture; but impressions had to range themselves, for the hour, as they could. I had come forth for a view of such parts of the condition as might peep out at the hour and on the spot, and it was clearly not going to be the restless analyst's own fault if conditions in general, everywhere, should strike him as peculiarly, as almost affectingly, at the mercy of observation. They came out to meet us, in their actuality, in the soft afternoon ; they stood, artless, unconscious, unshamed, at the very gates of Appearance; they might, verily, have been there, in their plenitude, at the call of some procession of drums and banners—the principal facts of the case being collected along our passage, to my fancy, quite as if they had been principal citizens. And then there was the further fact of the case, one's own ridiculous property and sign—the romantic, if not the pathetic, circumstance of one's having had to wait till now to read even such meagre meanings as this into a page at which one's geography might so easily have opened. It might have threatened, for twenty minutes, to be almost complicating, but the truth was recorded : it was an adventure, unmistakably, to have a revelation made so convenient —to be learning at last, in the maturity of one's powers, what New Jersey might "connote." This was nearer than I had ever come to any such experience ; and it was now as if, all my life, my curiosity had been greater than I knew. Such, for an excited sensibility, are the refinements of personal contact. These influences then were present, as a source of glamour, at every turn of our drive, and especially present, I imagined, during that longest perspective when the road took no turn, but showed us, with a large, calm consistency, the straight blue band of summer sea, between the sandy shore and the reclaimed margin of which the chain of big villas was stretched tight, or at least kept straight, almost as for the close stringing of more or less monstrous pearls. The association of the monstrous thrusts itself somehow into my retrospect, for all the decent humility of the low, quiet coast, where the shadows of the waning afternoon could lengthen at their will and the chariots of Israel, on the wide and admirable road, could advance, in the glittering eye of each array of extraordinarily exposed windows, as through an harmonious golden haze.

There was gold-dust in the air, no doubt—which would have been again an element of glamour if it had not rather lighted the scene with too crude a confidence. It was one of the phases, full of its own marks and signs, of New York, the immense, in *villeggiatura*—and, presently, with little room left for doubt of what particular phase it might be. The huge new houses, up and down, looked over their smart, short lawns as with a certain familiar prominence in their profiles, which was borne out by the accent, loud, assertive, yet benevolent withal, with which they confessed to their extreme expensiveness. " Oh, yes ; we were awfully dear, for what we are and for what we do "—it was proud, but it was rather rueful ; with the odd appearance everywhere as of florid creations waiting, a little bewilderingly, for their justification, waiting for the next clause in the sequence, waiting in short for life, for time, for interest, for character, for identity itself to come to them, quite as large spread tables or superfluous shops may wait for guests and customers. The scene overflowed with curious suggestion ; it comes back to me with the afternoon air and the amiable flatness, the note of the sea in a drowsy mood ; and I thus somehow think of the great white boxes as standing there with the silvered ghostliness (for all the silver involved) of a series of candid new moons. It could only be the occupants, moreover, who were driving on the vast, featureless highway, to and fro in front of their ingenuous palaces and as if pretending not to recognize them when they passed ; German Jewry— wasn't it conceivable ?—tending to the stout, the simple, the kind, quite visibly to the patriarchal, and with the old superseded shabbiness of Long Branch partly for the goal of their course ; the big brown wooden barracks of the hotels, the bold rotunda of the gaming-room—monuments already these, in truth, of a more artless age, and yet with too little history about them for dignity of ruin. Dignity, if not of ruin at least of reverence, was what, at other points, doubtless, we failed considerably less to read into the cottage where Grant lived and the cottage where Garfield died ; though they had, for all the world, those modest structures, exactly the effect of objects diminished by recession into space—as if to symbolize the rapidity of their recession into time. They have been left so far behind by the expensive, as the expensive is now practised ; in spite of having apparently been originally a sufficient expression of it.

This could pass, it seemed, for the greatest vividness of the picture—that the expensive, for New York in *villeggiatura*, even on such subordinate showing, is like a train covering ground at maximum speed and pushing on, at present, into regions unmeasurable. It included, however, other lights, some of which glimmered, to my eyes, as with the promise of great future intensity— hanging themselves as directly over the question of manners as if they had been a row of lustres reflected in the polished floor of a ball-room. Here was the expensive as a power by itself, a power unguided, undirected, practically unapplied, really exerting itself in a void that could make it no response, that had nothing—poor gentle, patient, rueful, but altogether helpless, void !— to offer in return. The game was that of its doing, each party to the whole combination, what it could, but with the result of the common effort's falling so short. Nothing could be of a livelier interest—with the question of manners always in view—than to note that the most as yet accomplished at such a cost was the air of unmitigated publicity, publicity as a condition, as a doom, from which there could be no appeal ; just as in all the topsy-turvy order, the defeated scheme, the misplaced confidence, or whatever one may call it, there was no achieved protection, no constituted mystery of retreat, no saving complexity, not so much as might be represented by a foot of garden wall or a preliminary sketch of interposing shade. The homely principle under which the picture held at all together was that of the famous freedom of the cat to look at the king; that seemed, so clearly, throughout, the only motto that would work. The ample villas, in their full dress, planted each on its little square of brightly-green carpet, and as with their stiff skirts pulled well down, eyed each other, at short range, from head to foot; while the open road, the chariots, the buggies, the motors, the pedestrians—which last number, indeed, was remarkably small —regarded at their ease both this reciprocity and the parties to it. It was in fact all *one* participation, with an effect deterrent to those ingenuities, or perhaps indeed rather to those commonplaces, of conjecture produced in general by the outward show of the fortunate life. That, precisely, appeared the answer to the question of manners: the fact that in such conditions there couldn't *be* any manners to speak of; that the basis of privacy was somehow wanting for them; and that nothing, accordingly, no image, no presumption of constituted relations, possibilities, amenities, in the social, the domestic order, was inwardly projected. It was as if the projection had been so completely outward that one could but find one's self almost uneasy about the mere perspective required for the common acts of the personal life, that minimum of vagueness as to what takes place in it for which the complete "home" aspires to provide.

What had it been their idea to *do*, the good people—do, exactly, *for* their manners, their habits, their intercourse, their relations, their pleasures, their general advantage and justification? Do, that is, in affirming their wealth with such innocent emphasis and yet not at the same time affirming anything else. It would have rested on the cold-blooded critic, doubtless, to explain why the crudity of wealth did strike him with so direct a force; accompanied after all with no paraphernalia, no visible redundancies of possession, not so much as a lodge at any gate, nothing but the scale of many of the houses and their candid look of having cost as much as they knew how. Unmistakably they all proclaimed it—they would have cost still more had the way but been shown them; and, meanwhile, they added as with one voice, they would take a fresh start as soon as ever it should be. "We are only instalments, symbols, stop-gaps," they practically admitted, and with no shade of embarrassment; "expensive as we are, we have nothing to do with continuity, responsibility, transmission, and don't in the least care what becomes of us after we have served our present purpose." On the detail of this impression, however, I needn't insist; the essence of it, which was all that was worth catching, was one's recognition of the odd treachery that may practically lie in wait for isolated opulence. The highest luxury of all, the supremely expensive thing, is constituted privacy—and yet it was the supremely expensive thing that the good people had supposed themselves to be getting : all of which, I repeat, enriched the case, for the restless analyst, with an illustrative importance. For what did it offer but the sharp interest of the match everywhere and everlastingly played between the short-cut and the long road?—an interest never so sharp as since the short-cut has been able to find itself so endlessly backed by money. Money in fact *is* the short-cut—or the short-cut money; and the long road having, in the instance before me, so little operated, operated for the effect, as we may say, of the cumulative, the game remained all in the hands of its adversary.

The example went straight to the point, and thus was

the drama presented : what turn, on the larger, the general stage, was the game going to take ?   The whole spectacle, with the question, opened out, diffusing positively a multitudinous murmur that was in my ears, for some of the more subtly-romantic parts of the drive, as who should say (the sweet American vaguenesses, hailed again, the dear old nameless, promiscuous lengths of woodside and waterside), like the collective afternoon hum of invisible insects.   Yes ; it was all actually going to be drama, and *that* drama ; than which nothing could be more to the occult purpose of the confirmed, the systematic story-seeker, or to that even of the mere ancient contemplative person curious of character.   The very *donnée* of the piece could be given, the subject formulated : the great adventure of a society reaching out into the apparent void for the amenities, the consummations, after having earnestly gathered in so many of the preparations and necessities.   " Into the apparent void "—I had to insist on that, since without it there would be neither comedy nor tragedy ; besides which so little was wanting, in the way of vacancy, to the completeness of the appearance.   What would lurk beneath this—or indeed what wouldn't, what mightn't—to thicken the plot from stage to stage and to intensify the action ? The story-seeker would be present, quite intimately present, at the general effort—showing, doubtless, as quite heroic in many a case—to gouge an interest *out* of the vacancy, gouge it with tools of price, even as copper and gold and diamonds are extracted, by elaborate processes, from earth-sections of small superficial expression.   What was such an effort, on its associated side, for the attentive mind, but a more or less adventurous fight, carried on from scene to scene, with fluctuations and variations, the shifting quantity of success and failure ?   Never would be such a chance to see how the short-cut works, and if there be really any substitute for roundabout experience, for troublesome history, for the long, the immitigable process of time. It was a promise, clearly, of the highest entertainment.

II

It was presently to come back to me, however, that there were other sorts, too—so many sorts, in fact, for the ancient contemplative person, that selection and omission, in face of them, become almost a pain, and the sacrifice of even the least of these immediate sequences of impression in its freshness a lively regret. But without much foreshortening is no representation, and I was promptly to become conscious, at all events, of quite a different part of the picture, and of personal perceptions, to match it, of a different order. I woke up, by a quick transition, in the New Hampshire mountains, in the deep valleys and the wide woodlands, on the forest-fringed slopes, the far-seeing crests of the high places, and by the side of the liberal streams and the lonely lakes; things full, at first, of the sweetness of belated recognition, that of the sense of some bedimmed summer of the distant prime flushing back into life and asking to give again as much as possible of what it had given before— all in spite, too, of much unacquaintedness, of the newness, to my eyes, through the mild September glow, of the particular rich region. I call it rich without compunction, despite its several poverties, caring little that half the charm, or half the response to it, may have been shamelessly "subjective"; since that but slightly shifts the ground of the beauty of the impression. When you wander about in Arcadia you ask as few questions as possible. That *is* Arcadia in fact, and questions drop, or at least get themselves deferred and shiftlessly shirked; in conformity with which truth the New England hills and woods—since they were not all, for the weeks to come, of mere New Hampshire—the mild September glow and even the clear October blaze were things to play on the chords of memory and association, to say nothing of those of surprise, with an admirable art of their own. The tune may have dropped at last, but it succeeded for a month in being strangely sweet, and in producing, quite with intensity, the fine illusion. Here, moreover, was "interest" of the sort that could come easily, and therefore not of the sort—quite the contrary —that involved a consideration of the millions spent ; a fact none the fainter, into the bargain, for having its curious, unexpected, inscrutable side.

Why was the whole connotation so *delicately* Arcadian, like that of the Arcadia of an old tapestry, an old legend, an old love-story in fifteen volumes, one of those of Mademoiselle de Scudéri? Why, in default of other elements of the higher finish, did all the woodwalks and nestled nooks and shallow, carpeted dells, why did most of the larger views themselves, the outlooks to purple crag and blue horizon, insist on referring themselves to the idyllic *type* in its purity ?—as if the higher finish, even at the hand of nature, were in some sort a perversion, and hillsides and rocky eminences and wild orchards, in short any common sequestered spot, could strike one as the more exquisitely and ideally Sicilian, Theocritan, poetic, romantic, academic, from their not bearing the burden of too much history. The history was there in its degree, and one came upon it, on sunny afternoons, in the form of the classic abandoned farm of the rude forefather who had lost patience with his fate. These scenes of old, hard New England effort, defeated by the soil and the climate and reclaimed by nature and time—the crumbled, lonely chimney-stack, the overgrown threshold, the dried-up well, the cart-track vague and lost—these seemed the only notes to interfere, in their

meagreness, with the queer *other*, the larger, eloquence
that one kept reading into the picture. Even the wild
legend, immediately local, of the Indian who, having, a
hundred years ago, murdered a husbandman, was pursued, by roused avengers, to the topmost peak of
Chocorua Mountain, and thence, to escape, took his leap
into the abyss—even so sharp an echo of a definite far-off
past, enriching the effect of an admirable silvered summit
(for Chocorua Mountain carries its grey head quite with
the grandest air), spent itself in the mere idleness of the
undiscriminated, tangled actual. There was one thinkable
reason, of course, for everything, which hung there as
a possible answer to any question, should any question
insist. Did one by chance exaggerate, did one rhapsodize
amiss, and was the apparent superior charm of the whole
thing mainly but an accident of one's own situation, the
state of having happened to be deprived to excess—that
is for too long—of naturalism in *quantity?* Here it was
in such quantity as one hadn't for years had to deal with;
and that might by itself be a luxury corrupting the
judgment.

It was absurd, perhaps, to have one's head so easily
turned ; but there was perfect convenience, at least, in
the way the parts of the impression fell together and
took a particular light. This light, from whatever source
proceeding, cast an irresistible spell, bathed the picture
in the confessed resignation of early autumn, the charming
sadness that resigned itself with a silent smile. I say
"silent" because the voice of the air had dropped as
forever, dropped to a stillness exquisite, day by day, for
a pilgrim from a land of stertorous breathing, one of the
windiest corners of the world ; the leaves of the forest
turned, one by one, to crimson and to gold, but never
broke off: all to the enhancement of this strange conscious hush of the landscape, which kept one in presence
as of a world created, a stage set, a sort of ample capacity

constituted, for—well, for things that wouldn't, after all, happen : more the pity for them, and for me and for you. This view of so many of the high places of the hills and deep places of the woods, the lost trails and wasted bowers, the vague, empty, rock-roughened pastures, the lonely intervals where the afternoon lingered and the hidden ponds over which the season itself seemed to bend as a young bedizened, a slightly melodramatic mother, before taking some guilty flight, hangs over the crib of her sleeping child—these things put you, so far as you were preoccupied with the human history of places, into a mood in which appreciation became a positive wantonness and the sense of quality, plucking up unexpectedly a spirit, fairly threatened to take the game into its hands. You discovered, when once it was stirred, an elegance in the commonest objects, and a mystery even in accidents that really represented, perhaps, mere plainness unashamed. Why otherwise, for instance, the inveterate charm of the silver-grey rock cropping through thinly-grassed acres with a placed and "composed" felicity that suggested the furniture of a drawing-room ? The great boulders in the woods, the pulpit-stones, the couchant and rampant beasts, the isolated cliffs and lichened cathedrals, had all, seen, as one passed, through their drizzle of forest light, a special New Hampshire beauty ; but I never tired of finding myself of a sudden in some lonely confined place, that was yet at the same time both wide and bright, where I could recognize, after the fashion of the old New Hampshire sociability, every facility for spending the day. There was the oddity—the place was furnished by its own good taste ; its bosky ring shut it in, the two or three gaps of the old forgotten enclosure made symmetrical doors, the sweet old stones had the surface of grey velvet, and the scattered wild apples were like figures in the carpet.

It might be an ado about trifles—and half the poetry,

roundabout, the poetry in solution in the air, was doubtless but the alertness of the touch of autumn, the imprisoned painter, the Bohemian with a rusty jacket, who
had already broken out with palette and brush ; yet the
way the colour begins in those days to be dabbed, the way,
here and there, for a start, a solitary maple on a woodside flames in single scarlet, recalls nothing so much as
the daughter of a noble house dressed for a fancy-ball,
with the whole family gathered round to admire her
before she goes. One speaks, at the same time, of the
orchards ; but there are properly no orchards where half
the countryside shows, all September, the easiest, most
familiar sacrifice to Pomona. The apple-tree, in New
England, plays the part of the olive in Italy, charges
itself with the effect of detail, for the most part otherwise
too scantly produced, and, engaged in this charming care,
becomes infinitely decorative and delicate. What it must
do for the too under-dressed land in May and June is
easily supposable ; but its office in the early autumn is to
scatter coral and gold. The apples are everywhere and
every interval, every old clearing, an orchard ; they have
"run down" from neglect and shrunken from cheapness
—you pick them up from under your feet but to bite into
them, for fellowship, and throw them away ; but as you
catch their young brightness in the blue air, where they
suggest strings of strange-coloured pearls tangled in the
knotted boughs, as you note their manner of swarming
for a brief and wasted gaiety, they seem to ask to be
praised only by the cheerful shepherd and the oaten pipe
The question of the encircled waters too, larger and
smaller—that again was perhaps an ado about trifles ; but
you can't, in such conditions, and especially at first, resist
the appeal of their extraordinarily mild faces and wooded
brims, with the various choice spots where the great
straight pines, interspaced beside them, and yielding to
small strands as finely curved as the eyebrows of beauty,

make the sacred grove and the American classic temple, the temple for the worship of the evening sky, the cult of the Indian canoe, of Fenimore Cooper, of W. C. Bryant, of the immortalizable water-fowl. They look too much alike, the lakes and the ponds, and this is, indeed, all over the world, too much a reproach to lakes and ponds—to all save the pick of the family, say, like George and Champlain ; the American idea, moreover, is too inveterately that woods shall grow thick to the water. Yet there is no feature of grace the landscape could so ill spare— let alone one's not knowing what other, what baser, promiscuity mightn't oppress the banks if that of the free overgrowth didn't. Each surface of this sort is a breathing-space in the large monotony ; the rich recurrence of water gives a polish to the manner itself, so to speak, of nature ; thanks to which, in any case, the memory of a characteristic perfection attaches, I find, to certain hours of declining day spent, in a shallow cove, on a fallen log, by the scarce-heard plash of the largest liquid expanse under Chocorua ; a situation interfused with every properest item of sunset and evening star, of darkening circle of forest, of boat that, across the water, put noiselessly out—of analogy, in short, with every typical triumph of the American landscape " school," now as rococo as so many squares of ingenious wool-work, but the remembered delight of our childhood. On *terra firma*, in New England, too often dusty or scrubby, the guarantee is small that some object at variance, cruelly at variance, with the glamour of the landscape school may not " put out." But that boat across the water is safe, is sustaining as far as it goes ; it puts out from the cove of romance, from the inlet of poetry, and glides straight over, with muffled oar, to the—well, to the right place.

The consciousness of quantity, rather, as opposed to quality, to which I just alluded, quantity inordinate, quantity duly impressive and duly, if need be, overwhelming, had been the form of vigilance posting itself at the window—whence, incontestably, after a little, yielding to the so marked agitation of its sister-sense, it stepped back into the shadow of the room. If memory, at any rate, with its message so far to carry, had played one a trick, imagination, or some finer faculty still, could play another to match it. If it had settled to a convenience of the mind that "New England scenery" was hard and dry and thin, scrubby and meagre and "plain," here was that comfort routed by every plea of fancy—though of a fancy indeed perhaps open to the charge of the morbid—and by every refinement of appeal. The oddest thing in the world would delightfully have happened—and happened just there—in case one had really found the right word for the anomaly of one's surprise. What would the right word be but that nature, in these lights, was no single one of the horrid things I have named, but was, instead of them all, that quite other happy and charming thing, *feminine?*—feminine from head to foot, in expression, tone and touch, mistress throughout of the feminine attitude and effect. That had by no means the figure recalled from far back, but when once it had fully glimmered out it fitted to perfection, it became the case like a crown of flowers and provided completely for one's relation to the subject.

"Oh Italy, thou woman-land!" breaks out Browning, more than once, straight at *that* mark, and with a force of example that, for this other collocation, served much more as an incitement than as a warning. Reminded vividly of the identities of latitude and living so much in the same relation to the sun, you never really in New Hampshire—nor in Massachusetts, I was soon able to observe—look out at certain hours for the violet spur of an Apennine or venture to speak, in your admiration, of Tuscan or Umbrian forms, without feeling that the ground has quite gratefully borne you. The matter, however, the matter of the insidious grace, is not at all only a question of amusing coincidence; something intrinsically lovable everywhere lurks—which most comes out indeed, no doubt, under the consummate art of autumn. How shall one lightly enough express it, how describe it 'or to what compare it?—since, unmistakably, after all, the numbered items, the few flagrant facts, fail perfectly to account for it. It is like some diffused, some slightly confounding, sweetness of voice, charm of tone and accent, on the part of some enormous family of rugged, of almost ragged, rustics—a tribe of sons and daughters too numerous to be counted and homogeneous perhaps to monotony. There was a voice in the air, from week to week, a spiritual voice: "Oh, the *land's* all right!"—it took on fairly a fondness of emphasis, it rebounded from other aspects, at times, with such a tenderness. Thus it sounded, the blessed note, under many promptings, but always in the same form and to the effect that the poor dear land itself—if that was all that was the matter—would beautifully "do." It seemed to plead, the pathetic presence, to be liked, to be loved, to be stayed with, lived with, handled with some kindness, shown even some courtesy of admiration. What was that but the feminine attitude?—not the actual, current, impeachable, but the old ideal and classic; the air of meeting you everywhere, standing in wait everywhere, yet always without conscious defiance, only in mild submission to your doing what you would with it. The mildness was of the very essence, the essence of all the forms and lines, all the postures and surfaces, all the slimness and thinness and elegance, all the consent, on the part of trees and rocks and streams, even of vague happy valleys and fine undistinguished hills, to be viewed, to their humiliation, in the mass, instead of being viewed in the piece.

It is perhaps absurd to have to hasten to add that doing what you would with it, in these irresponsible senses, simply left out of account, for the country in general, the proved, the notorious fact that nothing useful, nothing profitable, nothing directly economic, *could* be done at all. Written over the great New Hampshire region at least, and stamped, in particular, in the shadow of the admirable high-perched cone of Chocorua, which rears itself, all granite, over a huge interposing shoulder, quite with the *allure* of a minor Matterhorn—everywhere legible was the hard little historic record of agricultural failure and defeat. It had to pass for the historic background, that traceable truth that a stout human experiment had been tried, had broken down. One was in presence, everywhere, of the refusal to consent to history, and of the consciousness, on the part of every site, that this precious compound is in no small degree being insolently made, on the other side of the continent, at the expense of such sites. The touching appeal of nature, as I have called it therefore, the " Do something kind for me," is not so much a " Live upon me and thrive by me " as a " Live *with* me, somehow, and let us make out together what we may do for each other—something that is not merely estimable in more or less greasy greenbacks. See how 'sympathetic' I am," the still voice seemed everywhere to proceed, " and how I am therefore better than my fate ; see how I lend myself to poetry and sociability—positively to æsthetic use : give me that consolation." The appeal was thus not only from the rude absence of the company that had gone, and the still ruder presence of the company left, the scattered families, of poor spirit and loose habits, who had feared the risk of change ; it was to a listening ear, directly—that of the " summer people," to whom, in general, one soon began to figure so much of the country, in New England, as looking for its future ; with the consequence in fact that, from place to place, the summer people themselves almost promised to glow with a reflected light. It was a clue, at any rate, in the maze of contemplation, for this vision of the relation so established, the disinherited, the impracticable land throwing itself, as for a finer argument, on the non-rural, the intensely urban class, and the class in question throwing itself upon the land for reasons of its own. What would come of such an *entente*, on the great scale, for both parties?—that special wonderment was to strike me everywhere as in order. How populations with money to spare may extract a vulgar joy from " show " sections of the earth, like Switzerland and Scotland, we have seen abundantly proved, so that this particular lesson has little more to teach us ; in America, however, evidently, the difference in the conditions, and above all in the scale of demonstration, is apt to make lessons new and larger.

Once the whole question had ranged itself under that head—what would the "summer people," as a highly comprehensive term, do with the aspects (perhaps as a highly comprehensive term also), and what would the aspects do with the summer people?—it became conveniently portable and recurrently interesting. Perhaps one of the best reasons I can give for this last side of it was that it kept again and again presenting the idea of that responsibility for *appearances* which, in such an association as loomed thus large, was certain to have to fix itself somewhere. What was one to say of appearances as they actually prevailed—from the moment, I mean, they were not of the charming order that nature herself could care for? The appearances of man, the appearances of woman, and of their conjoined life, the general latent spectacle of their arrangements, appurtenances, manners, devices, opened up a different chapter, the leaves of which one could but musingly turn. A better expression of the effect of most of this imagery on the mind should really be sought, I think, in its seeming, through its sad consistency, a mere complete negation of

appearances—using the term in the sense of any familiar
and customary "care for looks." Even the recognition
that, the scattered summer people apart, the thin population was poor and bare had its bewilderment, on which I
shall presently touch ; but the poverty and the bareness
were, as we seemed to measure them, a straight admonition of all we had, from far back, so easily and comfortably
taken for granted, in the rural picture, on the other side
of the world. There was a particular thing that, more
than any other, had been pulled out of the view and that
left the whole show, humanly and socially, a collapse.
This particular thing was exactly the fact of the *importance*, the significance, imputable, in a degree, to appearances. In the region in which these observations first
languished into life that importance simply didn't exist
at all, and its absence was everywhere forlornly, almost
tragically, attested. There was the little white wooden
village, of course, with its houses in queer alignment and
its rudely-emphasized meeting-house, in particular, very
nearly as unconsecrated as the store or the town pump ;
but this represented, throughout, the highest tribute to
the amenities. A sordid ugliness and shabbiness hung,
inveterately, about the wayside "farms," and all their
appurtenances and incidents—above all, about their
inmates ; when the idea of appearance was anywhere
expressed (and its highest flights were but in the matter
of fresh paint or a swept dooryard), a summer person was
usually the author of the boon. The teams, the carts,
the conveyances in their kinds, the sallow, saturnine
natives in charge of them, the enclosures, the fences, the
gates, the wayside "bits," of whatever sort, so far as these
were referable to human attention or human neglect, kept
telling the tale of the difference made, in a land of long
winters, by the suppression of the two great factors of
the familiar English landscape, the squire and the parson.
What the squire and the parson do, between them, for

appearances (which is what I am talking of) in scenes, predominantly Anglo-Saxon, subject to their sway, is brought home, as in an ineffable glow, when the elements are reduced to "composing," in the still larger Anglo-Saxon light, without them. Here was no church, to begin with; and the shrill effect of the New England meeting-house, in general, so merely continuous and congruous, as to type and tone, with the common objects about it, the single straight breath with which it seems to blow the ground clear of the seated solidity of religion, is an impression that responds to the renewed sight of one of these structures as promptly as the sharp ring to the pressure of the electric button. One lives among English ancientries, for instance, as in a world toward the furnishing of which religion has done a large part. And here, immediately, was a room vast and vacant, with a vacancy especially reducible, for most of the senses, to the fact of that elimination. Perpetually, inevitably, moreover, as the restless analyst wandered, the eliminated thing *par excellence* was the thing most absent to sight— and for which, oh! a thousand times, the small substitutes, the mere multiplication of the signs of theological enterprise, in the tradition and on the scale of commercial and industrial enterprise, had no attenuation worth mentioning. The case, in the New Hampshire hills at least, was quite the same for the pervasive Patron, whose absence made such a hole. We went on counting up all the blessings we had, too unthankfully, elsewhere owed to him; we lost ourselves in the intensity of the truth that to compare a simplified social order with a social order in which feudalism had once struck deep was the right way to measure the penetration of feudalism. If there was no point here at which they had perceptibly begun, there was on the other side of the world no point at which they had perceptibly ceased. One's philosophy, one's logic might perhaps be muddled, but one clung to them for the convenience of their explanation of so much of the ugliness. The ugliness—one pounced, indeed, on this as on a talisman for the future—was the so complete abolition of *forms;* if, with so little reference to their past, present or future possibility, they could be said to have been even so much honoured as to be abolished.

The pounce at any rate was, for a guiding light, effectual; the guiding light worked to the degree of seeming at times positively to save the restless analyst from madness. He could make the absence of forms responsible, and he could thus react without bitterness—react absolutely with pity; he could judge without cruelty and condemn without despair; he could think of the case as perfectly definite and say to himself that, could forms only *be*, as a recognized accessory to manners, introduced and developed, the ugliness might begin scarcely to know itself. He could play with the fancy that the people might at last grow fairly to like them—far better, at any rate, than the class in question may in its actual ignorance suppose: the necessity would be to give it, on an adequate scale and in some lucid way, a taste of the revelation. What "form," meanwhile, *could* there be in the almost sophisticated dinginess of the present destitution? One thoughtfully asked that, though at the cost of being occasionally pulled up by odd glimpses of the underlying existence of a standard. There was the wage-standard, to begin with; the well-nigh awestruck view of the high rate of remuneration open to the most abysmally formless of "hired" men, indeed to field or house labour, expert or inexpert, on the part of either sex, in any connection: the ascertainment of which was one of the "bewilderments" I just now spoke of, one of the failures of consistency in the grey revelation. After this there was the standard, ah! the very high standard, of sensibility and propriety, so far as tribute on this ground was not owed by the parties themselves, but owed *to* them, not to be rendered, but to be received, and with a stiff, a warningly stiff, account kept of it. Didn't it appear at moments a theme for endless study, this queer range of the finer irritability in the breasts of those whose fastidiousness was compatible with the violation of almost every grace in life *but* that one ? " Are you the woman of the house ? " a rustic cynically squalid, and who makes it a condition of *any* intercourse that he be received at the front door of the house, not at the back, asks of a *maîtresse de maison*, a summer person trained to resignation, as preliminary to a message brought, as he then mentions, from the " washerlady." These are the phenomena, of course, that prompt the woman of the house, and perhaps still more the man, to throw herself, as I say, on the land, for what it may give her of balm and beauty—a character to which, as I also say, the land may affect these unfortunates as so consciously and tenderly playing up. The lesson had perhaps to be taught ; if the Patron is at every point so out of the picture, the end is none the less not yet of the demonstration, on the part of the figures peopling it, that they are not to be patronized. Once to see this, however, was again to focus the possible evolution of manners, the latent drama to come : the æsthetic enrichment of the summer people, so far as they should be capable or worthy of it, by contact with the consoling background, so full of charming secrets, and the forces thus conjoined for the production and the imposition of forms. Thrown back again almost altogether, as by the Jersey shore, on the excitement of the speculative, one could extend unlimitedly—by which I mean one could apply to a thousand phases of the waiting spectacle—the idea of the possible drama. So everything worked round, afresh, to the promise of the large interest.

III

If the interest then was large, this particular interest
of the "social" side of the general scene, more and more
likely to emerge, what better proof could I want again
than the differences of angle at which it continued to
present itself? The differences of angle—as obvious
most immediately, for instance, "north of the mountains,"
and first of all in the valley of the Saco—gathered into
their train a hundred happy variations. I kept tight hold
of my temporary clue, the plea of the country's amiability,
as I have called it, its insinuating appeal from too
rigorous a doom; but there was a certain strain in this,
from day to day, and relief was apparent as soon as the
conditions changed. They changed, notably, by the
rapid and complete drop of the sordid element from the
picture; it was, for all the world, of a sudden, as if
Appearance, precious principle, had again asserted its
rights. That confidence, clearly, at North Conway, had
come to it in the course of the long years, too many
to reckon over, that separated my late from my early
vision—though I recognized as disconcerting, toward the
close of the autumn day, to have to owe this perception,
in part, to the great straddling, bellowing railway, the
high, heavy, dominant American train that so reverses
the relation of the parties concerned, suggesting somehow
that the country exists for the "cars," which overhang it
like a conquering army, and not the cars for the country.
This presence had learned to penetrate the high valleys
and had altered, unmistakably, the old felicity of proportion. The old informal earthy coach-road was a firm
highway, wide and white—and ground to dust, for all its
firmness, by the whirling motor; without which I might
have followed it, back and back a little, into the near,
into the far, country of youth—left lying, however, as the

case stood, beyond the crest of a hill. Only the high rock-walls of the Ledges, the striking sign of the spot, were there; grey and perpendicular, with their lodged patches of shrub-like forest growth, and the immense floor, below them, where the Saco spreads and turns and the elms of the great general meadow stand about like candelabra (with their arms reversed) interspaced on a green table. There hung over these things the insistent hush of a September Sunday morning; nowhere greater than in the tended woods enclosing the admirable country home that I was able to enjoy as a centre for contemplation; woods with their dignity maintained by a large and artful clearance of undergrowth, and repaying this attention, as always, by something of the semblance of a sacred grove, a place prepared for high uses, even if for none rarer than high talk. There was a latent poetry— old echoes, ever so faint, that *would* come back; it made a general meaning, lighted the way to the great modern farm, all so contemporary and exemplary, so replete with beauty of beasts and convenience of man, with a positive dilettantism of care, but making one perhaps regret a little the big, dusky, heterogeneous barns, the more Bohemian bucolics, of the earlier time. I went down into the valley—that was an impression to woo by stages; I walked beside one of those great fields of standing Indian corn which make, to the eye, so perfect a note for the rest of the American rural picture, throwing the conditions back as far as our past permits, rather than forward, as so many other things do, into the age to come. The maker of these reflections betook himself at last, in any case, to an expanse of rock by a large bend of the Saco, and lingered there under the infinite charm of the place. The rich, full lapse of the river, the perfect brownness, clear and deep, as of liquid agate, in its wide swirl, the large indifferent ease in its pace and motion, as of some great benevolent institution smoothly working;

all this, with the sense of the deepening autumn about, gave I scarce know what pastoral nobleness to the scene, something raising it out of the reach of even the most restless of analysts. The analyst in fact could scarce be restless here ; the impression, so strong and so final, persuaded him perfectly to peace. This, on September Sunday mornings, was what American beauty *should* be ; it filled to the brim its idea and its measure—albeit Mount Washington, hazily overhung, happened not to contribute to the effect. It was the great, gay river, singing as it went, like some reckless adventurer, good-humoured for the hour and with his hands in his pockets, that argued the whole case and carried everything assentingly before it.

Who, for that matter, shall speak, who shall begin to speak, of the alacrity with which, in the New England scene (to confine ourselves for the moment only to that), the eye and the fancy take to the water?—take to it often for relief and security, the corrective it supplies to the danger of the common. The case is rare when it is not better than the other elements of the picture, even if these be at their best ; and its strength is in the fact that the common has, for the most part, to stop short at its brink ; no water being intrinsically less distinguished— save when it is dirty—than any other. By a fortunate circumstance, moreover, are not the objects usually afloat on American lakes and rivers, to say nothing of bays and sounds, almost always white and wonderful, high-piled, characteristic, fantastic things, begotten of the native conditions and shining in the native light? Let my question, however, not embroider too extravagantly my mere sense of driving presently, though after nightfall, and in the public conveyance, into a village that gave out, through the dusk, something of the sense of a flourishing Swiss village of the tourist season, as one recalls old Alpine associations : the swing of the coach, the cold, high air, the scattered hotels and their lighted windows, the loitering people who might be celebrated climbers or celebrated guides, the resonance of the bridge as one crossed, the gleam of the swift river under the lamps. My village had no happy name; it was, crudely speaking, but Jackson, N. H., just as the swift river that, later on, in the morning light, to the immediate vision, easily surpassed everything else, was only the river of the Wildcat—a superiority strictly comparative. The note of this superiority was in any case already there, for the first, for the nocturnal impression; scarce seen, only heard as yet, it could still give the gloom a larger lift than any derived from a tour of the piazzas of the hotels. This tour, undertaken while supper was preparing, in the interest of a study of manners, left room, all the same, for much support to the conviction I just expressed, the conviction that, name for name, the stream had got off better than the village, that streams *couldn't*, at the worst, have such cruel names as villages, and that this too, after all, was an intimation of their relative value. That inference was, for the actual case, to be highly confirmed; the Wildcat River, on the autumn morning, in its deep valley and its precipitous bed, was as headlong and romantic as one could desire; though, indeed, I am not, in frankness, prepared to say better things of it than of the great picture, the feature of the place, to a view of which I mounted an hour or two after breakfast.

Here, at least, where a small and charming country-house had seated itself very much as the best box, on the most expensive tier, rakes the prospect for grand opera— here might manners too be happily studied, save perhaps for their being enjoyed at too short range. Here, verily, were verandahs of contemplation, but admitting to such images of furnished peace, within, as could but illustrate a rare personal history. This was a felicity apart; whereas down in the valley, the night before, the story told at the lighted windows of the inns was precisely, was above all, of advantages impartially diffused and shared. That, at any rate, would seem in each instance the most direct message of the life displayed to the observer, on the fresher evenings, in the halls and parlours, the large, clean, bare spaces (almost penally clean and bare), where plain, respectable families seemed to sit and study in silence, with a kind of awe indeed, as from a sense of inevitable doom, their reflected resemblances, from group to group, their baffling identities of type and tone, their inability to escape from participations and communities. My figure of the opera-box, for the other, the removed, case, is justified meanwhile by the memory of the happy vision that was to make up to me for having missed Mount Washington at Intervale; the something splendidly scenic in the composition of the "Presidential range," hung in the air, across the valley, with its most eminent object holding exactly the middle of the stage and the grand effect stretching without a break to either wing. Mount Washington, seen from such a point of vantage, a kind of noble equality of intercourse, looks admirably, solidly *seated*, as with the other Presidential peaks standing at his chair; and the picture is especially sublime far off to the right, with the grand style of Carter's Dome, a masterly piece of drawing against the sky, and the romantic dip of Carter's Notch, the very ideal of the pass (other than Alpine) that announces itself to the winding wayfarer, for beauty and interest, from a distance. The names, "Presidential" and other, minister little to the poetry of association; but that, throughout the American scene, is a source of irritation with which the restless analyst has had, from far back, to count. Charming places, charming objects, languish, all round him, under designations that seem to leave on them the smudge of a great vulgar thumb—which is precisely a part of what the pleading land appears to hint to you

when it murmurs, in autumn, its intelligent refrain.   If it
feels itself better than so many of the phases of its fate,
so there are spots where you see it turn up at you, under
some familiar tasteless infliction of this order, the
plaintive eye of a creature wounded with a poisoned
arrow.

You learn, after a little, not to insist on names—that is
not to inquire of them ; and are happiest perchance when
the answer is made you as it was made me by a neighbour, in a railway train, on the occasion of my greatly
admiring, right and left of us, a tortuous brawling river.
I had supposed it for a moment, in my innocence, the
Connecticut—which it decidedly was not; it was only,
as appeared, a stream *quelconque*, a stream without an
identity.   That was better, somehow, than the adventure
of a little later—my learning, too definitely, that another
stream, ample, admirable, in every way distinguished, a
stream worthy of Ruysdael or Salvator Rosa, was known
but as the Farmington River.   This I could in no manner
put up with—this taking by the greater of the comparatively common little names of the less.   Farmington, as
I was presently to learn, is a delightful, a model village ;
but villages, fords, bridges are not the godparents of the
element that makes them possible, they are much rather
the godchildren.   So far as such reflections might be idle,
however, in an order so differently determined, they easily
lost themselves, on the morrow of Jackson, N. H., in an
impression of sharper intensity ; that of a drive away, on
the top of the coach, in the wondrous, lustrous early
morning and in company that positively gave what it had
to give quite as if it had had my curiosity on its conscience.
That curiosity held its breath, in truth, for fear of breaking the spell—the spell of the large liberty with which a
pair of summer girls and a summer youth, from the hotel,
took all nature and all society (so far as society was
present on the top of the coach) into the confidence of

their personal relation. Their personal relation—that of the young man was with the two summer girls, whose own was all with *him;* any other, with their mother, for instance, who sat speechless and serene beside me, with the other passengers, with the coachman, the guard, the quick-eared four-in-hand, being for the time completely suspended. The freedoms of the young three—who were, by the way, not in their earliest bloom either—were thus bandied in the void of the gorgeous valley without even a consciousness of its shriller, its recording echoes. The whole phenomenon was documentary; it started, for the restless analyst, innumerable questions, amid which he felt himself sink beyond his depth. The immodesty was too colossal to be anything but innocence—yet the innocence, on the other hand, was too colossal to be anything but inane. And they were alive, the slightly stale three: they talked, they laughed, they sang, they shrieked, they romped, they scaled the pinnacle of publicity and perched on it flapping their wings; whereby they were shown in possession of many of the movements of life. Life, however, involved in some degree experience—if only the experience, for instance, of the summer apparently just spent, at a great cost, in the gorgeous valley. How was *that*, how was the perception of any concurrent presence, how was the human or social function at all, compatible with the *degree* of the inanity? There was, as against this, the possibility that the inanity was feigned, if not the immodesty; and the fact that there would have been more immodesty in feigning it than in letting it flow clear. These were maddening mystifications, and the puzzle fortunately dropped with the arrival of the coach at the station.

IV

Clearly, none the less, there were puzzles and puzzles, and I had almost immediately the amusement of waking

up to another—this one of a different order altogether.
The point was that if the bewilderments I have just
mentioned had dropped, most other things had dropped
too : the challenge to curiosity here was in the extreme
simplification of the picture, a simplification on original
lines.   Not that there was not still much to think of—if
only because one had to stare at the very wonder of a
picture so simplified.   The thing now was to catch this
note, to keep it in the ear and see, really, how far and how
long it would sound.   The simplification, for that immediate vision, was to a broad band of deep and clear
blue sea, a blue of the deepest and clearest conceivable,
limited in one quarter by its far and sharp horizon of
sky, and in the other by its near and sharp horizon of
yellow sand overfringed with a low woody shore ; the
whole seen through the contorted cross-pieces of stunted,
wind-twisted, far-spreading, quite fantastic old pines and
cedars, whose bunched bristles, at the ends of long limbs,
produced, against the light, the most vivid of all reminders.
Cape Cod, on this showing, was exactly a pendent,
pictured Japanese screen or banner ; a delightful little
triumph of " impressionism," which, during my short visit
at least, never departed, under any provocation, from its
type.   Its type, so easily formulated, so completely filled,
was there the last thing at night and the first thing in
the morning ; there was rest for the mind—for that,
certainly, of the restless analyst—in having it so exactly
under one's hand.   After that one could read into it other
meanings without straining or disturbing it.   There was
a couchant promontory in particular, half bosky with the
evergreen boskage of the elegant kakemono, half bare
with the bareness of refined, the *most* refined, New
England decoration—a low, hospitable headland projected, as by some water-colourist master of the trick, into
a mere brave wash of cobalt.   It interfered, the sweet
promontory, with its generous Boston bungalow, its

verandahs still haunted with old summer-times, and so wide that the present could elbow and yet not jostle the past—it interfered no whit, for all its purity of style, with the human, the social question always dogging the steps of the ancient contemplative person and making him, before each scene, wish really to get *into* the picture, to cross, as it were, the threshold of the frame. It never lifts, verily, this obsession of the story-seeker, however often it may flutter its wings, it may bruise its breast, against surfaces either too hard or too blank. " The *manners*, the manners : where and what are they, and what have they to tell ? "—that haunting curiosity, essential to the honour of his office, yet making it much of a burden, fairly buzzes about his head the more pressingly in proportion as the social mystery, the lurking human secret, seems more shy.

Then it is that, as he says to himself, the secret must be most queer—and it might therefore well have had, so insidiously sounded, a supreme queerness on Cape Cod. For not the faintest echo of it trembled out of the blankness ; there were always the little white houses of the village, there were always the elegant elms, feebler and more feathery here than further inland ; but the life of the little community was practically locked up as tight as if it had *all* been a question of painted Japanese silk. And that was doubtless, for the story-seeker, absolutely the little story : the constituted blankness was the whole business, and one's opportunity was all, thereby, for a study of exquisite emptiness. This was stuff, in its own way, of a beautiful quality ; that impression came to me with a special sweetness that I have not forgotten. The help in the matter was that I had not forgotten, either, a small pilgrimage or two of far-away earlier years—the sense as of absent things in other summer-times, golden afternoons that referred themselves for their character simply to sandy roads and primitive " farms," crooked inlets of mild sea and, at the richest, large possibilities of worked cranberry-swamp. I remembered, in fine, Matta-poisett, I remembered Marion, as admirable examples of that frequent New England phenomenon, the case the consummate example of which I was soon again to recognize in Newport—the presence of an *unreasoned* appeal, in nature, to the sense of beauty, the appeal on a basis of items that failed somehow, count and recount them as one would, to justify the effect and make up the precious sum. The sum, at Newport above all, as I was soon again to see, is the exquisite, the irresistible; but you falter before beginning to name the parts of the explanation, conscious how short the list may appear. Thus everything, in the whole range of imagery, affirms itself and interposes; you will, you inwardly determine, arrive at some notation of manners even if you perish in the attempt. Thus, as I jogged southward, from Boston, in a train that stopped and stopped again, for my fuller enlightenment, and that insisted, the good old promiscuous American car itself, on having as much of its native character as possible for my benefit, I already knew I must fall back on old props of association, some revival of the process of seeing the land grow mild and vague and interchangeably familiar with the sea, all under the spell of the reported "gulf-stream," those mystic words that breathe a softness wherever they sound.

It was imperative here that they should do what they could for me, and they must have been in full operation when, on my arrival at the small station from which I was to drive across to Cotuit—"across the Cape," as who should say, romantic thought, though I strain a point geographically for the romance—I found initiation awaiting me in the form of minimized horse-and-buggy and minimized man. The man was a little boy in tight knickerbockers, the horse barely an animal at all, a mere ambling spirit in shafts on the scale of a hairpin, the

buggy disembodied save for its wheels, the whole thing
the barest infraction of the road, of the void : circumstances, altogether, that struck the note, the right, the
persistent one—that of my baffled endeavour, while in
the neighbourhood, to catch life in the fact, and of my
then having to recognize it as present *without* facts, or
with only the few (the little white houses, the feathery
elms, the band of ocean blue, the stripe of sandy yellow,
the tufted pines in angular silhouette, the cranberry-
swamps stringed across, for the picking, like the ruled
pages of ledgers), that fell, incorruptibly silent, into the
picture. We were still far from our goal, that first hour,
when I had recognized the full pictorial and other
" value " of my little boy and his little accessories ; had
seen, in the amiable waste that we continued to plough
till we struck, almost with a shock, the inconsistency
of a long stretch of new " stone " road, that, socially,
economically, every contributive scrap of this detail was
required. I drained my small companion, by gentle
pressure, of such side-lights as he could project, consisting
almost wholly, as they did, of a prompt and shrill, an
oddly-emphasized " Yes, *sir !* " to each interrogative
attempt to break ground. The summer people had
already departed—with, as it seemed to me, undue
precipitation ; the very hotel offered, in its many-
windowed bulk, the semblance of a mere huge brittle
sea-shell that children tired of playing with it have cast
again upon the beach ; the alignments of white cottages
were, once more, as if the children had taken, for a
change, to building houses of cards and then had
deserted *them.* I remember the sense that something
must be done for penetration, for discovery ; I remember
an earnest stroll, undertaken for a view of waterside life,
which resulted in the perception of a young man, in a
spacious but otherwise unpeopled nook, a clear, straight-
forward young man to converse with, for a grand

opportunity, across the water, waist-high in the quiet
tide and prodding the sea-bottom for oysters ; also in the
discovery of an animated centre of industry of which
oysters again were the motive : a mute citizen or two
packing them in boxes, on the beach, for the Boston
market, the hammer of some vague carpentry hard by,
and, filling the air more than anything else, the unabashed
discourse of three or four school-children at leisure,
visibly "prominent" and apparently in charge of the life
of the place.   I remember not less a longish walk, and a
longer drive, into low extensions of woody, piney, pondy
landscape, veined with blue inlets and trimmed, on
opportunity, with blond beaches—through all of which I
pursued in vain the shy spectre of a revelation.   The
only revelation seemed really to be that, quite as in New
Hampshire, so many people had "left" that the remaining characters, on the sketchy page, were too few to
form a word.   With this, accordingly, of what, in the
bright air, for the charmed visitor, were the softness and
sweetness of impression *made ?*   I had again to take it
for a mystery.

V

This was really, for that matter, but the first phase of
a resumed, or rather of a greatly-enlarged, acquaintance
with the New England village in its most exemplary
state : the state of being both sunned and shaded ; of
exhibiting more fresh white paint than can be found
elsewhere in equal areas, and yet of correcting that
conscious, that doubtless often somewhat embarrassed,
hardness of countenance with an art of its own.   The
descriptive term is of the simplest, the term that suffices
for the whole family when at its best : having spoken of
them as "elm-shaded," you have said so much about
them that little else remains.   It is but a question,

throughout, of the quantity, the density, of their shade; often so thick and ample, from May to November, that their function, in the social, in the economic, order would seem on occasion to consist solely of their being passive to that effect. To note the latter, accordingly, to praise it, to respond to its appeal for admiration, practically represents, as you pass beneath the great feathery arches, the only comment that may be addressed to the scene. The charming thing—if that be the best way to take it— is that the scene is everywhere the same; whereby tribute is always ready and easy, and you are spared all shocks of surprise and saved any extravagance of discrimination. These communities stray so little from the type, that you often ask yourself by what sign or difference you know one from the other. The goodly elms, on either side of the large straight "street," rise from their grassy margin in double, ever and anon in triple, file; the white paint, on wooden walls, amid open dooryards, reaffirms itself eternally behind them—though hanging back, during the best of the season, with a sun-checkered, " amusing " vagueness; while the great verdurous vista, the high canopy of meeting branches, has the air of consciously playing the trick and carrying off the picture. " See with how little we do it; count over the elements and judge how few they are : in other words come back in winter, in the months of the naked glare, when the white paint looks dead and dingy against the snow, the poor dear old white paint— immemorial, ubiquitous, save as venturing into brown or yellow—which is really all we have to build on!" Some such sense as that you may catch from the murmur of the amiable elms—if you are a very restless analyst indeed, that is a very indiscreet listener.

As you wouldn't, however, go back in winter on any account whatever, and least of all for any such dire discovery, the picture hangs undisturbed in your gallery, and you even, with extended study of it, class it among your best mementos of the great autumnal harmony. The truth is that, for six or seven weeks after the mid-September, among the mountains of Massachusetts and Connecticut, the mere *fusion* of earth and air and water, of light and shade and colour, the almost shameless tolerance of nature for the poor human experiment, are so happily effective that you lose all reckoning of the items of the sum, that you in short find in your draught, contentedly, a single strong savour. By all of which I don't mean to say that this sweetness of the waning year has not more taste in the presence of certain objects than in the presence of certain others. Objects remarkable enough, objects rich and rare perhaps, objects at any rate curious and interesting, emerge, for genial reference, from the gorgeous blur, and would commit me, should I give them their way, to excesses of specification. So I throw myself back upon the fusion, as I have called it—with the rich light hanging on but half-a-dozen spots. This renews the vision of the Massachusetts Berkshire—land beyond any other, in America, to-day, as one was much reminded, of leisure on the way to legitimation, of the social idyll, of the workable, the expensively workable, American form of country life; and, in especial, of a perfect consistency of surrender to the argument of the verdurous vista. This is practically the last word of such communities as Stockbridge, Pittsfield, Lenox, or of such villages as Salisbury and Farmington, over the Connecticut border. I speak of consistency in spite of the fact that it has doubtless here and there, under the planted elms, suffered some injury at the hands of the summer people; for really, beneath the wide mantle of parti-coloured Nature, nothing matters but the accidental liability of the mantle here and there to fall thickest. Thus it is then that you do, after a little, differentiate, from place to place, and compare and even prefer; thus it is that you recognize a scale and a range of amplitude —nay, more, wonderful to say, on occasion an emergence of detail ; thus it is, in fine, that, while accepting the just eminence of Stockbridge and Pittsfield, for instance, you treat yourself on behalf of Farmington to something like a luxury of discrimination.

I may perhaps not go the length of asserting that Farmington might brave undismayed the absolute removal of the mantle of charity ; since the great elm-gallery there struck me as not less than elsewhere essentially mistress of the scene.   Only there were particular felicities there within the general—and anything very particular, in the land at large, always gave the case an appearance of rarity.   When the great elm-gallery happens to be garnished with old houses, and the old houses happen to show style and form and proportion, and the hand of time, further, has been so good as to rest on them with all the pressure of protection and none of that of interference, then it is that the New England village may placidly await any comer.   Farmington sits with this confidence on the top of a ridge that presents itself in its fringed length—a straight avenue seen in profile—to the visitor taking his way from the station across a couple of miles of level bottom that speak, for New England, of a luxury of culture ; and nothing could be more fastidious and exceptional, and thereby more impressive in advance, than such upliftedness of posture.   What is it but the note of the aristocratic in an air that so often affects us as drained precisely, and well-nigh to our gasping, of any exception to the common?   The indication I here glance at secures for the place in advance, as you measure its detachment across the valley, a positively thrilled attention.   Then comes, under the canopy of autumn, your vision of the grounds of this mild haughtiness, every one of which you gratefully allow.   Stay as many hours as you will—and my stay was but of hours—they don't break down; you trace them into fifty minor titles and dignities, all charming aspects and high refinements of the older New England domestic architecture. Not only, moreover, are the best houses so "good"—the good ones are so surprisingly numerous. That is all they seem together to say. "We are good, yes—we are excellent; though, if we know it very well, we make no vulgar noise about it: we only just stand here, in our long double line, in the manner of mature and just slightly-reduced gentlewomen seated against the wall at an evening party (some party where mature gentlewomen unusually abound), and neither too boldly affront the light nor shrink from the favouring shade." That again, on the spot, is the discreet voice of the air—which quavered away, for me, into still other admissions.

It takes but the barest semitone to start the story-seeker curious of manners—the story-seeker impenitent and uncorrected, as happened in this case, by a lesson unmistakably received, or at least intended, a short time before. He had put a question, on that occasion, with an expectancy doubtless too crude; he had asked a resident of a large city of the middle West what might be, credibly, the conditions of the life "socially" led there. He had not, at Farmington, forgotten the ominous pause that had preceded the reply: "The conditions of the life? Why, the same conditions as everywhere else." He had not forgotten, either, the thrill of his sense of this collapse of his interlocutor: the case being, obviously, that it is of the very nature of conditions, as reported on by the expert—and it was to the expert he had appealed—to vary from place to place, so that they fall into as many groups, and constitute as many stamps, as there are different congregations of men. His interlocutor was not of the expert—*that* had really been the lesson; and it was with a far different poetry, the sweet shyness of veracity, that Farmington confessed to idiosyncrasies. I have too little space, however, as I had then too little time, to pretend to have lifted more than the smallest corner of this particular veil; besides which, if it is of the essence of the land, in these regions, to throw you back, after a little, upon the possible humanities, so it often results from the social study, too baffling in many a case, that you are thrown back upon the land. That agreeable, if sometimes bewildering, seesaw is perhaps the best figure, in such conditions, for the restless analyst's tenor of life. It was an effect of the fusion he has endeavoured to suggest; it is certainly true, at least, that, among the craggy hills, among little mountains that turned so easily, at any opening, to clearness of violet and blue, among the wood-circled dells that seemed to wait as for afternoon dances, among the horizons that recalled at their will the Umbrian note and the finer drawing, every ugliness melted and dropped, any wonderment at the other face of the medal seemed more trouble than it was worth. It was enough that the white village or the painted farm could gleam from afar, on the faintly purple slope, like a thing of mystery or of history; it was enough that the charming hill-mass, happily presented and foreshortened, should lie there like some beast, almost heraldic, resting his nose on his paws.

Those images, for retrospect, insistently supplant the others; though I have notes enough, I find, about the others too—about the inscrutability of the village street in general, for instance, in any relation but its relation to its elms. What *they* seemed to say is what I have mentioned; but what secrets, meanwhile, did the rest of the scene keep? *Were* there any secrets at all, or had the outward blankness, the quantity of absence, as it were, in the air, its inward equivalent as well? There was the high, thin church, made higher, made highest, and sometimes, as at Farmington, made as pretty as a monstrous Dutch toy, by its steeple of quaint and classic carpentry; but this monument appeared to *testify* scarce more than some large white card, embellished with a stencilled border, on which a message or a sentence, an invitation or a revelation, might be still to be inscribed. The present, the positive, was mainly represented, ever, by the level railway-crossing, gaining expression from its localization of possible death and destruction, where the great stilted, strident, yet so almost comically impersonal train, which, with its so often undesignated and so always unservanted stations, and its general air of "bossing" the neighbourhoods it warns, for climax of its characteristic curtness, to "look out" for its rush, is everywhere a large contribution to one's impression of a kind of monotony of acquiescence. This look as of universal acquiescence plays somehow through the visible vacancy—seems a part of the thinness, the passivity, of that absence of the settled standard which contains, as I more and more felt, from day to day, the germ of the most final of all my generalizations. I needn't be too prompt with it—so much higher may it hold its head, I foresee, when it flowers, perfectly, as a conclusion, than when it merely struggles through the side of the subject as a tuft for provisional clutching. It sprouts in that soil, none the less, betimes, this apprehension that the "common man" and the common woman have here their appointed paradise and sphere, and that the sign of it is the abeyance, on many a scene, of any wants, any tastes, any habits, any traditions but theirs. The bullying railway orders them off their own decent avenue without a fear that they will "stand up" to it; the tone of the picture is the pitch of their lives, and when you listen to what the village street seems to say, marking it, at the end, with your "Is that *all?*" it is as if you had had your account of a scheme fashioned preponderantly in their image.

I mean in *theirs* exactly, with as little provision for what is too foul for them as for what is too fair: the very middle, the golden mean, of the note of the common, to which the two extremes of condition are equally wanting; though with the mark strongest, if anywhere, against dusky misfortune and precarious dependence. The romance of costume, for better or worse, the implication of vices, accomplishments, manners, accents, attitudes, is as absent for evil as for good, for a low connection as for a high: which is why the simplification covers so much ground, that of public houses, that of kinds of people, that of suggestions, however faint, of discernible opportunity, of any deviation, in other words, into the *un*common. There are no "kinds" of people; there are simply people, very, very few, and all of one kind, the kind who thus simply invest themselves for you in the grey truth that they don't go to the public house. It's a negative garment, but it must serve you; which it makes shift to do while you keep on asking, from the force of acquired habit, what may be behind, what beneath, what within, what may represent, in such conditions, the appeal of the senses or the tribute to them; what, in such a show of life, may take the place (to put it as simply as possible) of amusement, of social and sensual margin, overflow and by-play. Of course there *is* by-play here and there; here and there, of course, extremes *are* touched: otherwise, the whole concretion, in its thinness, would crack, and the fact is that two or three of these strong patches of surface-embroidery remain with me as curious and interesting. Never was such by-play as in a great new house on a hilltop that overlooked the most composed of communities; a house apparently conceived—and with great felicity—on the lines of a magnified Mount Vernon, and in which an array of modern "impressionistic" pictures, mainly French, wondrous examples of Manet, of Degas, of

Claude Monet, of Whistler, of other rare recent hands, treated us to the momentary effect of a large slippery sweet inserted, without a warning, between the compressed lips of half-conscious inanition. One hadn't quite known one was starved, but the morsel went down by the mere authority of the thing consummately *prepared*. Nothing else had been, in all the circle, prepared to anything like the same extent; and though the consequent taste, as a mixture with the other tastes, was of the queerest, no proof of the sovereign power of art could have been, for the moment, sharper. It happened to be that particular art—it might as well, no doubt, have been another; it made everything else shrivel and fade: it was like the sudden trill of a nightingale, lord of the hushed evening.

These appeared to be, over the land, always possible adventures; obviously I should have others of the same kind; I could let them, in all confidence, accumulate and wait. But, if that was one kind of extreme, what meanwhile was the other kind, the kind portentously alluded to by those of the sagacious who had occasionally put it before me that the village street, the arched umbrageous vista, half so candid and half so cool, is too frequently, in respect to "morals," but a whited sepulchre? They had so put it before me, these advisers, but they had as well, absolutely and all tormentingly, so left it: partly as if the facts were too abysmal for a permitted distinctness, and partly, no doubt, as from the general American habit of indirectness, of positive primness, of allusion to those matters that are sometimes collectively spoken of as "the great facts of life." It had been intimated to me that the great facts of life are in high fermentation on the other side of the ground glass that never for a moment flushes, to the casual eye, with the hint of a lurid light: so much, at least, one had no alternative, under pressure, but to infer. The inference, however, still left the

question a prey to vagueness—it being obvious that
vice requires forms not less than virtue, or perhaps even
more, and that forms, up and down the prospect, were
exactly what one waited in vain for. The theory that
no community *can* live wholly without by-play, and the
confirmatory word, for the particular case, of more
initiated reporters, these things were all very well ; but
before a scene peeled as bare of palpable pretext as the
American sky is often peeled of clouds (in the interest of
the slightly acid juice of its light), where and how was
the application to be made? It came at last, the application—that, I mean, of the portentous hint ; and under it,
after a fashion, the elements fell together. Why the
picture *shouldn't* bristle with the truth—that was all
conceivable ; that the truth could only strike inward,
horribly inward, not playing up to the surface—this too
needed no insistence ; what was sharpest for reflection
being, meanwhile, a couple of minor appearances, which
one gathered as one went. That our little arts of pathetic,
of humorous, portrayal may, for all their claim to an
edifying " realism," have on occasion small veracity and
courage—that again was a remark pertinent to the matter.
But the strangest link in the chain, and quite the horridest,
was this other, of high value to the restless analyst—
that, as the " interesting " puts in its note but where it
can and where it will, so the village street and the lonely
farm and the hillside cabin became positively richer
objects under the smutch of imputation ; twitched with
a grim effect the thinness of their mantle, shook out of
its folds such crudity and levity as they might, and
borrowed, for dignity, a shade of the darkness of Cenci-
drama, of monstrous legend, of old Greek tragedy, and
thus helped themselves out for the story-seeker more
patient almost of anything than of flatness.

There was not flatness, accordingly, though there
might be dire dreariness, in some of those impressions

gathered, for a climax, in the Berkshire country of Massachusetts, which forced it upon the fancy that here at last, in far, deep mountain valleys, where the winter is fierce and the summer irresponsible, was that heart of New England which makes so pretty a phrase for print and so stern a fact, as yet, for feeling. During the great loops thrown out by the lasso of observation from the wonder-working motor-car that defied the shrinkage of autumn days, this remained constantly the best formula of the impression and even of the emotion ; it sat in the vehicle with us, but spreading its wings to the magnificence of movement, and gathering under them indeed most of the meanings of the picture. The heart of New England, at this rate, was an ample, a generous, heart, the largest demands on which, as to extent and variety, seemed not to overstrain its capacity. But it was where the mountain-walls rose straight and made the valleys happiest or saddest—one couldn't tell which, as to the felicity of the image, and it didn't much matter—that penetration was, for the poetry of it, deepest ; just as generalization, for an opposite sort of beauty, was grandest on those several occasions when we perched for a moment on the summit of a "pass," a real little pass, slowly climbed to and keeping its other side, with an art all but Alpine, for a complete revelation, and hung there over the full vertiginous effect of the long and steep descent, the clinging road, the precipitous fall, the spreading, shimmering land bounded by blue horizons. We liked the very vocabulary, reduced to whatever minimum, of these romanticisms of aspect ; again and again the land would do beautifully, if that were all that was wanted, and it deserved, the dear thing, thoroughly, any verbal caress, any tenderness of term, any share in a claim to the grand manner, to which we could responsively treat it. The grand manner was in the winding ascent, the rocky defile, the sudden rest for wonder, and

all the splendid reverse of the medal, the world belted
afresh as with purple sewn with pearls—melting, in other
words, into violet hills with vague white towns on their
breasts.

That was, at the worst, for October afternoons, the
motor helping, our frequent fare ; the habit of confidence
in which was, perhaps, on no occasion so rewarded as on
that of a particular plunge, from one of the highest places,
through an ebbing golden light, into the great Lebanon
" bowl," the vast, scooped hollow in one of the hither
depths of which (given the quarter of our approach) we
found the Shaker settlement once more or less, I believe,
known to fame, ever so grimly planted.   The grimness,
even, was all right, when once we had admiringly dropped
down and down and down ; it would have done for that
of a Buddhist monastery in the Himalayas—though more
savagely clean and more economically impersonal, we
seemed to make out, than the communities of older faiths
are apt to show themselves.   I remember the mere chill
of contiguity, like the breath of the sepulchre, as we
skirted, on the wide, hard floor of the valley, the rows of
gaunt windows polished for no whitest, stillest, meanest
face, even, to look out ; so that they resembled the
parallelograms of black paint criss-crossed with white lines
that represent transparency in Nuremberg dolls'-houses.
It wore, the whole settlement, as seen from without, the
strangest air of active, operative death ; as if the state of
extinction were somehow, obscurely, administered and
applied—the final hush of passions, desires, dangers,
converted into a sort of huge stiff brush for sweeping
away rubbish, or still more, perhaps, into a monstrous
comb for raking in profit.   The whole thing had the
oddest appearance of mortification made to "pay."
This was really, however, sounding the heart of New
England beyond its depth, for I am not sure that the
New York boundary had not been, just there, over-

passed ; there flowered out of that impression, at any rate, another adventure, the very bravest possible for a shortened day, of which the motive, whether formulated or not, had doubtless virtually been to feel, with a far-stretched arm, for the heart of New York. *Had* New York, the miscellaneous monster, a heart at all ?—this inquiry, amid so much encouraged and rewarded curiosity, might have been well on the way to become sincere, and we kept groping, between a prompt start and an extremely retarded return, for any stray sign of an answer.

The answer, perhaps, in the event, still eluded us, but the pursuit itself, away across State lines, through zones of other manners, through images of other ideals, through densities of other values, into a separate sovereign civil-ization in short—this, with "a view of the autumnal Hudson " for an added incentive, became, in all the conditions, one of the finer flowers of experience. To be on the lookout for differences was, not unnaturally, to begin to meet them just over the border and see them increase and multiply ; was, indeed, with a mild con-sistency, to feel it steal over us that we were, as we advanced, in a looser, shabbier, perhaps even rowdier world, where the roads were of an easier virtue and the " farms " of a scantier pride, where the absence of the ubiquitous sign-post of New England, joy of lonely corners, left the great spaces with an accent the less ; where, in fine, the wayside bravery of the common-wealth of Massachusetts settled itself, for memory, all serenely, to suffer by no comparison whatever. And yet it wasn't, either, that this other was not also a big, bold country, with ridge upon ridge and horizon by horizon to deal with, insistently, pantingly, puffingly, pausingly, before the great river showed signs of taking up the tale with its higher hand ; it wasn't, above all, that the most striking signs by which the nearness of the river was first announced, three or four fine old houses overlooking the long road, reputedly Dutch manors, seats of patriarchs and patroons, and unmistakably rich " values " in the vast, vague scene, had not a nobler archaic note than even the best of the New England colonial; it wasn't that, finally, the Hudson, when we reached the town that repeats in so minor a key the name of the stream, was not autumnal indeed, with majestic impenetrable mists that veiled the waters almost from sight, showing only the dim Catskills, off in space, as perfunctory graces, cheaply thrown in, and leaving us to roam the length of a large straight street which was, yes, decidedly, for comparison, for curiosity, not as the streets of Massachusetts.

The best here, to speak of, was that the motor underwent repair and that its occupants foraged for dinner— finding it indeed excellently at a quiet cook-shop, about the middle of the long-drawn way, after we had encountered coldness at the door of the main hotel by reason of our French poodle. This personage had made our group, admirably composed to our own sense as it was, only the more illustrious; but minds indifferent to an opportunity of intercourse, if but the intercourse of mere vision, with fine French poodles, may be taken always as suffering where they have sinned. The hospitality of the cook-shop was meanwhile touchingly, winningly unconditioned, yet full of character, of local, of national truth, as we liked to think: documentary, in a high degree—we talked it over—for American life. Wasn't it interesting that with American life so personally, so freely affirmed, the superstition of cookery should yet be so little denied? It was the queer old complexion of the long straight street, however, that most came home to me: Hudson, in the afternoon quiet, seemed to stretch back, with fumbling friendly hand, to the earliest outlook of my consciousness. Many matters had come and gone, innumerable impressions had supervened; yet here, in the stir of the senses, a whole range of small forgotten things revived, things intensely Hudsonian, more than Hudsonian ; small echoes and tones and sleeping lights, small sights and sounds and smells that made one, for an hour, *as* small—carried one up the rest of the river, the very river of life indeed, as a thrilled, roundabouted pilgrim, by primitive steamboat, to a mellow, mediæval Albany.

VI

It is a convenience to be free to confess that the play of perception during those first weeks was quickened, in the oddest way, by the wonderment (which was partly also the amusement) of my finding how many corners of the general, of the local, picture had anciently never been unveiled for me at all, and how many unveiled too briefly and too scantly, with quite insufficient bravery of gesture. That might make one ask by what strange law one had lived in the other time, with gaps, to that number, in one's experience, in one's consciousness, with so many muffled spots in one's general vibration—and the answer indeed to such a question might carry with it an infinite penetration of retrospect, a penetration productive of ghostly echoes as sharp sometimes as aches or pangs. So many had been the easy things, the contiguous places, the conspicuous objects, to right or to left of the path, that had been either unaccountably or all too inevitably left undiscovered, and which were to live on, to the inner vision, through the long years, as mere blank faces, round, empty, metallic, senseless disks dangling from familiar and reiterated names. Why, at the same time, one might ask, had the consciousness of irritation from these vain forms not grown greater ? why had the inconvenience, or the disgrace, of early privation become an accepted memory ? All, doubtless, in the very interest, precisely, of this eventual belated romance, and so that adventures, even of minor type, so preposterously postponed should be able to deck themselves at last with a kind of accumulation of freshness.

So the freshness, all the autumn, kept breaking through the staleness—when the staleness, so agreeably flavoured with hospitality, and indeed with new ingredients, was a felt element at all. There was after all no moment perhaps at which one element stood out so very sharply from the other—the hundred emendations and retouches of the old picture, its greater depth of tone, greater show of detail, greater size and scale, tending by themselves to confound and mislead, in a manner, the lights and shades of remembrance. Very promptly, in the Boston neighbourhoods, the work of time loomed large, and the difference made by it, as one might say, for the general richness. The richness might have its poverties still and the larger complexity its crudities ; but, all the same, to look back was to seem to have been present at an extraordinary general process, that of the rapid, that of the ceaseless relegation of the *previous* (on the part of the whole visible order) to one of the wan categories of misery. What was taking place was a perpetual repudiation of the past, so far as there had been a past to repudiate, so far as the past was a positive rather than a negative quantity. There had been plenty in it, assuredly, of the negative, and that was but a shabbiness to disown or a deception to expose ; yet there had been an old conscious commemorated life too, and it was this that had become the victim of supersession. The pathos, so to call it, of the impression was somehow that it didn't, the earlier, simpler condition, still resist or protest, or at all expressively flush through ; it was consenting to become a past with all the fine candour with which it had tried to affirm itself, in its day, as a present—and very much, for that matter, as with a due ironic forecast of the fate in store for the hungry, triumphant actual.

This savours perhaps of distorted reflection, but there was really a light over it in which the whole spectacle was to shine. *The will to grow* was everywhere written large, and to grow at no matter what or whose expense. I had naturally seen it before, I had seen it, on the other side of the world, in a thousand places and forms, a thousand hits and misses: these things are the very screeches of the pipe to which humanity is actually dancing. But here, clearly, it was a question of scale and space and chance, margin and elbow-room, the quantity of floor and loudness of the dance-music; a question of the ambient air, above all, the permitting medium, which had at once, for the visitor's personal inhalation, a dry taste in the mouth. Thin and clear and colourless, what would it ever say "no" to? or what would it ever paint thick, indeed, with sympathy and sanction? With so little, accordingly, within the great frame of the picture, to prevent or to prescribe, it was as if anything might be done there that any sufficient number of subscribers to any sufficient number of sufficiently noisy newspapers might want. That, moreover, was but another name for the largest and straightest perception the restless analyst had yet risen to—the perception that awaits the returning absentee from this great country, on the wharf of disembarkation, with an embodied intensity that no superficial confusion, no extremity of chaos any more than any brief mercy of accident, avails to mitigate. The waiting observer need be little enough of an analyst, in truth, to arrive at that consciousness, for the phenomenon is vivid in direct proportion as the ship draws near. The great presence that bristles for him on the sounding dock, and that shakes the planks, the loose boards of its theatric stage to an inordinate unprecedented rumble, is the monstrous form of Democracy, which is thereafter to project its shifting angular shadow, at one time and another, across every inch of the field of his vision. It is the huge democratic broom that has made the clearance and that one seems to see brandished in the empty sky.

That is of course on one side no great discovery, for what does even the simplest soul ever sail westward for, at this time of day, if not to profit, so far as possible, by "the working of democratic institutions"? The political, the civic, the economic view of them is a study that may be followed, more or less, at a distance; but the way in which they determine and qualify manners, feelings, communications, modes of contact and conceptions of life —this is a revelation that has its full force and its lively interest only on the spot, where, when once caught, it becomes the only clue worth mentioning in the labyrinth. The condition, notoriously, represents an immense boon, but what does the enjoyment of the boon represent? The clue is never out of your hands, whatever other objects, extremely disconnected from it, may appear at the moment to fill them. The democratic consistency, consummately and immitigably complete, shines through with its hard light, whatever equivocal gloss may happen momentarily to prevail. You may talk of other things, and you do, as much as possible; but you are really thinking of that one, which has everything else at its mercy. What indeed is this circumstance that the condition is thus magnified but the commanding value of the picture, its message and challenge to intelligent curiosity? Curiosity is fairly fascinated by the sense of the immensity of the chance, and by the sense that the whole of the chance has been taken. It is rarely given to us to see a great game played as to the very end—and that was where, with his impression of nothing to prevent, of nothing, anywhere around him, to prevent anything, the ancient contemplative person, floating serenely in his medium, had yet occasionally to gasp before the assault of the quantity of illustration.

The illustration might be, enormously, of something deficient, absent—in which case it was for the aching void to be (as an aching void) striking and interesting. As an explication or an implication the democratic intensity could always figure.

VII

There was little need, for that matter, to drag it into the foreground on the evening of my renewed introduction to the particular Boston neighbourhood—the only one of them all—with which I had been formerly somewhat acquainted. I had alighted in New York but three days before, and my senses were all so full of it that as I look back I can again feel it, under the immediate Cambridge impression, assert itself by turning quite to insidious softness, to confused and surprised recognition. I had driven out from Boston through the warm September night and through a town-picture as of extraordinary virtuous vacancy (without so much as the figure of a policeman in sight from the South Station to the region of Harvard Square), and I remember how the odorous hour—charged with the old distinctively American earth-smell, which in the darkness fairly poetized the suburbs, and with the queer, far, wild throb of shrilling insects—prescribed to me the exact form of the response to the question as to one's sense of a " great change" already so often sounded. " A great change? No change at all. Where then would the 'intensity' be? But *changes*—ever so many and so amusing and so agreeable. The intensity is compatible with *them*—nothing, clearly, is going to be so interesting as to make out, with plenty of good-will, how compatible!" There was unmistakably everywhere a more embroidered surface —the new free figures played over the canvas; so that at this rate, in the time to come, how far might the embroidery not go, what silk and gold mightn't it weave into the pattern? It wasn't of course a question of rhapsodizing—Cambridge was Cambridge still, and all faithful to its type; but the rustle of the trees in the summer night had a larger tone, the more frequent lamplight slept on ampler walls, the body of impression was greater and the University, above all, seemed in more confident possession. It massed there in multiplied forms, with new and strange architectures looming through the dark; it appeared to have wandered wide and to be stretching forth, in many directions, long, acquisitive arms.

This vision, for the moment, of a great dim, clustered but restlessly expansive Harvard, hushed to vacation stillness as to a deep ambitious dream, was, for the impressible story-seeker, practically the germ of the most engaging of the generalized images of reassurance, the furniture, so to speak, of the *other* scale, that the extension of his view was to cause him to cultivate. Reassurance is required, before the spectacle of American manners at large, whenever one most acutely perceives how little honour they tend to heap on the art of discrimination, and it is at such hours that, turning in his frequent stupefaction, the restless analyst reaches out for support to the nearest faint ghost of a constituted Faculty. It takes no exceptional exposure to the promiscuous life to show almost any institution pretending to university form as stamped here with the character and function of the life-saving monasteries of the dark ages. They glow, the humblest of them, to the imagination—the imagination that fixes the surrounding scene as a huge Rappacini-garden, rank with each variety of the poison-plant of the money-passion—they glow with all the vividness of the defined alternative, the possible antidote, and seem to call on us to blow upon the flame till it is made inextinguishable. So little time had it taken, at any rate, to suggest to me that a new and higher price, in American conditions, is attaching to the cloister, literally—the place inaccessible (to put it most pertinently) to the shout of the newspaper, the place to perambulate, the place to think, apart from the crowd. Doubtless indeed I was not all aware of it at the time, but the image I touch upon in connection with those first moments was to remain with me, the figure of the rich old Harvard organism brooding, exactly, through the long vacation, brooding through the summer night, on discriminations, on insistences, on sublime and exquisite heresies to come.

After that arrived daylight recognitions, but they were really for the most part offered me, as in a full cup, by the accident of a couple of hours that were to leave me the pure essence, the finer sense of them. These were a matter of a fortnight later, as I had had immediately to make an absence, and the waning September afternoon of the second occasion took on a particular quality for this deferred surrender of a dozen stored secrets. "Secrets" I call them because the total impression was of the production of some handful of odds and ends that had lurked, for long, in a locked drawer, and which, being brought out, might promote, by their blinking consciousness, either derision or respect. They excited, as befell, an extraordinary tenderness—on which conclusion it was fortunate to be able afterwards to rest. I wandered, for the day's end, with a young modern for whom the past had not been and who was admirably unconscious of the haunting moral of the whole mutation —the tune to which the pampered present made the other time look comparatively grim. Each item of the pampered state contributed to this effect—the finer *mise en scène*, the multiplied resources, halls, faculties, museums, undergraduate and postgraduate habitations (these last of so large a luxury); the pompous little club-houses, visited, all vacant, in the serious tell-tale twilight that seemed to give them, intellectually, "away"; the beautiful new Union, with its great grave noble hall, of which there would be so much more to be said; and above all, doubtless, the later majesties of the Law School, in the near presence of which the tiny old disinherited seat of that subject, outfaced and bedimmed, seemed unable to make even a futile plea for quaintness. I went into the new Law Library, immense and supreme—in the shadow of which I caught myself sniffing the very dust, prehistoric but still pungent, of the old. I saw in the distance a distinguished friend, all alone, belatedly working there, but to go to him I should have had to cross the bridge that spans the gulf of time, and, with a suspicion of weak places, I was nervous about its bearing me.

What such delicacies came to, then and afterwards, for the whole impression, was the instinct not to press, not to push on, till forced, through any half-open door of the real. The real was there, certainly enough, outside and all round, but there was standing-ground, more immediately, for a brief idyll, and one would walk in the idyll, if only from hour to hour, while one could. This could but mean that one would cultivate the idyllic, for the social, for the pictorial illusion, by every invoking and caressing art; and in fact, as a consequence, the reflection of our observer's experience for the next few weeks —that is so long as the spell of the autumn lasted— would be but the history of his more or less ingenious arts. With the breaking of the autumn, later on, everything broke, everything went—everything was transposed at least into another key. But for the time so much had been gained—the happy trick had been played.

VIII

It was after all in the great hall of the Union perhaps (to come back to that delicate day's end) that the actual vibration of response seemed most to turn to audible music—repeated, with all its suggestiveness, on another occasion or two. For the case was unmistakably that just there, more than anywhere, by a magnificent stroke, an inspiration working perhaps even beyond its consciousness, the right provision had been made for the remembering mind. The place was addressed in truth so largely to an enjoying and producing future that it might seem to frown on mere commemoration, on the backward vision ; and yet, at the moment I speak of, its very finest meaning might have been that of a liberal monument to those who had come and gone, to the company of the lurking ghosts. The air there was full of them, and this was its service, that it cared for them *all*, and so eased off the intensity of their appeal. And yet it appeared to play that part for a reason more interesting than reducible to words—a reason that mainly came out for me while, in the admirable hall aforesaid, I stood before Sargent's high portrait of Major Henry Lee Higginson, *donatorio* of the house (as well as author, all round about, of innumerable other civil gifts) ; a representation of life and character, a projection of genius, which even that great painter has never outdone. Innumerable, ever, are the functions performed and the blessings wrought by the supreme work of art, but I know of no case in which it has been so given to such a work to make the human statement with a great effect, to interfuse a group of public acts with the personality, with the characteristics, of the actor. The acts would still have had all their value if the portrait had had less, but they would not assuredly have been able to become so interesting, would not have grown to affect each beneficiary, however obscure, as proceeding, for him, from a possible relation, a possible intimacy. It is to the question of intimacy with somebody or other that all great practical public recognition is finally carried back—but carried only by the magic carpet, when the magic carpet happens to be there. Mr. Sargent's portrait of Henry Higginson is exactly the magic carpet.

That was the "pull" (one kept on feeling) that this happy commemorative creation of the Union had over the great official, the great bristling brick Valhalla of the early "seventies," that house of honour and of hospitality which, under the name of the Alumni Hall, dispenses (apart from its containing a noble auditorium) laurels to the dead and dinners to the living. The recording tablets of the members of the University sacrificed, on the Northern side, in the Civil War, are too impressive not to retain here always their collective beauty ; but the monumental office and character suffer throughout from the too scant presence of the massive and the mature. The great structure speads and soars with the best will in the world, but succeeds in resembling rather some high-masted ship at sea, in slightly prosaic equilibrium, than a thing of builded foundations and embrasured walls. To which it is impossible not immediately to add that these distinctions are relative and these comparisons almost odious, in face of the recent generations, gathered in from beneath emptier skies, who must have found in the big building as it stands an admonition and an ideal. So much the better for the big building, assuredly, and none so calculably the worse for the generations themselves. The reflection follows close moreover that, tactfully speaking, criticism has no close concern with Alumni Hall; it is as if that grim visitor found the approaches closed to him—had to enter, to the loss of all his identity, some relaxing air of mere sentimental, mere shameless association. He turns his back, a trifle ruefully whistling, and wanders wide ; so at least I seemed to see him do, all September, all October, and hereabouts in particular : I felt him resignedly reduced, for the time, to looking over, to looking through, the fence—all the more that at Cambridge there was at last something in the nature of a fence so to be dealt with.

The smaller aspects, the sight of mere material arrears made up, may seem unduly to have held me when I say that few fresh circumstances struck me as falling more happily into the picture than this especial decency of the definite, the palpable affirmation and belated delimitation of College Yard. The high, decorated, recurrent gates and the still insufficiently high iron palings—representing a vast ring and even now incomplete—may appear, in spots, extemporized and thin ; but that signifies little in presence of the precious idea on the side of which, in the land of the "open door," the all-abstract outline, the timid term and the general concession, they bravely range themselves. The open door—as it figures here in respect to everything but trade—may make a magnificent place, but it makes poor places ; and in places, despite our large mistrust of privacy, and until the national ingenuity shall have invented a substitute for them, we must content ourselves with living. This especial drawing of the belt at Harvard is an admirably interesting example of the way in which the formal enclosure of objects at all interesting immediately refines upon their interest, immediately establishes values. The enclosure may be impressive from without, but from within it is sovereign ; nothing is more curious than to trace in the aspects so controlled the effect of their established relation to it. This resembles, in the human or social order, the improved situation of the foundling who has discovered his family or of the actor who has mastered his part.

The older buildings, in the Yard, profit indeed, on the spot, to the story-seeking mind, by the fact of their comparative exhibition of the tone of time—so prompt an ecstasy and so deep a relief reward, in America, everywhere, any suggested source of interest that is not the interest of importunate newness. That source overflows, all others run thin ; but the wonder and the satisfaction are that in College Yard more than one of these should have finally been set to running thick. The best pieces of the earlier cluster, from Massachusetts to Stoughton, emerge from their elongation of history with a paler archaic pink in their brickwork ; their scant primitive details, small "quaintnesses" of form, have turned, each, to the expressive accent that no short-cut of "style" can ever successfully imitate, and from their many-paned windows, where, on the ensconced benches, so many generations have looked out, they fall, in their minor key, into the great main current of ghostly gossip. "See, see, we are getting on, we are getting almost ripe, ripe enough to justify the question of taste about us. We are growing a complexion—which takes almost as long, and is in fact pretty well the same thing, as growing a philosophy ; but we are putting it on and entering into the dignity of time, the beauty of life. We are in a word beginning to begin, and we have that best sign of it, haven't we ? that we make the vulgar, the very vulgar, think we are beginning to end."

That moreover was not the only relation thus richly promoted ; there could be no unrest of analysis worthy of the name that failed to perceive how, after term had opened, the type of the young men coming and going in the Yard gained, for vivacity of appeal, through this more marked constitution of a *milieu* for it. Here, verily, questions could swarm ; for there was scarce an impression of the local life at large that didn't play into them. One thing I had not yet done—I had not been, under the best guidance, out to Ellis Island, the seat of the Commissioner of Immigration, in the bay of New York, to catch in the fact, as I was to catch later on, a couple of hours of the ceaseless process of the recruiting of our race, of the plenishing of our huge national *pot au feu*, of the introduction of fresh—of perpetually fresh so far it isn't perpetually stale—foreign matter into our heterogeneous system. But even without that a haunting wonder as to what might be becoming of us all, "typically," ethnically, and thereby physiognomically, linguistically, *personally*, was always in order. The young men in their degree, as they flocked candidly up to college, struck me as having much to say about it, and there was always the sense of light on the subject, for comparison and reference, that a long experience of other types and other manners could supply. Swarming ingenuous youths, *whom did they look like the sons of?*— that inquiry, as to any group, any couple, any case, represented a game that it was positively thrilling to play out. There was plenty to make it so, for there was, to begin with, both the forecast of the thing that might easily settle the issue and the forecast of the thing that might easily complicate it.

No impression so promptly assaults the arriving visitor of the United States as that of the overwhelming preponderance, wherever he turns and twists, of the unmitigated "business man" face, ranging through its various possibilities, its extraordinary actualities, of intensity. And I speak here of facial cast and expression alone, leaving out of account the questions of voice, tone, utterance and attitude, the chorus of which would vastly swell the testimony and in which I seem to discern, for these remarks at large, a treasure of illustration to come. Nothing, meanwhile, is more concomitantly striking than the fact that the women, over the land—allowing for every element of exception

—appear to be of a markedly finer texture than the men, and that one of the liveliest signs of this difference is precisely in their less narrowly specialized, their less commercialized, distinctly more generalized, physiognomic character. The superiority thus noted, and which is quite another matter from the universal fact of the mere usual female femininity, is far from constituting absolute distinction, but it constitutes relative, and it is a circumstance at which interested observation snatches, from the first, with an immense sense of its *portée*. There are, with all the qualifications it is yet open to, fifty reflections to be made upon the truth it seems to represent, the appearance of a queer deep split or chasm between the two stages of personal polish, the two levels of the conversible state, at which the sexes have arrived. It is at all events no exaggeration to say that the imagination at once embraces it as *the* feature of the social scene, recognizing it as a subject fruitful beyond the common, and wondering even if for pure drama, the drama of manners, anything anywhere else touches it. If it be a "subject," verily—with the big vision of the intersexual relation as, at such an increasing rate, a prey to it—the right measure for it would seem to be offered in the art of the painter of life by the concrete example, the art of the dramatist or the novelist, rather than in that of the talker, the reporter at large. The only thing is that, from the moment the painter begins to look at American life brush in hand, he is in danger of seeing, in comparison, almost nothing else in it—nothing, that is, so characteristic as this apparent privation, for the man, of his right kind of woman, and this apparent privation, for the woman, of her right kind of man.

The right kind of woman for the American man may really be, of course, as things are turning out with him, the woman as to whom his most workable relation is to support her and bear with her—just as the right kind of man for the American woman may really be the man who intervenes in her life only by occult, by barely divinable, by practically disavowed courses. But the ascertainment and illustration of these truths would be, exactly, very conceivably high sport for the ironic poet— who has surely hitherto neglected one of his greatest current opportunities. It in any case remains vivid that American life may, as regards much of its manifestation, fall upon the earnest view as a society ot women "located" in a world of men, which is so different a matter from a collection of men of the world ; the men supplying, as it were, all the canvas, and the women all the embroidery. Just this vividness it was that held up the torch, through the Cambridge autumn, to that question of the affiliation of the encountered Harvard undergraduate which I may not abandon. In what proportion of instances would it stick out that the canvas, rather than the embroidery, was what he had to show ? In what proportion would he wear the stamp of the unredeemed commercialism that should betray his paternity ? In what proportion, in his appearance, would the different social "value" imputable to his mother have succeeded in interposing ? The discerned answer to these inquiries is really, after all, too precious (in its character of contribution to one's total gathered wisdom) to be given away prematurely ; but there was at least always the sense, to which the imagination reverted, that in the collegiate cloisters and academic shades of other countries this absence of a possible *range* of origin and breeding in a young type had not been so felt. The question of origin, the question of breeding, had been large—never settled in advance ; there had been fifty *sorts* of persons, fifty representatives of careers, to whom the English, the French, the German universitarian of tender years might refer you for a preliminary account of him.

I speak of my keeping back, for the present, many of my ultimate perceptions, but I may none the less recall my having had, all the season, from early, the ring in my ears of a reply I had heard made, on the spot, to a generous lady offering entertainment to a guest, a stranger to the scene, whose good impression she had had at heart. "What kind of people should I like to meet? Why, my dear madam, have you more than *one* kind?" At the same time that I could remember this, however, I could also remember that the consistently *bourgeois* fathers must themselves in many cases have had mothers whose invitation to their male offspring to clutch at their relatively finer type had not succeeded in getting itself accepted. That constituted a fatal precedent, and it would have to be in the female offspring, probably, that one should look for evidences of the clutching—an extension of the inquiry for which there was plenty of time. What did escape from submersion, meanwhile, as is worth mentioning, was the golden state of being reminded at moments that there are no such pleasure-giving accidents, for the mind, as violations of the usual in conditions that make them really precarious and rare. As the usual, in our vast crude democracy of trade, is the new, the simple, the cheap, the common, the commercial, the immediate, and, all too often, the ugly, so any human product that those elements fail conspicuously to involve or to explain, any creature, or even any feature, not turned out to pattern, any form of suggested rarity, subtlety, ancientry, or other pleasant perversity, prepares for us a recognition akin to rapture. These lonely ecstasies of the truly open sense make up often, in the hustling, bustling desert, for such "sinkings" of the starved stomach as have led one too often to have to tighten one's æsthetic waistband.

IX

All of which is sufficiently to imply, again, that for adventurous contemplation, at any of the beguiled hours of which I pretend here but to give the general happier drift, there was scarce such a thing as a variation of insistence. As every fact was convertible into a fancy, there was only an encouraged fusion of possible felicities and possible mistakes, stop-gaps before the awful advent of a "serious sense of critical responsibility." Or say perhaps rather, to alter the image, that there was only a builded breakwater against the assault of matters demanding a *literal* notation. I walked, at the best, but on the breakwater—looking down, if one would, over the flood of the real, but much more occupied with the sight of the old Cambridge ghosts, who seemed to advance one by one, even at that precarious eminence, to meet me. My small story would gain infinitely in richness if I were able to name them, but they swarmed all the while too thick, and of but two or three of them alone is it true that they push their way, of themselves, through any silence. It was thus at any rate a question —as I have indeed already sufficiently shown—of what one read *into* anything, not of what one read out of it; and the occasions that operated for that mild magic resolve themselves now into three or four of an intrinsic colour so dim as to be otherwise well-nigh indistinguishable. Why, if one could tell it, would it be so wonderful, for instance, to have stood on the low cliff that hangs over the Charles, by the nearer side of Mount Auburn, and felt the whole place bristle with merciless memories? It was late in the autumn and in the day—almost evening; with a wintry pink light in the west, the special shade, fading into a heartless prettiness of grey, that shows with a polar chill through the grim tracery of November. Just opposite, at a distance, beyond the

river and its meadows, the white face of the great empty
Stadium stared at me, as blank as a rising moon—with
Soldiers' Field squaring itself like some flat memorial
slab that waits to be inscribed. I had seen it inscribed a
week or two before in the fantastic lettering of a great
intercollegiate game of football, and that impression had
been so documentary, as to the capacity of the American
public for momentary gregarious emphasis, that I regret
having to omit here all the reflections it prompted.

They were not, however, what was now relevant, save
in so far as the many-mouthed uproar they recalled was
a voice in the more multitudinous modern hum through
which one listened almost in vain for the sound of the
old names. One of these in particular rose to my lips—
it was impossible to stand there and not reach out a
hand to J. R. L. as to a responsive personal presence,
the very genius of the spot, who had given it from so
early the direct literary consecration without which even
the most charming seats of civilization go through life
awkwardly and ruefully, after the manner of unchristened
children. They lack thus, for the great occasions, the
great formal necessities, their "papers." It was thanks
to Lowell even more immediately than to Longfellow
that Cambridge *had* its papers—though if I find myself
putting that word into the past tense it is perhaps
because of the irresistible admonition, too (proceeding
so from a thousand local symptoms), that titles embodied
in literary form are less and less likely, in the Harvard
air, to be asked for. That is clearly not the way the
wind sets : we see the great University sit and look very
hard, at blue horizons of possibility, across the high
table-land of her future ; but the light of literary desire
is not perceptibly in her eye (nothing is more striking
than the recent drop in her of any outward sign of
literary curiosity) ; precisely for which reason it was,
doubtless, in part, that the changed world seemed

reflected with a certain tragic intensity even in faces ever so turned to cheerful lights as those of my two constructive companions.

I had passed high, square, sad old Elmwood on the way to my cliff over the Charles, and had wonderingly lingered a little about it. I had passed Mr. Longfellow's immemorial, historical, admired residence, still ample and symmetrical and visibly tourist-haunted (the only detected ruffle of its noble calm); elements of the picture that had rekindled for an hour the finer sensibility, the finer continuity and piety. It was because of these things, again, that I felt the invoked pair beside me presently turn away, as under a chill, from that too spectral (in its own turn) stare of the Stadium—perceived as a portent of the more *roaring*, more reported and excursionized scene; and in particular seemed to see J. R. L.'s robust humour yield to the recognition of the irony of fate, dear to every poet, in one of its most pointed forms. That humour had played of old, charmingly, over the thesis that Cambridge, Mass., was, taken altogether, the most inwardly civilized, most intimately humane, among the haunts of men; whereby it had committed itself, this honest adventurer, to a patient joy in the development of the *genius loci*, and was therefore without provision, either of poetry or of prose, against the picture of proportions and relations overwhelmingly readjusted. If the little old place, with its accessible ear, had been so brave, what was the matter with the big new one, going in, as it would itself say, for greater braveries still? Nothing, no doubt, but that the possession of an ear would be ceasing to count as an advantage. In what produced form, for instance, if he had been right, was now represented the love of letters of which he had been so distinguished an example? If he had on the other hand *not* been right—well, it would all be rather dreadful. Such, at all events, may be the disconcertments of a revisiting spirit—when he has happened to revisit too ingenious an old friend.

The old friend moreover had meanwhile had, and in relation to this large loose fringe of the town, there so freely disposed, one of his very own disconcertments; he had turned his steps, for the pleasure of memory, to Fresh Pond, dear to the muses of youth, the Sunday afternoons of spring, and had to accept there his clearest vision perhaps of the new differences and indifferences. The little nestling lake of other days had ceased to nestle; there was practically no Fresh Pond any more, and I seemed somehow to see why the muses had fled even as from the place at large. The light flutter of their robes had surrounded far-away walks and talks: one could at this day, on printed, on almost faded pages, give chapter and verse for the effect, audible on the Sunday afternoons, of their habit, of murmurous hinted approval. Other things had come by makeweight; the charming Country Club on toward Watertown, all verandahs and golf-links and tennis-lawns, all tea and ices and self-consciousness; and there had come, thereabouts too, the large extension of the "Park System," the admirable commissioners' roads that reach across the ruder countryside like the arms of carnivorous giants stretching over a tea-table of blackberries and buns. But these things were in the eternal American note, the note of the gregarious, the concentric, and pervaded moreover by the rustle of petticoats too distinguishable from any garment-hem of the sacred nine. The desecrated, the destroyed resort had favoured, save on rare feast-days, the single stroll, or at the worst the double, dedicated to shared literary secrets; which was why I almost angrily missed, among the ruins, what I had mainly gone back to recover—some echo of the dreams of youth, the titles of tales, the communities of friendship, the sympathies and patiences, in fine, of dear W. D. H.

2

New York Revisited

THE single impression or particular vision most answering to the greatness of the subject would have been, I think, a certain hour of large circumnavigation that I found prescribed, in the fulness of the spring, as the almost immediate crown of a return from the Far West. I had arrived at one of the transpontine stations of the Pennsylvania Railroad; the question was of proceeding to Boston, for the occasion, without pushing through the terrible town—why "terrible," to my sense, in many ways, I shall presently explain—and the easy and agreeable attainment of this great advantage was to embark on one of the mightiest (as appeared to me) of train-bearing barges and, descending the western waters, pass round the bottom of the city and remount the other current to Harlem; all without "losing touch" of the Pullman that had brought me from Washington. This absence of the need of losing touch, this breadth of effect, as to the whole process, involved in the prompt floating of the huge concatenated cars not only without arrest or confusion, but as for positive prodigal beguilement of the artless traveller, had doubtless much to say to the ensuing state of mind, the happily-excited and amused view of the great face of New York. The extent, the ease, the energy, the quantity and number, all notes scattered about as if, in the whole business and

in the splendid light, nature and science were joyously
romping together, might have been taking on again,
for their symbol, some collective presence of great
circling and plunging, hovering and perching sea-
birds, white-winged images of the spirit, of the restless
freedom of the Bay. The Bay had always, on other
opportunities, seemed to blow its immense character
straight into one's face—coming "at" you, so to speak,
bearing down on you, with the full force of a thousand
prows of steamers seen exactly on the line of their
longitudinal axis; but I had never before been so
conscious of its boundless cool assurance or seemed to
see its genius so grandly at play. This was presumably
indeed because I had never before enjoyed the remarkable adventure of taking in so much of the vast bristling
promontory from the water, of ascending the East River,
in especial, to its upper diminishing expanses.

Something of the air of the occasion and of the mood
of the moment caused the whole picture to speak with
its largest suggestion; which suggestion is irresistible
when once it is sounded clear. It is all, absolutely, an
expression of things lately and currently *done*, done on
a large impersonal stage and on the basis of inordinate
gain—it is not an expression of any other matters whatever; and yet the sense of the scene (which had at
several previous junctures, as well, put forth to my
imagination its power) was commanding and thrilling,
was in certain lights almost charming. So it befell,
exactly, that an element of mystery and wonder entered
into the impression—the interest of trying to make out,
in the absence of features of the sort usually supposed
indispensable, the reason of the beauty and the joy. It
is indubitably a "great" bay, a great harbour, but no
one item of the romantic, or even of the picturesque, as
commonly understood, contributes to its effect. The
shores are low and for the most part depressingly

furnished and prosaically peopled; the islands, though numerous, have not a grace to exhibit, and one thinks of the other, the real flowers of geography in this order, of Naples, of Capetown, of Sydney, of Seattle, of San Francisco, of Rio, asking how if *they* justify a reputation, New York should seem to justify one. Then, after all, we remember that there are reputations and reputations; we remember above all that the imaginative response to the conditions here presented may just happen to proceed from the intellectual extravagance of the given observer. When this personage is open to corruption by almost any large view of an intensity of life, his vibrations tend to become a matter difficult even for *him* to explain. He may have to confess that the group of evident facts fails to account by itself for the complacency of his appreciation. Therefore it is that I find myself rather backward with a perceived sanction, of an at all proportionate kind, for the fine exhilaration with which, in this free wayfaring relation to them, the wide waters of New York inspire me. There is the beauty of light and air, the great scale of space, and, seen far away to the west, the open gates of the Hudson, majestic in their degree, even at a distance, and announcing still nobler things. But the real appeal, unmistakably, is in that note of vehemence in the local life of which I have spoken, for it is the appeal of a particular type of dauntless power.

The aspect the power wears then is indescribable; it is the power of the most extravagant of cities, rejoicing, as with the voice of the morning, in its might, its fortune, its unsurpassable conditions, and imparting to every object and element, to the motion and expression of every floating, hurrying, panting thing, to the throb of ferries and tugs, to the plash of waves and the play of winds and the glint of lights and the shrill of whistles and the quality and authority of breeze-borne cries—all,

practically, a diffused, wasted clamour of *detonations*—
something of its sharp free accent and, above all, of its
sovereign sense of being "backed" and able to back.
The universal *applied* passion struck me as shining
unprecedentedly out of the composition ; in the bigness
and bravery and insolence, especially, of everything that
rushed and shrieked ; in the air as of a great intricate
frenzied dance, half merry, half desperate, or at least half
defiant, performed on the huge watery floor. This appearance of the bold lacing-together, across the waters, of
the scattered members of the monstrous organism—lacing
as by the ceaseless play of an enormous system of steam-
shuttles or electric bobbins (I scarce know what to call
them), commensurate in form with their infinite work—
does perhaps more than anything else to give the pitch
of the vision of energy. One has the sense that the
monster grows and grows, flinging abroad its loose limbs
even as some unmannered young giant at his "larks,"
and that the binding stitches must for ever fly further and
faster and draw harder ; the future complexity of the
web, all under the sky and over the sea, becoming thus
that of some colossal set of clockworks, some steel-souled
machine-room of brandished arms and hammering fists
and opening and closing jaws. The immeasurable
bridges are but as the horizontal sheaths of pistons
working at high pressure, day and night, and subject,
one apprehends with perhaps inconsistent gloom, to
certain, to fantastic, to merciless multiplication. In the
light of this apprehension indeed the breezy brightness
of the Bay puts on the semblance of the vast white
page that awaits beyond any other perhaps the black
overscoring of science.

Let me hasten to add that its present whiteness is
precisely its charming note, the frankest of the signs you
recognize and remember it by. That is the distinction
I was just feeling my way to name as the main ground

of its doing so well, for effect, without technical scenery. There are great imposing ports—Glasgow and Liverpool and London—that have already their page blackened almost beyond redemption from any such light of the picturesque as can hope to irradiate fog and grime, and there are others, Marseilles and Constantinople say, or, for all I know to the contrary, New Orleans, that contrive to abound before everything else in colour, and so to make a rich and instant and obvious show. But memory and the actual impression keep investing New York with the tone, predominantly, of summer dawns and winter frosts, of sea-foam, of bleached sails and stretched awnings, of blanched hulls, of scoured decks, of new ropes, of polished brasses, of streamers clear in the blue air; and it is by this harmony, doubtless, that the projection of the individual character of the place, of the candour of its avidity and the freshness of its audacity, is most conveyed. The "tall buildings," which have so promptly usurped a glory that affects you as rather surprised, as yet, at itself, the multitudinous sky-scrapers standing up to the view, from the water, like extravagant pins in a cushion already overplanted, and stuck in as in the dark, anywhere and anyhow, have at least the felicity of carrying out the fairness of tone, of taking the sun and the shade in the manner of towers of marble. They are not all of marble, I believe, by any means, even if some may be, but they are impudently new and still more impudently "novel"—this in common with so many other terrible things in America—and they are triumphant payers of dividends; all of which uncontested and unabashed pride, with flash of innumerable windows and flicker of subordinate gilt attributions, is like the flare, up and down their long, narrow faces, of the lamps of some general permanent "celebration."

You see the pin-cushion in profile, so to speak, on passing between Jersey City and Twenty-third Street, but you get it broadside on, this loose nosegay of architectural flowers, if you skirt the Battery, well out, and embrace the whole plantation. Then the "American beauty," the rose of interminable stem, becomes the token of the cluster at large — to that degree that, positively, this is all that is wanted for emphasis of your final impression. Such growths, you feel, have confessedly arisen but to be "picked," in time, with a shears; nipped short off, by waiting fate, as soon as "science," applied to gain, has put upon the table, from far up its sleeve, some more winning card. Crowned not only with no history, but with no credible possibility of time for history, and consecrated by no uses save the commercial at any cost, they are simply the most piercing notes in that concert of the expensively provisional into which your supreme sense of New York resolves itself. They never begin to speak to you, in the manner of the builded majesties of the world as we have heretofore known such—towers or temples or fortresses or palaces—with the authority of things of permanence or even of things of long duration. One story is good only till another is told, and sky-scrapers are the last word of economic ingenuity only till another word be written. This shall be possibly a word of still uglier meaning, but the vocabulary of thrift at any price shows boundless resources, and the consciousness of that truth, the consciousness of the finite, the menaced, the essentially *invented* state, twinkles ever, to my perception, in the thousand glassy eyes of these giants of the mere market. Such a structure as the comparatively windowless bell-tower of Giotto, in Florence, looks supremely serene in its beauty. You don't feel it to have risen by the breath of an interested passion that, restless beyond all passions, is for ever seeking more pliable forms. Beauty has been the object of its creator's idea, and, having found beauty, it has found the form in which it splendidly rests.

Beauty indeed was the aim of the creator of the spire of Trinity Church, so cruelly overtopped and so barely distinguishable, from your train-bearing barge, as you stand off, in its abject helpless humility; and it may of course be asked how much of this superstition finds voice in the actual shrunken presence of that laudable effort. Where, for the eye, is the felicity of simplified Gothic, of noble pre-eminence, that once made of this highly-pleasing edifice the pride of the town and the feature of Broadway? The answer is, as obviously, that these charming elements are still there, just where they ever were, but that they have been mercilessly deprived of their visibility. It aches and throbs, this smothered visibility, we easily feel, in its caged and dishonoured condition, supported only by the consciousness that the dishonour is no fault of its own. We commune with it, in tenderness and pity, through the encumbered air; our eyes, made, however unwillingly, at home in strange vertiginous upper atmospheres, look down on it as on a poor ineffectual thing, an architectural object addressed, even in its prime aspiration, to the patient pedestrian sense and permitting thereby a relation of intimacy. It was to speak to me audibly enough on two or three other occasions—even through the thick of that frenzy of Broadway just where Broadway receives from Wall Street the fiercest application of the maddening lash; it was to put its tragic case there with irresistible lucidity. "Yes, the wretched figure I am making is as little as you see my fault—it is the fault of the buildings whose very first care is to deprive churches of their visibility. There are but two or three—two or three outward and visible churches—left in New York 'anyway,' as you must have noticed, and even they are hideously threatened : a fact at which no one, indeed, appears to be shocked, from which no one draws the least of the inferences that stick straight out of it, which every one seems in short to take for granted either with remarkable stupidity or with remarkable cynicism." So, at any rate, they may still effectively communicate, ruddy-brown (where not browny-black) old Trinity and any pausing, any attending survivor of the clearer age—and there is yet more of the bitterness of history to be tasted in such a tacit passage, as I shall presently show.

Was it not the bitterness of history, meanwhile, that on that day of circumnavigation, that day of highest intensity of impression, of which I began by speaking, the ancient rotunda of Castle Garden, viewed from just opposite, should have lurked there as a vague nonentity? One had known it from far, far back and with the indelibility of the childish vision—from the time when it was the commodious concert-hall of New York, the firmament of long-extinguished stars ; in spite of which extinction there outlives for me the image of the infant phenomenon Adelina Patti, whom (another large-eyed infant) I had been benevolently taken to hear : Adelina Patti, in a fan-like little white frock and "pantalettes" and a hussar-like red jacket, mounted on an armchair, its back supporting her, wheeled to the front of the stage and warbling like a tiny thrush even in the nest. Shabby, shrunken, barely discernible to-day, the ancient rotunda, adjusted to other uses, had afterwards, for many decades, carried on a conspicuous life—and it was the present remoteness, the repudiated barbarism of all this, foreshortened by one's own experience, that dropped the acid into the cup. The sky-scrapers and the league-long bridges, present and to come, marked the point where the age—the age for which Castle Garden could have been, in its day, a "value"—had come out. That in itself was nothing— ages do come out, as a matter of course, so far from where they have gone in. But it had done so, the latter half of the nineteenth century, in one's own more or less immediate presence; the difference, from pole to pole, was so vivid and concrete that no single shade of any one of its aspects was lost. This impact of the whole condensed past at once produced a horrible, hateful sense of personal antiquity.

Yet was it after all that those monsters of the mere market, as I have called them, had more to say, on the question of "effect," than I had at first allowed?—since they are the element that looms largest for me through a particular impression, with remembered parts and pieces melting together rather richly now, of "down-town" seen and felt from the inside. "Felt"—I use that word, I dare say, all presumptuously, for a relation to matters of magnitude and mystery that I could begin neither to measure nor to penetrate, hovering about them only in magnanimous wonder, staring at them as at a world of immovably-closed doors behind which immense "material" lurked, material for the artist, the painter of life, as we say, who shouldn't have begun so early and so fatally to fall away from possible initiations. This sense of a baffled curiosity, an intellectual adventure forever renounced, was surely enough a state of feeling, and indeed in presence of the different half-hours, as memory presents them, at which I gave myself up both to the thrill of Wall Street (by which I mean that of the whole wide edge of the whirlpool), and the too accepted, too irredeemable ignorance, I am at a loss to see what intensity of response was wanting. The imagination might have responded more if there had been a slightly less settled inability to understand what every one, what any one, was really doing; but the picture, as it comes back to me, is, for all this foolish subjective poverty, so crowded with its features that I rejoice, I confess, in not having more of them to handle. No open apprehension, even if it be as open as a public vehicle plying for hire, can carry more than a certain amount of life, of a kind; and there was nothing at play in the outer air, at least, of the scene, during these glimpses, that didn't scramble for admission into mine very much as I had seen the mob seeking entrance to an up-town or a down-town electric car fight for life at one of the apertures.   If it had been the final function of the Bay to make one feel one's age, so, assuredly, the mouth of Wall Street proclaimed it, for one's private ear, distinctly enough; the breath of existence being taken, wherever one turned, as that of youth on the run and with the prize of the race in sight, and the new landmarks crushing the old quite as violent children stamp on snails and caterpillars.

The hour I first recall was a morning of winter drizzle and mist, of dense fog in the Bay, one of the strangest sights of which I was on my way to enjoy; and I had stopped in the heart of the business quarter to pick up a friend who was to be my companion.   The weather, such as it was, worked wonders for the upper reaches of the buildings, round which it drifted and hung very much as about the flanks and summits of emergent mountain-masses—for, to be just all round, there *was* some evidence of their having a message for the eyes.   Let me parenthesize, once for all, that there are other glimpses of this message, up and down the city, fre-quently to be caught; lights and shades of winter and summer air, of the literally "finishing" afternoon in particular, when refinement of modelling descends from the skies and lends the white towers, all new and crude and commercial and over-windowed as they are, a fleeting distinction.   The morning I speak of offered me my first chance of seeing one of them from the inside—which was an opportunity I sought again, repeatedly, in respect to others; and I became conscious of the force with which this vision of their prodigious working, and of the multitudinous life, as if each were a swarming city in itself, that they are capable of housing, may beget, on the part of the free observer, in other words of the restless analyst, the impulse to describe and present the facts and express the sense of them. Each of these huge constructed and compressed communities, throbbing, through its myriad arteries and pores, with a single passion, even as a complicated watch throbs with the one purpose of telling you the hour and the minute, testified overwhelmingly to the *character* of New York—and the passion of the restless analyst, on his side, is for the extraction of character. But there would be too much to say, just here, were this incurable eccentric to let himself go ; the impression in question, fed by however brief an experience, kept overflowing the cup and spreading in a wide waste of speculation. I must dip into these depths, if it prove possible, later on ; let me content myself for the moment with remembering how from the first, on all such ground, my thought went straight to poor great wonder-working Émile Zola and *his* love of the human aggregation, the artificial microcosm, which had to spend itself on great shops, great businesses, great " apartment-houses," of inferior, of mere Parisian scale. His image, it seemed to me, really asked for compassion—in the presence of this material that his energy of evocation, his alone, would have been of a stature to meddle with. What if *Le Ventre de Paris*, what if *Au Bonheur des Dames*, what if *Pot-Bouille* and *L'Argent*, could but have come into being under the New York inspiration ?

The answer to that, however, for the hour, was that, in all probability, New York was not going (as it turns such remarks) to produce both the maximum of " business " spectacle and the maximum of ironic reflection of it. Zola's huge reflector got itself formed, after all, in a far other air ; it had hung there, in essence, awaiting the scene that was to play over it, long before the scene really approached it in scale. The reflecting surfaces, of the ironic, of the epic order, suspended in the New York atmosphere, have yet to show symptoms of shining out, and the monstrous phenomena themselves, meanwhile, strike me as having, with their immense momentum, got the start, got ahead of, in proper parlance, any possibility of poetic, of dramatic capture. That conviction came to me most perhaps while I gazed across at the special sky-scraper that overhangs poor old Trinity to the north—a south face as high and wide as the mountain-wall that drops the Alpine avalanche, from time to time, upon the village, and the village spire, at its foot; the interest of this case being above all, as I learned, to my stupefaction, in the fact that the very creators of the extinguisher are the churchwardens themselves, or at least the trustees of the church property. What was the case but magnificent for pitiless ferocity?—that inexorable law of the growing invisibility of churches, their everywhere reduced or abolished *presence*, which is nine-tenths of their virtue, receiving thus, at such hands, its supreme consecration. This consecration was positively the greater that just then, as I have said, the vast money-making structure quite horribly, quite romantically justified itself, looming through the weather with an insolent cliff-like sublimity. The weather, for all that experience, mixes intimately with the fulness of my impression; speaking not least, for instance, of the way "the state of the streets" and the assault of the turbid air seemed all one with the look, the tramp, the whole quality and *allure*, the consummate monotonous commonness, of the pushing male crowd, moving in its dense mass—with the confusion carried to chaos for any intelligence, any perception; a welter of objects and sounds in which relief, detachment, dignity, meaning, perished utterly and lost all rights. It appeared,

the muddy medium, all one with every other element
and note as well, all the signs of the heaped industrial
battle-field, all the sounds and silences, grim, pushing,
trudging silences too, of the universal will to move—to
move, move, move, as an end in itself, an appetite at any
price.

In the Bay, the rest of the morning, the dense raw
fog that delayed the big boat, allowing sight but of
the immediate ice-masses through which it thumped its
way, was not less of the essence. Anything blander, as
a medium, would have seemed a mockery of the facts
of the terrible little Ellis Island, the first harbour of
refuge and stage of patience for the million or so of
immigrants annually knocking at our official door.
Before this door, which opens to them there only
with a hundred forms and ceremonies, grindings and
grumblings of the key, they stand appealing and waiting,
marshalled, herded, divided, subdivided, sorted, sifted,
searched, fumigated, for longer or shorter periods—the
effect of all which prodigious process, an intendedly
"scientific" feeding of the mill, is again to give the
earnest observer a thousand more things to think of
than he can pretend to retail. The impression of Ellis
Island, in fine, would be—as I was to find throughout
that so many of my impressions would be—a chapter
by itself; and with a particular page for recognition of
the degree in which the liberal hospitality of the eminent
Commissioner of this wonderful service, to whom I had
been introduced, helped to make the interest of the
whole watched drama poignant and unforgettable. It
is a drama that goes on, without a pause, day by day
and year by year, this visible act of ingurgitation on
the part of our body politic and social, and constituting
really an appeal to amazement beyond that of any
sword-swallowing or fire-swallowing of the circus. The
wonder that one couldn't keep down was the thought

that these two or three hours of one's own chance vision of the business were but as a tick or two of the mighty clock, the clock that never, never stops—least of all when it strikes, for a sign of so much winding-up, some louder hour of our national fate than usual. I think indeed that the simplest account of the action of Ellis Island on the spirit of any sensitive citizen who may have happened to "look in" is that he comes back from his visit not at all the same person that he went. He has eaten of the tree of knowledge, and the taste will be for ever in his mouth. He had thought he knew before, thought he had the sense of the degree in which it is his American fate to share the sanctity of his American consciousness, the intimacy of his American patriotism, with the inconceivable alien; but the truth had never come home to him with any such force. In the lurid light projected upon it by those courts of dismay it shakes him—or I like at least to imagine it shakes him—to the depths of his being; I like to think of him, I positively *have* to think of him, as going about ever afterwards with a new look, for those who can see it, in his face, the outward sign of the new chill in his heart. So is stamped, for detection, the questionably privileged person who has had an apparition, seen a ghost in his supposedly safe old house. Let not the unwary, therefore, visit Ellis Island.

The after-sense of that acute experience, however, I myself found, was by no means to be brushed away; I felt it grow and grow, on the contrary, wherever I turned: other impressions might come and go, but this affirmed claim of the alien, however immeasurably alien, to share in one's supreme relation was everywhere the fixed element, the reminder not to be dodged. One's supreme relation, as one had always put it, was one's relation to one's country—a conception made up so largely of one's countrymen and one's countrywomen.

Thus it was as if, all the while, with such a fond tradition of what these products predominantly were, the idea of the country itself underwent something of that profane overhauling through which it appears to suffer the indignity of change. Is not our instinct in this matter, in general, essentially the safe one—that of keeping the idea simple and strong and continuous, so that it shall be perfectly sound? To touch it over-much, to pull it about, is to put it in peril of weakening; yet on this free assault upon it, this readjustment of it in *their* monstrous, presumptuous interest, the aliens, in New York, seemed perpetually to insist. The combination there of their quantity and their quality—that loud primary stage of alienism which New York most offers to sight—operates, for the native, as their note of settled possession, something they have nobody to thank for; so that *un*settled possession is what we, on our side, seem reduced to—the implication of which, in its turn, is that, to recover confidence and regain lost ground, we, not they, must make the surrender and accept the orientation. We must go, in other words, *more* than half-way to meet them; which is all the difference, for us, between possession and dispossession. This sense of dispossession, to be brief about it, haunted me so, I was to feel, in the New York streets and in the packed trajectiles to which one clingingly appeals from the streets, just as one tumbles back into the streets in appalled reaction from *them*, that the art of beguiling or duping it became an art to be cultivated—though the fond alternative vision was never long to be obscured, the imagination, exasperated to envy, of the ideal, in the order in question; of the luxury of some such close and sweet and *whole* national consciousness as that of the Switzer and the Scot.

II

My recovery of impressions, after a short interval, yet with their flush a little faded, may have been judged to involve itself with excursions of memory—memory directed to the antecedent time—reckless almost to extravagance. But I recall them to-day, none the less, for that value in them which ministered, at happy moments, to an artful evasion of the actual. There was no escape from the ubiquitous alien into the future, or even into the present; there was an escape but into the past. I count as quite a triumph in this interest an unbroken ease of frequentation of that ancient end of Fifth Avenue to the whole neighbourhood of which one's earlier vibrations, a very far-away matter now, were attuned. The precious stretch of space between Washington Square and Fourteenth Street had a value, had even a charm, for the revisiting spirit—a mild and melancholy glamour which I am conscious of the difficulty of "rendering" for new and heedless generations. Here again the assault of suggestion is too great; too large, I mean, the number of hares started, before the pursuing imagination, the quickened memory, by this fact of the felt moral and social value of this comparatively unimpaired morsel of the Fifth Avenue heritage. Its reference to a pleasanter, easier, hazier past is absolutely comparative, just as the past in question itself enjoys as such the merest courtesy-title. It is all recent history enough, by the measure of the whole, and there are flaws and defacements enough, surely, even in its appearance of decency of duration. The tall building, grossly tall and grossly ugly, has failed of an admirable chance of distinguished consideration for it, and the dignity of many of its peaceful fronts has succumbed to the presence of those industries whose

foremost need is to make "a good thing" of them.
The good thing is doubtless being made, and yet this
lower end of the once agreeable street still just escapes
being a wholly bad thing. What held the fancy in
thrall, however, as I say, was the admonition, proceeding
from all the facts, that values of this romantic order
are at best, anywhere, strangely relative. It was an
extraordinary statement on the subject of New York
that the space between Fourteenth Street and Washington Square *should* count for "tone," figure as the old
ivory of an overscored tablet.

True wisdom, I found, was to let it, to make it, so
count and figure as much as it would, and charming
assistance came for this, I also found, from the young
good-nature of May and June. There had been neither
assistance nor good-nature during the grim weeks of
mid-winter ; there had been but the meagre fact of a
discomfort and an ugliness less formidable here than
elsewhere. When, toward the top of the town, circulation, alimentation, recreation, every art of existence, gave
way before the full onset of winter, when the upper
avenues had become as so many congested bottle-necks,
through which the wine of life simply refused to be
decanted. getting back to these latitudes resembled really
a return from the North Pole to the Temperate Zone :
it was as if the wine of life had been poured for you,
in advance, into some pleasant old punch-bowl that
would support you through the temporary stress. Your
condition was not reduced to the endless vista of a
clogged tube, of a thoroughfare occupied as to the
narrow central ridge with trolley-cars stuffed to suffocation, and as to the mere margin, on either side, with
snow-banks resulting from the cleared rails and offering
themselves as a field for all remaining action. Free
existence and good manners, in New York, are too
much brought down to a bare rigour of marginal

relation to the endless electric coil, the monstrous chain that winds round the general neck and body, the general middle and legs, very much as the boa-constrictor winds round the group of the Laocoon. It struck me that when these folds are tightened in the terrible stricture of the snow-smothered months of the year, the New York predicament leaves far behind the anguish represented in the Vatican figures. To come and go where East Eleventh Street, where West Tenth, opened their kind short arms was at least to keep clear of the awful hug of the serpent. And this was a grace that grew large, as I have hinted, with the approach of summer, and that made in the afternoons of May and of the first half of June, above all, an insidious appeal. There, I repeat, was the delicacy, there the mystery, there the wonder, in especial, of the unquenchable intensity of the impressions received in childhood. They are made then once for all, be their intrinsic beauty, interest, importance, small or great; the stamp is indelible and never wholly fades. This in fact gives it an importance when a lifetime has intervened. I found myself intimately recognizing every house my officious tenth year had, in the way of imagined adventure, introduced to me— incomparable master of ceremonies after all ; the privilege had been offered since to millions of other objects that had made nothing of it, that had gone as they came ; so that here were Fifth Avenue corners with which one's connection was fairly exquisite. The lowered light of the days' ends of early summer became them, moreover, exceedingly, and they fell, for the quiet northward perspective, into a dozen delicacies of composition and tone.

One could talk of "quietness" now, for the shrinkage of life so marked, in the higher latitudes of the town, after Easter, the visible early flight of that "society" which, by the old custom, used never to budge before

June or July, had almost the effect of clearing some of the streets, and indeed of suggesting that a truly clear New York might have an unsuspected charm or two to put forth. An approach to peace and harmony might have been, in a manner, promised, and the sense of other days took advantage of it to steal abroad with a ghostly tread. It kept meeting, half the time, to its discomfiture, the lamentable little Arch of Triumph which bestrides these beginnings of Washington Square— lamentable because of its poor and lonely and unsupported and unaffiliated state. With this melancholy monument it could make no terms at all, but turned its back to the strange sight as often as possible, helping itself thereby, moreover, to do a little of the pretending required, no doubt, by the fond theory that nothing hereabouts was changed. Nothing *was*, it could occasionally appear to me—there was no new note in the picture, not one, for instance, when I paused before a low house in a small row on the south side of Waverley Place and lived again into the queer mediæval costume (preserved by the daguerreotypist's art) of the very little boy for whom the scene had once embodied the pangs and pleasures of a dame's small school. The dame must have been Irish, by her name, and the Irish tradition, only intensified and coarsened, seemed still to possess the place, the fact of the survival, the sturdy sameness, of which arrested me, again and again, to fascination. The shabby red house, with its mere two storeys, its lowly "stoop," its dislocated ironwork of the forties, the early fifties, the record, in its face, of blistering summers and of the long stages of the loss of self-respect, made it as consummate a morsel of the old liquor-scented, heated-looking city, the city of no pavements, but of such a plenty of politics, as I could have desired. And neighbouring Sixth Avenue, overstraddled though it might be with feats of engineering unknown to the

primitive age that otherwise so persisted, wanted only,
to carry off the illusion, the warm smell of the bakery
on the corner of Eighth Street, a blessed repository
of doughnuts, cookies, cream-cakes and pies, the slow
passing by which, on returns from school, must have
had much in common with the experience of the ship-
men of old who came, in long voyages, while they
tacked and hung back, upon those belts of ocean that
are haunted with the balm and spice of tropic islands.

These were the felicities of the backward reach, which,
however, had also its melancholy checks and snubs;
nowhere quite so sharp as in presence, so to speak,
of the rudely, the ruthlessly suppressed birth-house on
the other side of the Square. That was where the
pretence that nearly nothing was changed had most
to come in; for a high, square, impersonal structure,
proclaiming its lack of interest with a crudity all
its own, so blocks, at the right moment for its own
success, the view of the past, that the effect for me,
in Washington Place, was of having been amputated
of half my history. The grey and more or less "hallowed"
University building—wasn't it somehow, with a desperate
bravery, both castellated and gabled?—has vanished from
the earth, and vanished with it the two or three adjacent
houses, of which the birthplace was one. This was the
snub, for the complacency of retrospect, that, whereas
the inner sense had positively erected there for its private
contemplation a commemorative mural tablet, the very
wall that should have borne this inscription had been
smashed as for demonstration that tablets, in New York,
are unthinkable. And I have had indeed to permit
myself this free fantasy of the hypothetic rescued identity
of a given house—taking the vanished number in
Washington Place as most pertinent—in order to invite
the reader to gasp properly with me before the fact that
we not only fail to remember, in the whole length of the

city, one of these frontal records of birth, sojourn, or death, under a celebrated name, but that we have only to reflect an instant to see any such form of civic piety inevitably and for ever absent. The form is cultivated, to the greatly quickened interest of street-scenery, in many of the cities of Europe; and is it not verily bitter, for those who feel a poetry in the noted passage, longer or shorter, here and there, of great lost spirits, that the institution, the profit, the glory of any such association is denied in advance to communities tending, as the phrase is, to "run" preponderantly to the sky-scraper? Where, in fact, is the point of inserting a mural tablet, at any legible height, in a building certain to be destroyed to make room for a sky-scraper? And from where, on the other hand, in a façade of fifty floors, does one "see" the pious plate recording the honour attached to one of the apartments look down on a responsive people? We have but to ask the question to recognize our necessary failure to answer it as a supremely characteristic local note —a note in the light of which the great city is projected into its future as, practically, a huge, continuous fifty-floored conspiracy against the very idea of the ancient graces, those that strike us as having flourished just in proportion as the parts of life and the signs of character have *not* been lumped together, not been indistinguishably sunk in the common fund of mere economic convenience. So interesting, as object-lessons, may the developments of the American gregarious ideal become; so traceable, at every turn, to the restless analyst at least, are the heavy footprints, in the finer texture of life, of a great commercial democracy seeking to abound supremely in its own sense and having none to gainsay it.

Let me not, however, forget, amid such contemplations, what may serve here as a much more relevant instance of the operation of values, the price of the as yet un-diminished dignity of the two most southward of the

Fifth Avenue churches. Half the charm of the prospect, at that extremity, is in their still being there, and being as they are; this charm, this serenity of escape and survival positively works as a blind on the side of the question of their architectural importance. The last shade of pedantry or priggishness drops from your view of that element; they illustrate again supremely your grasped truth of the *comparative* character, in such conditions, of beauty and of interest. The special standard they may or may not square with signifies, you feel, not a jot: all you know, and want to know, is that they are probably menaced—some horrible voice of the air has murmured it—and that with them will go, if fate overtakes them, the last cases worth mentioning (with a single exception), of the modest felicity that sometimes used to be. Remarkable certainly the state of things in which mere exemption from the "squashed" condition can shed such a glamour; but we may accept the state of things if only we can keep the glamour undispelled. It reached its maximum for me, I hasten to add, on my penetrating into the Ascension, at chosen noon, and standing for the first time in presence of that noble work of John La Farge, the representation, on the west wall, in the grand manner, of the theological event from which the church takes its title. Wonderful enough, in New York, to find one's self, in a charming and considerably dim "old" church, hushed to admiration before a great religious picture; the sensation, for the moment, upset so all the facts. The hot light, outside, might have been that of an Italian *piazzetta;* the cool shade, within, with the important work of art shining through it, seemed part of some other-world pilgrimage—all the more that the important work of art itself, a thing of the highest distinction, spoke, as soon as one had taken it in, with that authority which makes the difference, ever afterwards, between the remembered and the forgotten quest.

A rich note of interference came, I admit, through the splendid window-glass, the finest of which, unsurpassably fine, to my sense, is the work of the same artist; so that the church, as it stands, is very nearly as commemorative a monument as a great reputation need wish. The deeply pictorial windows, in which clearness of picture and fulness of expression consort so successfully with a tone as of magnified gems, did not strike one as looking into a yellow little square of the south— they put forth a different implication; but the flaw in the harmony was, more than anything else, that sinister voice of the air of which I have spoken, the fact that one *could* stand there, vibrating to such impressions, only to remember the suspended danger, the possibility of the doom. Here was the loveliest cluster of images, begotten on the spot, that the preoccupied city had ever taken thought to offer itself; and here, to match them, like some black shadow they had been condemned to cast, was this particular prepared honour of " removal " that appeared to hover about them.

One's fear, I repeat, was perhaps misplaced—but what an air to live in, the shuddering pilgrim mused, the air in which such fears are not misplaced only when we are conscious of very special reassurances! The vision of the doom that does descend, that had descended all round, was at all events, for the half-hour, all that was wanted to charge with the last tenderness one's memory of the transfigured interior. Afterwards, outside, again and again, the powers of removal struck me as looming, awfully, in the newest mass of multiplied floors and windows visible at this point. *They*, ranged in this terrible recent erection, were going to bring in money— and was not money the only thing a self-respecting structure could be thought of as bringing in? Hadn't one heard, just before, in Boston, that the security, that the sweet serenity of the Park Street Church, charmingest,

there, of aboriginal notes, the very light, with its perfect
position and its dear old delightful Wren-like spire, of
the starved city's eyes, had been artfully practised against,
and that the question of saving it might become, in the
near future, acute? Nothing, fortunately, I think, is so
much the "making" of New York, at its central point,
for the visual, almost for the romantic, sense, as the
Park Street Church is the making, by its happy coming-
in, of Boston; and, therefore, if it were thinkablé that
the peculiar rectitude of Boston might be laid in the
dust, what mightn't easily come about for the reputedly
less austere conscience of New York? Once such
questions had obtained lodgment, to take one's walks
was verily to look at almost everything in their light;
and to commune with the sky-scraper under this influence
was really to feel worsted, more and more, in any magnanimous attempt to adopt the æsthetic view of it. I
may appear to make too much of these invidious presences,
but it must be remembered that they represent, for our
time, the only claim to any consideration other than
merely statistical established by the resounding growth
of New York. The attempt to take the æsthetic view
is invariably blighted sooner or later by their most salient
characteristic, *the* feature that speaks loudest for the
economic idea. Window upon window, at any cost, is
a condition never to be reconciled with any grace of
building, and the logic of the matter here happens to put
on a particularly fatal front. If quiet interspaces, always
half the architectural battle, exist no more in such a
structural scheme than quiet tones, blest breathing-spaces,
occur, for the most part, in New York conversation, so the
reason is, demonstrably, that the building can't afford them.
(It is by very much the same law, one supposes, that
New York conversation cannot afford stops.) The building can only afford lights, each light having a superlative
value as an aid to the transaction of business and the

conclusion of sharp bargains. Doesn't it take in fact acres of window-glass to help even an expert New Yorker to get the better of another expert one, or to see that the other expert one doesn't get the better of *him*? It is easy to conceive that, after all, with this origin and nature stamped upon their foreheads, the last word of the mercenary monsters should not be their address to our sense of formal beauty.

Still, as I have already hinted, there was always the case of the one other rescued identity and preserved felicity, the happy accident of the elder day still un-grudged and finally legitimated. When I say ungrudged, indeed, I seem to remember how I had heard that the divine little City Hall had *been* grudged, at a critical moment, to within an inch of its life; had but just escaped, in the event, the extremity of grudging. It lives on securely, by the mercy of fate—lives on in the delicacy of its beauty, speaking volumes again (more volumes, distinctly, than are anywhere else spoken) for the exquisite truth of the *conferred* value of interesting objects, the value derived from the social, the civilizing function for which they have happened to find their opportunity. It is the opportunity that gives them their price, and the luck of there being, round about them, nothing greater than themselves to steal it away from them. They strike thus, virtually, the supreme note, and—such is the mysterious play of our finer sensibility! —one takes this note, one is glad to work it, as the phrase goes, for all it is worth. I so work the note of the City Hall, no doubt, in speaking of the spectacle there constituted as "divine"; but I do it precisely by reason of the spectacle taken *with* the delightful small facts of the building: largely by reason, in other words, of the elegant, the gallant little structure's situation and history, the way it has played, artistically, ornamentally, its part, has held out for the good cause, through the long years, alone and unprotected. The fact is it has been the very centre of that assault of vulgarity of which the innumerable mementos rise within view of it and tower, at a certain distance, over it; and yet it has never parted with a square inch of its character, it has forced them, in a manner, to stand off. I hasten to add that in expressing thus its uncompromised state I speak of its outward, its æsthetic character only. So, at all events, it has discharged the civilizing function I just named as inherent in such cases—that of representing, to the community possessed of it, all the Style the community is likely to get, and of making itself responsible for the same.

The consistency of this effort, under difficulties, has been the story that brings tears to the eyes of the hovering kindly critic, and it is through his tears, no doubt, that such a personage reads the best passages of the tale and makes out the proportions of the object. Mine, I recognize, didn't prevent my seeing that the pale yellow marble (or whatever it may be) of the City Hall has lost, by some late excoriation, the remembered charm of its old surface, the pleasant promiscuous patina of time; but the perfect taste and finish, the reduced yet ample scale, the harmony of parts, the just proportions, the modest classic grace, the living look of the type aimed at, these things, with gaiety of detail undiminished and "quaintness" of effect augmented, are all there; and I see them, as I write, in that glow of appreciation which made it necessary, of a fine June morning, that I should somehow pay the whole place my respects. The simplest, in fact the only way, was, obviously, to pass under the charming portico and brave the consequences: this impunity of such audacities being, in America, one of the last of the lessons the repatriated absentee finds himself learning. The crushed spirit he brings back from European discipline never quite rises to the height of the native argument, the brave sense that the public, the civic building is his very own, for any honest use, so that he may tread even its most expensive pavements and staircases (and very expensive, for the American citizen, these have lately become,) without a question asked. This further and further unchallenged penetration begets in the perverted person I speak of a really romantic thrill: it is like some assault of the dim seraglio, with the guards bribed, the eunuchs drugged and one's life carried in one's hand. The only drawback to such freedom is that penetralia it is so easy to penetrate fail a little of a due impressiveness, and that if stationed sentinels are bad for the temper of the freeman they are good for the "prestige" of the building.

Never, in any case, it seemed to me, had any freeman made so free with the majesty of things as I was to make on this occasion with the mysteries of the City Hall—even to the point of coming out into the presence of the Representative of the highest office with which City Halls are associated, and whose thoroughly gracious condonation of my act set the seal of success upon the whole adventure. Its dizziest intensity in fact sprang precisely from the unexpected view opened into the old official, the old so thick-peopled local, municipal world: upper chambers of council and state, delightfully of their nineteenth-century time, as to design and ornament, in spite of rank restoration; but replete, above all, with portraits of past worthies, past celebrities and city fathers, Mayors, Bosses, Presidents, Governors, Statesmen at large, Generals and Commodores at large, florid ghosts, looking so unsophisticated now, of years not remarkable, municipally, for the absence of sophistication. Here were types, running mainly to ugliness and all bristling with the taste of their day and the quite touching provincialism of their conditions, as to many of which nothing would be more interesting than a study of New York annals in the light of their personal look, their very

noses and mouths and complexions and heads of hair—
to say nothing of their waistcoats and neckties; with
such colour, such sound and movement would the thick
stream of local history then be interfused. Wouldn't its
thickness fairly become transparent? since to walk through
the collection was not only to see and feel so much that
had happened, but to understand, with the truth again
and again inimitably pointed, why nothing could have
happened otherwise; the whole array thus presenting
itself as an unsurpassed demonstration of the real reasons
of things. The florid ghosts look out from their exceedingly gilded frames—all that *that* can do is bravely
done for them—with the frankest responsibility for
everything; their collective presence becomes a kind of
copious tell-tale document signed with a hundred names.
There are few of these that at this hour, I think, we
particularly desire to repeat; but the place where they
may be read is, all the way from river to river and from
the Battery to Harlem, the place in which there is most
of the terrible town.

III

If the Bay had seemed to me, as I have noted, most
to help the fond observer of New York aspects to a sense,
through the eyes, of embracing possession, so the part
played there for the outward view found its match for the
inward in the portentous impression of one of the great
caravansaries administered to me of a winter afternoon.
I say with intention "administered": on so assiduous a
guide, through the endless labyrinth of the Waldorf-
Astoria was I happily to chance after turning out of the
early dusk and the January sleet and slosh into permitted,
into enlightened contemplation of a pandemonium not
less admirably ordered, to all appearance, than rarely
intermitted. The seer of great cities is liable to easy

error, I know, when he finds this, that or the other caught glimpse the supremely significant one—and I am willing to preface with that remark my confession that New York told me more of her story at once, then and there, than she was again and elsewhere to tell.   With this apprehension that she was in fact fairly shrieking it into one's ears came a curiosity, corresponding, as to its kind and its degree of interest ; so that there was nought to do, as we picked our tortuous way, but to stare with all our eyes and miss as little as possible of the revelation.   That harshness of the essential conditions, the outward, which almost any large attempt at the amenities, in New York, has to take account of and make the best of, has at least the effect of projecting the visitor with force upon the spectacle prepared for him at this particular point and of marking the more its sudden high pitch, the character of violence which all its warmth, its colour and glitter so completely muffle.   There is violence outside, mitigating sadly the frontal majesty of the monument, leaving it exposed to the vulgar assault of the street by the operation of those dire facts of absence of margin, of meagreness of site, of the brevity of the block, of the inveteracy of the near thoroughfare, which leave " style," in construction, at the mercy of the impertinent cross-streets, make detachment and independence, save in the rarest cases, an insoluble problem, preclude without pity any element of court or garden, and open to the builder in quest of distinction the one alternative, and the great adventure, of seeking his reward in the sky.

Of their licence to pursue it there to any extent whatever New Yorkers are, I think, a trifle too assertively proud ; no court of approach, no interspace worth mention, ever forming meanwhile part of the ground-plan or helping to receive the force of the breaking public wave.   New York pays at this rate the penalty of her primal topographic curse, her old inconceivably bourgeois scheme of composition and distribution, the uncorrected labour of minds with no imagination of the future and blind before the opportunity given them by their two magnificent water-fronts. This original sin of the longitudinal avenues perpetually, yet meanly intersected, and of the organized sacrifice of the indicated alternative, the great perspectives from East to West, might still have earned forgiveness by some occasional departure from its pettifogging consistency. But, thanks to this consistency, the city is, of all great cities, the least endowed with any blest item of stately square or goodly garden, with any happy accident or surprise, any fortunate nook or casual corner, any deviation, in fine, into the liberal or the charming. That way, however, for the regenerate filial mind, madness may be said to lie—the way of imagining what might have been and putting it all together in the light of what so helplessly is. One of the things that helplessly are, for instance, is just this assault of the street, as I have called it, upon any direct dealing with our caravansary. The electric cars, with their double track, are everywhere almost as tight a fit in the narrow channel of the roadway as the projectile in the bore of a gun ; so that the Waldorf-Astoria, sitting by this absent margin for life with her open lap and arms, is reduced to confessing, with a strained smile, across the traffic and the danger, how little, outside her mere swing-door, she can do for you. She seems to admit that the attempt to get at her may cost you your safety, but reminds you at the same time that any good American, and even any good inquiring stranger, is supposed willing to risk that boon for her. " *Un bon mouvement,* therefore : you must make a dash for it, but you'll see I'm worth it." If such a claim as this last be ever justified, it would indubitably be justified here ; the survivor scrambling out of the current and up the bank finds in the amplitude of the entertainment awaiting him an instant sense as of applied restoratives. The amazing hotel-world quickly closes round him ; with the process of transition reduced to its minimum he is transported to conditions of extraordinary complexity and brilliancy, operating—and with proportionate perfection—by laws of their own and expressing after their fashion a complete scheme of life. The air swarms, to intensity, with the *characteristic*, the characteristic condensed and accumulated as he rarely elsewhere has had the luck to find it. It jumps out to meet his every glance, and this unanimity of its spring, of all its aspects and voices, is what I just now referred to as the essence of the loud New York story. That effect of violence in the whole communication, at which I thus hint, results from the inordinate mass, the quantity of presence, as it were, of the testimony heaped together for emphasis of the wondrous moral.

The moral in question, the high interest of the tale, is that you are in presence of a revelation of the possibilities of the hotel—for which the American spirit has found so unprecedented a use and a value ; leading it on to express so a social, indeed positively an æsthetic ideal, and making it so, at this supreme pitch, a synonym for civilization, for the capture of conceived manners themselves, that one is verily tempted to ask if the hotel-spirit may not just *be* the American spirit most seeking and most finding itself. That truth—the truth that the present is more and more the day of the hotel—had not waited to burst on the mind at the view of this particular establishment ; we have all more or less been educated to it, the world over, by the fruit-bearing action of the American example : in consequence of which it has been opened to us to see still other societies moved by the same irresistible spring and trying, with whatever grace and ease they may bring to the business, to unlearn as many as possible of their old social canons, and in especial their old discrimination in favour of the private life. The business for them—for communities to which the American ease in such matters is not native—goes much less of itself and produces as yet a scantier show ; the great difference with the American show being that in the United States every one is, for the lubrication of the general machinery, practically in everything, whereas in Europe, mostly, it is only certain people who are in anything ; so that the machinery, so much less generalized, works in a smaller, stiffer way. This one caravansary makes the American case vivid, gives it, you feel, that quantity of illustration which renders the place a new thing under the sun. It is an expression of the gregarious state breaking down every barrier but two— one of which, the barrier consisting of the high pecuniary tax, is the immediately obvious. The other, the rather more subtle, is the condition, for any member of the flock, that he or she—in other words especially she—be presumably " respectable," be, that is, not discoverably anything else. The rigour with which any appearance of pursued or desired adventure is kept down—adventure in the florid sense of the word, the sense in which it remains an euphemism—is not the least interesting note of the whole immense promiscuity. Protected at those two points the promiscuity carries, through the rest of the range, everything before it.

It sat there, it walked and talked, and ate and drank, and listened and danced to music, and otherwise revelled and roamed, and bought and sold, and came and went there, all on its own splendid terms and with an encompassing material splendour, a wealth and variety of constituted picture and background, that might well feed it with the finest illusions about itself. It paraded through halls and saloons in which art and history, in masquerading dress, muffled almost to suffocation as in the gold brocade of their pretended majesties and their conciliatory graces, stood smirking on its passage with the last cynicism of hypocrisy. The exhibition is wonderful for that, for the suggested sense of a promiscuity which manages to be at the same time an inordinate untempered monotony ; manages to be so, on such ground as this, by an extraordinary trick of its own, wherever one finds it. The combination forms, I think, largely, the very interest, such as it is, of these phases of the human scene in the United States—if only for the pleasant puzzle of our wondering how, when types, aspects, conditions, have so much in common, they should seem at all to make up a conscious miscellany. That question, however, the question of the play and range, the practical elasticity, of the social sameness, in America, will meet us elsewhere on our path, and I confess that all questions gave way, in my mind, to a single irresistible obsession. This was just the ache of envy of the spirit of a society which had found there, in its prodigious public setting, so exactly what it wanted. One was in presence, as never before, of a realized ideal and of that childlike rush of surrender to it and clutch at it which one was so repeatedly to recognize, in America, as the note of the supremely gregarious state. It made the whole vision unforgettable, and I am now carried back to it, I confess, in musing hours, as to one of my few glimpses of perfect human felicity. It had the admirable sign that it was, precisely, so comprehensively collective —that it made so vividly, in the old phrase, for the greatest happiness of the greatest number. Its rare beauty, one felt with instant clarity of perception, was that it was, for a " mixed " social manifestation, blissfully exempt from any principle or possibility of disaccord with itself. It was absolutely a fit to its conditions, those conditions which were both its earth and its heaven, and every part of the picture, every item of the immense sum, every wheel of the wondrous complexity, was on the best terms with all the rest.

The sense of these things became for the hour as the golden glow in which one's envy burned, and through which, while the sleet and the slosh, and the clangorous charge of cars, and the hustling, hustled crowds held the outer world, one carried one's charmed attention from one chamber of the temple to another. For that is how the place speaks, as great constructed and achieved harmonies mostly speak—as a temple builded, with clustering chapels and shrines, to an idea. The hundreds and hundreds of people in circulation, the innumerable huge-hatted ladies in especial, with their air of finding in the gilded and storied labyrinth the very firesides and pathways of home, became thus the serene faithful, whose rites one would no more have sceptically brushed than one would doff one's disguise in a Mohammedan mosque. The question of who they all might be, seated under palms and by fountains, or communing, to some inimitable New York tune, with the shade of Marie Antoinette in the queer recaptured actuality of an easy Versailles or an intimate Trianon—such questions as that, interesting in other societies and at other times, insisted on yielding here to the mere eloquence of the general truth. Here was a social order in positively stable equilibrium. Here was a world whose relation to its form and medium was practically imperturbable ; here was a conception of publicity *as* the vital medium organized with the authority with which the American genius for organization, put on its mettle, alone could organize it. The whole thing remains for me, however, I repeat, a gorgeous golden blur, a paradise peopled with unmistakable American shapes, yet in which, the general and the particular, the organized and the extemporized, the element of ingenuous joy below and of consummate management above, melted together and left one uncertain which of them one was, at a given turn of the maze, most admiring. When I reflect indeed that without my

clue I should not have even known the maze—should
not have known, at the given turn, whether I was engulfed,
for instance, in the *vente de charité* of the theatrical profession and the onset of persuasive peddling actresses, or
in the annual tea-party of German lady-patronesses (of I
know not what) filling with their Oriental opulence and
their strange idiom a playhouse of the richest rococo,
where some other expensive anniversary, the ball of a
guild or the carouse of a club, was to tread on their heels
and instantly mobilize away their paraphernalia—when
I so reflect I see the sharpest dazzle of the eyes as
precisely the play of the genius for organization.

There are a thousand forms of this ubiquitous American force, the most ubiquitous of all, that I was in no
position to measure ; but there was often no resisting a
vivid view of the form it may take, on occasion, under
pressure of the native conception of the hotel.   Encountered embodiments of the gift, in this connection,
master-spirits of management whose influence was as the
very air, the very expensive air, one breathed, abide
with me as the intensest examples of American character ; indeed as the very interesting supreme examples
of a type which has even on the American ground,
doubtless, not said its last word, but which has at least
treated itself there to a luxury of development.   It gives
the impression, when at all directly met, of having at its
service something of that fine flame that makes up
personal greatness ; so that, again and again, as I found,
one would have liked to see it more intimately at work.
Such failures of opportunity and of penetration, however,
are but the daily bread of the visionary tourist.   Whenever I dip back, in fond memory, none the less, into the
vision I have here attempted once more to call up, I see
the whole thing overswept as by the colossal extended
arms, waving the magical bâton, of some high-stationed
orchestral leader, the absolute presiding power, conscious

of every note of every instrument, controlling and commanding the whole volume of sound, keeping the whole effect together and making it what it is. What may one say of such a spirit if not that he understands, so to speak, the forces he sways, understands his boundless American material and plays with it like a master indeed? One sees it thus, in its crude plasticity, almost in the likeness of an army of puppets whose strings the wealth of his technical imagination teaches him innumerable ways of pulling, and yet whose innocent, whose always ingenuous agitation of their members he has found means to make them think of themselves as delightfully free and easy. Such was my impression of the perfection of the concert that, for fear of its being spoiled by some chance false note, I never went into the place again.

It might meanwhile seem no great adventure merely to walk the streets; but (beside the fact that there is, in general, never a better way of taking in life), this pursuit irresistibly solicited, on the least pretext, the observer whose impressions I note—accustomed as he had ever been conscientiously to yield to it: more particularly with the relenting year, when the breath of spring, mildness being really installed, appeared the one vague and disinterested presence in the place, the one presence not vociferous and clamorous. Any definite presence that doesn't bellow and bang takes on in New York by that simple fact a distinction practically exquisite; so that one goes forth to meet it as a guest of honour, and that, for my own experience, I remember certain aimless strolls as snatches of intimate communion with the spirit of May and June—as abounding, almost to enchantment, in the comparatively *still* condition. Two secrets, at this time, seemed to profit by that influence to tremble out; one of these to the effect that New York would really have been " meant" to be charming, and the other to the effect that the restless analyst, willing at the lightest persuasion to let so much of its ugliness edge away unscathed from his analysis, must have had for it, from far back, one of those loyalties that are beyond any reason.

" It's all very well," the voice of the air seemed to say, if I may so take it up; " it's all very well to 'criticize,' but you distinctly take an interest and are the victim of your interest, be the grounds of your perversity what they will. You can't escape from it, and don't you see that this, precisely, is what *makes* an adventure for you (an adventure, I admit, as with some strident, battered, questionable beauty, truly some 'bold bad' charmer), of almost any odd stroll, or waste half-hour, or other promiscuous passage, that results for you in an impression? There is always your bad habit of receiving through almost any accident of vision more impressions than you know what to do with; but that, for common convenience, is your eternal handicap and may not be allowed to plead here against your special responsibility. You *care* for the terrible town, yea even for the 'horrible,' as I have overheard you call it, or at least think it, when you supposed no one would know; and you see now how, if you fly such fancies as that it was conceivably meant to be charming, you are tangled by that weakness in some underhand imagination of its possibly, one of these days, as a riper fruit of time, becoming so. To do that, you indeed sneakingly provide, it must get away from itself; but you are ready to follow its hypothetic dance even to the mainland and to the very end of its tether. What makes the general relation of your adventure with it is that, at bottom, you are all the while wondering, in presence of the aspects of its genius and its shame, what elements or parts, if any, would be worth its saving, worth carrying off for the fresh embodiment and the better life, and which of them would have, on the other hand, to face the notoriety of going *first* by the board. I have literally heard you qualify the monster as 'shameless'—though that was wrung from you, I admit, by the worst of the winter conditions, when circulation, in any fashion consistent with personal decency or dignity, was merely mocked at, when the stony-hearted 'trolleys,' cars of Juggernaut in their power to squash, triumphed all along the line, when the February blasts became as cyclones in the darkened gorges of masonry (which down-town, in particular, put on, at their mouths, the semblance of black rat-holes, holes of gigantic rats, inhabited by whirlwinds;) when all the pretences and impunities and infirmities, in fine, had massed themselves to be hurled at you in the fury of the elements, in the character of the traffic, in the unadapted state of the place to almost *any* dense movement, and, beyond everything, in that pitch of all the noises which acted on your nerves as so much wanton provocation, so much conscious cynicism. The fury of sound took the form of derision of the rest of your woe, and thus it *might*, I admit, have struck you as brazen that the horrible place should, in such confessed collapse, still be swaggering and shouting. It might have struck you that great cities, with the eyes of the world on them, as the phrase is, should be capable either of a proper form or (failing this) of a proper compunction ; which tributes to propriety were, on the part of New York, equally wanting. This made you remark, precisely, that nothing was wanting, on the other hand, to that analogy with the character of the bad bold beauty, the creature the most blatant of whose pretensions is that she is one of those to whom everything is always forgiven. On what ground 'forgiven'? of course you ask ; but note that you ask it while you're in the very act of forgiving. Oh yes, you are ; you've as much as said so yourself. So there it all is ; arrange it as you can. Poor dear bad bold beauty ; there must indeed be something about her——!"

Let me grant then, to get on, that there *was* doubtless,

in the better time, something about her; there was enough about her, at all events, to conduce to that distinct cultivation of her company for which the contemplative stroll, when there was time for it, was but another name. The analogy was in truth complete; since the repetition of such walks, and the admission of the beguiled state contained in them, resembled nothing so much as the visits so often still incorrigibly made to compromised charmers. I defy even a master of morbid observation to perambulate New York unless he be interested; so that in a case of memories so gathered the interest must be taken as a final fact. Let me figure it, to this end, as lively in every connection—and so indeed no more lively at one mild crisis than at another. The crisis—even of observation at the morbid pitch—is inevitably mild in cities intensely new; and it was with the quite peculiarly insistent newness of the upper reaches of the town that the spirit of romantic inquiry had always, at the best, to reckon. There are new cities enough about the world, goodness knows, and there are new parts enough of old cities—for examples of which we need go no farther than London, Paris and Rome, all of late so mercilessly renovated. But the newness of New York—unlike even that of Boston, I seemed to discern—had this mark of its very own, that it affects one, in every case, as having treated itself as still more provisional, if possible, than any poor dear little interest of antiquity it may have annihilated. The very sign of its energy is that it doesn't believe in itself; it fails to succeed, even at a cost of millions, in persuading you that it does. Its mission would appear to be, exactly, to gild the temporary, with its gold, as many inches thick as may be, and then, with a fresh shrug, a shrug of its splendid cynicism for its freshly detected inability to convince, give up its actual work, however exorbitant, as the merest of stop-gaps. The difficulty with the compromised charmer is just this constant inability to convince; to convince ever, I mean, that she is serious, serious about any form whatever, or about anything but that perpetual passionate pecuniary purpose which plays with all forms, which derides and devours them, though it may pile up the cost of them in order to rest a while, spent and haggard, in the illusion of their finality.

The perception of this truth grows for you by your simply walking up Fifth Avenue and pausing a little in presence of certain forms, certain exorbitant structures, in other words, the elegant domiciliary, as to which the illusion of finality was within one's memory magnificent and complete, but as to which one feels to-day that their life wouldn't be, as against any whisper of a higher interest, worth an hour's purchase. They sit there in the florid majesty of the taste of their time—a light now, alas, generally clouded ; and I pretend of course to speak, in alluding to them, of no individual case of danger or doom. It is only a question of that unintending and unconvincing expression of New York everywhere, as yet, on the matter of the *maintenance* of a given effect—which comes back to the general insincerity of effects, and truly even (as I have already noted) to the insincerity of the effect of the sky-scrapers themselves. There results from all this—and as much where the place most smells of its millions as elsewhere—that unmistakable New York admission of unattempted, impossible maturity. The new Paris and the new Rome do at least propose, I think, to be old—one of these days ; the new London even, erect as she is on leaseholds destitute of dignity, yet does, for the period, appear to believe in herself. The vice I glance at is, however, when showing, in our flagrant example, on the forehead of its victims, much more a cause for pitying than for decrying them. Again and again, in the upper reaches, you pause with that pity ; you learn, on the occasion of a kindly glance up and down a quiet cross-street (there being objects and aspects in many of them appealing to kindness), that such and such a house, or a row, is "coming down"; and you gasp, in presence of the elements involved, at the strangeness of the moral so pointed. It rings out like the crack of that lash in the sky, the play of some mighty teamster's whip, which ends by affecting you as the poor New Yorker's one association with the idea of "powers above." "No"—this is the tune to which the whip seems flourished—"there's no step at which you shall rest, no form, as I'm constantly showing you, to which, consistently with my interests, you *can*. I build you up but to tear you down, for if I were to let sentiment and sincerity once take root, were to let any tenderness of association once accumulate, or any 'love of the old' once pass unsnubbed, what would become of *us*, who have our hands on the whipstock, please? Fortunately we've learned the secret for keeping association at bay. We've learned that the great thing is not to suffer it to so much as begin. Wherever it does begin we find we're lost; but as that takes some time we get in ahead. It's the reason, if you must know, why you shall 'run,' all, without exception, to the fifty floors. We defy you even to aspire to venerate shapes so grossly constructed as the arrangement in fifty floors. You may have a feeling for keeping on with an old staircase, consecrated by the tread of generations—especially when it's 'good,' and old staircases are often so lovely; but how can you have a feeling for keeping on with an old elevator, how can you have it any more than for keeping on with an old omnibus? You'd be ashamed to venerate the arrangement in fifty floors, accordingly, even if you could; whereby, saving you any moral trouble or struggle, they are conceived and constructed—and you must do us the justice of this care for your sensibility—in a manner to put the thing out of the question. In such a manner, moreover, as that there shall be immeasurably more of them, in quantity, to tear down than of the actual past that we are now sweeping away.   Wherefore we shall be kept in precious practice.   The word will perhaps be then—who knows?—for building from the earth-surface downwards ; in which case it will be a question of tearing, so to speak, 'up.'   It little matters, so long as we blight the superstition of rest."

Yet even in the midst of this vision of eternal waste, of conscious, sentient-looking houses and rows, full sections of streets, to which the rich taste of history is forbidden even while their fresh young lips are just touching the cup, something charmingly done, here and there, some bid for the ampler permanence, seems to say to you that the particular place only asks, as a human home, to lead the life it has begun, only asks to enfold generations and gather in traditions, to show itself capable of growing up to character and authority.   Houses of the best taste are like clothes of the best tailors—it takes their age to show us how good they are ; and I frequently recognized, in the region of the upper reaches, this direct appeal of the individual case of happy construction.   Construction at large abounds in the upper reaches, construction indescribably precipitate and elaborate—the latter fact about it always so oddly hand in hand with the former ; and we should exceed in saying that felicity is always its mark. But some highly liberal, some extravagant intention almost always is, and we meet here even that happy accident, already encountered and acclaimed, in its few examples, down-town, of the object shining almost absurdly in the light of its merely comparative distinction.   All but lost in the welter of instances of sham refinement, the shy little case of real refinement detaches itself ridiculously, as being (like the saved City Hall, or like the pleasant old garden-walled house on the north-west corner of Washington Square and Fifth Avenue) of so beneficent an admonition as to show, relatively speaking, for priceless. These things, which I may not take time to pick out, are the salt that saves, and it is enough to say for their delicacy that they are the direct counterpart of those other dreadful presences, looming round them, which embody the imagination of new kinds and new clustered, emphasized quantities of vulgarity. To recall these fine notes and these loud ones, the whole play of wealth and energy and untutored liberty, of the movement of a breathless civilization reflected, as brick and stone and marble may reflect, through all the contrasts of prodigious flight and portentous stumble, is to acknowledge, positively, that one's rambles were delightful, and that the district abutting on the east side of the Park, in particular, never engaged my attention without, by the same stroke, making the social question dance before it in a hundred interesting forms.

The social question quite fills the air, in New York, for any spectator whose impressions at all follow themselves up; it wears, at any rate, in what I have called the upper reaches, the perpetual strange appearance as of Property perched high aloft and yet itself looking about, all ruefully, in the wonder of what it is exactly doing there. We see it perched, assuredly, in other and older cities, other and older social orders; but it strikes us in those situations as knowing a little more where it is. It strikes us as knowing how it has got up and why it must, infallibly, stay up; it has not the frightened look, measuring the spaces around, of a small child set on a mantelshelf and about to cry out. If old societies are interesting, however, I am far from thinking that young ones may not be more so—with their collective countenance so much more presented, precisely, to observation, as by their artless need to get themselves explained. The American world produces almost everywhere the impression of appealing to any attested interest for the word, the *fin mot*, of what it may mean ; but I somehow see those parts of it most at a loss that are already explained not a little by the ample possession of money. This is the amiable side there of the large developments of private ease in general—the amiable side of those numerous groups that are rich enough and, in the happy vulgar phrase, bloated enough, to be candidates for the classic imputation of haughtiness. The amiability proceeds from an essential vagueness ; whereas real haughtiness is never vague about itself—it is only vague about others. That is the human note in the huge American rattle of gold—so far as the "social" field is the scene of the rattle. The "business" field is a different matter—as to which the determination of the audibility in it of the human note (so interesting to try for if one had but the warrant) is a line of research closed to me, alas, by my fatally uninitiated state. My point is, at all events, that you cannot be "hard," really, with any society that affects you as ready to learn from you, and from this resource for it of your detachment combining with your proximity, what in the name of all its possessions and all its destitutions it would honestly be "at."

3

New York
and the Hudson

A SPRING IMPRESSION

It was a concomitant, always, of the down-town hour that it could be felt as *most* playing into the surrendered consciousness and making the sharpest impression ; yet, since the up-town hour was apt, in its turn, to claim the same distinction, I could only let each of them take its way with me as it would. The oddity was that they seemed not at all to speak of different things—by so quick a process does any one aspect, in the United States, in general, I was to note, connect itself with the rest ; so little does any link in the huge looseness of New York, in especial, appear to come as a whole, or as final, out of the fusion. The fusion, as of elements in solution in a vast hot pot, is always going on, and one stage of the process is as typical or as vivid as another. Whatever I might be looking at, or be struck with, the object or the phase was an item in the pressing conditions of the place, and as such had more in common with its sister items than it had in difference from them. It mattered little, moreover, whether this might be a proof that New York, among cities, most deeply languishes and palpitates, or vibrates and flourishes (whichever way one may put it) under the breath of her conditions, or whether, simply, this habit of finding a little of *all* my impressions reflected in any one of them testified to the enjoyment of a real relation with the subject. I like indeed to think of my relation to New York as, in that manner, almost inexpressibly intimate, and as hence making, for daily sensation, a keyboard as continuous, and as free from hard transitions, as if swept by the fingers of a master-pianist. You cannot, surely, say more for your sense of the underlying unity of an occasion than that the taste of each dish in the banquet recalls the taste of most of the others; which is what I mean by the "continuity," not to say the affinity, on the island of Manhattan, between the fish and the sweets, between the soup and the game.   The whole feast affects one as eaten—that is the point—with the general queer sauce of New York; a preparation as freely diffused, somehow, on the East side as on the West, in the quarter of Grand Street as in the quarter of Murray Hill. No fact, I hasten to add, would appear to make the place more amenable to delineations of the order that may be spoken of as hanging together.

I must confess, notwithstanding, to not being quite ready to point directly to the common element in the dense Italian neighbourhoods of the lower East side, and in the upper reaches of Fifth and of Madison Avenues; though indeed I wonder at this inability in recollecting two or three of those charming afternoons of early summer, in Central Park, which showed the fruit of the foreign tree as shaken down there with a force that smothered everything else. The long residential vistas I have named were within a quarter of an hour's walk, but the alien was as truly in possession, under the high "aristocratic" nose, as if he had had but three steps to come. If it be asked why, the alien still striking you so as an alien, the singleness of impression, throughout the place, should still be so marked, the answer, close at hand, would seem to be that the alien himself fairly *makes* the singleness of impression.   Is not the universal sauce essentially *his* sauce, and do we not feel ourselves feeding, half the time, from the ladle, as greasy as he chooses to leave it for us, that he holds out ? Such questions were in my ears, at all events, with the cheerful hum of that babel of tongues established in the vernal Park, and they supplied, beyond doubt, the livelier interest of any hour of contemplation there. I hate to drift into dealing with them at the expense of a proper tribute, kept distinct and vivid, to the charming bosky precinct itself, the great field of recreation with which they swarmed ; but it could not be the fault of the brooding visitor, and still less that of the restored absentee, if he was conscious of the need of mental adjustment to phenomena absolutely fresh. He could remember still how, months before, a day or two after his restoration, a noted element of one of his first impressions had been this particular revealed anomaly. He had been, on the Jersey shore, walking with a couple of friends through the grounds of a large new rural residence, where groups of diggers and ditchers were working, on those lines of breathless haste which seem always, in the United States, of the essence of any question, toward an expensive effect of landscape gardening. To pause before them, for interest in their labour, was, and would have been everywhere, instinctive ; but what came home to me on the spot was that whatever *more* would have been anywhere else involved had here inevitably to lapse.

What lapsed, on the spot, was the element of communication with the workers, as I may call it for want of a better name ; that element which, in a European country, would have operated, from side to side, as the play of mutual recognition, founded on old familiarities and heredities, and involving, for the moment, some impalpable exchange. The men, in the case I speak of, were Italians, of superlatively southern type, and any impalpable exchange struck me as absent from the air to positive intensity, to mere unthinkability. It was as if contact were out of the question and the sterility of the passage between us recorded, with due dryness, in our staring silence. This impression was for one of the party a shock—a member of the party for whom, on the other side of the world, the imagination of the main furniture, as it might be called, of any rural excursion, of *the* rural in particular, had been, during years, the easy sense, for the excursionist, of a social relation with any encountered type, from whichever end of the scale proceeding. Had that not ever been, exactly, a part of the vague warmth, the intrinsic colour, of any honest man's rural walk in his England or his Italy, his Germany or his France, and was not the effect of its so suddenly dropping out, in the land of universal brotherhood—for I was to find it drop out again and again—rather a chill, straightway, for the heart, and rather a puzzle, not less, for the head ? Shortly after the spring of this question was first touched for me I found it ring out again with a sharper stroke. Happening to have lost my way, during a long ramble among the New Hampshire hills, I appealed, for information, at a parting of the roads, to a young man whom, at the moment of my need, I happily saw emerge from a neighbouring wood. But his stare was blank, in answer to my inquiry, and, seeing that he failed to understand me and that he had a dark-eyed " Latin " look, I jumped to the inference of his being a French Canadian. My repetition of my query in French, however, forwarded the case as little, and my trying him with Italian had no better effect. " What *are* you then ? " I wonderingly asked—on which my accent loosened in him the faculty of speech. " I'm an Armenian," he replied, as if it were the most natural thing in the world for a wage-earning youth in the heart of New England to be—so that all I could do was to try and make my profit of the lesson. I could have made it better, for the occasion, if, even on the Armenian basis, he had appeared to expect brotherhood; but this had been as little his seeming as it had been that of the diggers by the Jersey shore.

To inquire of these things on the spot, to betray, that is, one's sense of the " chill " of which I have spoken, is of course to hear it admitted, promptly enough, that there is no claim to brotherhood with aliens in the first grossness of their alienism. The material of which they consist is being dressed and prepared, at this stage, for brotherhood, and the consummation, in respect to many of them, will not be, can not from the nature of the case be, in any lifetime of their own. Their children are another matter—as in fact the children throughout the United States, are an immense matter, are almost the greatest matter of all ; it is the younger generation who will fully profit, rise to the occasion and enter into the privilege. The machinery is colossal—nothing is more characteristic of the country than the development of this machinery, in the form of the political and social habit, the common school and the newspaper ; so that there are always millions of little transformed strangers growing up in regard to whom the idea of intimacy of relation may be as freely cherished as you like. *They* are the stuff of whom brothers and sisters are made, and the making proceeds on a scale that really need leave nothing to desire. All this you take in, with a wondering mind, and in the light of it the great " ethnic " question rises before you on a corresponding scale and with a corresponding majesty. Once it has set your observation, to say nothing of your imagination, working, it becomes for you, as you go and come, the wonderment to which everything ministers and that is quickened well-nigh to madness, in some places and on some occasions, by every face and every accent that meet your eyes and ears. The sense of the elements in

the cauldron—the cauldron of the "American" character—becomes thus about as vivid a thing as you can
at all quietly manage, and the question settles into a
form which makes the intelligible answer further and
further recede. "What meaning, in the presence of
such impressions, can continue to attach to such a term
as the 'American' character?—what type, as the result
of such a prodigious amalgam, such a hotch-potch of
racial ingredients, is to be conceived as shaping itself?"
The challenge to speculation, fed thus by a thousand
sources, is so intense as to be, as I say, irritating; but
practically, beyond doubt, I should also say, you take
refuge from it—since your case would otherwise be
hard; and you find your relief not in the least in any
direct satisfaction or solution, but absolutely in that blest
general drop of the immediate need of conclusions, or
rather in that blest general feeling for the impossibility
of them, to which the philosophy of any really fine
observation of the American spectacle must reduce itself,
and the large intellectual, quite even the large æsthetic,
margin supplied by which accompanies the spectator as
his one positively complete comfort.

It is more than a comfort to him, truly, in all the conditions, this accepted vision of the too-defiant scale of
numerosity and quantity—the effect of which is so to
multiply the possibilities, so to open, by the million,
contingent doors and windows: he rests in it at last as
an absolute luxury, converting it even into a substitute,
into *the* constant substitute, for many luxuries that are
absent. He doesn't *know*, he can't *say*, before the facts,
and he doesn't even want to know or to say; the facts
themselves loom, before the understanding, in too large
a mass for a mere mouthful: it is as if the syllables were
too numerous to make a legible word. The *il*legible
word, accordingly, the great inscrutable answer to questions, hangs in the vast American sky, to his imagination,

as something fantastic and *abracadabrant*, belonging to no known language, and it is under this convenient ensign that he travels and considers and contemplates, and, to the best of his ability, enjoys. The interesting point, in the connection, is moreover that this particular effect of the scale of things is the only effect that, throughout the land, is not directly adverse to joy. Extent and reduplication, the multiplication of cognate items and the continuity of motion, are elements that count, there, in general, for fatigue and satiety, prompting the earnest observer, overburdened perhaps already a little by his earnestness, to the reflection that the country is too large for any human convenience, that it can scarce, in the scheme of Providence, have been meant to be dealt with as we are trying, perhaps all in vain, to deal with it, and that its very possibilities of population themselves cause one to wince in the light of the question of intercourse and contact. That relation to its superficies and content—the relation of flat fatigue—is, with the traveller, a constant quantity; so that he feels himself justified of the inward, the philosophic, escape into the immensity. And as it is the restored absentee, with his acquired habit of nearer limits and shorter journeys and more muffled concussions, who is doubtless most subject to flat fatigue, so it is this same personage who most avails himself of the liberty of waiting to see. It is an advantage—acting often in the way of a compensation, or of an appeal from the immediate—that he becomes, early in his period of inquiry, conscious of intimately invoking, in whatever apparent inconsistency it may lodge him. There is too much of the whole thing, he sighs, for the personal relation with it ; and yet he would desire no inch less for the relation that he describes to himself best perhaps either as the provisionally-imaginative or as the distantly-respectful. Diminution of quantity, even by that inch, might mark the difference of his having to begin to recognize from afar, as through a rift in the obscurity, the gleam of some propriety of opinion.   What would a man make, many things still being as they are, he finds himself asking, of a *small* America?—and what may a big one, on the other hand, still not make of itself? Goodness be thanked, accordingly, for the bigness.   The state of flat fatigue, obviously, is not an opinion, save in the sense attributed to the slumber of the gentleman of the anecdote who had lost consciousness during the reading of the play—it belongs to the order of mere sensation and impression ; and as to these the case is quite different : he may have as many of each as he can carry.

II

The process of the mitigation and, still more, of the conversion of the alien goes on, meanwhile, obviously, not by leaps and bounds or any form of easy magic, but under its own mystic laws and with an outward air of quite declining to be unduly precipitated.   How little it may be thought of in New York as a quick business we readily perceive as the effect of merely remembering the vast numbers of their kind that the arriving reinforcements, from whatever ends of the earth, find already in possession of the field.   There awaits the disembarked Armenian, for instance, so warm and furnished an Armenian corner that the need of hurrying to get rid of the sense of it must become less and less a pressing preliminary.   The corner growing warmer and warmer, it is to be supposed, by rich accretions, he may take his time, more and more, for becoming absorbed in the surrounding element, and he may in fact feel more and more that he can do so on his own conditions.   I seem to find indeed in this latter truth a hint for the best expression of a whole side of New York—the best expression of much of the medium in which one consciously moves. It is formed by this fact that the alien is taking his time, and that you go about with him meanwhile, sharing, all respectfully, in his deliberation, waiting on his convenience, watching him at his interesting work. The vast foreign quarters of the city present him as thus engaged in it, and they are curious and portentous and "picturesque" just by reason of their doing so. You recognize in them, freely, those elements that are not elements of swift convertibility, and you lose yourself in the wonder of what becomes, as it were, of the obstinate, the unconverted residuum. The country at large, as you cross it in different senses, keeps up its character for you as the hugest thinkable organism for successful "assimilation"; but the assimilative force itself has the residuum still to count with. The operation of the immense machine, identical after all with the total of American life, trembles away into mysteries that are beyond our present notation and that reduce us in many a mood to renouncing analysis.

Who and what is an alien, when it comes to that, in a country peopled from the first under the jealous eye of history?—peopled, that is, by migrations at once extremely recent, perfectly traceable and urgently required. They are still, it would appear, urgently required—if we look about far enough for the urgency; though of that truth such a scene as New York may well make one doubt. Which is the American, by these scant measures? —which is *not* the alien, over a large part of the country at least, and where does one put a finger on the dividing line, or, for that matter, "spot" and identify any particular phase of the conversion, any one of its successive moments? The sense of the interest of so doing is doubtless half the interest of the general question—the possibility of our seeing lucidly presented some such phenomenon, in a given group of persons, or even in a felicitous individual, as the dawn of the American spirit while the declining rays of the Croatian, say, or of the Calabrian, or of the Lusitanian, still linger more or less pensively in the sky. Fifty doubts and queries come up, in regard to any such possibility, as one circulates in New York, with the so ambiguous element in the *launched* foreign personality always in one's eyes ; the wonder, above all, of whether there be, comparatively, in the vastly greater number of the representatives of the fresh contingent, any spirit that the American does not find an easy prey. Repeatedly, in the electric cars, one seemed invited to take that for granted—there being occasions, days and weeks together, when the electric cars offer you nothing else to think of. The carful, again and again, is a foreign carful ; a row of faces, up and down, testifying, without exception, to alienism unmistakable, alienism undisguised and unashamed. You do here, in a manner perhaps, discriminate; the launched condition, as I have called it, is more developed in some types than in others ; but I remember observing how, in the Broadway and the Bowery conveyances in especial, they tended, almost alike, to make the observer gasp with the sense of isolation. It was not for this that the observer on whose behalf I more particularly write had sought to take up again the sweet sense of the natal air.

The great fact about his companions was that, foreign as they might be, newly inducted as they might be, they were *at home*, really more at home, at the end of their few weeks or months or their year or two, than they had ever in their lives been before ; and that *he* was at home too, quite with the same intensity : and yet that it was this very equality of condition that, from side to side, made the whole medium so strange. Here again, however, relief may be sought and found—and I say this at the risk of perhaps picturing the restored absentee as too constantly requiring it ; for there is fascination in the study of the innumerable ways in which this sense of being at home, on the part of all the types, may show forth. New York offers to such a study a well-nigh unlimited field, but I seem to recall winter days, harsh, dusky, sloshy winter afternoons, in the densely-packed East-side street-cars, as an especially intimate surrender to it. It took its place thus, I think, under the general American law of *all* relief from the great equalizing pressure : it took on that last disinterestedness which consists of one's getting away from one's subject by plunging into it, for sweet truth's sake, still deeper. If I speak, moreover, of this general first grossness of alienism as presented in "types," I use that word for easy convenience and not in respect to its indicating marked variety. There are many different ways, certainly, in which obscure fighters of the battle of life may look, under new high lights, queer and crude and unwrought ; but the striking thing, precisely, in the crepuscular, tunnel-like avenues that the " Elevated " overarches—yet without quenching, either, that constant power of any American exhibition rather luridly to light itself—the striking thing, and the beguiling, was always the manner in which figure after figure and face after face already betrayed the common consequence and action of their whereabouts. Face after face, unmistakably, was " low "—particularly in the men, squared all solidly in their new security and portability, their vague but growing sense of many unprecedented things ; and as signs of the reinforcing of a large local conception of manners and relations it was difficult to say if they most affected one as promising or as portentous.

The great thing, at any rate, was that they were all together so visibly on the new, the lifted level—that of consciously not being what they *had* been, and that this immediately glazed them over as with some mixture, of indescribable hue and consistency, the wholesale varnish of consecration, that might have been applied, out of a bottomless receptacle, by a huge white-washing brush. Here, perhaps, was the nearest approach to a seizable step in the evolution of the oncoming citizen, the stage of his no longer being for you—for any complacency of the romantic, or even verily of the fraternizing, sense in you—the foreigner of the quality, of the kind, that he might have been *chez lui.* Whatever he might see himself becoming, he was never to see himself that again, any more than you were ever to see him. He became then, to my vision (which I have called fascinated for want of a better description of it), a creature promptly despoiled of those " manners " which were the grace (as I am again reduced to calling it) by which one had best known and, on opportunity, best liked him. He presents himself thus, most of all, to be plain—and not only in New York, but throughout the country—as wonderingly conscious that his manners of the other world, that everything you have there known and praised him for, have been a huge mistake : to that degree that the sense of this luminous discovery is what we mainly imagine his weighted communications to those he has left behind charged with ; those rich letters home as to the number and content of which the Post Office gives us so remarkable a statistic. If there are several lights in which the great assimilative organism itself may be looked at, does it not still perhaps loom largest as an agent for revealing to the citizen-to-be the error in question ? He hears it, under this ægis, proclaimed in a thousand voices, and it is as listening to these and as, according to the individual, more or less swiftly, but always infallibly, penetrated and convinced by them, that I felt myself see him go about his business, see him above all, for some odd reason, sit there in the street-car, and with a slow, brooding gravity, a dim calculation of bearings, which yet never takes a backward step, expand to the full measure of it.

So, in New York, largely, the "American" value of the immigrant who arrives at all mature is restricted to the enjoyment (all prepared to increase) of that important preliminary truth; which makes him for us, we must own, till more comes of it, a tolerably neutral and colourless image. He resembles for the time the dog who sniffs round the freshly-acquired bone, giving it a push and a lick, betraying a sense of its possibilities, but not— and quite as from a positive deep tremor of consciousness —directly attacking it. There are categories of foreigners, truly, meanwhile, of whom we are moved to say that only a mechanism working with scientific force could have performed this feat of making them colourless. The Italians, who, over the whole land, strike us, I am afraid, as, after the Negro and the Chinaman, the human value most easily produced, the Italians meet us, at every turn, only to make us ask what has become of that element of the agreeable address in *them* which has, from far back, so enhanced for the stranger the interest and pleasure of a visit to their beautiful country. They shed it utterly, I couldn't but observe, on their advent, after a deep inhalation or two of the clear native air; shed it with a conscientious completeness which leaves one looking for any faint trace of it. "Colour," of that pleasant sort, was what they had appeared, among the races of the European family, most to have; so that the effect I speak of, the rapid action of the ambient air, is like that of the tub of hot water that reduces a piece of bright-hued stuff, on immersion, to the proved state of not "washing": the only fault of my image indeed being that if the stuff loses its brightness the water of the tub at least is more or less agreeably dyed with it. That is doubtless not the case for the ambient air operating after

the fashion I here note—since we surely fail to observe
that the property washed out of the new subject begins
to tint with its pink or its azure his fellow-soakers in the
terrible tank.   If this property that has quitted him—the
general amenity of attitude in the absence of provocation
to its opposite—could be accounted for by its having
rubbed off on any number of surrounding persons, the
whole process would be easier and perhaps more com-
forting to follow.   It will not have been his first occasion
of taking leave of short-sighted comfort in the United
States, however, if the patient inquirer postpones that
ideal to the real solicitation of the question I here touch
on.

What *does* become of the various positive properties,
on the part of certain of the installed tribes, the good
manners, say, among them, as to which the process of
shedding and the fact of eclipse come so promptly into
play?   It has taken long ages of history, in the other
world, to produce them, and you ask yourself, with independent curiosity, if they may really be thus extinguished
in an hour.   And if they are not extinguished, into what
pathless tracts of the native atmosphere do they virtually,
do they provisionally, and so all undiscoverably, melt?
Do they burrow underground, to await their day again?
—or in what strange secret places are they held in deposit
and in trust?   The "American" identity that has profited
by their sacrifice has meanwhile acquired (in the happiest
cases) all apparent confidence and consistency; but may
not the doubt remain of whether the extinction of qualities ingrained in generations is to be taken for quite
complete?   Isn't it conceivable that, for something like
a final efflorescence, the business of slow comminglings
and makings-over at last ended, they may rise again to
the surface, affirming their vitality and value and playing
their part?   It would be for them, of course, in this event,
to attest that they had been worth waiting so long for;

but the speculation, at any rate, irresistibly forced upon us, is a sign of the interest, in the American world, of what I have called the "ethnic" outlook.   The cauldron, for the great stew, has such circumference and such depth that we can only deal here with ultimate syntheses, ultimate combinations and possibilities.   Yet I am well aware that if these vague evocations of them, in their nebulous remoteness, may charm the ingenuity of the student of the scene, there are matters of the foreground that they have no call to supplant.   Any temptation to let them do so is meanwhile, no doubt, but a proof of that impulse irresponsibly to escape from the formidable foreground which so often, in the American world, lies in wait for the spirit of intellectual dalliance.

III

New York really, I think, is all formidable foreground ; or, if it be not, there is more than enough of this pressure of the present and the immediate to cut out the close sketcher's work for him.   These things are a thick growth all round him, and when I recall the intensity of the material picture in the dense Yiddish quarter, for instance, I wonder at its not having forestalled, on my page, mere musings and, as they will doubtless be called, moonings.   There abides with me, ineffaceably, the memory of a summer evening spent there by invitation of a high public functionary domiciled on the spot —to the extreme enhancement of the romantic interest his visitor found him foredoomed to inspire—who was to prove one of the most liberal of hosts and most luminous of guides.   I can scarce help it if this brilliant personality, on that occasion the very medium itself through which the whole spectacle showed, so colours my impressions that if I speak, by intention, of the facts that played into them I may really but reflect the rich talk and the general privilege of the hour. That accident moreover must take its place simply as the highest value and the strongest note in the total show—so much did it testify to the quality of appealing, surrounding life. The sense of this quality was already strong in my drive, with a companion, through the long, warm June twilight, from a comparatively conventional neighbourhood; it was the sense, after all, of a great swarming, a swarming that had begun to thicken, infinitely, as soon as we had crossed to the East side and long before we had got to Rutgers Street. There is no swarming like that of Israel when once Israel has got a start, and the scene here bristled, at every step, with the signs and sounds, immitigable, unmistakable, of a Jewry that had burst all bounds. That it has burst all bounds in New York, almost any combination of figures or of objects taken at hazard sufficiently proclaims; but I remember how the rising waters, on this summer night, rose, to the imagination, even above the housetops and seemed to sound their murmur to the pale distant stars. It was as if we had been thus, in the crowded, hustled roadway, where multiplication, multiplication of everything, was the dominant note, at the bottom of some vast sallow aquarium in which innumerable fish, of over-developed proboscis, were to bump together, for ever, amid heaped spoils of the sea.

The children swarmed above all—here was multiplication with a vengeance; and the number of very old persons, of either sex, was almost equally remarkable; the very old persons being in equal vague occupation of the doorstep, pavement, curbstone, gutter, roadway, and every one alike using the street for overflow. As overflow, in the whole quarter, is the main fact of life—I was to learn later on that, with the exception of some shy corner of Asia, no district in the world known to the statistician has so many inhabitants to the yard—the scene hummed with the human presence beyond any I had ever faced in quest even of refreshment; producing part of the impression, moreover, no doubt, as a direct consequence of the intensity of the Jewish aspect. This, I think, makes the individual Jew more of a concentrated person, savingly possessed of everything that is in him, than any other human, noted at random—or is it simply, rather, that the unsurpassed strength of the race permits of the chopping into myriads of fine fragments without loss of race-quality? There are small strange animals, known to natural history, snakes or worms, I believe, who, when cut into pieces, wriggle away contentedly and live in the snippet as completely as in the whole. So the denizens of the New York Ghetto, heaped as thick as the splinters on the table of a glass-blower, had each, like the fine glass particle, his or her individual share of the whole hard glitter of Israel. This diffused intensity, as I have called it, causes any array of Jews to resemble (if I may be allowed another image) some long nocturnal street where every window in every house shows a maintained light. The advanced age of so many of the figures, the ubiquity of the children, carried out in fact this analogy; they were all there for race, and not, as it were, for reason: that excess of lurid meaning, in some of the old men's and old women's faces in particular, would have been absurd, in the conditions, as a really directed attention—it could only be the gathered past of Israel mechanically pushing through. The way, at the same time, this chapter of history did, all that evening, seem to push, was a matter that made the "ethnic" apparition again sit like a skeleton at the feast. It was fairly as if I could see the spectre grin while the talk of the hour gave me, across the board, facts and figures, chapter and verse, for the extent of the Hebrew conquest of New York. With a reverence for intellect, one should doubtless have drunk in tribute to an intellectual people; but I remember being at no time more conscious of that merely portentous element, in the aspects of American growth, which reduces to inanity any marked dismay quite as much as any high elation. The portent is one of too many—you always come back, as I have hinted, with your easier gasp, to *that*: it will be time enough to sigh or to shout when the relation of the particular appearance to all the other relations shall have cleared itself up. Phantasmagoric for me, accordingly, in a high degree, are the interesting hours I here glance at content to remain—setting in this respect, I recognize, an excellent example to all the rest of the New York phantasmagoria. Let me speak of the remainder only as phantasmagoric too, so that I may both the more kindly recall it and the sooner have done with it.

I have not done, however, with the impression of that large evening in the Ghetto; there was too much in the vision, and it has left too much the sense of a rare experience. For what did it all really come to but that one had seen with one's eyes the New Jerusalem on earth? What less than that could it all have been, in its far-spreading light and its celestial serenity of multiplication? There it was, there it is, and when I think of the dark, foul, stifling Ghettos of other remembered cities, I shall think by the same stroke of the city of redemption, and evoke in particular the rich Rutgers Street perspective—rich, so peculiarly, for the eye, in that complexity of fire-escapes with which each house-front bristles and which gives the whole vista so modernized and appointed a look. Omnipresent in the "poor" regions, this neat applied machinery has, for the stranger, a common side with the electric light and the telephone, suggests the distance achieved from the old Jerusalem. (These frontal iron ladders and platforms, by the way, so numerous throughout New York, strike more New York notes than can be parenthetically named—and among them perhaps most sharply the note of the ease with which, in the terrible town, on opportunity, "architecture" goes by the board; but the appearance to which they often most conduce is that of the spaciously organized cage for the nimbler class of animals in some great zoological garden. This general analogy is irresistible—it seems to offer, in each district, a little world of bars and perches and swings for human squirrels and monkeys. The very name of architecture perishes, for the fire-escapes look like abashed afterthoughts, staircases and communications forgotten in the construction; but the inhabitants lead, like the squirrels and monkeys, all the merrier life.) It was while I hung over the prospect from the windows of my friend, however, the presiding genius of the district, and it was while, at a later hour, I proceeded in his company, and in that of a trio of contributive fellow-pilgrims, from one "characteristic" place of public entertainment to another: it was during this rich climax, I say, that the city of redemption was least to be taken for anything less than it was. The windows, while we sat at meat, looked out on a swarming little square in which an ant-like population darted to and fro; the square consisted in part of a "district" public garden, or public lounge rather, one of those small backwaters or refuges, artfully economized for rest, here and there, in the very heart of the New York whirlpool, and which spoke louder than anything else of a Jerusalem disinfected. What spoke loudest, no doubt, was the great overtowering School which formed a main boundary and in the shadow of which we all comparatively crouched.

But the School must not lead me on just yet—so colossally has its presence still to loom for us; that presence which profits so, for predominance, in America, by the failure of concurrent and competitive presences, the failure of any others looming at all on the same scale

save that of Business, those in particular of a visible
Church, a visible State, a visible Society, a visible Past;
those of the many visibilities, in short, that warmly
cumber the ground in older countries. Yet it also spoke
loud that my friend was quartered, for the interest of the
thing (from his so interesting point of view), in a
"tenement-house"; the New Jerusalem would so have
triumphed, had it triumphed nowhere else, in the fact
that this charming little structure *could* be ranged, on the
wonderful little square, under that invidious head. On
my asking to what latent vice it owed its stigma, I was
asked in return if it didn't sufficiently pay for its name
by harbouring some five-and-twenty families. But this,
exactly, was the way it testified—this circumstance of the
simultaneous enjoyment by five-and-twenty families, on
"tenement" lines, of conditions so little sordid, so highly
"evolved." I remember the evolved fire-proof staircase,
a thing of scientific surfaces, impenetrable to the microbe,
and above all plated, against side friction, with white
marble of a goodly grain. The white marble was surely
the New Jerusalem note, and we followed that note, up
and down the district, the rest of the evening, through
more happy changes than I may take time to count.
What struck me in the flaring streets (over and beyond
the everywhere insistent, defiant, unhumorous, exotic face)
was the blaze of the shops addressed to the New
Jerusalem wants and the splendour with which these
were taken for granted; the only thing indeed a little
ambiguous was just this look of the trap too brilliantly,
too candidly baited for the wary side of Israel itself. It
is not *for* Israel, in general, that Israel so artfully shines
—yet its being moved to do so, at last, in that luxurious
style, might be precisely the grand side of the city of
redemption. Who can ever tell, moreover, in any conditions and in presence of any apparent anomaly, what the
genius of Israel may, or may not, really be "up to"?

The grateful way to take it all, at any rate, was with the sense of its coming back again to the inveterate rise, in the American air, of every value, and especially of the lower ones, those most subject to multiplication; such a wealth of meaning did this keep appearing to pour into the value and function of the country at large. Importances are all strikingly shifted and reconstituted, in the United States, for the visitor attuned, from far back, to "European" importances; but I think of no other moment of my total impression as so sharply working over my own benighted vision of them. The scale, in this light of the New Jerusalem, seemed completely rearranged; or, to put it more simply, the wants, the gratifications, the aspirations of the "poor," as expressed in the shops (which were the shops of the "poor"), denoted a new style of poverty; and this new style of poverty, from street to street, stuck out of the possible purchasers, one's jostling fellow-pedestrians, and made them, to every man and woman, individual throbs in the larger harmony. One can speak only of what one has seen, and there were grosser elements of the sordid and the squalid that I doubtless never saw. That, with a good deal of observation and of curiosity, I should have failed of this, the country over, affected me as by itself something of an indication. To miss that part of the spectacle, or to know it only by its having so unfamiliar a pitch, was an indication that made up for a great many others. It is when this one in particular is forced home to you—this immense, vivid *general* lift of poverty and general appreciation of the living unit's paying property in himself—that the picture seems most to clear and the way to jubilation most to open. For it meets you there, at every turn, as the result most definitely attested. You are as constantly reminded, no doubt, that these rises in enjoyed value shrink and dwindle under the icy breath of Trusts and the weight of the new remorseless monopolies that operate as no madnesses of ancient personal power thrilling us on the historic page ever operated; the living unit's property in himself becoming more and more merely such a property as may consist with a relation to properties overwhelmingly greater and that allow the asking of no questions and the making, for co-existence with them, of no conditions.   But that, in the fortunate phrase, is another story, and will be altogether, evidently, a new and different drama.   There is such a thing, in the United States, it is hence to be inferred, as freedom to grow up to be blighted, and it may be the only freedom in store for the smaller fry of future generations. If it is accordingly of the smaller fry I speak, and of how large they massed on that evening of endless admonitions, this will be because I caught them thus in their comparative humility and at an early stage of their American growth.   The life-thread has, I suppose, to be of a certain thickness for the great shears of Fate to feel for it.   Put it, at the worst, that the Ogres were to devour them, they were but the more certainly to fatten into food for the Ogres.

Their dream, at all events, as I noted it, was meanwhile sweet and undisguised—nowhere sweeter than in the half-dozen picked beer-houses and cafés in which our ingenuous *enquête*, that of my fellow-pilgrims and I, wound up.   These establishments had each been selected for its playing off some facet of the jewel, and they wondrously testified, by their range and their individual colour, to the spread of that lustre.   It was a pious rosary of which I should like to tell each bead, but I must let the general sense of the adventure serve.   Our successive stations were in no case of the " seamy " order, an inquiry into seaminess having been unanimously pronounced futile, but each had its separate social connotation, and it was for the number and variety of these connotations, and their individual plenitude and prosperity, to set one thinking. Truly the Yiddish world was a vast world, with its own deeps and complexities, and what struck one above all was that it sat there at its cups (and in no instance vulgarly the worse for them) with a sublimity of good conscience that took away the breath, a protrusion of elbow never aggressive, but absolutely proof against jostling. It was the incurable man of letters under the skin of one of the party who gasped, I confess; for it was in the light of letters, that is in the light of our language as literature has hitherto known it, that one stared at this all-unconscious impudence of the agency of future ravage. The man of letters, in the United States, has his own difficulties to face and his own current to stem—for dealing with which his liveliest inspiration may be, I think, that they are still very much his own, even in an Americanized world, and that more than elsewhere they press him to intimate communion with his honour. For that honour, the honour that sits astride of the consecrated English tradition, to his mind, quite as old knighthood astride of its caparisoned charger, the dragon most rousing, over the land, the proper spirit of St. George, is just this immensity of the alien presence climbing higher and higher, climbing itself into the very light of publicity.

I scarce know why, but I saw it that evening as in some dim dawn of that promise to its own consciousness, and perhaps this was precisely what made it a little exasperating. Under the impression of the mere mob the question doesn't come up, but in these haunts of comparative civility we saw the mob sifted and strained, and the exasperation was the sharper, no doubt, because what the process had left most visible was just the various possibilities of the waiting spring of intelligence. Such elements constituted the germ of a "public," and it was impossible (possessed of a sensibility worth speaking of) to be exposed to them without feeling how new a thing under the sun the resulting public would be. That was

where one's "lettered" anguish came in—in the turn of
one's eye from face to face for some betrayal of a pre-
hensile hook for the linguistic tradition as one had known
it. Each warm lighted and supplied circle, each group
of served tables and smoked pipes and fostered decencies
and unprecedented accents, beneath the extravagant
lamps, took on thus, for the brooding critic, a likeness to
that terrible modernized and civilized room in the Tower
of London, haunted by the shade of Guy Fawkes, which
had more than once formed part of the scene of the
critic's taking tea there.   In this chamber of the present
urbanities the wretched man had been stretched on the
rack, and the critic's ear (how else should it have been a
critic's?) could still always catch, in pauses of talk, the
faint groan of his ghost.   Just so the East side cafés—
and increasingly as their place in the scale was higher—
showed to my inner sense, beneath their bedizenment,
as torture-rooms of the living idiom ; the piteous gasp of
which at the portent of lacerations to come could reach
me in any drop of the surrounding Accent of the Future.
The accent of the very ultimate future, in the States,
may be destined to become the most beautiful on the
globe and the very music of humanity (here the "ethnic"
synthesis shrouds itself thicker than ever) ; but whatever
we shall know it for, certainly, we shall not know it for
English—in any sense for which there is an existing
literary measure.

IV

The huge jagged city, it must be nevertheless said,
has always at the worst, for propitiation, the resource of
its easy reference to its almost incomparable river.   New
York may indeed be jagged, in her long leanness, where
she lies looking at the sky in the manner of some colossal
hair-comb turned upward and so deprived of half its teeth

that the others, at their uneven intervals, count doubly
as sharp spikes; but, unmistakably, you can bear with
some of her aspects and her airs better when you have
really taken in that reference—which I speak of as easy
because she has in this latter time begun to make it with
an appearance of some intention. She has come at last,
far up on the West side, into possession of her birthright,
into the roused consciousness that some possibility of a
river-front may still remain to her; though, obviously, a
justified pride in this property has yet to await the birth
of a more responsible sense of style in her dealings with
it, the dawn of some adequate plan or controlling idea.
Splendid the elements of position, on the part of the new
Riverside Drive (over the small suburbanizing name of
which, as at the effect of a second-rate shop-worn article,
we sigh as we pass); yet not less irresistible the pang of
our seeing it settle itself on meagre, bourgeois, happy-
go-lucky lines. The pity of this is sharp in proportion
as the "chance" has been magnificent, and the soreness
of perception of what merely might have been is as
constant as the flippancy of the little vulgar "private
houses" or the big vulgar "apartment hotels" that are
having their own way, so unchallenged, with the whole
question of composition and picture. The fatal "tall"
pecuniary enterprise rises where it will, in the candid
glee of new worlds to conquer; the intervals between
take whatever foolish little form they like; the sky-line,
eternal victim of the artless jumble, submits again to the
type of the broken hair-comb turned up; the streets that
abut from the East condescend at their corners to any
crudity or poverty that may suit their convenience. And
all this in presence of an occasion for noble congruity
such as one scarce knows where to seek in the case of
another great city.

A sense of the waste of criticism, however, a sense
that is almost in itself consoling, descends upon the fond

critic after his vision has fixed the scene awhile in this light of its lost accessibility to some informed and bene-volent despot, some power working in one great way and so that the interest of beauty should have been better saved. Is not criticism wasted, in other words, just by the reason of the constant remembrance, on New York soil, that one is almost impudently cheated by any part of the show that pretends to prolong its actuality or to rest on its present basis? Since every part, however blazingly new, fails to affect us as doing more than hold the ground for something else, some conceit of the bigger dividend, that is still to come, so we may bind up the æsthetic wound, I think, quite as promptly as we feel it open. The particular ugliness, or combination of ugli-nesses, is no more final than the particular felicity (since there are several even of these up and down the town to be noted), and whatever crudely-extemporized look the Riverside heights may wear to-day, the spectator of fifty years hence will find his sorrow, if not his joy, in a different extemporization. The whole thing is the vividest of lectures on the subject of individualism, and on the strange truth, no doubt, that this principle may in the field of art—at least if the art be architecture—often conjure away just that mystery of distinction which it sometimes so markedly promotes in the field of life. It is also quite as suggestive perhaps on the ever-interest-ing question, for the artist, of the entirely relative nature and value of "treatment." A manner so right in one relation may be so wrong in another, and a house-front so "amusing" for its personal note, or its perversity, in a short perspective, may amid larger elements merely dishonour the harmony. And yet why *should* the charm ever fall out of the "personal," which is so often the very condition of the exquisite? Why should conformity and subordination, that acceptance of control and assent to collectivism in the name of which our age has seen such dreary things done, become on a given occasion the one *not* vulgar way of meeting a problem?

Inquiries these, evidently, that are answerable only in presence of the particular cases provoking them; when indeed they may hold us as under a spell. Endless for instance the æsthetic nobleness of such a question as that of the authority with which the spreading Hudson, at the opening of its gates, would have imposed on the constructive powers, if listened to, some proportionate order —would, in other words, have admirably given us collectivism at its highest. One has only to stand there and *see*—of such value are lessons in "authority." But the great vista of the stream alone speaks of it—save in so far at least as the voice is shared, and to so different, to so dreadful a tune, by the grossly-defacing railway that clings to the bank. The authority of railways, in the United States, sits enthroned as none other, and has always, of course, in any vision of aspects, to be taken into account. Here, at any rate, it is the rule that has prevailed; the other, the high interest of the possible picture, is one that lapses; so that the cliffs overhang the water, and at various points descend to it in green slopes and hollows (where the landscape-gardener does what he can), only to find a wealth of visible baseness installed there before them. That so familiar circumstance, in America, of the completion of the good thing ironically and, as would often seem for the time, insuperably baffled, meets here one of its liveliest illustrations. It at all events helps to give meanwhile the mingled pitch of the whole concert that Columbia College (to sound the old and easier name) should have "moved up"—moved up twice, if I am not mistaken—to adorn with an ampler presence this very neighbourhood. It has taken New York to invent, for the thickening of classic shades, the "moving" University; and does not that quite mark the tune of the dance, of the local unwritten law that forbids almost *any* planted object to gather in a history where it stands, forbids in fact any accumulation that may not be recorded in the mere bank-book? This last became long ago *the* historic page.

It is, however, just because the beauty of the Hudson seems to speak of other matters, and because the sordid city has the honour, after all, of sitting there at the Beautiful Gate, that I alluded above to her profiting in a manner, even from the point of view of "taste," by this close and fortunate connection. The place puts on thus, not a little, the likeness of a large loose family which has had queer adventures and fallen into vulgar ways, but for which a glorious cousinship never quite repudiated by the indifferent princely cousin—*bon prince* in this as in other matters—may still be pleaded. At the rate New York is growing, in fine, she will more and more "command," in familiar intercourse, the great perspective of the River; so that here, a certain point reached, her whole case must change and her general opportunity, swallowing up the mainland, become a new question altogether. Let me hasten to add that in the light of this opportunity even the most restless analyst can but take the hopeful view of her. I fear I am finding too many personal comparisons for her—than which indeed there can be no greater sign of a confessed pre-occupation; but she figures, once again, as an heir whose expectations are so vast and so certain that no temporary sowing of wild oats need be felt to endanger them. As soon as the place begins to spread at ease real responsibility of all sorts will begin, and the good-natured feeling must surely be that the civic conscience in her, at such a stage, will fall into step. Of the spreading woods and waters amid which the future in question appears still half to lurk, that mainland region of the Bronx, vast above all in possibilities of Park, out of which it already appears half to emerge, I unluckily failed of occasion to take the adequate measure. But my confused impression was of a kind of waiting abundance, an extraordinary quantity of "nature," for the reformed rake, that is the sobered heir, to play with. It is the fashion in the East to speak of New York as poor of environment, unpossessed of the agreeable, accessible countryside that crowns the convenience not only of London and of Paris, but even, with more humiliating promptitude, that of Boston, of Philadelphia, of Baltimore. In spite, however, of the memory, from far back, of a hundred marginal Mahattanese miseries, an immediate belt of the most sordid character, I cannot but think of this invidious legend as attempting to prove too much.

The countryside is there, on the most liberal of scales —it is the townside, only, that, having the great waters and the greater distances generally to deal with, has worn so rude and demoralized a face as to frighten the country away. And if the townside is now making after the countryside fast, as I say, and with a little less of the mere roughness of the satyr pursuing the nymph, what finer warrant could be desired than such felicities of position as those enjoyed, on the Riverside heights, by the monument erected to the soldiers and sailors of the Civil War and, even in a greater degree, by the tomb of General Grant? These are verily monumental sites of the first order, and I confess that, though introduced to them on a bleak winter morning, with no ingratiation in any element, I felt the critical question, as to the structures themselves, as to taste or intention, as to the amount of involved or achieved consecration or profanation, carried off in the general greatness of the effect. I shall in fact always remember that icy hour, with the temple-crowned headlands, the wide Hudson vista white with the cold, all nature armour-plated and grim, as an extraordinarily strong and simple composition; made stern and kept simple as for some visit of the God of Battles to his chosen. He might have been riding there, on the north wind, to look down at them, and one caught for the moment, the true hard light in which military greatness should be seen. It shone over the miles of ice with its lustre of steel, and if what, thus attested, it makes one think of was its incomparable, indestructible "prestige," so that association affected me both then and on a later occasion as with a strange indefinable consequence—an influence in which the æsthetic consideration, the artistic value of either memorial, melted away and became irrelevant. For here, if ever, was a great democratic demonstration caught in the fact, the nakedest possible effort to strike the note of the august. The tomb of the single hero in particular presents itself in a manner so opposed to our common ideas of the impressive, to any past vision of sepulchral state, that we can only wonder if a new kind and degree of solemnity may not have been arrived at in this complete rupture with old consecrating forms.

The tabernacle of Grant's ashes stands there by the pleasure-drive, unguarded and unenclosed, the feature of the prospect and the property of the people, as open as an hotel or a railway-station to any coming and going, and as dedicated to the public use as builded things in America (when not mere closed churches) only can be. Unmistakable its air of having had, all consciously, from the first, to raise its head and play its part without pomp and circumstance to "back" it, without mystery or ceremony to protect it, without Church or State to intervene on its behalf, with only its immediacy, its familiarity of interest to circle it about, and only its proud outlook to preserve, so far as possible, its character. The tomb of Napoleon at the Invalides is a great national property, and the play of democratic manners sufficiently surrounds it; but as compared to the small pavilion on the Riverside bluff it is a holy of holies, a great temple jealously guarded and formally approached. And yet one doesn't conclude, strange to say, that the Riverside pavilion fails of its expression a whit more than the Paris dome; one perhaps even feels it triumph by its use of its want of reserve as a very last word.   The admonition of all of which possibly is—I confess I but grope for it—that when there has been in such cases a certain other happy combination, an original sincerity of intention, an original propriety of site, and above all an original high value of name and fame, something in this line really supreme, publicity, familiarity, immediacy, as I have called them, *carried far enough*, may stalk in and out of the shrine with their hands in their pockets and their hats on their heads, and yet not dispel the Presence.   The question at any rate puts itself—as new questions in America are always putting themselves : Do certain impressions there represent the absolute extinction of old sensibilities, or do they represent only new forms of them?   The inquiry would be doubtless easier to answer if so many of these feelings were not mainly known to us just *by* their attendant forms.   At this rate, or on such a showing, in the United States, attendant forms being, in every quarter, remarkably scarce, it would indeed seem that the sentiments implied *are* extinct; for it would be an abuse of ingenuity, I fear, to try to read mere freshness of form into some of the more rank failures of observance. There are failures of observance that stand, at the best, for failures of sense—whereby, however, the question grows too great.   One must leave the tomb of Grant to its conditions and its future with the simple note for it that if it be not in fact one of the most effective of commemorations it is one of the most missed.   On the whole I distinctly "liked" it.

V

It is still vivid to me that, returning in the spring-time from a few weeks in the Far West, I re-entered New

York State with the absurdest sense of meeting again a
ripe old civilization and travelling through a country
that showed the mark of established manners. It will
seem, I fear, one's perpetual refrain, but the moral `was
yet once more that values of a certain order are, in such
conditions, all relative, and that, as some wants of the
spirit *must* somehow be met, one knocks together any
substitute that will fairly stay the appetite. We had
passed great smoky Buffalo in the raw vernal dawn—
with a vision, for me, of curiosity, character, charm,
whatever it might be, too needfully sacrificed, opportunity
perhaps forever missed, yet at the same time a vision in
which the lost object failed to mock at me with the last
concentration of shape; and history, as we moved Eastward, appeared to meet us, in the look of the land, in its
more overwrought surface and thicker detail, quite as if
she had ever consciously declined to cross the border
and were aware, precisely, of the queer feast we should
find in her. The recognition, I profess, was a preposterous ecstasy: one couldn't have felt more if one
had passed into the presence of some seated, placid,
rich-voiced gentlewoman after leaving that of an honest
but boisterous hoyden. .It was doubtless a matter only
of degrees and shades, but never was such a pointing of
the lesson that a sign of any sort may count double if it
be but artfully placed. I spent that day, literally, in the
company of the rich-voiced gentlewoman, making my
profit of it even in spite of a second privation, the doom
I was under of having only, all wistfully, all ruefully, to
avert my lips from the quaint silver bowl, as I here quite
definitely figured it, in which she offered me the entertainment of antique Albany. At antique Albany, to a
certainty, the mature matron involved in my metaphor
would have put on a particular grace, and as our train
crossed the river for further progress I almost seemed to
see her stand at some gable-window of Dutch association,

one of the two or three impressed there on my infantile imagination, to ask me why then I had come so far at all.

I could have replied but in troubled tones, and I looked at the rest of the scene for some time, no doubt, as through the glaze of all-but filial tears. Thus it was, possibly, that I saw the River shine, from that moment on, as a great romantic stream, such as could throw not a little of its glamour, for the mood of that particular hour, over the city at its mouth. I had not even known, in my untravelled state, that we were to "strike" it on our way from Chicago, so that it represented, all that afternoon, so much beauty thrown in, so much benefit beyond the bargain—the so hard bargain, for the traveller, of the American railway-journey at its best. That ordeal was in any case at its best here, and the perpetually interesting river kept its course, by my right elbow, with such splendid consistency that, as I recall the impression, I repent a little of having just now reflected with acrimony on the cost of the obtrusion of track and stations to the Riverside view. One must of course choose between dispensing with the ugly presence and enjoying the scenery by the aid of the same—which but means, really, that to use the train at all had been to put one's self, for any proper justice to the scenery, in a false position. That, however, takes us too far back, and one can only save one's dignity by laying all such blames on our detestable age. A decent respect for the Hudson would confine us to the use of the boat—all the more that American river-steamers have had, from the earliest time, for the true *raffiné*, their peculiar note of romance. A possible commerce, on the other hand, with one's time—which is always also the time of so many other busy people—has long since made mincemeat of the rights of contemplation; rights as reduced, in the United States, to-day, and by quite the same argument, as those of the noble savage whom we have banished to his narrowing reservation.   Letting that pass, at all events, I still remember that I was able to put, from the car-window, as many questions to the scene as it could have answered in the time even had its face been clearer to read.

Its face was veiled, for the most part, in a mist of premature spring heat, an atmosphere draping it indeed in luminous mystery, hanging it about with sun-shot silver and minimizing any happy detail, any element of the definite, from which the romantic effect might here and there have gained an accent.   There was not an accent in the picture from the beginning of the run to Albany to the end—for which thank goodness! one is tempted to say on remembering how often, over the land in general, the accents are wrong.   Yet if the romantic effect as we know it elsewhere mostly depends on them, why *should* that glamour have so shimmered before me in their absence?—how should the picture have managed to be a constant combination of felicities?   Was it just *because* the felicities were all vaguenesses, and the "beauties," even the most celebrated, all blurs?—was it perchance on that very account that I could meet my wonder so promptly with the inference that what I had in my eyes on so magnificent a scale was simply, was famously, "style"?   I was landed by that conclusion in the odd further proposition that style could then exist without accents—a quandary soon after to be quenched, however, in the mere blinding radiance of a visit to West Point.   I was to make that memorable pilgrimage a fortnight later—and I was to find my question, when it in fact took place, shivered by it to mere silver atoms. The very powers of the air seemed to have taken the case in hand and positively to have been interested in making it transcend all argument.   Our Sunday of mid-May, wet and windy, let loose, over the vast stage, the whole procession of storm-effects; the raw green of wooded heights and hollows was only everywhere rain-brightened, the weather playing over it all day as with some great grey water-colour brush. The essential character of West Point and its native nobleness of position can have been but intensified, I think, by this artful process; yet what was mainly unmistakable was the fact again of the suppression of detail as in the positive interest of the grand style. One had therefore only to take detail as another name for accent, the accent that might prove compromising, in order to see it made good that style *could* do without them, and that the grand style in fact almost always must. How on this occasion the trick was played is more than I shall attempt to say; it is enough to have been conscious of our being, from hour to hour, literally bathed in that high element, with the very face of nature washed, so to speak, the more clearly to express and utter it.

Such accordingly is the strong silver light, all simplifying and ennobling, in which I see West Point; see it as a cluster of high promontories, of the last classic elegance, overhanging vast receding reaches of river, mountain-guarded and dim, which took their place in the geography of the ideal, in the long perspective of the poetry of association, rather than in those of the State of New York. It was as if the genius of the scene had said: "No, you *shan't* have accent, because accent is, at the best, local and special, and might here by some perversity —how do I know after all?—interfere. I want you to have something unforgettable, and therefore you shall have *type*—yes, absolutely have type, and even tone, without accent; an impossibility, you may hitherto have supposed, but which you have only to look about you now really to see expressed. And type and tone of the very finest and rarest; type and tone good enough for Claude or Turner, if they could have walked by these

rivers instead of by their thin rivers of France and Italy ;
type and tone, in short, that gather in shy detail under
wings as wide as those with which a motherly hen covers
her endangered brood.   So there you are—deprived of
all ' accent' as a peg for criticism, and reduced thereby,
you see, to asking me no more questions." I was able
so to take home, I may add, this formula of the matter,
that even the interesting facts of the School of the
Soldier which have carried the name of the place about
the world almost put on the shyness, the air of conscious
evasion and escape, noted in the above allocution : they
struck me as forsaking the foreground of the picture.
It was part of the play again, no doubt, of the grey
water-colour brush : there was to be no consent of the
elements, that day, to anything but a generalized elegance
—in which effect certainly the clustered, the scattered
Academy played, on its high green stage, its part.   But,
of all things in the world, it massed, to my vision, more
mildly than I had somehow expected ; and I take that
for a feature, precisely, of the pure poetry of the impression.   It lurked there with grace, it insisted without
swagger—and I could have hailed it just for this reason
indeed as a presence of the last distinction.   It is doubtless too much to say, in fine, that the Institution, at
West Point, "suffers" comparatively, for vulgar individual emphasis, from the overwhelming liberality of
its setting—and I perhaps chanced to see it in the very
conditions that most invest it with poetry.   The fact
remains that, both as to essence and as to quantity, its
prose seemed washed away, and I shall recall it in the
future much less as the sternest, the world over, of all the
seats of Discipline, than as some great Corot-composition
of young, vague, wandering figures in splendidly-classic
shades.

VI

I make that point, for what it is worth, only to remind myself of another occasion on which the romantic note sounded for me with the last intensity, and yet on which the picture swarmed with accents—as, absent or present, I must again call them—that contributed alike to its interest and to its dignity. The proof was complete, on this second Sunday, with the glow of early summer already in possession, that affirmed detail was not always affirmed infelicity—since the scene here bristled with detail (and detail of the importance that frankly *constitutes* accent) only to the enhancement of its charm. It was a matter once more of hanging over the Hudson on the side opposite West Point, but further down; the situation was founded, as at West Point, on the presence of the great feature and on the consequent general lift of foreground and distance alike, and yet infinitely sweet was it to gather that style, in such conditions and for the success of such effects, had not really to depend on mere kind vaguenesses, on any anxious deprecation of distinctness. There was no vagueness now; a wealth of distinctness, in the splendid light, met the eyes—but with the very result of showing them how happily it could play. What it came back to was that the accents, in the delightful old pillared and porticoed house that crowned the cliff and commanded the stream, were as right as they were numerous; so that there immediately followed again on this observation a lively recognition of the ground of the rightness. To wonder what this was could be but to see, straightway, that, though many reasons had worked together for them, mere time had done more than all; that beneficence of time enjoying in general, in the United States, so little even of the chance that so admirably justifies itself, for the most part,

when interference happens to have spared it. Cases of
this rare mercy yet exist, as I had had occasion to note,
and their consequent appeal to the touched sense within
us comes, as I have also hinted, with a force out of all
proportion, comes with a kind of accepted insolence of
authority. The things that have lasted, in short, whatever they may be, "succeed" as no newness, try as it
will, succeeds, inasmuch as their success is a created
interest.

There we catch the golden truth which so much of
the American world strikes us as positively organized to
gainsay, the truth that production takes time, and that
the production of interest, in particular, takes *most* time.
Desperate again and again the ingenuity of the offered,
the obtruded substitute, and pathetic in many an instance
its confessed failure ; this remark being meanwhile relevant to the fact that my charming old historic house of
the golden Sunday put me off, among its great trees,
its goodly gardens, its acquired signs and gathered
memories, with no substitute whatever, even the most
specious, but just paid cash down, so to speak, ripe
ringing gold, over the counter, for all the attention it
invited. It had character, as one might say, and character is scarce less precious on the part of the homes of
men in a raw medium than on the part of responsible
persons at a difficult crisis. This virtue was there within
and without and on every face ; but perhaps nowhere so
present, I thought, as in the ideal refuge for summer
days formed by the wide north porch, if porch that
disposition may be called—happiest disposition of the
old American country-house—which sets tall columns in
a row, under a pediment suitably severe, to present them
as the "making" of a high, deep gallery. I know not
what dignity of old afternoons suffused with what languor
seems to me always, under the murmur of American
trees and by the lap of American streams, to abide in

these mild shades ; there are combinations with depths of congruity beyond the plummet, it would seem, even of the most restless of analysts, and rather than try to say why my whole impression here melted into the general iridescence of a past of Indian summers hanging about mild ghosts half asleep, in hammocks, over still milder novels, I would renounce altogether the art of refining.   For the iridescence consists, in this connection, of a shimmer of association that still more refuses to be reduced to terms ; some sense of legend, of aboriginal mystery, with a still earlier past for its dim background and the insistent idea of the River as above all romantic for its warrant.   Helplessly analyzed, perhaps, this amounts to no more than the very childish experience of a galleried house or two round about which the views and the trees and the peaches and the pony seemed prodigious, and to the remembrance of which the wonder of Rip Van Winkle and that of the " Hudson River School " of landscape art were, a little later on, to contribute their glamour.

If Rip Van Winkle had been really at the bottom of it all, nothing could have furthered the whole case more, on the occasion I speak of, than the happy nearness of the home of Washington Irving, the impression of which I was thus able, in the course of an hour, to work in— with the effect of intensifying more than I can say the old-time charm and the general legendary fusion. These are beautiful, delicate, modest matters, and how can one touch them with a light enough hand ?   How can I give the comparatively coarse reasons for my finding at Sunnyside, which contrives, by some grace of its own, to be at once all ensconced and embowered in relation to the world, and all frank and uplifted in relation to the river, a perfect treasure of mild moralities ?   The highway, the old State road to Albany, bristling now with the cloud-compelling motor, passes at the head of a deep, long lane, winding, embanked, overarched, such an old-world lane as one scarce ever meets in America; but if you embrace this chance to plunge away to the left you come out for your reward into the quite indefinable air of the little American literary past. The place is inevitably, to-day, but a qualified Sleepy Hollow—the Sleepy Hollow of the author's charming imagination was, as I take it, off somewhere in the hills, or in some dreamland of old autumns, happily unprofanable now; for "modernity," with its terrible power of working its will, of abounding in its sense, of gilding its toy—modernity, with its pockets full of money and its conscience full of virtue, its heart really full of tenderness, has seated itself there under pretext of guarding the shrine. What has happened, in a word, is very much what has happened in the case of other shy retreats of anchorites doomed to celebrity—the primitive cell has seen itself encompassed, in time, by a temple of many chambers, all dedicated to the history of the hermit. The cell is still there at Sunnyside, and there is even yet so much charm that one doesn't attempt to say where the parts of it, all kept together in a rich conciliatory way, begin or end—though indeed, I hasten to add, the identity of the original modest house, the shrine within the gilded shell, has been religiously preserved.

One has, in fact, I think, no quarrel whatever with the amplified state of the place, for it is the manner and the effect of this amplification that enable us to read into the scene its very most interesting message. The "little" American literary past, I just now said—using that word—(whatever the real size of the subject) because the caressing diminutive, at Sunnyside, is what rises of itself to the lips; the small uncommodious study, the limited library, the "dear" old portrait-prints of the first half of the century—very dear to-day when properly signed and properly sallow—these things, with the beauty of the site, with the sense that the man of letters of the unimproved age, the age of processes still comparatively slow, could have wanted no deeper, softer dell for mulling material over, represent the conditions that encounter now on the spot the sharp reflection of our own increase of arrangement and loss of leisure. This is the admirable interest of the exhibition of which Wolfert's Roost had been, a hundred years before the date of Irving's purchase, the rudimentary principle—that it throws the facts of our earlier "intellectual activity" into a vague golden perspective, a haze as of some unbroken spell of the same Indian summer I a moment ago had occasion to help myself out with; a fond appearance than which nothing could minister more to envy. If we envy the spinners of prose and tellers of tales to whom our American air anciently either administered or refused sustenance, this is all, and quite the best thing, it would seem, that we need do for them: it exhausts, or rather it forestalls, the futilities of discrimination. Strictly critical, mooning about Wolfert's Roost of a summer Sunday, I defy even the hungriest of analysts to be: his predecessors, the whole connected company, profit so there, to his rueful vision, by the splendour of their possession of better conditions than his. It has taken *our* ugly era to thrust in the railroad at the foot of the slope, among the masking trees; the railroad that is part, exactly, of the pomp and circumstance, the quickened pace, the heightened fever, the narrowed margin expressed within the very frame of the present picture, as I say, and all in the perfect good faith of collateral piety. I had hoped not to have to name the railroad—it seems so to give away my case. There was no railroad, however, till long after Irving's settlement—he survived the railroad but by a few years, and my case is simply that, disengaging *his* Sunnyside from its beautiful extensions and arriving thus at the

sense of his easy elements, easy for everything but
rushing about and being rushed at, the sense of his
" command " of the admirable river and the admirable
country, his command of all the mildness of his life, of
his pleasant powers and his ample hours, of his friends
and his contemporaries and his fame and his honour and
his temper and, above all, of his delightful fund of
reminiscence and material, I seemed to hear, in the
summer sounds and in the very urbanity of my enter-
tainers, the last faint echo of a felicity forever gone.
That is the true voice of such places, and not the imputed
challenge to the chronicler or the critic.

4

New York

SOCIAL NOTES

Were I not afraid of appearing to strike to excess the so-called pessimistic note, I should really make much of the interesting, appealing, touching vision of waste—I know not how else to name it—that flung its odd melancholy mantle even over one's walks through the parts of the town supposedly noblest and fairest. For it proceeded, the vision, I think, from a source or two still deeper than the most obvious, the constant shocked sense of houses and rows, of recent expensive construction (that had cost thought as well as money, that had taken birth presumably as a *serious*, demonstration, and that were thereby just beginning to live into history) marked for removal, for extinction, in their prime, and awaiting it with their handsome faces so fresh and yet so wan and so anxious. The most tragic element in the French Revolution, and thence surely the most tragic in human annals, was the so frequent case of the very young sent to the scaffold—the youths and maidens, all bewildered and stainless, lately born into a world decked for them socially with flowers, and for whom, none the less suddenly, the horror of horrors uprose. They were literally the victims I thought of, absurd as it may seem, under the shock in question ; in spite of which, however, even this is not what I mean by my impression of the squandered effort. I have had occasion to speak—and one can only speak with sympathy—of the really human, the communicative, side of that vivid show of a society trying to build itself, with every elaboration, into some coherent sense *of* itself, and literally putting forth interrogative feelers, as it goes, into the ambient air ; literally reaching out (to the charmed beholder, say) for some measure and some test of its success. This effect of certain of the manifestations of wealth in New York is, so far as I know, unique ; nowhere else does pecuniary power so beat its wings in the void, and so look round it for the charity of some hint as to the possible awkwardness or possible grace of its motion, some sign of whether it be flying, for good taste, too high or too low. In the other American cities, on the one hand, the flights are as yet less numerous—though already promising no small diversion ; and amid the older congregations of men, in the proportionately rich cities of Europe, on the other hand, good taste is present, for reference and comparison, in a hundred embodied and consecrated forms. Which is why, to repeat, I found myself recognizing in the New York predicament a particular character and a particular pathos. The whole costly up-town demonstration was a record, in the last analysis, of individual loneliness ; whence came, precisely, its insistent testimony to waste—waste of the still wider sort than the mere game of rebuilding.

That quite different admonition of the general European spectacle, the effect, in the picture of things, as of a large, consummate economy, traditionally practised, springs from the fact that old societies, old, and even new, aristocracies, are arranged exactly to supply functions, forms, the whole element of custom and perpetuity, to any massiveness of private ease, however great. Massive private ease attended with no force of assertion beyond the hour is an anomaly rarely encountered, therefore, in countries where the social arrangements strike one as undertaking, by their very nature and pretension, to make the future as interesting as the past. These conditions, the romantic ones for the picture-seeker, are generally menaced, one is reminded; they tend to alter everywhere, partly by the very force of the American example, and it may be said that in France, for instance, they have done nothing but alter for a hundred years. It none the less remains true that for once that we ask ourselves in " Europe " what is going to become of a given piece of property, whether family " situation," or else palace, castle, picture, *parure*, other attribute of wealth, we indulge in the question twenty times in the United States—so scant an engagement does the visible order strike us as taking to provide for it. *There* comes in the note of loneliness on the part of these loose values—deep as the look in the eyes of dogs who plead against a change of masters. The visible order among ourselves undertakes at the most that they shall change hands, and the meagreness and indignity of this doom affect them as a betrayal just in proportion as they have grown great. Uppermost Fifth Avenue, for example, is lined with dwellings the very intention both of the spread and of the finish of which would seem to be to imply that they are " entailed " as majestically as red tape can entail them. But we know how little they enjoy any such courtesy or security; and, but for our tender heart and our charming imagination, we would blight them in their bloom with our restless analysis. " It's all very well for you to look as if, since you've had no past, you're going in, as the next best thing, for a magnificent compensatory future. What are you going to make your future *of*, for all your airs, we want to know?—what elements of a future, as futures have gone in the great world, are at all assured to you? Do what you will, you sit here only in the lurid light of 'business,' and you know, without our reminding you, what guarantees, what majestic continuity and heredity, that represents. Where are not only your eldest son and *his* eldest son, those prime indispensables for any real projection of your estate, unable as they would be to get rid of you even if they should wish; but where even is the old family stocking, properly stuffed and hanging so heavy as not to stir, some dreadful day, in the cold breath of Wall Street? No, what you are reduced to for 'importance' is the present, pure and simple, squaring itself between an absent future and an absent past as solidly as it can. You overdo it for what you are—you overdo it still more for what you may be; and don't pretend, above all, with the object-lesson supplied you, close at hand, by the queer case of Newport, don't pretend, we say, not to know what we mean."

"We say," I put it, but the point is that we say nothing, and it is that very small matter of Newport exactly that keeps us compassionately silent. The present state of Newport shall be a chapter by itself, which I long to take in hand, but which must wait its turn; so that I may mention it here only for the supreme support it gives to this reading of the conditions of New York opulence. The show of the case to-day—oh, so vividly and pathetically!—is that New York and other opulence, creating the place, for a series of years, as part of the effort of "American society" to find out, by experiment, what it would be at, now has no further use for it—has only learned from it, at an immense expenditure, how to get rid of an illusion. "We've found out, after all (since it's a question of what we would be 'at'), that we wouldn't be at Newport—if we can possibly be anywhere else; which, with our means, we indubitably *can* be: so that we leave poor dear Newport just ruefully to show it." That remark is written now over the face of the scene, and I can think nowhere of a mistake confessed to so promptly, yet in terms so exquisite, so charmingly cynical; the terms of beautiful houses and delicate grounds closed, condemned and forsaken, yet so "kept up," at the same time, as to cover the retreat of their projectors. The very air and light, soft and discreet, seem to speak, in tactful fashion, for people who would be embarrassed to be there—as if it might shame them to see it proved against them that they could once have been so artless and so bourgeois. The point is that they have learned not to be by the rather terrible process of exhausting the list of mistakes. Newport, for them—or for us others—is only one of these mistakes; and we feel no confidence that the pompous New York houses, most of them so flagrantly tentative, and tentative only, bristling with friezes and pinnacles, but discernibly deficient in reasons, shall not collectively form another. It is the hard fate of new aristocracies that the element of error, with them, has to be contemporary—not relegated to the dimness of the past, but receiving the full modern glare, a light fatal to the fond theory that the best society, everywhere, has grown, in all sorts of ways, in spite of itself. We see it in New York trying, trying its very hardest, to grow, not yet knowing (by so many indications) what to grow *on*.

There comes back to me again and again, for many reasons, a particular impression of this interesting struggle in the void—a constituted image of the upper social organism floundering there all helplessly, more or less floated by its immense good-will and the splendour of its immediate environment, but betrayed by its paucity of real resource. The occasion I allude to was simply a dinner-party, of the most genial intention, but at which the note of high ornament, of the general uplifted situation, was so consistently struck that it presented itself, on the page of New York life, as a purple patch without a possible context—as consciously, almost painfully, un-accompanied by passages in anything like the same key. The scene of our feast was a palace and the perfection of setting and service absolute; the ladies, beautiful, gracious and glittering with gems, were in tiaras and a semblance of court-trains, a sort of prescribed official magnificence; but it was impossible not to ask one's self with what, in the wide American frame, such great matters might be supposed to consort or to rhyme. The material pitch was so high that it carried with it really no social sequence, no application, and that, as a tribute to the ideal, to the exquisite, it wanted company, support, some sort of consecration. The difficulty, the irony, of the hour was that so many of the implications of complete-ness, that is, of a sustaining social order, were absent. There was nothing for us to do at eleven o'clock—or for the ladies at least—but to scatter and go to bed. There was nothing, as in London or in Paris, to go " on " to ; the going " on " is, for the New York aspiration, always the stumbling-block. A great court-function would alone have met the strain, met the terms of the case—would alone properly have crowned the hour. When I speak of the terms of the case I must remind myself indeed that they were not all of one complexion ; which is but another sign, however, of the inevitable jaggedness of the purple patch in great commercial democracies. The high colour required could be drawn in abundance from the ladies, but in a very minor degree, one easily perceived, from the men. The impression was singular, but it was there : had there been a court-function the ladies must have gone on to it alone, trusting to have the proper partners and mates supplied them on the premises—supplied, say, with the checks for recovery of their cloaks. The high pitch, all the exalted reference, was of the palatial house, the would-be harmonious women, the tiaras and the trains ; it was not of the amiable gentlemen, delightful in their way, in whose so often quaint presence, yet without whose immediate aid, the effort of American society to arrive at the "best" consciousness still goes forward.

This failure of the sexes to keep step socially is to be noted, in the United States, at every turn, and is perhaps more suggestive of interesting "drama," as I have already hinted, than anything else in the country. But it illustrates further that foredoomed *grope* of wealth, in the conquest of the amenities—the strange necessity under which the social interest labours of finding out for itself, as a preliminary, what civilization really *is*. If the men are not to be taken as contributing to it, but only the women, what new case is *that*, under the sun, and under what strange aggravations of difficulty therefore is the problem not presented? We should call any such treatment of a different order of question the empirical treatment—the limitations and aberrations of which crop up, for the restless analyst, in the most illustrative way. Its presence is felt unmistakably, for instance, in the general extravagant insistence on the Opera, which plays its part as the great vessel of social salvation, the comprehensive substitute for all other conceivable vessels; the *whole* social consciousness thus clambering into it, under stress, as the whole community crams into the other public receptacles, the desperate cars of the Subway or the vast elevators of the tall buildings. The Opera, indeed, as New York enjoys it, one promptly perceives, is worthy, musically and picturesquely, of its immense function; the effect of it is splendid, but one has none the less the oddest sense of hearing it, as an institution, groan and creak, positively almost split and crack, with the extra weight thrown upon it—the weight that in worlds otherwise arranged is artfully scattered, distributed over all the ground. In default of a court-function our ladies of the tiaras and court-trains might have gone on to the opera-function, these occasions

offering the only approach to the implication of the tiara
known, so to speak, to the American law. Yet even
here there would have been no one for them, in congruity and consistency, to curtsey to—their only possible
course becoming thus, it would seem, to make obeisance,
clingingly, to each other. This truth points again the
effect of a picture poor in the male presence ; for to what
male presence of native growth is it thinkable that the
wearer of an American tiara *should* curtsey ? Such a
vision gives the measure of the degree in which we see
the social empiricism in question putting, perforce, the
cart before the horse. In worlds otherwise arranged,
besides there being always plenty of subjects for genu-
flection, the occasion itself, with its character fully turned
on, produces the tiara. In New York this symbol has,
by an arduous extension of its virtue, to produce the
occasion.

II

I found it interesting to note, furthermore, that the
very Clubs, on whose behalf, if anywhere, expert
tradition might have operated, betrayed with a *bonhomie*
touching in the midst of their magnificence the empirical
character. Was not their admirable, their unique, hospitality, for that matter, an empirical note—a departure
from the consecrated collective egoism governing such
institutions in worlds, as I have said, otherwise arranged ?
Let the hospitality in this case at least stand for the
prospective discovery of a new and better law, under
which the consecrated egoism itself will have become the
" provincial " sign. Endless, at all events, the power of
one or two of these splendid structures to testify to the
state of manners—of manners undiscourageably seeking
the superior stable equilibrium. There had remained with
me as illuminating, from years before, the confidential

word of a friend on whom, after a long absence from New York, the privilege of one of the largest clubs had been conferred. "The place is a palace, for scale and decoration, but there is only one kind of letter-paper." There would be more kinds of letter-paper now, I take it—though the American club struck me everywhere, oddly, considering the busy people who employ it, as much less an institution for attending to one's correspondence than others I had had knowledge of; generally destitute, in fact, of copious and various appliances for that purpose. There is such a thing as the imagination of the writing-table, and I nowhere, save in a few private houses, came upon its fruits; to which I must add that this is the one connection in which the provision for ease has not an extraordinary amplitude, an amplitude unequalled anywhere else. One emphatic reservation, throughout the country, the restored absentee finds himself continually making, but the universal custom of the house with almost no one of its indoor parts distinguishable from any other is an affliction against which he has to learn betimes to brace himself. This diffused vagueness of separation between apartments, between hall and room, between one room and another, between the one you are in and the one you are not in, between place of passage and place of privacy, is a provocation to despair which the public institution shares impartially with the luxurious "home." To the spirit attuned to a different practice these dispositions can only appear a strange perversity, an extravagant aberration of taste; but I may here touch on them scarce further than to mark their value for the characterization of manners.

They testify at every turn, then, to those of the American people, to the prevailing "conception of life"; they correspond, within doors, to the as inveterate suppression of almost every outward exclusory arrangement. The instinct is throughout, as we catch it at play, that of minimizing, for any "interior," the guilt or odium or responsibility, whatever these may appear, of its *being* an interior. The custom rages like a conspiracy for nipping the interior in the bud, for denying its right to exist, for ignoring and defeating it in every possible way, for wiping out successively each sign by which it may be known from an exterior. The effacement of the difference has been marvellously, triumphantly brought about; and, with all the ingenuity of young, fresh, frolicsome architecture aiding and abetting, has been made to flourish, alike in the small structure and the great, as the very law of the structural fact. Thus we have the law fulfilled that every part of every house shall be, as nearly as may be, visible, visitable, penetrable, not only from every other part, but from as many parts of as many other houses as possible, if they only be near enough. Thus we see systematized the indefinite extension of all spaces and the definite merging of all functions; the enlargement of every opening, the exaggeration of every passage, the substitution of gaping arches and far perspectives and resounding voids for enclosing walls, for practicable doors, for controllable windows, for all the rest of the essence of the room-character, that room-suggestion which is so indispensable not only to occupation and concentration, but to conversation itself, to the play of the social relation at any other pitch than the pitch of a shriek or a shout. This comprehensive canon has so succeeded in imposing itself that it strikes you as reflecting inordinately, as positively serving you up for convenient inspection, under a clear glass cover, the social tone that has dictated it. But I must confine myself to recording, for the moment, that it takes a whole new discipline to put the visitor at his ease in so merciless a medium; he finds himself looking round for a background or a limit, some localizing fact or two, in the interest of talk, of that " good " talk which always

falters before the complete proscription of privacy. He
sees only doorless apertures, vainly festooned, which
decline to tell him where he is, which make him still
a homeless wanderer, which show him other apertures,
corridors, staircases, yawning, expanding, ascending,
descending, and all as for the purpose of giving his
presence "away," of reminding him that what he says
must be said for the house. He is beguiled in a
measure by reading into these phenomena, ever so
sharply, the reason of many another impression; he is
beguiled by remembering how many of the things said
in America *are* said for the house ; so that if all that he
wants is to keep catching the finer harmony of effect and
cause, of explanation and implication, the cup of his
perception is full to overflowing.

That satisfaction does represent, certainly, much of
his quest ; all the more that what he misses, in the
place—the comfort and support, for instance, of windows,
porches, verandahs, lawns, gardens, "grounds," that, by
not taking the whole world into their confidence, have
not the whole world's confidence to take in return—
ranges itself for him in that large mass of American
idiosyncrasy which contains, unmistakably, a precious
principle of future reaction. The desire to rake and be
raked has doubtless, he makes out, a long day before it
still ; but there are too many reasons why it should not
be the last word of *any* social evolution. The social
idea has too inevitably secrets in store, quite other
constructive principles, quite other refinements on the
idea of intercourse, with which it must eventually reckon.
It will be certain at a given moment, I think, to head
in a different direction altogether ; though obviously
many other remarkable things, changes of ideal, of habit,
of key, will have to take place first. The conception of
the home, and *a fortiori* of the club, as a combination of
the hall of echoes and the toy "transparency" held

against the light, will meanwhile sufficiently prevail to have made my reference to it not quite futile.   Yet I must after all remember that the reservation on the ground of comfort to which I just alluded applies with its smallest force to the interchangeability of club compartments, to the omnipresence of the majestic open arch in club conditions.   Such conditions more or less prescribe that feature, and criticism begins only when private houses emulate the form of clubs.   What I had mainly in mind was another of these so inexhaustible values of my subject ; with which the question of rigour of comfort has nothing to do.   I cherish certain remembered aspects for their general vivid eloquence—for the sake of my impression of the type of great generous club-establishments in which the " empiricism " of that already-observed idea of the conquest of splendour could richly and irresponsibly flower.   It is of extreme interest to be reminded, at many a turn of such an exhibition, that it takes an endless amount of history to make even a little tradition, and an endless amount of tradition to make even a little taste, and an endless amount of taste, by the same token, to make even a little tranquillity.   Tranquillity results largely from taste tactfully applied, taste ighted above all by experience and possessed of a clue for its labyrinth.   There is no such clue, for club-felicity, as some view of congruities and harmonies, completeness of correspondence between aspects and uses.   A sense for that completeness is a thing of slow growth, one of the flowers of tradition precisely ; of the good conservative tradition that walks apart from the extravagant use of money and the unregulated appeal to " style "—passes in fact, at its best, quite on the other side of the way.   This discrimination occurs when the ground has the good fortune to be already held by some definite, some transmitted conception of the adornments and enhancements that consort, and that do not consort, with the presence, the habits, the tone, of lounging, gossiping, smoking, newspaper-reading, bridge-playing, cocktail-imbibing men. The club-developments of New York read here and there the lesson of the strange deserts in which the appeal to style may lose itself, may wildly and wantonly stray, without a certain light of the fine old gentlemanly prejudice to guide it.

III

But I should omit half my small story were I not meanwhile to make due record of the numerous hours at which one ceased consciously to discriminate, just suffering one's sense to be flooded with the large clean light and with that suggestion of a crowded "party" of young persons which lurked in the general aspect of the handsomer regions—a great circle of brilliant and dowered *débutantes* and impatient youths, expert in the cotillon, waiting together for the first bars of some wonderful imminent dance-music, something "wilder" than any ever yet. It is such a wait for something more, these innocents scarce know what, it is this, distinctly, that the upper New York picture seems to cause to play before us; but the wait is just that collective alertness of bright-eyed, light-limbed, clear-voiced youth, without a doubt in the world and without a conviction; which last, however, always, may perfectly be absent without prejudice to confidence. The confidence and the innocence are those of children whose world has ever been practically a safe one, and the party so imaged is thus really even a child's party, enormously attended, but in which the united ages of the company make up no formidable sum. In the light of that analogy the New York social movement of the day, I think, always shines —as the whole show of the so-called social life of the

country does, for that matter ; since it comes home to
the restless analyst everywhere that this " childish "
explanation is the one that meets the greatest number
of the social appearances. To arrive—and with tolerable
promptitude—at that generalization is to find it, right
and left, immensely convenient, and thereby quite to
cling to it : the newspapers alone, for instance, doing so
much to feed it, from day to day, as with their huge
playfully brandished wooden spoon. We seem at
moments to see the incoherence and volatility of childhood, its living but in the sense of its hour and in the
immediacy of its want, its instinctive refusal to be
brought to book, its boundless liability to contagion and
boundless incapacity for attention, its ingenuous blankness to-day over the appetites and clamours of yesterday,
its chronic state of besprinklement with the sawdust
of its ripped-up dolls, which it scarce goes even through
the form of shaking out of its hair—we seem at moments
to see these things, I say, twinkle in the very air, as by
reflection of the movement of a great, sunny playroom
floor. The immensity of the native accommodation,
socially speaking, for the childish life, is not that exactly
the key of much of the spectacle ?—the safety of the vast
flat expanse where every margin abounds and nothing
too untoward need happen. The question is interesting,
but I remember quickly that I am concerned with it only
so far as it is part of the light of New York.

It appeared at all events, on the late days of spring,
just a response to the facility of things, and to much of
their juvenile pleasantry, to find one's self "liking,"
without more ado, and very much even at the risk of
one's life, the heterogeneous, miscellaneous apology for a
Square marking the spot at which the main entrance, as
I suppose it may be called, to the Park opens toward
Fifth Avenue ; opens toward the glittering monument to
Sherman, toward the most death-dealing, perhaps, of

all the climaxes of electric car cross-currents, toward the loosest of all the loose distributions of the over-topping "apartment" and other hotel, toward the most jovial of all the sacrifices of preconsidered composition, toward the finest of all the reckless revelations, in short, of the brave New York humour. The best thing in the picture, obviously, is Saint-Gaudens's great group, splendid in its golden elegance and doing more for the scene (by thus giving the beholder a point of such dignity for his orientation) than all its other elements together. Strange and seductive for any lover of the reasons of things this inordinate value, on the spot, of the dauntless refinement of the Sherman image; the comparative vulgarity of the environment drinking it up, on one side, like an insatiable sponge, and yet failing at the same time sensibly to impair its virtue. The refinement prevails and, as it were, succeeds; holds its own in the medley of accidents, where nothing else is refined unless it be the amplitude of the "quiet" note in the front of the Metropolitan Club; amuses itself in short with being as extravagantly "intellectual" as it likes. Why, therefore, given the surrounding medium, does it so triumphantly impose itself, and impose itself not insidiously and gradually, but immediately and with force? Why does it not pay the penalty of expressing an idea and being founded on one?—such scant impunity seeming usually to be enjoyed among us, at this hour, by any artistic intention of the finer strain? But I put these questions only to give them up—for what I feel beyond anything else is that Mr. Saint-Gaudens somehow takes care of himself.

To what measureless extent he does this on occasion one was to learn, in due course, from his magnificent Lincoln at Chicago—the lesson there being simply that of a mystery exquisite, the absolute inscrutable; one of the happiest cases known to our time, known doubtless

to any time, of the combination of intensity of effect with
dissimulation, with deep disavowal, of process. After
seeing the Lincoln one consents, for its author, to the
drop of questions—that is the lame truth ; a truth in the
absence of which I should have risked another word or
two, have addressed perhaps even a brief challenge to a
certain ambiguity in the Sherman. Its idea, to which I
have alluded, strikes me as equivocal, or more exactly as
double ; the image being, on the one side, and splendidly
rendered, that of an overwhelming military advance, an
irresistible march into an enemy's country—the strain
forward, the very inflation of drapery with the rush,
symbolizing the very breath of the Destroyer. But the
idea is at the same time—which part of it is also
admirably expressed—that the Destroyer is a messenger
of peace, with the olive branch too waved in the blast
and with embodied grace, in the form of a beautiful
American girl, attending his business. And I confess
to a lapse of satisfaction in the presence of this inter-
weaving—the result doubtless of a sharp suspicion of
all attempts, however glittering and golden, to confound destroyers with benefactors. The military monument in the City Square responds evidently, wherever
a pretext can be found for it, to a desire of men's hearts ;
but I would have it always as military as possible, and I
would have the Destroyer, in intention at least, not
docked of one of his bristles. I would have him deadly
and terrible, and, if he be wanted beautiful, beautiful
only as a war-god and crested not with peace, but with
snakes. Peace is a long way round from him, and blood
and ashes in between. So, with a less intimate perversity, I think, than that of Mr. Saint-Gaudens's brilliant
scheme, I would have had a Sherman of the terrible
march (the "immortal" march, in all abundance, if that
be the needed note), not irradiating benevolence, but
signifying, by every ingenious device, the misery, the

ruin and the vengeance of his track. It is not one's affair to attempt to teach an artist how such horrors may be monumentally signified; it is enough that their having been perpetrated is the very ground of the monument. And monuments should always have a clean, clear meaning.

IV

I must positively get into the gate of the Park, however—even at the risk of appearing to have marched round through Georgia to do so. I found myself, in May and June, getting into it whenever I could, and if I spoke just now of the loud and inexpensive charm (inexpensive in the æsthetic sense) of the precinct of approach to it, that must positively have been because the Park diffuses its grace. One grasped at every pretext for finding it inordinately amiable, and nothing was more noteworthy than that one felt, in doing so, how this was the only way to play the game in fairness. The perception comes quickly, in New York, of the singular and beautiful but almost crushing mission that has been laid, as an effect of time, upon this limited territory, which has risen to the occasion, from the first, so consistently and bravely. It is a case, distinctly, in which appreciation and gratitude for a public function admirably performed are twice the duty, on the visitor's part, that they may be in other such cases. We may even say, putting it simply and strongly, that if he doesn't here, in his thought, keep patting the Park on the back, he is guilty not alone of a failure of natural tenderness, but of a real deviation from social morality. For this mere narrow oblong, much *too* narrow and very much too short, had directly prescribed to it, from its origin, to "do," officially, on behalf of the City, the publicly amiable, and *all* the publicly amiable—all there could be any question of in the conditions: incurring thus a heavier charge, I respectfully submit, than one has ever before seen so gallantly carried. Such places, the municipally-instituted pleasure-grounds of the greater and the smaller cities, abound about the world and everywhere, no doubt, agreeably enough play their part; but is the part anywhere else as heroically played in proportion to the difficulty? The difficulty in New York, *that* is the point for the restless analyst; conscious as he is that other cities even in spite of themselves lighten the strain and beguile the task—a burden which here on the contrary makes every inch of its weight felt. This means a good deal, for the space comprised in the original New York scheme represents in truth a wonderful economy and intensity of effort. It would go hard with us not to satisfy ourselves, in other quarters (and it is of the political and commercial capitals we speak), of some such amount of "general" outside amenity, of charm in the town at large, as may here and there, even at widely-scattered points, relieve the o'erfraught heart. The sense of the picturesque often finds its account in strange and unlikely matters, but has none the less a way of finding it, and so, in the coming and going, takes the chance. But the New York problem has always resided in the absence of any chance to take, however one might come and go—come and go, that is, before reaching the Park.

To the Park, accordingly, and to the Park only, hitherto, the æsthetic appetite has had to address itself, and the place has therefore borne the brunt of many a peremptory call, acting out year after year the character of the cheerful, capable, bustling, even if overworked, hostess of the one inn, somewhere, who has to take all the travel, who is often at her wits' end to know how to deal with it, but who, none the less, has, for the honour of the house, never once failed of hospitality.   That is how we see Central Park, utterly overdone by the "run" on its resources, yet also never having had to make an excuse.   When once we have taken in thus its remarkable little history, there is no endearment of appreciation that we are not ready to lay, as a tribute, on its breast; with the interesting effect, besides, of our recognizing in this light how the place has had to be, in detail and feature, exactly what it is.   It has had to have something for everybody, since everybody arrives famished; it has had to multiply itself to extravagance, to pathetic little efforts of exaggeration and deception, to be, breathlessly, everywhere and everything at once, and produce on the spot the particular romantic object demanded, lake or river or cataract, wild woodland or teeming garden, boundless vista or bosky nook, noble eminence or smiling valley.   It has had to have feature at any price, the clamour of its customers being inevitably *for* feature; which accounts, as we forgivingly see, for the general rather eruptive and agitated effect, the effect of those old quaint prints which give in a single view the classic, gothic and other architectural wonders of the world. That is its sole defect—its being inevitably too self-conscious, being afraid to be just vague and frank and quiet.   I should compare her again—and the propriety is proved by this instinctively feminine pronoun—to an actress in a company destitute, through an epidemic or some other stress, of all other feminine talent; so that she assumes on successive nights the most dissimilar parts and ranges in the course of a week from the tragedy queen to the singing chambermaid.   That valour by itself wins the public and brings down the house—it being really a marvel that she should in no part fail of a hit.   Which is what I mean, in short, by the sweet *ingratiation* of the Park.   You are perfectly aware, as you hang about her in May and June, that you *have*, as a travelled person, beheld more remarkable scenery and communed with nature in ampler or fairer forms; but it is quite equally definite to you that none of those adventures have counted more to you for experience, for stirred sensibility—inasmuch as you can be, at the best, and in the showiest countries, only thrilled by the pastoral or the awful, and as to pass, in New York, from the discipline of the streets to this so different many-smiling presence is to be thrilled at every turn.

The strange thing, moreover, is that the crowd, in the happiest seasons, at favouring hours, the polyglot Hebraic crowd of pedestrians in particular, has, for what it is, none but the mildest action on the nerves. The nerves are too grateful, the intention of beauty everywhere too insistent; it "places" the superfluous figures with an art of its own, even when placing them in heavy masses, and they become for you practically as your fellow-spectators of the theatre, whose proximity you take for granted, while the little overworked *cabotine* we have hypothesized, the darling of the public, is vocalizing or capering. I recall as singularly contributive in all this sense the impression of a splendid Sunday afternoon of early summer, when, during a couple of hours spent in the mingled medium, the variety of accents with which the air swarmed seemed to make it a question whether the Park itself or its visitors were most polyglot. The condensed geographical range, the number of kinds of scenery in a given space, competed with the number of languages heard, and the whole impression was of one's having had but to turn in from the Plaza to make, in the most agreeable manner possible, the tour of the little globe. And that, frankly, I think, was the best of all impressions—was seeing New York at its best; for if ever one could feel at one's ease about the "social question," it would be surely, somehow, on such an occasion. The number of persons in circulation was enormous—so great that the question of how they had got there, from their distances, and would get away again, in the so formidable public conveyances, loomed, in the background, rather like a skeleton at the feast ; but the general note was thereby, intensely, the "popular," and the brilliancy of the show proportionately striking. That is the great and only brilliancy worth speaking of, to my sense, in the general American scene —the air of hard prosperity, the ruthlessly pushed-up and promoted look worn by men, women and children alike. I remember taking that appearance, of the hour or two, for a climax to the sense that had most remained with me after a considerable previous moving about over the land, the sense of the small quantity of mere human sordidness of state to be observed.

One is liable to observe it in *any* best of all possible worlds, and I had not, in truth, gone out of my way either to avoid it or to look for it ; only I had met it enough, in other climes, without doing so, and had, to be veracious, not absolutely and utterly missed it in the American. Images of confirmed (though, strangely, of active, occupied and above all "sensitive") squalor had I encountered in New Hampshire hills ; also, below the Southern line, certain special, certain awful examples, in Black and White alike, of the last crudity of condition. These spots on the picture had, however, lost themselves in the general attestation of the truth most forced home, the vision of the country as, supremely, a field for the unhampered revel, the unchecked *essor*, material and moral, of the "common man" and the common woman. How splendidly they were making it all answer, for the most part, or to the extent of the so rare public collapse of the individual, had been an observation confirmed for me by a rapid journey to the Pacific coast and back ; yet I had doubtless not before seen it so answer as in this very concrete case of the swarming New York afternoon.

It was little to say, in that particular light, that such grossnesses as want or tatters or gin, as the unwashed face or the ill-shod, and still less the unshod, foot, or the mendicant hand, became strange, unhappy, far-off things —it would even have been an insult to allude to them or to be explicitly complacent about their absence. The case was, unmistakably, universally, of the common, the very common man, the very common woman and the very common child; but all enjoying what I have called their promotion, their rise in the social scale, with that absence of acknowledging flutter, that serenity of assurance, which marks, for the impressed class, the school-boy or the school-girl who is accustomed, and who always quite expects, to "move up." The children at play, more particularly the little girls, formed the characters, as it were, in which the story was written largest; frisking about over the greenswards, grouping together in the vistas, with an effect of the exquisite in attire, of delicacies of dress and personal "keep-up," as through the shimmer of silk, the gloss of beribboned hair, the gleam of cared-for teeth, the pride of varnished shoe, that might well have created a doubt as to their "popular" affiliation. This affiliation was yet established by sufficiencies of context, and might well have been, for that matter, by every accompanying vocal or linguistic note, the swarm of queer sounds, mostly not to be interpreted, that circled round their pretty heads as if they had been tamers of odd, outlandish, perching little birds. They fell moreover into the vast category of those ubiquitous children of the public schools who occupy everywhere, in the United States, so much of the forefront of the stage, and at the sight of whose so remarkably clad and shod condition the brooding analyst, with the social question never, after all, too much in abeyance, could clap, in private, the most reactionary hands.

The brooding analyst had in fact, from the first of his

return, recognized in the mere detail of the testimony
everywhere offered to the high pitch of the American
shoe-industry, a lively incentive to cheerful views; the
population showing so promptly, in this connection, as
the best equipped in the world.   The impression at first
had been irresistible: two industries, at the most, seemed
to rule the American scene.   The dentist and the shoe-
dealer divided it between them; to that degree, positively,
that in public places, in the perpetual electric cars which
seem to one's desperation at times (so condemned is one
to live in them) all there measurably *is* of the American
scene, almost any other typical, any other personal fact
might be neglected, for consideration, in the interest of
the presentable foot and the far-shining dental gold.   It
was a world in which every one, without exception, no
matter how "low" in the social scale, wore the best and
the newest, the neatest and the smartest, boots; to be
added to which (always for the brooding analyst) was
the fascination, so to speak, of noting how much more
than any other single thing this may do for a possibly
compromised appearance.   And if my claim for the
interest of this exhibition seems excessive, I refer the
objector without hesitation to a course of equivalent
observation in other countries, taking an equally miscellaneous show for his basis.   Nothing was more curious
than to trace, on a great ferry-boat, for instance, the
effect of letting one's eyes work up, as in speculation,
from the lower to the higher extremities of some seated
row of one's fellow passengers.   The testimony of the
lower might preponderantly have been, always, to their
comparative conquest of affluence and ease; but this
presumption gave way, at successive points, with the
mounting vision, and was apt to break down entirely
under the evidence of face and head.   When I say
"head," I mean more particularly, where the men were,
concerned, hat; this feature of the equipment being

almost always at pains, and with the oddest, most inveterate perversity, to defeat and discredit whatever
might be best in the others.   Such are the problems in
which a restless analysis may land us.

Why should the general "feeling" for the boot, in the
United States, be so mature, so evolved, and the feeling
for the hat lag at such a distance behind it?   The
standard as to that article of dress struck me as, everywhere, of the lowest; governed by no consensus of view,
custom or instinct, no sense of its "vital importance" in
the manly aspect.   And yet the wearer of any loose
improvisation in the way of a head-cover will testify as
frankly, in his degree, to the extreme consideration given
by the community at large, as I have intimated, to the
dental question.   The terms in which this evidence is
presented are often, among the people, strikingly artless,
but they are a marked advance on the omnipresent
opposite signs, those of a systematic detachment from
the chair of anguish, with which any promiscuous
"European" exhibition is apt to bristle.   I remember
to have heard it remarked by a French friend, of a
young woman who had returned to her native land after
some years of domestic service in America, that she
had acquired there, with other advantages, *le sourire
Californien*, and the "Californian" smile, indeed, expressed, more or less copiously, in undissimulated cubes
of the precious metal, plays between lips that render
scant other tribute to civilization.   The greater interest,
in this connection, however, is that impression of the
state and appearance of the teeth viewed among the
"refined" as supremely important, which the restored
absentee, long surrounded elsewhere with the strangest
cynicisms of indifference on this article, makes the
subject of one of his very first notes.   Every one, in
"society," has good, handsome, pretty, has above all
cherished and tended, teeth ; so that the offered spectacle,

frequent in other societies, of strange irregularities, protrusions, deficiencies, fangs and tusks and cavities, is quite refreshingly and consolingly absent. The consequences of care and forethought, from an early age, thus write themselves on the facial page distinctly and happily, and it is not too much to say that the total show is, among American aspects, cumulatively charming. One sees it sometimes balance, for charm, against a greater number of less fortunate items, in that totality, than one would quite know how to begin estimating.

But I have strayed again far from my starting-point and have again, I fear, succumbed to the danger of embroidering my small original proposition with too many, and scarce larger, derivatives. I left the Plaza, I left the Park steeped in the rose-colour of such a brightness of Sunday and of summer as had given me, on a couple of occasions, exactly what I desired—a simplified attention, namely, and the power to rest for the time in the appearance that the awful aliens were flourishing there in perfections of costume and contentment. One had only to take them in as more completely, conveniently and expensively *endimanchés* than one had ever, on the whole, seen any other people, in order to feel that one was calling down upon all the elements involved the benediction of the future—and calling it down most of all on one's embraced permission not to worry any more. It was by way of not worrying, accordingly, that I found in another presentment of the general scene, chanced upon at a subsequent hour, all sorts of interesting and harmonious suggestions. These adventures of the critical spirit were such mere mild walks and talks as I almost blush to offer, on this reduced scale, as matter of history ; but I draw courage from the remembrance that history is never, in any rich sense, the immediate crudity of what "happens," but the much finer complexity of what we read into it and think of in connection with it.

If a walk across the Park, with a responsive friend, late
on the golden afternoon of a warm week-day, and if a
consequent desultory stroll, for speculation's sake, through
certain northward and eastward streets and avenues, of
an identity a little vague to me now, save as a blur of
builded evidence as to proprietary incomes—if such an
incident ministered, on the spot, to a boundless evocation,
it then became history of a splendid order: though I
perhaps must add that it became so for the two participants alone, and with an effect after all not easy to
communicate. The season was over, the recipients of
income had retired for the summer, and the large clear
vistas were peopled mainly with that conscious hush and
that spectral animation characteristic of places kept, as
with all command of time and space, for the indifferent,
the all but insolent, absentee. It was a vast, costly,
empty newness, redeemed by the rare quiet and coloured
by the pretty light, and I scare know, I confess, why it
should have had anything murmurous or solicitous to
say at all, why its eloquence was not over when it had
thus defined itself as intensely rich and intensely
modern.

If I have spoken, with some emphasis, of what it
"evoked," I might easily be left, it would appear, with
that emphasis on my hands—did I not catch, indeed, for
my explanation, the very key to the anomaly. Ransack-
ing my brain for the sources of the impressiveness, I see
them, of a sudden, locked up in that word "modern";
the mystery clears in the light of the fact that one was .
perhaps, for that half-hour, more intimately than ever
before in touch with the sense of the term. It was
exactly because I seemed, with the ear of the spirit, to
hear the whole quarter bid, as with one penetrating
voice, for the boon of the future, for some guarantee, or
even mere hinted promise, of history and opportunity,
that the attitude affected me as the last revelation of

modernity. What made the revelation was the collective sharpness, so to speak, of this vocal note, offering any price, offering everything, wanting only to outbid and prevail, at the great auction of life. "See how ready we are"—one caught the tone : "ready to buy, to pay, to promise ; ready to place, to honour, our purchase. We have everything, don't you see ? every capacity and appetite, every advantage of education and every susceptibility of sense ; no 'tip' in the world, none that our time is capable of giving, has been lost on us : so that all we now desire is what you, Mr. Auctioneer, have to dispose of, the great 'going' chance of a time to come." That was the sound unprecedentedly evoked for me, and in a form that made sound somehow overflow into sight. It was as if, in their high gallery, the bidders, New Yorkers every one, were before one's eyes ; pressing to the front, hanging over the balustrade, holding out clamorous importunate hands. It was not, certainly, for general style, pride and colour, a Paul Veronese company ; even the women, in spite of pearls and brocade and golden hair, failed of that type, and still more inevitably the men, without doublet, mantle, ruff or sword ; the nearest approach might have been in the great hounds and the little blackamoors. But my vision had a kind of analogy ; for what were the Venetians, after all, but the children of a Republic and of trade? It was, however, mainly, no doubt, an affair of the supporting marble terrace, the platform of my crowd, with as many columns of onyx and curtains of velvet as any great picture could need. About these there would be no difficulty whatever ; though this luxury of vision of the matter had meanwhile no excuse but the fact that the hour was charming, the waning light still lucid, the air admirable, the neighbourhood a great empty stage, expensively, extravagantly set, and the detail in frontage and cornice and architrave, in every feature of every edifice, as sharp as the uttered words of the plea I have just imagined.

V

The American air, I take advantage of this connection to remember, lends a felicity to all the exactitudes of architecture and sculpture, favours sharp effects, disengages differences, preserves lights, defines projected shadows.   Sculpture, in it, never either loses a value or conceals a loss, and it is everywhere full of help to discriminated masses.   This remark was to be emphatically made, I found myself observing, in presence of so distinct an appeal to high clearness as the great Palladian pile just erected by Messrs. Tiffany on one of the upper corners of Fifth Avenue, where it presents itself to the friendly sky with a great nobleness of white marble.   One is so thankful to it, I recognize, for not having twenty-five stories, which it might easily have had, I suppose, in the wantonness of wealth or of greed, that one gives it a double greeting, rejoicing to excess perhaps at its merely remaining, with the three fine arched and columned stages above its high basement, within the conditions of sociable symmetry.   One may break one's heart, certainly, over its only being, for "interest," a great miscellaneous shop—if one has any heart left in New York for such adventures.   One may also reflect, if any similar spring of reflection will still serve, on its being, to the very great limitation of its dignity, but a more or less pious *pastiche* or reproduction, the copy of a model that sits where Venetian water-steps keep—or used to keep!—vulgar invasion at bay.   But I hasten to add that one will do these things only at the cost of not "putting in" wherever one can the patch of optimism, the sigh of relief, the glow of satisfaction, or whatever else the pardonably factitious emotion may be called—which in New York is very bad economy. Look for interest where you may, cultivate a working felicity, press the spring hard, and you will see that, to whatever air Palladian piles may have been native, they can nowhere tell their great cold calculated story, in measured chapter and verse, better than to the strong sea-light of New York. This medium has the abundance of some ample childless mother who consoles herself for her sterility by an unbridled course of adoption — as I seemed again to make out in presence of the tiers of white marble that are now on their way to replace the granitic mass of the old Reservoir, *ultima Thule* of the northward walk of one's early time.

The reservoir of learning here taking form above great terraces—which my mind's eye makes as great as it would like—lifts, once more, from the heart the weight of the "tall" building it apparently doesn't propose to become. I could admire, in the unfinished state of the work, but the lower courses of this inestimable structure, the Public Library that is to gather into rich alliance and splendid ease the great minor Libraries of the town; it was enough for my delight, however, that the conditions engage for a covering of the earth rather than an invasion of the air—of so supreme an effect, at the pitch things have reached, is this single element of a generous area. It offers the best of reasons for speaking of the project as inestimable. Any building that, being beautiful, presents itself as seated rather than as standing, can do with your imagination what it will ; you ask it no question, you give it a free field, content only if it will sit and sit and sit. And if you interrogate your joy, in the connection, you will find it largely founded, I think, on all the implications thus conveyed of a proportionately smaller quantity of the great religion of the Elevator. The lateral development of great buildings is as yet, in the United States, but an opportunity for the legs, is in fact almost their sole opportunity—a circumstance that, taken alone, should eloquently plead; but it has another blest value, for the imagination, for the nerves, as a check on the constant obsession of one's living, of every one's living, by the packed and hoisted basket. The sempiternal lift, for one's comings and goings, affects one at last as an almost intolerable symbol of the herded and driven state and of that malady of preference for gregarious ways, of insistence on gregarious ways only, by which the people about one seem ridden. To wait, perpetually, in a human bunch, in order to be hustled, under military drill, the imperative order to "step lively," into some tight mechanic receptacle, fearfully and wonderfully working, is conceivable, no doubt, as a sad liability of our nature, but represents surely, when cherished and sacrificed to, a strange perversion of sympathies and ideals. Anything that breaks the gregarious spell, that relieves one of one's share, however insignificant, of the abject collective consciousness of being pushed and pressed in, with something that one's shoulders and one's heels must dodge at their peril, something that slides or slams or bangs, operating, in your rear, as ruthlessly as the guillotine—anything that performs this office puts a price on the lonely sweetness of a step or two taken by one's self, of deviating into some sense of independent motive power, of climbing even some grass-grown staircase, with a dream perhaps of the thrill of fellow-feeling *then* taking, then finding, place—something like Robinson Crusoe's famous thrill before Friday's footprint in the sand.

However these things might be, I recall further, as an incident of that hour of "evocation," the goodly glow, under this same illumination, of an immense red building, off in the clear north-east quarter, which had hung back, with all success, from the perpendicular form, and which actually covered ground with its extensions of base, its wide terrestrial wings. It had, I remember, in the early evening light, a homely kindness of diffused red brick, and to make out then that it was a great exemplary Hospital, one of the many marvels of New York in this general order, was to admire the exquisite art with which, in such a medium, it had so managed to invest itself with stillness. It was as quiet there, on its ample interspace, as if the clamorous city, round-about, as if the passion of the Elevated and of the Elevator in especial, were forever at rest and no one were stepping lively for miles and miles away; so that visibly, it had a spell to cast and a character to declare—things I was won over, on the spot, to desire a nearer view of. Fortune presently favoured this purpose, and almost my last impression of New York was gathered, on a very hot June morning, in the long, cool corridors of the Presbyterian Hospital, and in those "halls of pain," the high, quiet, active wards, silvery-dim with their whiteness and their shade, where the genius of the terrible city seemed to filter in with its energy sifted and softened, with its huge good-nature refined. There were reasons beyond the scope of these remarks for the interest of that hour, but it is at least within the scope that I recall noting there, all responsively, as not before, that if the *direct* pressure of New York is too often to ends that strike us as vulgar, the indirect is capable, and perhaps to an unlimited degree, of these lurking effects of delicacy. The immediate expression is the expression of violence, but you may find there is something left, something kept back for you, if that has not from the first fatally deafened you. It carries with it an after-sense which put on for me, under several happy in-timations, the image of some garden of the finest flowers—or of such as might be on the way to become the finest—masked by an enormous bristling hedge of defensive and aggressive vegetation, lacerating, defiant, not to be touched without blood. One saw the garden itself, behind its hedge and approachable only by those in the secret—one divined it to contain treasures of delicacy, many of them perhaps still to be developed, but attesting the possibilities of the soil. My Presbyterian Hospital was somehow in the garden, just where the soil, the very human soil itself, was richest, and—though this may appear an odd tribute to an institution founded on the principle of instant decision and action—it affected me, amid its summer airs and its boundless, soundless business, as surpassingly delicate. *There*, if nowhere else, was adjustment of tone ; there was the note of mildness and the sense of manners ; under the impression of which I am not sure of not having made up my mind that, were I merely alone and disconcerted, merely unprepared and unwarned, in the vast, dreadful place, as must happen to so many a helpless mortal, I should positively desire or " elect," as they say, to become the victim of some such mischance as would put me into relation again, the ambulance or the police aiding, with these precious. saving presences. They might re-establish for me, before the final extinction or dismissal, some belief in manners and in tone.

Was it in the garden also, as I say, that the Metropolitan Museum had meanwhile struck me as standing ?—the impression of a quite other hazard of *flânerie* this, and one of those memories, once more, that I find myself standing off from, as under the shadow of their too numerous suggestion. That institution *is*, decidedly, to-day, part of the inner New York harmony that I have described as a touched after-sense ; so that if there were, scattered about the place, elements prompting rich, if vague, evocations, this was recognizably one of the spots over which such elements would have most freedom to play. The original Museum was a thing of the far past ;

hadn't I the vision of it, from ancient days, installed, stately though scrappy, in a large eccentric house in West Fourteenth Street, a house the prior period, even the early, impressive construction of which one recalled from days still more ancient, days so far away that to be able to travel back to them was almost as good, or as bad, as being a centenarian? This superfluous consciousness of the original seat of the Museum, of where and what it had been, was one of those terrible traps to memory, about the town, which baited themselves with the cheese of association, so to speak, in order to exhibit one after-wards as "caught," or, otherwise expressed, as old; such being the convicted state of the unfortunate who knows the *whole* of so many of his stories. The case is never really disguisable; we get off perhaps when we only know the ends of things, but beyond that our historic sense betrays us. We have known the beginnings, we have been present, in the various connections, at the birth, the life and the death, and it is wonderful how traceably, in such a place as New York, careers of importance may run their course and great institutions, while you are just watching, rise, prosper and fall. I had had my shudder, in that same Fourteenth Street, for the complete dis-appearance of a large church, as massive as brown stone could make it, at the engaging construction of which one's tender years had "assisted" (it exactly faced the parental home, and nefarious, perilous play was found possible in the works), but which, after passing from youth to middle age and from middle age to antiquity, has vanished as utterly as the Assyrian Empire.

So, it was to be noted, had the parental home, and so the first home of the Museum, by what I made out, beyond Sixth Avenue—after which, for the last-named, had there not been a second seat, long since superseded too, a more prolonged *étape* on the glorious road? This also gave out a shimmer from the middle time, but with

the present favouring stage of the journey the glorious
road seems to stretch away.   It is a palace of art, truly,
that sits there on the edge of the Park, rearing itself with
a radiance, yet offering you expanses to tread ; but I found
it invite me to a matter of much more interest
than any mere judging of its dispositions.   It spoke
with a hundred voices of that huge process of historic
waste that the place in general keeps putting before
you ; but showing it in a light that drew out the harshness or the sadness, the pang, whatever it had seemed
elsewhere, of the reiterated sacrifice to pecuniary profit.
For the question here was to be of the advantage to the
spirit, not to the pocket ; to be of the æsthetic advantage
involved in the wonderful clearance to come.   From
the moment the visitor takes in two or three things
—first, perhaps, the scale on which, in the past, bewildering tribute has flowed in ; second, the scale on
which it must absolutely now flow out ; and, third, the
presumption created by the vivacity of these two movements for a really fertilizing stir of the ground—he sees
the whole place as the field of a drama the nearer view
of the future course of which he shall be sorry to lose.
One never winces after the first little shock, when Education is expensive—one winces only at the expense which,
like so much of the expense of New York, doesn't educate ;
and Education, clearly, was going to seat herself in these
marble halls—admirably prepared for her, to all appearance—and issue her instructions without regard to cost.
The obvious, the beautiful, the thrilling thing was that,
without regard to cost either, they were going to be
obeyed : that inference was somehow irresistible, the disembodied voices I have spoken of quite forcing it home
and the palace roof arching to protect it as the dome of
the theatre protects the performance.   I know not if all past
purchase, in these annals (putting the Cesnola Collection
aside), has been without reproach, but it struck me as safe

to gather that (putting aside again Mr. Marquand's rare munificence) almost no past acceptance of gifts and bequests "in kind" had been without weakness. In the light of Sargent's splendid portrait, simply, there would have been little enough weakness to associate with Mr. Marquand's collection; but the gifts and bequests in general, even when speciously pleasing or interesting, constitute an object-lesson in the large presence of which the New York mind will perform its evolution—an evolution traceable, and with sharpness, in advance. I shall nevertheless not attempt to foretell it; for sufficient to the situation, surely, is the appearance, represented by its announcing shadow, that Acquisition—acquisition if need be on the highest terms—may, during the years to come, bask here as in a climate it has never before enjoyed. There was money in the air, ever so much money—that was, grossly expressed, the sense of the whole intimation. And the money was to be all for the most exquisite things—for *all* the most exquisite except creation, which was to be off the scene altogether; for art, selection, criticism, for knowledge, piety, taste. The intimation—which was somehow, after all, so pointed—would have been detestable if interests other, and smaller, than these had been in question. The Education, however, was to be exclusively that of the sense of beauty; this defined, romantically, for my evoked drama, the central situation. What left me wondering a little, all the same, was the contradiction involved in one's not thinking of some of its prospective passages as harsh. Here it is, no doubt, that one catches the charm of rigours that take place all in the æsthetic and the critical world. They would be invidious, would be cruel, if applied to personal interests, but they take on a high benignity as soon as the values concerned become values mainly for the mind. (If they happen to have also a trade-value this is pure superfluity and excess.) The thought of the acres of canvas and the tons of marble to be turned out into the cold world as the penalty of old error and the warrant for a clean slate ought to have drawn tears from the eyes. But these impending incidents affected me, in fact, on the spot, as quite radiant demonstrations. The Museum, in short, was going to be great, and in the geniality of the life to come such sacrifices, though resembling those of the funeral-pile of Sardanapalus, dwindled to nothing.

5

The Bowery
and Thereabouts

I SCARCE know, once more, if such a matter be a sign of the city itself, or only another perversity on the part of a visitor apt to press a little too hard, everywhere, on the spring of the show ; but wherever I turned, I confess, wherever any aspect seemed to put forth a freshness, there I found myself saying that this aspect was one's strongest impression. It is impossible, as I now recollect, not to be amused at the great immediate differences of scene and occasion that could produce such a judgment, and this remark directly applies, no doubt, to the accident of a visit, one afternoon of the dire midwinter, to a theatre in the Bowery at which a young actor in whom I was interested had found for the moment a fine melodramatic opportunity. This small adventure—if the adventures of rash observation be ever small—was to remain embalmed for me in all its odd, sharp notes, and perhaps in none more than in its element of contrast with an image antediluvian, the memory of the conditions of a Bowery theatre, *the* Bowery Theatre in fact, contemporary with my more or less gaping youth. Was that vast dingy edifice, with its illustrious past, still standing ?—a point on which I was to remain vague while I electrically travelled through a strange, a sinister over-roofed clangorous darkness, a wide thoroughfare beset, for all its width, with sound and fury, and bristling, amid the traffic, with posts and piles

that were as the supporting columns of a vast cold, yet
also uncannily-animated, sepulchre. It was like moving
the length of an interminable cage, beyond the remoter
of whose bars lighted shops, struggling dimly under
other pent-house effects, offered their Hebrew faces and
Hebrew names to a human movement that affected one
even then as a breaking of waves that had rolled, for
their welter on this very strand, from the other side
of the globe. I was on my way to enjoy, no doubt,
some peculiarly "American" form of the theatric
mystery, but my way led me, apparently, through
depths of the Orient, and I should clearly take my
place with an Oriental public.

I took it in fact in such a curtained corner of a private
box as might have appeared to commit me to the most
intimate interest possible—might have done so, that is, if
all old signs had not seemed visibly to fail and new
questions, mockingly insoluble, to rise. The old signs
would have been those of some "historic" community,
so to speak, between the play and the public, between
those opposed reciprocal quantities: such a consciousness of the same general terms of intercourse for
instance, as I seemed to have seen prevail, long years
ago, under the great dim, bleak, sonorous dome of the
old Bowery. Nothing so much imposed itself at first
as this suggestive contrast—the vision of the other big
bare ranting stupid stage, the grey void, smelling of dust
and tobacco-juice, of a scene on which realism was yet
to dawn, but which addressed itself, on the other hand,
to an audience at one with it. Audience and "production" had been then of the same stripe and the same
"tradition"; the pitch, that is, had been of our own
domestic and romantic tradition (to apply large words
to a loose matter, a matter rich in our very own
æsthetic idiosyncrasy). I should say, in short, if it
didn't savour of pedantry, that if this ancient "poetic"

had been purely a home-grown thing, nursed in the English intellectual cradle, and in the American of a time when the American resembled the English closely enough, so the instincts from which it sprang were instincts familiar to the whole body of spectators, whose dim sense of art (to use again the big word) was only not thoroughly English because it must have been always so abundantly Irish. The foreign note, in that thinner air, was, at the most, the Irish, and I think of the elements of the " Jack Sheppard" and " Claude Duval" Bowery, including the peanuts and the orange-peel, as quite harmoniously Irish. From the corner of the box of my so improved playhouse further down, the very name of which moreover had the cosmopolite lack of point, I made out, in the audience, the usual mere monotony of the richer exoticism. No single face, beginning with those close beside me (for my box was a shared luxury), but referred itself, by my interpretation, to some such strange outland form as we had not dreamed of in my day. There they all sat, the representatives of the races we have nothing " in common" with, as naturally, as comfortably, as munchingly, as if the theatre were their constant practice—and, as regards the munching, I may add, I was struck with the appearance of quality and cost in the various confections pressed from moment to moment upon our notice by the little playhouse peddlers.

It comes over me under this branch of my reminiscence, that these almost " high-class" luxuries, circulating in such a company, were a sort of supreme symbol of the *promoted* state of the aspirant to American conditions. He, or more particularly she, had been promoted, and, more or less at a bound, to the habitual use of chocolate-creams, and indeed of other dainties, refined and ingenious, compared with which these are quite *vieux jeu*. This last remark might in fact open up for us, had

I space, a view, interesting to hold a moment, or to follow
as far as it might take us, of the wondrous consumption
by the "people," over the land, of the most elaborate
solid and liquid sweets, such products as form in other
countries an expensive and select dietary.   The whole
phenomenon of this omnipresent and essentially "popular" appeal of the confectioner and pastry-cook, I can
take time but to note, is more significant of the economic,
and even of the social situation of the masses than many
a circumstance honoured with more attention.   I found
myself again and again—in presence, for example, of the
great glittering temples, the bristling pagodas, erected to
the worship in question wherever men and women, perhaps
particularly women, most congregate, and above all under
the high domes of the great modern railway stations—
I found myself wondering, I say, what such facts represented, what light they might throw upon manners and
wages.   Wages, in the country at large, *are* largely
manners—the only manners, I think it fair to say, one
mostly encounters; the market and the home therefore
look alike dazzling, at first, in this reflected, many-
coloured lustre.   It speaks somehow, beyond anything
else, of the diffused sense of material ease—since the
solicitation of sugar couldn't be so hugely and artfully
organized if the response were not clearly proportionate.
But how is the response itself organized, and what are
the other items of that general budget of labour, what in
especial are the attenuations of that general state of
fatigue, in which so much purchasing-power can flow to
the supposedly superfluous?   The wage-earners, the
toilers of old, notably in other climes, were known by the
wealth of their songs; and has it, on these lines, been
given to the American people to be known by the number
of their " candies " ?

I must not let the question, however, carry me too
far—quite away from the point I was about to make

of my sense of the queer chasm over which, on the Saturday afternoon at the Windsor Theatre, I seemed to see the so domestic drama reach out to the so exotic audience and the so exotic audience reach out to the so domestic drama. The play (a masterpiece of its type, if I may so far strain a point, in such a case, and in the interest of my young friend's excellent performance, as to predicate "type") was American, to intensity, in its blank conformity to convention, the particular implanted convention of the place. This convention, simply expressed, was that there should never be anything different in a play (the most conservative of human institutions) from what there had always been before ; that *that place*, in a word, should always know the very same theatric thing, any deviation from which might be phrenology, or freemasonry, or ironmongery, or anything else in the world, but would never be drama, especially drama addressed to the heart of the people. The tricks and the traps, the *trucs*, the whole stage-carpentry, might freely renew themselves, to create for artless minds the illusion of a difference ; but the sense of the business would still have to reside in our ineradicable Anglo-Saxon policy, or our seemingly deep-seated necessity, of keeping, where "representation" is concerned, so far away from the truth and the facts of life as really to betray a fear in us of possibly doing something like them should we be caught nearer. "Foreigners," in general, unmistakably, in any attempt to render life, obey the instinct of keeping closer, positively recognize the presence and the solicitation of the deep waters ; yet here was my houseful of foreigners, physiognomically branded as such, confronted with our pale poetic—fairly caught for schooling in our art of making the best of it. Nothing (in the texture of the occasion) could have had a sharper interest than this demonstration that, since what we most pretend to do with them is thoroughly to school them, the schooling, by our system, cannot begin too soon nor pervade their experience too much. Were they going to rise to it, or rather to fall to it—to *our* instinct, as distinguished from their own, for picturing life ? Were they to take our lesson, submissively, in order to get with it our smarter traps and tricks, our superior Yankee machinery (illustrated in the case before them, for instance, by a wonderful folding bed in which the villain of the piece, pursuing the virtuous heroine round and round the room and trying to leap over it after her, is, at the young lady's touch of a hidden spring, engulfed as in the jaws of a crocodile ?) Or would it be their dim intellectual resistance, a vague stir in them of some unwitting heritage—of the finer irony, that I should make out, on the contrary, as withstanding the effort to corrupt them, and thus perhaps really promising to react, over the head of our offered mechanic bribes, on our ingrained intellectual platitude ?

One had only to formulate that question to seem to see the issue hang there, for the excitement of the matter, quite as if the determination were to be taken on the spot. For the opposition over the chasm of the footlights, as I have called it, grew intense truly, as I took in on one side the hue of the Galician cheek, the light of the Moldavian eye, the whole pervasive facial mystery, swaying, at the best, for the moment, over the gulf, on the vertiginous bridge of American confectionery—and took in on the other the perfect " Yankee " quality of the challenge which stared back at them as in the white light of its hereditary thinness. I needn't say that when I departed—perhaps from excess of suspense—it was without seeing the balance drop to either quarter, and I am afraid I think of the odd scene as still enacted in many places and many ways, the inevitable rough union in discord of the two groups of instincts, the fusion of the two camps by a queer, clumsy, wasteful social chemistry.

Such at all events are the roundabout processes of peaceful history, the very history that succeeds, for our edification, in *not* consisting of battles and blood and tears.

II

I was happily to find, at all events, that I had not, on that occasion, done with the Bowery, or with its neighbourhood—as how could one not rejoice to return to an air in which such infinite suggestion might flower? The season had advanced, though the summer night was no more than genial, and the question, for this second visit, was of a "look-in," with two or three friends, at three or four of the most "characteristic" evening resorts (for reflection and conversation) of the dwellers on the East side. It was definitely not, the question, of any gaping view of the policed underworld—unanimously pronounced an imposture, in general, at the best, and essentially less interesting than the exhibition of public manners. I found on the spot, in harmony with this preference, that nothing better could have been desired, in the way of pure presentable picture, subject always to the swinging lantern-light of the individual imagination, than the first (as I think it was, for the roaming hour) of our penetrated "haunts"—a large semi-subterranean establishment, a beer-cellar rich in the sporting note, adorned with images of strong men and lovely women, prize-fighters and *ballerine*, and finding space in its deep bosom for a billiard-room and a bowling-alley, all sociably squeezed together; finding space, above all, for a collection of extraordinarily equivocal types of consumers : an intensity of equivocation indeed planted, just as if to await direct and convenient study, in the most typical face of the collection, a face which happened, by good fortune, to be that of the most officious presence. When the element of the equivocal in personal character and history takes on, in New York, an addition from all the rest of the swarming ambiguity and fugacity of race and tongue, the result becomes, for the picture-seeker, indescribably, luridly strong. There always comes up, at view of the "low" physiognomy shown in conditions that denote a measure of impunity and ease, the question—than which few, I think, are more interesting to the psychologist—of the forms of ability *consistent* with lowness ; the question of the quality of intellect, the sublety of character, the mastery of the art of life, with which the extremity of baseness may yet be associated. That question held me, I confess, so under its spell during those almost first steps of our ingenuous *enquête*, that I would gladly have prolonged, just there, my opportunity to sound it.

The fascination was of course in the perfection of the baseness, and the puzzle in the fact that it could be subject, without fatally muddling, without tearing and rending them, to those arts of life, those quantities of conformity, the numerous involved accommodations and patiences, that are *not* in the repertory of the wolf and the snake. Extraordinary, we say to ourselves on such occasions, the amount of formal tribute that civilization is after all able to gouge out of apparently hopeless stuff; extraordinary that it can make a presentable sheath for such fangs and such claws. The mystery is in the *how* of the process, in the wonderful little wavering borderland between nature and art, the place of the crooked seam where, if psychology had the adequate lens, the white stitches would show. All this played through one's thought, to the infinite extension of the sufficiently close and thoroughly *banal* beer-cellar. There happened to be reasons, not to be shaded over, why one of my companions should cause a particular chord of recognition to vibrate, and the very convergence of hushed looks, in the so "loud" general medium, seemed to lay bare, from table to table, the secret of the common countenance (common to that place) put off its guard by curiosity, almost by amiability. The secret was doubtless in many cases but the poor familiar human secret of the vulgar mind, of the soul unfurnished, so to speak, in respect to delicacy, probity, pity, with a social decoration of the mere bleak walls of instinct; but it was the unforgettable little personality that I have referred to as the presiding spirit, it was the spokesman of our welcome, the master of the scene himself, who struck me as presenting my question in its finest terms. To conduct a successful establishment, to *be* a spokesman, an administrator, an employer of labour and converser on subjects, let alone a citizen and a tax-payer, was to have an existence abounding in relations and to be subject to the law that a relation, however imperfectly human or social, is at the worst a matter that can only be described as delicate. Well, in presence of the abysmal obliquity of such a face, of the abysmal absence of traceability or coherency in such antecedents, where did the different delicacies involved come in at all?—how did intercourse emerge at all, and, much more, emerge so brilliantly, as it were, from its dangers? The answer had to be, for the moment, no doubt, that if there be such a state as that of misrepresenting your value and use, there is also the rarer condition of being so sunk beneath the level of appearance as not to be able to represent them at all. Appearance, in you, has thus not only no notes, no language, no authority, but is literally condemned to operate *as* the treacherous sum of your poverties.

The jump was straight, after this, to a medium so different that I seem to see, as the one drawback to evoking it again, however briefly, the circumstance that it started the speculative hare for even a longer and straighter run. This irrepressible animal covered here,

however, a much goodlier country, covered it in the
interest of a happy generalization—the bold truth that
even when apparently done to death by that property
of the American air which reduces so many aspects to
a common denominator, certain finer shades of saliency
and consistency do often, by means known to themselves,
recover their rights.   They are like swimmers who
have had to plunge, to come round and under water,
but who pop out a panting head and shine for a moment
in the sun.   My image is perhaps extravagant, for the
question is only of the kept recollection of a café pure
and simple, particularly pure and particularly simple in
fact, inasmuch as it dispensed none but "soft" drinks
and presented itself thus in the light, the quiet,
tempered, intensely individual light, of a beerhouse
innocent of beer.   I have indeed no other excuse for
calling it a beerhouse than the fact that it offered to
every sense such a deep Germanic peace as abides, for
the most part (though not always even then), where the
deep-lidded tankard balances with the scarce shallower
bowl of the meditative pipe.   This modest asylum had
its tone, which I found myself, after a few minutes,
ready to take for exquisite, if on no other ground than
its almost touching suggestion of discriminations made
and preserved in the face of no small difficulty.   That
is what I meant just now by my tribute to the occasional
patience of unquenched individualism—the practical
subtlety of the spirit unashamed of its preference for
the minor key, clinging, through thick and thin, to its
conception of decency and dignity, and finding means
to make it good even to the exact true shade.   These
are the real triumphs of art—the discriminations in
favour of taste produced not by the gilded and guarded
"private room," but by making publicity itself delicate,
making your barrier against vulgarity consist but in a
few tables and chairs, a few coffee-cups and boxes of

dominoes. Money in quantities enough can always create tone, but it had been created here by mere unbuyable instinct. The charm of the place in short was that its note of the exclusive had been arrived at with such a beautifully fine economy. I try, in memory, and for the value of the lesson, to analyze, as it were, the elements, and seem to recall as the most obvious the contemplative stillness in which the faint click of the moved domino could be heard, and into which the placid attention of the quiet, honest men who were thus testifying for the exquisite could be read. The exquisite, yes, *was* the triumph of their tiny temple, with all the loud surrounding triumphs, those of the coarse and the common, making it but stick the faster, like a well-inserted wedge. And fully to catch this was to catch by the same stroke the main ground of the effect, to see that it came most of all from felicity of suppression and omission. There was so visibly too much everywhere else of everything vulgar, that there reigned here, for the difference, the learnt lesson that there could scarce be in such an air of infection little enough, in quantity and mass, of anything. The felicity had its climax in the type, or rather in the individual character, of our host, who, officiating alone, had apparently suppressed all aids to service and succeeded, as by an inspiration of genius, in omitting, for all his years, to learn the current American. He spoke but a dozen words of it, and that was doubtless how he best kept the key of the old Germanic peace—of the friendly stillness in which, while the East side roared, a new metaphysic might have been thought out or the scheme of a new war intellectualized.

III

After this there were other places, mostly higher in the scale, and but a couple of which my memory recovers.

There was also, as I recall, a snatched interlude—an associated dash into a small crammed convivial theatre, an oblong hall, bristling with pipe and glass, at the end of which glowed for a moment, a little dingily, some broad passage of a Yiddish comedy of manners. It hovered there, briefly, as if seen through a spy-glass reaching, across the world, to some far-off dowdy Jewry; then our sense of it became too mixed a matter—it was a scent, literally, not further to be followed. There remained with me none the less the patch of alien comedy, with all it implied of esoteric vision on the part of the public. Something of that admonition had indeed, earlier in the season, been sharp—so much had one heard of a brilliant Yiddish actress who was drawing the town to the East side by the promise of a new note. This lady, however, had disconcerted my own purpose by suddenly appearing, in the orthodox quarter, in a language only definable as not in *intention* Yiddish—not otherwise definable; and I also missed, through a like alarm, the opportunity of hearing an admired actor of the same school. He was Yiddish on the East side, but he cropped up, with a wild growth, in Broadway as well, and his auditors seemed to know as little as care to what idiom they supposed themselves to be listening. Marked in New York, by many indications, this vagueness of ear as to differences, as to identities, of idiom.

I must not, however, under that interference, lose the echo of a couple of other of the impressions of my crowded summer night—and all the less that they kept working it, as I seem to remember, up to a higher and higher pitch. It had been intimated to me that one of these scenes of our climax had entered the sophisticated phase, that of sacrificing to a self-consciousness that was to be regretted—that of making eyes, so to speak, at the larger, the up-town public; that pestilent favour of "society" which is fatal to everything it touches and

which so quickly leaves the places of its passage unfit
for its own use and uninteresting for any other. This
establishment had learned to lay on local colour with
malice prepense—the local colour of its " Slav " origin—
and was the haunt, on certain evenings of the week, of
yearning groups from Fifth Avenue sated with familiar
horizons. Yet there were no yearning groups—none,
that is, save our own—at the time of our visit ; there was
only, very amply and pleasantly presented, another
aspect of the perpetual process of the New York inter-
marriage. As the Venetian Republic, in the person of
the Doge, used to go forth, on occasion, to espouse the
Adriatic, so it is quite as if the American, incarnate in its
greatest port, were for ever throwing the nuptial ring to
the still more richly-dowered Atlantic. I speak again
less of the nuptial rites themselves than of those
immediate fruits that struck me everywhere as so
characteristic—so equally characteristic, I mean, of each
party to the union. The flourishing establishment of my
present reference offered distinctly its outland picture,
but showed it in an American frame, and the features of
frame and picture arranged themselves shrewdly together.
Quiet couples, elderly bourgeois husbands and wives,
sat there over belated sausage and cheese, potato-salad
and Hungarian wine, the wife with her knitting produced
while the husband finished his cigar ; and the indication,
for the moment, might have been of some evening note
of Dantzig or of Buda-Pesth. But the conditioning
foreign, and the visibility of their quite so happily
conjugal give-and-take, in New York, is my reason for
this image of the repeated espousals. Why were the
quiet easy couples, with their homely café habit (kept in
the best relation to the growth, under the clicking
needles, of the marital stocking), such remote and indirect
results of our local anecdotic past, our famous escape, at
our psychological moment, from King George and his

works, with all sorts of inevitable lapses and hitches in any grateful consciousness they might ever have of that prime cause of their new birth? Yet why, on the other hand, could they affect one, even with the Fatherland planked under them in the manner of the praying-carpet spread beneath the good Mahometan, as still more disconnected from the historic consciousness implied in their own type, and with the mere moral identity of German or Slav, or whatever it might be, too extinct in them for any possibility of renewal? The exotic boss here did speak, I remember, fluent East-side New Yorkese, and it was in this wonderful tongue that he expressed to us his superior policy, his refined philosophy, announced his plans for the future and presented himself, to my vision, as a possibly far-reaching master-spirit. What remains with me is this expression, and the colour and the quality of it, and the free familiarity and the " damned foreign impudence," with so much taken for granted, and all the hitches and lapses, all the solutions of continuity, in *his* inward assimilation of our heritage and point of view, matched as these were, on our own side, by such signs of large and comparatively witless concession. What, oh, what again, were he and his going to make of us?

Well, there was the impression, and that was a question on which, for a certain intensity in it, our adventure might have closed; but it was so far from closing that, late though the hour, it presently opened out into a vast and complicated picture which I find myself thinking of, after an interval, as the splendid crown of the evening. Here were we still on the East side, but we had moved up, by stages artfully inspired, into the higher walks, into a pavilion of light and sound and savoury science that struck one as vaguely vast, as possibly gardened about, and that, blazing into the stillness of the small hours, dazzled one with the show of its copious and various activity. The whole vision was less intimate than elsewhere, but it was a world of custom quite away from any mere Delmonico tradition of one's earlier time, and rich, as one might reckon it, in its own queer marks, marks probably never yet reduced—inspiring thought!—to literary notation; with which it would seem better to form a point of departure for fresh exploration than serve as tail-piece to the end of a chapter. Who were all the people, and whence and whither and why, in the good New York small hours? Where *was* the place after all, and what might it, or might it not, truly, represent to slightly-fatigued feasters who, in a recess like a privileged opera-box at a *bal masqué*, and still communing with polyglot waiters, looked down from their gallery at a multitudinous supper, a booming orchestra, an elegance of disposed plants and flowers, a perfect organization and an abyss of mystery? Was it "on" Third Avenue, on Second, on fabulous unattempted First? Nothing would induce me to cut down the romance of it, in remembrance, to a mere address, least of all to an awful New York one; New York addresses falling so below the grace of a city where the very restaurants may on occasion, under restless analysis, flash back the likeness of Venetian palaces flaring with the old carnival. The ambiguity is the element in which the whole thing swims for me—so nocturnal, so bacchanal, so hugely hatted and feathered and flounced, yet apparently so innocent, almost so patriarchal again, and matching, in its mixture, with nothing one had elsewhere known. It breathed its simple "New York! New York!" at every impulse of inquiry; so that I can only echo contentedly, with analysis for once quite agreeably baffled, "Remarkable, unspeakable New York!"

6

The Sense of Newport

NEWPORT, on my finding myself back there, threatened me sharply, quite at first, with that predicament at which I have glanced in another connection or two—the felt condition of having known it too well and loved it too much for description or definition. What was one to say about it except that one *had* been so affected, so distraught, and that discriminations and reasons were buried under the dust of use? There was a chance indeed that the breath of the long years (of the interval of absence, I mean) would have blown away this dust—and that, precisely, was what one was eager to see. To go out, to look about, to recover the sense, was accordingly to put the question, without delay, to the proof—and with the happy consequence, I think, of an escape from a grave discomfiture. The charm was there again, unmistakably, the little old strange, very simple charm—to be expressed, as a fine proposition, or to be given up ; but the answer came in the fact that to have walked about for half-an-hour was to have felt the question clear away. It cleared away so conveniently, so blissfully, in the light of the benign little truth that nothing had been less possible, even in the early, ingenuous, infatuated days, than to describe or define Newport. It had clearly had nothing about it *to* describe or define, so that one's fondness had fairly rested on this sweet oddity in it.

One had only to look back to recognize that it had never condescended to give a scrap of reasoned account of itself (as a favourite of fortune and the haunt of the *raffiné*); it had simply lain there like a little bare, white, open hand, with slightly-parted fingers, for the observer with a presumed sense for hands to take or to leave. The observer with a real sense never failed to pay this image the tribute of quite tenderly grasping the hand, and even of raising it, delicately, to his lips; having no less, at the same time, the instinct of not shaking it too hard, and that above all of never putting it to any rough work.

Such had been from the first, under a chastened light and in a purple sea, the dainty isle of Aquidneck; which might have avoided the weak mistake of giving up its pretty native name and of becoming thereby as good as nameless—with an existence as Rhode Island practically monopolized by the State and a Newport identity borrowed at the best and applicable but to a corner. Does not this vagueness of condition, however, fitly symbolize the small virtual promontory, of which, superficially, nothing could be predicated but its sky and its sea and its sunsets? One views it as placed there, by some refinement in the scheme of nature, just as a touchstone of taste—with a beautiful little sense to be read into it by a few persons, and nothing at all to be made of it, as to its essence, by most others. I come back, for its essence, to that figure of the little white hand, with the gracefully-spread fingers and the fine grain of skin, even the dimples at the joints and the shell-like delicacy of the pink nails—all the charms in short that a little white hand may have. I see all the applications of the image—I see a special truth in each. It is the back of the hand, rising to the swell of the wrist, that is exposed —which is the way, I think, the true lover takes and admires it. He makes out in it, bending over it—or he used to in the old days—innumerable shy and subtle beauties, almost requiring, for justice, a magnifying-glass; and he winces at the sight of certain other obtruded ways of dealing with it. The touchstone of taste was indeed to operate, for the critical, the tender spirit, from the moment the pink palm was turned up on the chance of what might be "in" it. For nine persons out of ten, among its visitors, its purchasers of sites and builders of (in the old parlance) cottages, there had never been anything in it at all—except of course an opportunity: an opportunity for escaping the summer heat of other places, for bathing, for boating, for riding and driving, and for many sorts of more or less expensive riot. The pink palm being empty, in other words, to their vision, they had begun, from far back, to put things into it, things of their own, and of all sorts, and of many ugly, and of more and more expensive, sorts; to fill it substantially, that is, with gold, the gold that they have ended by heaping up there to an amount so oddly out of proportion to the scale of nature and of space.

This process, one was immediately to perceive with that renewal of impression, this process of injection and elaboration, of creating the palpable pile, had been going on for years to such a tune that the face of nature was now as much obliterated as possible, and the original shy sweetness as much as possible bedizened and bedevilled: all of which, moreover, might also at present be taken as having led, in turn, to the most unexpected climax, a matter of which I shall presently speak. The original shy sweetness, however, that range of effect which I have referred to as practically too latent and too modest for notation, had meanwhile had its votaries, the fond pedestrian minority, for whom the little white hand (to return for an instant to my figure, with which, as you see, I am charmed) had always been so full of treasures of its own as to discredit, from the point of view of taste, any attempt, from without, to stuff it fuller. Such attempts had, in the nature of the case, and from far back, been condemned to show for violations; violations of taste and discretion, to begin with—violations, more intimately, as the whole business became brisker, of a thousand delicate secret places, dear to the disinterested rambler, small, mild "points" and promontories, far away little lonely, sandy coves, rock-set, lily-sheeted ponds, almost hidden, and shallow Arcadian summer-haunted valleys, with the sea just over some stony shoulder: a whole world that called out to the long afternoons of youth, a world with its scale so measured and intended and happy, its detail so finished and pencilled and stippled (certainly for American detail!) that there comes back to me, across the many years, no better analogy for it than that of some fine foreground in an old "line" engraving. There remained always a sense, of course, in which the superimpositions, the multiplied excrescences, were a tribute to the value of the place; where no such liberty was ever taken save exactly *because* (as even the most blundering builder would have claimed) it was all so beautiful, so solitary and so "sympathetic." And that indeed has been, thanks to the "pilers-on" of gold, the fortune, the history of its beauty : that it now bristles with the villas and palaces into which the cottages have all turned, and that these monuments of pecuniary power rise thick and close, precisely, in order that their occupants may constantly remark to each other, from the windows to the "grounds," and from house to house, that it *is* beautiful, it *is* solitary and sympathetic. The thing has been done, it is impossible not to perceive, with the best faith in the world—though not altogether with the best light, which is always so different a matter ; and it is with the general consequence only, at the end of the story, that I find myself to-day concerned.

So much concerned I found myself, I profess, after I had taken in this fact of a very distinct general consequence, that the whole interest of the vision was quickened by it; and that when, in particular, on one of the last days of June, among the densely-arrayed villas, I had followed the beautiful "ocean drive" to its uttermost reach and back without meeting either another vehicle or a single rider, let alone a single pedestrian, I recognized matter for the intellectual thrill that attests a social revolution foreseen and completed. The term I use may appear extravagant, but it was a fact, none the less, that I seemed to take full in my face, on this occasion, the cold stir of air produced when the whirligig of time has made one of its liveliest turns. It is always going, the whirligig, but its effect is so to blow up the dust that we must wait for it to stop a moment, as it now and then does with a pant of triumph, in order to see what it has been at. I saw, beyond all doubt, on the spot— and *there* came in, exactly, the thrill; I could remember far back enough to have seen it begin to blow all the artless buyers and builders and blunderers into their places, leaving them there for half a century or so of fond security, and then to see it, of a sudden, blow them quite out again, as with the happy consciousness of some new amusing use for them, some other game still to play with them. This acquaintance, as it practically had been, with the whole rounding of the circle (even though much of it from a distance), was tantamount to the sense of having sat out the drama, the social, the local, that of a real American period, from the rise to the fall of the curtain —always assuming that truth of the reached catastrophe or *dénouement*. *How* this climax or solution had been arrived at—that, clearly, for the spectator, would have been worth taking note of; but what he made of it I shall not glance at till I have shown him as first of all, on the spot, quite modestly giving in to mere primary beguilement. It had been certain in advance that he would find the whole picture overpainted, and the question could only be, at the best, of how much of the ancient surface would here and there glimmer through. The ancient surface had been the concern, as I have hinted, of the small fond minority, the comparatively few people for whom the lurking shy charm, all there, but all to be felt rather than published, did in fact constitute a surface. The question, as soon as one arrived, was of whether some ghost of that were recoverable.

II

There was always, to begin with, the Old Town—we used, before we had become Old ourselves, to speak of it that way, in the manner of an allusion to Nuremberg or to Carcassonne, since it had been leading its little historic life for centuries (as we implied) before " cottages " and house-agents were dreamed of. It was not that we had great illusions about it or great pretensions for it ; we only thought it, without interference, very "good of its kind," and we had as to its *being* of that kind no doubt whatever. Would it still be of that kind, and what had the kind itself been ?—these questions made one's heart beat faster as one went forth in search of it. Distinctly, if it had been of a kind it *would* still be of it ; for the kind wouldn't at the worst or at the best (one scarce knew how to put it) have been worth changing : so that the question for the restored absentee, who so palpitated with the sense of it, all hung, absolutely, on the validity of the past. One might well hold one's breath if the past, with the dear little blue distances in it, were in danger now of being given away. One might well pause before the possible indication that a cherished impression of youth had been

but a figment of the mind. Fortunately, however, at Newport, and especially where the antiquities cluster, distances
are short, and the note of reassurance awaited me almost
round the first corner. One had been a hundred times
right—for how *was* one to think of it all, as one went
on, if one didn't think of it as Old? There played before
one's eyes again, in fine, in that unmistakable silvery
shimmer, a particular property of the local air, the exquisite law of the relative—the application of which, on
the spot, is required to make even such places as Viterbo
and Bagdad not seem new. One may sometimes be
tired of the word, but anything that has succeeded in
living long enough to become conscious of its *note*, is
capable on occasion of making that note effectively sound.
It *will* sound, we gather, if we listen for it, and the small
silver whistle of the past, with its charming quaver of
weak gaiety, quite played the tune I asked of it up and
down the tiny, sunny, empty Newport vistas, perspectives
coming to a stop like the very short walks of very old
ladies. What indeed but little very old ladies did they
resemble, the little very old streets? with the same
suggestion of present timidity and frugality of life, the
same implication in their few folds of drab, of mourning,
of muslin still mysteriously starched, the implication of
no adventure at any time, however far back, that mightn't
have been suitable to a lady.

The whole low promontory, in its wider and remoter
measurements, is a region of jutting tide-troubled "points,"
but we had admired the Old Town too for the emphasis
of its peculiar point, *the* Point; a quarter distinguished,
we considered, by a really refined interest. Here would
have been my misadventure, if I was to have any—that
of missing, on the grey page of to-day, the suggestive
passages I remembered; but I was to find, to my satisfaction, that there was still no more mistaking their
pleasant sense than there had ever been: a quiet, mild

waterside sense, not that of the bold, bluff outer sea, but one in which shores and strands and small coast things played the greater part; with overhanging back verandahs, with little private wooden piers, with painted boat-houses and boats laid up, with still-water bathing (the very words, with their old slightly prim discrimination, as of ladies and children jumping up and down, reach me across the years), with a wide-curving Bay and dim landward distances that melted into a mysterious, rich, superior, but quite disconnected and not at all permittedly patronizing Providence. There were stories, anciently, for the Point—so prescribed a feature of it that one made them up, freely and handsomely, when they were not otherwise to be come by; though one was never quite sure if they ought most to apply to the rather blankly and grimly Colonial houses, fadedly drab at their richest and mainly, as the legend ran, appurtenant to that Quaker race whom Massachusetts and Connecticut had prehistorically cast forth and the great Roger Williams had handsomely welcomed, or to the other habitations, the felicitous cottages, with their galleries on the Bay and toward the sunset, their pleasure-boats at their little wharves, and the supposition, that clung to them, of their harbouring the less fashionable of the outer Great, but also the more cultivated and the more artistic. Everything was there still, as I say, and quite as much as anything the prolonged echo of that ingenuous old-time distinction. It was a marvel, no doubt, that the handful of light elements I have named should add up to any total deserving the name of *picture*, and if I must produce an explanation I seek it with a certain confidence in the sense of the secret enjoyed by that air for bathing or, as one figures, for dipping, the objects it deals with. It takes them uninteresting, but feels immediately what submersion can do for them; tips them in, keeps them down, holds them under, just for

the proper length of time : after which they come up, as
I say, irradiating vague silver—the reflection of which
I have perhaps here been trying to catch even to
extravagance.

I did nothing, at any rate, all an autumn morning, but
discover again how " good " everything had been—
positively better than one had ventured to suppose in
one's care to make the allowance for one's young simplicity. Some things indeed, clearly, had been better
than one knew, and now seemed to surpass any fair
probability : else why, for instance, should I have been
quite awestruck by the ancient State House that over-
looks the ancient Parade ?—an edifice ample, majestic,
archaic, of the finest proportions and full of a certain
public Dutch dignity, having brave, broad, high
windows, in especial, the distinctness of whose innumerable square white-framed panes is the recall of
some street view of Haarlem or Leyden. Here was the
charming impression of a treasure of antiquity to the
vague image of which, through the years, one hadn't
done justice—any more than one had done it, positively,
to three or four of the other old-time ornaments of the
Parade (which, with its wide, cobbly, sleepy space, of
those years, in the shadow of the State House, must
have been much more of a Van der Heyden, or somebody of that sort, than one could have dreamed). There
was a treasure of modernity to reckon with, in the form
of one of the Commodores Perry (they are somehow
much multiplied at Newport, and quite monumentally
ubiquitous) engaged in his great naval act ; but this was
swept away in the general flood of justice to be done. I
continued to do it all over the place, and I remember
doing it next at a certain ample old-time house which
used to unite with the still prettier and archaic Vernon,
near it, to form an honourable pair. In this mild town-
corner, where it was so indicated that the grass should be

growing between the primitive paving-stones, and where indeed I honestly think it mainly is, amid whatever remains of them, ancient peace had appeared formerly to reign—though attended by the ghost of ancient war, inasmuch as these had indubitably been the haunts of our auxiliary French officers during the Revolution, and no self-respecting legend could fail to report that it was in the Vernon house Washington would have visited Rochambeau. There had hung about this structure, which is, architecturally speaking, all "rusticated" and indefinable decency, the implication of an inward charm that refined even on its outward, and this was the tantalizing message its clean, serious windows, never yet debased, struck me as still giving. But it was still (something told me) a question of not putting, anywhere, too many presumptions to the touch; so that my hand quitted the knocker when I was on the point of a tentative tap, and I fell back on the neighbour and mate, as to which there was unforgotten acquaintance to teach me certainty. Here, alas, cold change was installed; the place had become a public office—none of the "artistic" super-civilized, no *raffiné* of them all, among the passing fanciers or collectors, having, strangely enough, marked it for his own. This mental appropriation it is, or it was a few months ago, really impossible not to make, at sight of its delightful hall and almost "grand" staircase, its charming recessed, cupboarded, window-seated parlours, its general panelled amplitude and dignity: the due taster of such things putting himself straight into possession on the spot, and, though wondering at the indifference and neglect, breathing thanks for the absence of positive ravage. For me there were special ghosts on the staircase, known voices in the brown old rooms—presences that one would have liked, however, to call a little to account. " People don't do those things"; people didn't let so clear a case — clear for sound curiosity—go like that; they didn't, somehow, even if they were only ghosts. But I thought too, as I turned away, of all the others of the foolish, or at least of the responsible, those who for so long have swarmed in the modern quarter and who make profession of the finer sense.

This impression had been disturbing, but it had served its purpose in reconstituting, with a touch, a link—in laying down again every inch of the train of association with the human, the social, personal Newport of what I may call the middle years. To go further afield, to measure the length of the little old Avenue and tread again the little old cliff-walk, to hang over, from above, the little old white crescent of the principal bathing-sands, with the big pond, behind them, set in its stone-walled featureless fields; to do these things and many others, every one of them thus accompanied by the admission that all that *had* been had been little, was to feel dead and buried generations push off even the trans-parence of their shroud and get into motion for the peopling of a scene that a present posterity has outgrown. The company of the middle years, the so considerably prolonged formative, tentative, imaginative Newport time, hadn't outgrown it—this catastrophe was still to come, as it constitutes, precisely, the striking dramatic *dénouement* I have already referred to. American society—so far as that free mixture was to have arrived at cohesion—had for half a century taken its whole relation with the place seriously (which was by intention very gaily); it long remained, for its happiness, quite at one with this most favoured resort of its comparative innocence. In the attesting presence of all the constant elements, of natural conditions that have, after all, persisted more than changed, a hundred far-away passages of the extinct life and joy, and of the comparative innocence, came back to me with an inevitable grace. A glamour as of the flushed ends of beautiful old summers, making a quite rich medium, a red sunset haze, as it were, for a processional throng of charioteers and riders, fortunate folk, fortunate above all in their untouched good faith, adjourning from the pleasures of the day to those of the evening—this benignity in particular overspread the picture, hanging it there as the Newport aspect that most lived again. Those good people all could make discoveries within the frame itself—beginning of course to push it out, in all directions, so as sufficiently to enlarge it, as they fondly fancied, even for the experience of a sophisticated world. They danced and they drove and they rode, they dined and wined and dressed and flirted and yachted and polo'd and Casino'd, responding to the subtlest inventions of their age; on the old lawns and verandahs I saw them gather, on the old shining sands I saw them gallop, past the low headlands I saw their white sails verily flash, and through the dusky old shrubberies came the light and sound of their feasts.

It had all been in truth a history—for the imagination that could take it so; and when once that kindly stage was offered them it was a wonder how many figures and faces, how many names and voices, images and embodiments of youth mainly, and often of Beauty, and of felicity and fortune almost always, or of what then passed for such, pushed, under my eyes, in blurred gaiety, to the front. Hadn't it been above all, in its good faith, the Age of Beauties—the blessed age when it was so easy to *be*, "on the Avenue," a Beauty, and when it was so easy, not less, not to doubt of the unsurpassability of such as appeared there? It was through the fact that the whole scheme and opportunity satisfied them, the fact that the place was, as I say, good enough for them—it was through this that, with ingenuities and audacities and refinements of their own (some of the more primitive of which are still touching to think of) they extended the boundaries of civilization, and fairly taught themselves to believe they were doing it in the interest of nature.   Beautiful the time when the Ocean Drive had been hailed at once as a triumph of civilization and as a proof of the possible appeal of Scenery even to the dissipated.   It was spoken of as of almost boundless extent—as one of the wonders of the world ; as indeed it does turn often, in the gloaming, to purple and gold, and as the small sea-coves then gleam on its edge like barbaric gems on a mantle.   Yet if it was a question of waving the wand and of breathing again, till it stirred, on the quaintness of the old manners —I refer to those of the fifties, sixties, seventies, and don't exclude those of the eighties—it was most touching of all to go back to dimmest days, days, such as now appear antediluvian, when ocean-drives, engineered by landscape artists and literally macadamized all the way, were still in the lap of time ; when there was only an afternoon for the Fort, and another for the Beach, and another for the " Boat-house "—inconceivable innocence ! —and even the shortness of the Avenue seemed very long, and even its narrowness very wide, and even its shabbiness very promising for the future, and when, in fine, chariots and cavaliers took their course, across country, to Bateman's, by inelegant precarious tracts and returned, through the darkling void, with a sense of adventure and fatigue.   That, I can't but think, was the *pure* Newport time, the most perfectly guarded by a sense of margin and of mystery.

It was the time of settled possession, and yet furthest removed from these blank days in which margin has been consumed and the palaces, on the sites but the other day beyond price, stare silently seaward, monuments

to the *blasé* state of their absent proprietors. Purer
still, however, I remind myself, was that stretch of
years which I have reasons for thinking sacred, when
the custom of seeking hibernation on the spot partly
prevailed, when the local winter inherited something of
the best social grace (as it liked at least to think) of the
splendid summer, and when the strange sight might be
seen of a considerable company of Americans, not
gathered at a mere rest-cure, who confessed brazenly
to not being in business. Do I grossly exaggerate in
saying that this company, candidly, quite excitedly self-
conscious, as all companies not commercial, in America,
may be pleasantly noted as being, formed, for the time
of its persistence, an almost unprecedented small body—
unprecedented in American conditions ; a collection of
the detached, the slightly disenchanted and casually
disqualified, and yet of the resigned and contented, of
the socially orthodox : a handful of mild, oh delightfully
mild, cosmopolites, united by three common circumstances, that of their having for the most part more or
less lived in Europe, that of their sacrificing openly to
the ivory idol whose name is leisure, and that, not least,
of a formed critical habit. These things had been felt
as making them excrescences on the American surface,
where nobody ever criticized, especially after the grand
tour, and where the great black ebony god of business
was the only one recognized. So I see them, at all
events, in fond memory, lasting as long as they could
and finding no successors ; and they are most embalmed
for me, I confess, in that scented, somewhat tattered, but
faintly spiced, wrapper of their various " European "
antecedents. I see them move about in the light of
these, and I understand how it was this that made them
ask what would have become of them, and where in the
world, the hard American world, they *could* have hiber-

nated, how they could even, in the Season, have bowed their economic heads and lurked, if it hadn't been for Newport. I think of that question as, in their reduced establishments, over their winter whist, under their private theatricals, and pending, constantly, their loan and their return of the *Revue des Deux Mondes*, their main conversational note. I find myself in fact tenderly evoking them as special instances of the great—or perhaps I have a right only to say of the small—American complication; the state of one's having been so pierced, betimes, by the sharp outland dart as to be able ever afterwards but to move about, vaguely and helplessly, with the shaft still in one's side.

Their nostalgia, however exquisite, was, I none the less gather, sterile, for they appear to have left no seed. They must have died, some of them, in order to " go back "—to go back, that is, to Paris. If I make, at all events, too much of them, it is for their propriety as a delicate subjective value matching with the intrinsic Newport delicacy. They must have felt that they, obviously, notably, notoriously, did match—the proof of which was in the fact that to them alone, of the customary thousands, was the beauty of the good walk, over the lovely little land, revealed. The customary thousands here, as throughout the United States, never set foot to earth—yet this had happened so, of old, to be the particular corner of *their* earth that made that adventure most possible. At Newport, as the phrase was, in autumnal, in vernal hibernation, you *could* walk —failing which, in fact, you failed of impressions the most consolatory ; and it is mainly to the far ends of the low, densely shrubbed and perfectly finished little headlands that I see our friends ramble as if to stretch fond arms across the sea. There used to be distant places beyond Bateman's, or better still on the opposite isle of Conanicut, now blighted with ugly uses, where nursing a nostalgia on the sun-warmed rocks was almost as good as having none at all. So it was not only not our friends who had overloaded and overcrowded, but it was they at last, I infer, who gave way before that grossness. How should they have wished to leave seed only to be trampled by the white elephants?

The white elephants, as one may best call them, all cry and no wool, all house and no garden, make now, for three or four miles, a barely interrupted chain, and I dare say I think of them best, and of the distressful, inevitable waste they represent, as I recall the impression of a divine little drive, roundabout them and pretty well everywhere, taken, for renewal of acquaintance, while November was still mild. I sought another renewal, as I have intimated, in the vacant splendour of June, but the interesting evidence then only refined on that already gathered. The place itself, as man—and often, no doubt, alas, as woman, with her love of the immediate and contiguous—had taken it over, was more than ever, to the fancy, like some dim, simplified ghost of a small Greek island, where the clear walls of some pillared portico or pavilion, perched afar, looked like those of temples of the gods, and where Nature, deprived of that ease in merely massing herself on which "American scenery," as we lump it together, is too apt to depend for its effect, might have shown a piping shepherd on any hillside or attached a mythic image to any point of rocks. What an idea, originally, to have seen this miniature spot of earth, where the sea-nymphs on the curved sands, at the worst, might have chanted back to the shepherds, as a mere breeding-ground for white elephants! They look queer and conscious and lumpish—some of them, as with an air of the brandished proboscis, really grotesque—while their averted owners, roused from a witless dream, wonder what in the world is to be done with them. The answer to which, I think, can only be that there is absolutely nothing to be done; nothing but to let them stand there always, vast and blank, for reminder to those concerned of the prohibited degrees of witlessness, and of the peculiarly awkward vengeances of affronted proportion and discretion.

7

Boston

It sometimes uncomfortably happens for a writer, consulting his remembrance, that he remembers too much and finds himself knowing his subject too well; which is but the case of the bottle too full for the wine to start. There has to be room for the air to circulate between one's impressions, between the parts of one's knowledge, since it is the air, or call it the intervals on the sea of one's ignorance, of one's indifference, that sets these floating fragments into motion. This is more or less what I feel in presence of the invitation—even the invitation written on the very face of the place itself, of its actual aspects and appearances—to register my "impression" of Boston. Can one *have*, in the conditions, an impression of Boston, any that has not been for long years as inappreciable as a "sunk" picture?— that dead state of surface which requires a fresh application of varnish. The situation I speak of is the consciousness of "old" knowledge, knowledge so compacted by the years as to be unable, like the bottled wine, to flow. The answer to such questions as these, no doubt, however, is the practical one of trying a shake of the bottle or a brushful of the varnish. My "sunk" sense of Boston found itself vigorously varnished by mere renewal of vision at the end of long years; though I confess that under this favouring influence I ask myself why I should have had, after all, the notion of overlaid deposits of experience. The experience had anciently been small—so far as smallness may be imputed to any of our prime initiations; yet it had left consequences out of proportion to its limited seeming self. Early contacts had been brief and few, and the slight bridge had long ago collapsed; wherefore the impressed condition that acquired again, on the spot, an intensity, struck me as but half explained by the inordinate power of assimilation of the imaginative young. I should have had none the less to content myself with this evidence of the magic of past sensibilities had not the question suddenly been lighted for me as by a sudden flicker of the torch—and for my special benefit—carried in the hand of history. This light, waving for an instant over the scene, gave me the measure of my relation to it, both as to immense little extent and to quite subjective character.

I

It was in strictness only a matter of noting the harshness of change—since I scarce know what else to call it —on the part of the approaches to a particular spot I had wished to revisit. I made out, after a little, the entrance to Ashburton Place; but I missed on that spacious summit of Beacon Hill more than I can say the pleasant little complexity of the other time, marked with its share of the famous old-world "crookedness" of Boston, that element of the mildly tortuous which did duty, for the story-seeker, as an ancient and romantic note, and was half envied, half derided by the merely rectangular criticism. Didn't one remember the day when New Yorkers, when Philadelphians, when pilgrims from the West, sated with their eternal equidistances, with the quadrilateral scheme of life, "raved" about Cornhill and appeared to find in the rear of the State House a recall of one of the topographical, the architectural jumbles of Europe or Asia? And did not indeed the small happy accidents of the disappearing Boston exhale in a comparatively sensible manner the warm breath of history, the history of something as against the history of nothing? —so that, being gone, or generally going, they enabled one at last to feel and almost to talk about them as one had found one's self feeling and talking about the sacrificed relics of old Paris and old London. In this immediate neighbourhood of the enlarged State House, where a great raw clearance has been made, memory met that pang of loss, knew itself sufficiently bereft to see the vanished objects, a scant but adequate cluster of "nooks," of such odds and ends as parochial schemes of improvement sweep away, positively overgrown, within one's own spirit, by a wealth of legend. There was at least the gain, at any rate, that one was now going to be free to picture them, to embroider them, at one's ease— to tangle them up in retrospect and make the real romantic claim for them. This accordingly is what I am doing, but I am doing it in particular for the sacrificed end of Ashburton Place, the Ashburton Place that I anciently knew. This eminently respectable by-way, on my return to question it, opened its short vista for me honestly enough, though looking rather exposed and undermined, since the mouth of the passage to the west, formerly measured and narrow, had begun to yawn into space, a space peopled in fact, for the eye of appreciation, with the horrific glazed perpendiculars of the future. But the pair of ancient houses I was in quest of kept their tryst; a pleasant individual pair, mated with nothing else in the street, yet looking at that hour as if their old still faces had lengthened, their shuttered, lidded eyes had closed, their brick complexions had paled, above the good granite basements, to a fainter red—all as with the cold consciousness of a possible doom.

That possibility, on the spot, was not present to me, occupied as I was with reading into one of them a short page of history that I had my own reasons for finding of supreme interest, the history of two years of far-away youth spent there at a period—the closing-time of the War—full both of public and of intimate vibrations. The two years had been those of a young man's, a very young man's earliest fond confidence in a "literary career," and the effort of actual attention was to recover on the spot some echo of ghostly footsteps—the sound as of taps on the window-pane heard in the dim dawn. The place itself was meanwhile, at all events, a conscious memento, with old secrets to keep and old stories to witness for, a saturation of life as closed together and preserved in it as the scent lingering in a folded pocket-handkerchief. But when, a month later, I returned again (a justly-rebuked mistake) to see if another whiff of the fragrance were not to be caught, I found but a gaping void, the brutal effacement, at a stroke, of every related object, of the whole precious past. Both the houses had been levelled and the space to the corner cleared ; hammer and pickaxe had evidently begun to swing on the very morrow of my previous visit—which had moreover been precisely the imminent doom announced, without my understanding it, in the poor scared faces. I had been present, by the oddest hazard, at the very last moments of the victim in whom I was most interested ; the act of obliteration had been breathlessly swift, and if I had often seen how fast history could be made I had doubtless never so felt that it could be unmade still faster. It was as if the bottom had fallen out of one's own biography, and one plunged backward into space without meeting anything. That, however, seemed just to give me, as I have hinted, the whole figure of my connection with everything about, a connection that had been sharp, in spite of brevity, and then had broken short off. Thus it was the sense of the rupture, more than of anything else, that I was, and for a still much briefer time, to carry with me. It seemed to leave me with my early impression of the place on my hands, inapt, as might be, for use; so that I could only try, rather vainly, to fit it to present conditions, among which it tended to shrink and stray.

It was on two or three such loitering occasions, wondering and invoking pauses that had, a little vaguely and helplessly perhaps, the changed crest of Beacon Hill for their field—it was at certain of these moments of charged, yet rather chilled, contemplation that I felt my small cluster of early associations shrivel to a scarce discernible point. I recall a Sunday afternoon in particular when I hung about on the now vaster platform of the State House for a near view of the military monuments erected there, the statues of Generals Hooker and Devens, and for the charm at once and the pang of feeling the whole backward vista, with all its features, fall from that eminence into grey perspective. The top of Beacon Hill quite rakes, with a but slightly shifting range, the old more definite Boston; for there seemed no item, nor any number, of that remarkable sum that it would not anciently have helped one to distinguish or divine. There all these things essentially were at the moment I speak of, but only again as something ghostly and dim, something overlaid and smothered by the mere modern thickness. I lingered half-an-hour, much of the new disposition of the elements here involved being duly impressive, and the old uplifted front of the State House, surely, in its spare and austere, its ruled and pencilled kind, a thing of beauty, more delightful and harmonious even than I had remembered it; one of the inestimable values again, in the eye of the town, for taste and temperance, as the perfectly felicitous "Park Street" Church hard by, was another. The irresistible spell, however, I think, was something sharper yet—the coercion, positively, of feeling one's case, the case of one's deeper discomfiture, completely made out. The day itself, toward the winter's end, was all benignant, like the immense majority of the days of the American year, and there went forward across the top of the hill a continuous passage of men and women, in couples and talkative companies, who struck me as labouring wage-earners, of the simpler sort, arrayed, very comfortably, in their Sunday best and decently enjoying their leisure. They came up as from over the Common, they passed or they paused, exchanging remarks on the beauty of the scene, but rapidly presenting themselves to me as of more interest, for the moment, than anything it contained.

For no sound of English, in a single instance, escaped their lips; the greater number spoke a rude form of Italian, the others some outland dialect unknown to me— though I waited and waited to catch an echo of antique refrains. No note of any shade of American speech struck my ear, save in so far as the sounds in question represent to-day so much of the substance of that idiom The types and faces bore them out; the people before me were gross aliens to a man, and they were in serene and triumphant possession. Nothing, as I say, could have been more effective for figuring the hitherward bars of a grating through which I might make out, far-off in space, "my" small homogeneous Boston of the more interesting time. It was not of course that our gross little aliens were immediate "social" figures in the narrower sense of the term, or that any personal commerce of which there might be question could colour itself, to its detriment, from their presence; but simply that they expressed, as everywhere and always, the great cost at which every place on my list had become braver and louder, and that they gave the measure of the distance by which the general movement was *away*—away, always and everywhere, from the old presumptions and conceivabilities. Boston, the bigger, braver, louder Boston, was "away," and it was quite, at that hour, as if each figure in my procession were there on purpose to leave me no doubt of it.   Therefore had I the vision, as filling the sky, no longer of the great Puritan "whip," the whip for the conscience and the nerves, of the local legend, but that of a huge applied sponge, a sponge saturated with the foreign mixture and passed over almost everything I remembered and might still have recovered.   The detail of this obliteration would take me too far, but I had even then (on a previous day as well as only half-an-hour before) caught at something that might stand for a vivid symbol of the general effect of it.   To come up from School Street into Beacon was to approach the Athenæum —exquisite institution, to fond memory, joy of the aspiring prime; yet to approach the Athenæum only to find all disposition to enter it drop as dead as if from quick poison, what did *that* denote but the dreadful chill of change, and of the change in especial that was most completely dreadful?   For had not this honoured haunt of all the most civilized—library, gallery, temple of culture, the place that was to Boston at large as Boston at large was to the rest of New England—had it not with peculiar intensity had a "value," the most charming of its kind, no doubt, in all the huge country, and had not this value now, evidently, been brought so low that one shrank, in delicacy, from putting it to the test?

It was a case of the detestable "tall building" again, and of its instant destruction of quality in everything it overtowers.   Put completely out of countenance by the mere masses of brute ugliness beside it, the temple of culture looked only rueful and snubbed, hopelessly down in the world; so that, far from being moved to hover or to penetrate, one's instinct was to pass by on the other side, averting one's head from an humiliation one could do nothing to make less.   And this indeed though one would have liked to do something; the brute masses, above the comparatively small refined façade (one saw how happy one had always thought it) having for the inner ear the voice of a pair of school-bullies who hustle and pummel some studious little boy. "'Exquisite' was what they called you, eh? We'll teach you, then, little sneak, to be exquisite! We allow none of that rot round here." It was heart-breaking, this presentation of a Boston practically void of an Athenæum; though perhaps not without interest as showing how much one's own sense of the small city of the earlier time had been dependent on that institution. I found it of no use, at any rate, to think, for a compensatory sign of the new order, of the present Public Library; the present Public Library, however remarkable in its pomp and circumstance, and of which I had at that hour received my severe impression, being neither exquisite nor on the way to become so—a difficult, an impassable way, no doubt, for Public Libraries. Nor did I cast about, in fact, very earnestly, for consolation—so much more was I held by the vision of the closed order which shaped itself, continually, in the light of the differing present; an order gaining an interest for this backward view precisely as one felt that all the parts and tokens of it, while it lasted, had hung intimately together. Missing those parts and tokens, or as many of them as one could, became thus a constant slightly painful joy: it made them fall so into their place as items of the old character, or proofs, positively, as one might say, of the old distinction. It was impossible not to see Park Street itself, for instance—while I kept looking at the matter from my more "swagger" hilltop as violently vulgarized; and it was incontestable that, whatever might be said, there had anciently not been, on the whole continent, taking everything together, an equal animated space more exempt from vulgarity. There had probably been comparable spaces—impressions, in New York, in Philadelphia, in Baltimore, almost as good ; but only almost, by reason of their lacking (which was just the point) the indefinable perfection of Park Street.

It seems odd to have to borrow from the French the right word in this association—or would seem so, rather, had it been less often indicated that that people have better names than ours even for the qualities we are apt to suppose ourselves more in possession of than they. Park Street, in any case, had been magnificently *honnête* —the very type and model, for a pleasant street-view, of the character. The aspects that might elsewhere have competed were *honnêtes* and weak, whereas Park Street was *honnête* and strong—strong as founded on *all* the moral, material, social solidities, instead of on some of them only ; which made again all the difference. Personal names, as notes of that large emanation, need scarcely be invoked—they might even have a weakening effect ; the force of the statement was in its collective, cumulative look, as if each member of the row, from the church at the Tremont Street angle to the amplest, squarest, most purple presence at the Beacon Street corner (where it always had a little the air of a sturdy proprietor with back to the fire, legs apart and thumbs in the armholes of an expanse of high-coloured plush waist-coat), was but a syllable in the word Respectable several times repeated. One had somehow never heard it uttered with so convincing an emphasis. But the shops, up and down, are making all this as if it had never been, pleasant "premises" as they have themselves acquired ; and it was to strike me from city to city, I fear, that the American shop in general pleads but meagrely—whether on its outer face or by any more intimate art—for indulgence to its tendency to swarm, to bristle, to vociferate. The shop-front, observed at random, pro-duced on me from the first, and almost everywhere alike, a singular, a sinister impression, which left me uneasy till I had found a name for it : the sense of an economic law of which one had not for years known the unholy rigour, the vision of "protected" production and of commodities requiring certainly, in many cases, every advantage Protection could give them.   They looked to me always, these exhibitions, consciously and defiantly protected—insolently safe, able to be with impunity anything they would ; and when once that lurid light had settled on them I could see them, I confess, in none other ; so that the objects composing them fell, throughout, into a vicious and villainous category—quite as if audibly saying : " Oh come ; don't look among us for what you won't, for what you shan't find, the best quality attainable ; but only for that quite other matter, the best value we allow you.   You must take us or go without, and if you feel your nose thus held to the grindstone by the hard fiscal hand, it's no more than you deserve for harbouring treasonable thoughts."

So it was, therefore, that while the imagination and the memory strayed—strayed away to other fiscal climates, where the fruits of competition so engagingly ripen and flush—the streets affected one at moments as a prolonged show-case for every arrayed vessel of humiliation.   The fact that several classes of the protected products appeared to consist of articles that one might really anywhere have preferred did little, oddly enough, to diminish the sense of severe discipline awaiting the restored absentee on contact with these occasions of traffic. The discipline indeed is general, proceeding as it does from so many sources, but it earns its name, in particular, from the predicament of the ingenuous inquirer who asks himself if he can "really bear" the combination of such general manners and such general prices, of such general prices and such general manners.   He has a helpless bewildered moment during which he wonders if he mightn't bear the prices a little better if he were a little better addressed, or bear the usual form of address a little better if the prices were in themselves, given the commodity offered, a little less humiliating to the purchaser. Neither of these elements of his dilemma strikes him as likely to abate—the general cost of the things to drop, or the general grimness of the person he deals with over the counter to soften ; so that he reaches out again for balm to where he has had to seek it under other wounds, falls back on the cultivation of patience and regret, on large international comparison. He is confronted too often, to his sense, with the question of what may be " borne " ; but what does he see about him if not a vast social order in which the parties to certain relations are all the while marvellously, inscrutably, desperately "bearing" each other ? He may wonder, at his hours, how, under the strain, social cohesion does not altogether give way ; but that is another question, which belongs to a different plane of speculation. For he asks himself quite as much as anything else how the shopman or the shoplady can bear to be barked at in the manner he constantly hears used to them by customers —he recognizes that no agreeable form of intercourse *could* survive a day in such air : so that what is the only relation finding ground there but a necessary vicious circle of gross mutual endurance ?

These reflections connect themselves moreover with that most general of his restless hauntings in the United States—not only with the lapse of all wonderment at the immense number of absentees unrestored and making their lives as they may in other countries, but with the preliminary American postulate or basis for any successful accommodation of life. This basis is that of active pecuniary gain and of active pecuniary gain only—that of one's making the conditions so triumphantly pay that the prices, the manners, the other inconveniences, take their place as a friction it is comparatively easy to salve, wounds directly treatable with the wash of gold. What prevails, what sets the tune, is the American scale of gain, more magnificent than any other, and the fact that the whole assumption, the whole theory of life, is that of the individual's participation in it, that of his being more or less punctually and more or less effectually " squared." To make so much money that you won't, that you don't " mind," don't mind anything—that is absolutely, I think, the main American formula. Thus your making no money—or so little that it passes there for none—and being thereby distinctly reduced to minding, amounts to your being reduced to the knowledge that America is no place for you. To mind as one minds, for instance, in Europe, under provocation or occasion offered, and yet to have to live under the effect of American pressure, is speedily to perceive that the knot can be untied but by a definite pull of one or the other string. The immense majority of people pull, luckily for the existing order, the string that consecrates their connection with it; the minority (small, however, only in comparison) pull the string that loosens that connection. The existing order is meanwhile safe, inasmuch as the faculty of making money is in America the commonest of all and fairly runs the streets : so simple a matter does it appear there, among vast populations, to make betimes enough *not* to mind. Yet the withdrawal of the considerable group of the pecuniarily disqualified seems no less, for the present, an assured movement ; there will always be scattered individuals condemned to mind on a scale beyond any scale of making. The relation of this modest body to the country of their birth, which asks so much, on the whole—so many surrenders and compromises, and the possession above all of such a prodigious head for figures—before it begins, in its wonderful way, to give or to " pay," would appear to us supremely touching, I think, as a case of communion baffled and blighted, if we had time to work it out. It would bathe in something of a tragic light the vivid truth that the "great countries" are all, more and more, happy lands (so far as any can be called such) for any, for every sort of person rather than the middle sort. The upper sort—in the scale of wealth, the only scale now—can to their hearts' content build their own castles and move by their own motors; the lower sort, masters of gain in *their* degree, can profit, also to their hearts' content, by the enormous extension of those material facilities which may be gregariously enjoyed; they are able to rush about, as never under the sun before, in promiscuous packs and hustled herds, while to the act of so rushing about all felicity and prosperity appear for them to have been comfortably reduced. The frustrated American, as I have hinted at him, scraping for *his* poor practical solution in the depleted silver-mine of history, is the American who "makes" too little for the castle and yet "minds" too much for the hustled herd, who can neither achieve such detachment nor surrender to such society, and who most of all accordingly, in the native order, fails of a working basis. The salve, the pecuniary salve, in Europe, is sensibly less, but less on the other hand also the excoriation that makes it necessary, whether from above or below.

II

Let me at all events say for the Park Street Church, while I may still, on my hilltop, keep more or less in line with it, that this edifice persistently "holds the note," as yet, the note of the old felicity, and remains by so doing a precious public servant. Strange enough, doubtless, to find one's self pleading sanctity for a theological structure sanctified only by such a name—as who should say the Park Street Hotel or the Park Street Post-office; so much clearer would the claim seem to come were it the case of another St. Clement Danes or of another St. Mary-le-Strand. But in America we get our sanctity as we can, and we plead it, if we are wise, wherever the conditions suffer the faintest show of colour for it to flush through. Again and again it is a question, on behalf of the memorial object (and especially when preservation is at stake), of an interest and an appeal proceeding exactly *from* the conditions, and thereby not of an absolute, but of a relative force and weight; which is exactly the state of the matter with the Park Street Church. This happy landmark is, in strictness, with its mild recall, by its spire, of Wren's bold London examples, the comparatively thin echo of a far-away song—playing its part, however, for harmonious effect, as perfectly as possible. It is admirably placed, quite peculiarly *present*, on the Boston scene, and thus, for one reason and another, points its moral as not even the State House does. So we see afresh, under its admonition, that charm is a flower of wild and windblown seed—often not to be counted on when most anxiously planted, but taking its own time and its own place both for enriching and for mocking us. It mocks assuredly, above all, our money and our impatience, elements addressed to buying or "ordering" it, and only asks that when it does come we shall know it and love it. When we fail of this intelligence it simply, for its vengeance, boycotts us— makes us vulgar folk who have no concern with it. Then if we ever miss it we can never get it back— though our deepest depth of punishment of course is to go on fatuously not missing it, the joy of ourselves and of each other and the derision of those who know. These reflections were virtually suggested to me, on the eve of my leaving Boston, by ten words addressed to my dismay; the effect of which was to make Park Street

Church, for the hour, the most interesting mass of brick and mortar and (if I may risk the supposition) timber in America.

The words had been spoken, in the bright July air, by a friend encountered in the very presence of the mild monument, on the freshly-perceived value of which, for its position, for its civil function, I had happened irrepressibly to exclaim. Thus I learned that its existence might be spoken of as gravely menaced—menaced by a scheme for the erection of a "business block," a huge square of innumerable tiers and floors, thousands of places of trade, the trade that in such a position couldn't fail to be roaring. In the eye of financial envy the church was but a cumberer of the ground, and where, about us, had we seen financial envy fail when it had once really applied the push of its fat shoulder? Drunk as it was with power, what was to be thought of as resisting it? This was a question, truly, to frighten answers away—until I presently felt the most pertinent of all return as if on tiptoe. The perfect force of the case *as* a case, as an example, that was the answer of answers; the quite ideal pitch of the opportunity for virtue. Ideal opportunities are rare, and this occasion for not sacrificing the high ornament and cynosure of the town to the impudence of private greed just happens to be one, and to have the finest marks of the character. One had but to imagine a civilized community reading these marks, feeling that character, and then consciously and cynically falling below its admirable chance, to take in the impossibility of any such blot on the page of honour, any such keen appetite for the base alternative. It would be verily the end—the end of the old distinguished life, of the common intelligence that had flowered formerly, for attesting fame, from so strong a sap and into so thick and rich a cluster. One had thought of these things as one came and went—so interesting to-day in Boston are such informal consultations of the oracle (that of the very air and "tone"), such puttings to it of the question of what the old New England spirit may have still, intellectually, æsthetically, or for that matter even morally, to give; of what may yet remain, for productive scraping, of the formula of the native Puritanism educated, the formula once capacious enough for the "literary constellation" of the Age of Emerson. Is that cornucopia empty, or does some handful of strong or at least sound fruit lurk to this day, a trifle congested by keeping, up in the point of the horn? What, if so, are, in the ambient air, the symptoms of this possibility? what are the signs of intellectual promise, poetic, prosaic, philosophic, in the current generations, those actually learning their principal lesson, as one assumes, from the great University hard by? The old formula, that of Puritanism educated, has it, in fine, except for "business," anything more to communicate?—or do we perhaps mistake the case in still speaking, by reason of the projected shadow of Harvard, of "education" as at all involved?

Oh, for business, for a commercial, an organizing energy of the first order, the indications would seem to abound; the air being full of them as of one loud voice, and nowhere so full perhaps as at that Park Street corner, precisely, where it was to be suggested to me that their meaning was capable on occasion of turning to the sinister. The commercial energy at least was educated, up to the eyes—Harvard was still caring for that more than for anything else—but the wonderments, or perhaps rather the positive impressions I have glanced at, bore me constant company, keeping the last word, all emphasis of answer, back as if for the creation of a dramatic suspense. I liked the suspense, none the less, for what it had in common with "intellectual curiosity," and it gave me a light, moreover, which was highly convenient, helping me to look at everything in some related state to this proposition of the value of the Puritan residuum—the question of whether value *is* expressed, for instance, by the little tales, mostly by ladies, and about and for children romping through the ruins of the Language, in the monthly magazines. Some of my perceptions of relation might seem forced, for other minds, but it sufficed me that they were straight and clear for myself—straight and clear again, for example, when (always on my hilltop and raking the prospect over for memories) I quite assented to the tacit intimation that a long æsthetic period had closed with the disappearance of the old Museum Theatre. This had been the threatre of the "great" period—so far as such a description may fit an establishment that never produced during that term a play either by a Bostonian or by any other American; or it had at least, with however unequal steps, kept the great period company, made the Boston of those years quite complacently participate in its genial continuity. This character of its *being* an institution, its really being a theatre, with a repertory and a family of congruous players, not one of them the baleful actor-manager, head and front of all the so rank and so acclaimed vulgarities of our own day—this nature in it of not being the mere empty shell, the indifferent cave of the winds, that yields a few nights' lodging, under stress, to the passing caravan, gave it a dignity of which I seemed to see the ancient city gratefully conscious, fond and jealous, and the thought of which invites me to fling over it now perhaps too free a fold of the mantle of romance. And yet why too free ? is what I ask myself as I remember that the Museum had for long years a repertory—the repertory of its age—a company and a cohesion, theatrical trifles of the cultivation of which no present temple of the drama from end to end of the country appears to show a symptom. Therefore I spare a sigh to its memory, and, though I doubtless scarce think of it as the haunt of Emerson, of Hawthorne or of Mr. Ticknor, the common conscience of the mid-century in the New England capital insists on showing, at this distance of time, as the richer for it.

That then was one of the missed elements, but the consequent melancholy, I ought promptly to add, formed the most appropriate soil for stray sprouts of tenderness in respect to the few aspects that had not suffered. The old charm of Mount Vernon Street, for instance, wandering up the hill, almost from the waterside, to the rear of the State House, and fairly hanging about there to rest like some good flushed lady, of more than middle age, a little spent and "blown"—this ancient grace was not only still to be felt, but was charged, for depth of interest, with intenser ghostly presences, the rich growth of time, which might have made the ample slope, as one mounted, appear as beautifully peopled as Jacob's Ladder. That was exactly the kind of impression to be desired and welcomed; since ghosts belong only to places and suffer and perish with them. It was as if they themselves moreover were taking pleasure in this place, fairly indeed commending to me the fine old style of the picture. Nothing less appeared to account for my not having, in the other age, done it, as the phrase is, full justice, recognized in it so excellent a peace, such a clear Boston bravery—all to the end that it should quite strike me, on the whole, as not only, for the minor stretch and the domestic note, the happiest street-scene the country could show, but as pleasant, on those respectable lines, in a degree not surpassed even among outland pomps. Oh, the wide benignity of brick, the goodly, friendly, ruddy fronts, the felicity of scale, the solid *seat* of everything, even to the handful of happy deviations from the regular produced, we may fancy, by one of those "historic" causes which so rarely complicate, for humanization, the blankness of the American street-page, and the occasional occurrence of which, in general, as I am perhaps too repeatedly noting, excites on the part of the starved story-seeker a fantastic insistence.   I find myself willing, after all, to let my whole estimate of these mere mild monuments of private worth pass for extravagant if it but leave me a perch for musing on the oddity of our nature which makes us still like the places we have known or loved to grow old, when we can scarcely bear it in the people.   To walk down Mount Vernon Street to Charles was to have a brush with that truth, to recognize at least that we like the sense of age to come, locally, when it comes with the right accompaniments, with the preservation of character and the continuity of tradition, merits I had been admiring on the brow of the eminence.   From the other vision, the sight of the "decline in the social scale," the lapse into shabbiness and into bad company, we only suffer, for the ghosts in that case either refuse to linger, or linger at the most with faces ashamed and as if appealing against their association.

Such was the condition of the Charles Street ghosts, it seemed to me—shades of a past that had once been so thick and warm and happy ; they moved, dimly, through a turbid medium in which the signs of their old life looked soiled and sordid.   Each of them was there indeed, from far, far back ; they met me on the pavement, yet it was as if we could pass but in conscious silence, and nothing could have helped us, for any courage of communion, if we had not enjoyed the one merciful refuge that remained, where indeed we could breathe again, and with intensity, our own liberal air. Here, behind the effaced anonymous door, was the little ark of the modern deluge, here still the long drawing-room that looks over the water and toward the sunset, with a seat for every visiting shade, from far-away Thackeray down, and relics and tokens so thick on its walls as to make it positively, in all the town, the votive temple to memory. Ah, if it hadn't been for *that* small patch of common ground, with its kept echo of the very accent of the past, the revisiting spirit, at the bottom of the hill, could but have muffled his head, or but have stifled his heart, and turned away for ever. Let me even say that—always now at the bottom of the hill—it was in this practical guise he afterwards, at the best, found himself roaming. It is from about that point southward that the new splendours of Boston spread, and will clearly continue to spread, but it opened out to me as a tract pompous and prosaic, with which the little interesting city, the city of character and genius, exempt as yet from the Irish yoke, had had absolutely nothing to do. This disconnection was complete, and the southward, the westward territory made up, at the most, a platform or stage from which the other, the concentrated Boston of history, the Boston of Emerson, Thoreau, Hawthorne, Longfellow, Lowell, Holmes, Ticknor, Motley, Prescott, Parkman and the rest (in the sense either of birthplace or of central or sacred city) could be seen in as definite, and indeed now in almost as picturesquely mediæval, a concretion, appear to make as black and minute and "composed" a little pyramidal image, as the finished background of a Dürer print. It seemed to place itself there, in the middle distance, on the sharp salience of its commingled Reforms and Reserves—reformers and reservists rubbing shoulders in the common distinctness of their detachment from an inexpressive generation, and the composition rounding itself about as with the very last of its loose ends snipped off or tucked in.

III

There are neither loose ends nor stray flutters, whether of the old prose or the old poetry, to be encountered on the large lower level, though there are performances of a different order, in the shadow of which such matters tend to look merely, and perhaps rather meagrely, subjective. It is all very rich and prosperous and monotonous, the large lower level, but oh, so inexpressibly vacant! Where the "new land" corresponds most to its name, rejoices most visibly and complacently in its newness, its dumped and shovelled foundations, the home till recently of a mere vague marine backwater, there the long, straight residential avenues, vistas quite documentary, as one finds one's self pronouncing them, testify with a perfection all their own to a whole vast side of American life. The winter winds and snows, and the eternal dust, run races in them over the clearest course anywhere provided for that grim competition; the league-long brick pavements mirror the expansive void, for many months of the year, in their smooth, tight ice-coats (and ice over brick can only be described as heels over head), and the innumerable windows, up and down, watch each other, all hopelessly, as for revelations, indiscretions, audible, resonant, rebellious or explosive breakages of the pane from within, that never disturb the peace. (No one will begin, and the buried hatchet, in spite of whatever wistful looks to where it lies, is never dug up.) So it is that these sustained affirmations of one of the smoothest and the most settled social states "going" excite perversely, on the part of the restless analyst, questions that would seem logically the very last involved. We call such aspects "documentary" because they strike us, more than any others, as speaking volumes for the possible *serenity*, the common decency, the quiet cohesion, of a vast commercial and professional bourgeoisie left to itself. Here was such an order caught in the very fact, the fact of its living maximum. A bourgeoisie without an aristocracy to worry it is of course a very different thing from a bourgeoisie struggling *in* that shade, and nothing could express more than these interminable perspectives of security the condition of a community leading its life in the social sun.

Why, accordingly, of December afternoons, did the restless analyst, pausing at eastward-looking corners, find on his lips the vague refrain of Tennyson's "long, unlovely street"? Why, if Harley Street, if Wimpole, is unlovely, should Marlborough Street, Boston, be so—beyond the mere platitude of its motiveless name? Here is no monotony of black leasehold brick, no patent disavowal, in the interest of stale and strictly subordinate gentilities, of expression, animation, variety, curiosity; here, on the contrary, is often the individual house-front in all its independence and sometimes in all its felicity: this whole region being, like so many such regions in the United States to-day, the home of the free hand, a field for the liveliest architectural experiment. There are interesting, admirable houses—though always too much of the detestable vitreous "bow"—and there is above all what there is everywhere in America for saving, or at least for propping up, the situation, that particular look of the clear course and large opportunity ahead, which, when taken in conjunction with all the will to live, all the money to spend, all the knowledge to acquire and apply, seems to marshal the material possibilities in glittering illimitable ranks. Beacon Street, moreover, used to stretch back like a workable telescope for the focussing, at its higher extremity, in an air of which the positive defect is to be too seldom prejudicial, of the gilded dome of the State House—fresh as a Christmas toy seen across the floor of a large salubrious nursery. This made a civic vignette that furnished a little the desert of cheerful family life. But Marlborough Street, for imperturbable reasons of its own, used periodically to break my heart. It was of no use to make a vow of hanging about till I should have sounded my mystery —learned to say *why* black, stale Harley Street, for instance, in featureless row after row, had character and depth, while what was before me fell upon my sense with the thinness of tone of a precocious child—and still more why this latter effect should have been, as it were, so insistently irritating. If there be strange ways of producing an interest, to the critical mind, there are doubtless still stranger ways of not producing one, and it was important to me, no doubt, to make " my " defunct and compact and expressive little Boston appear to don all the signs of that character that the New Land, and what is built thereon, miss. How could one consider the place at all unless in a light ?—so that one had to decide definitely on one's light.

This it was after all easy to do from the moment one had determined to concede to the New Land the fact of possession of everything convenient and handsome under heaven. Peace could always come with this recognition of all the accessories and equipments, a hundred costly things, parks and palaces and institutions, that the earlier community had lacked ; and there was an individual connection—only one, presently to be noted—in which the actual city might seem for an hour to have no capacity for the uplifting *idea*, no aptitude for the finer curiosity, to envy the past. But meanwhile it was strange that even so fine a conception, finely embodied, as the new Public Library, magnificently superseding all others, was committed to speak to one's inner perception still more of the power of the purse and of the higher turn for business than of the old intellectual, or even of the old moral, sensibility. Why else then should one have thought of some single, some admirable hour of Emerson, in one of the dusky, primitive lecture-halls that have ceased to be, or of some large insuperable anti-slavery eloquence of Wendell Phillips's, during the same term and especially during the War, as breathing more of the consciousness of literature and of history than all the promiscuous bustle of the Florentine palace by Copley Square? Not that this latter edifice, the fruit of immense considerations, has not its honourable interest too ; which it would have if only in the light of the constant truth that almost any American application or practice of a general thought puts on a new and original aspect. Public libraries are a thoroughly general thought, and one has seen plenty of them, one is seeing dreadfully many, in these very days, the world over ; yet to be confronted with an American example is to have sight straightway of more difference than community, and to glean on the spot fresh evidence of that democratic way of dealing which it has been the American office to translate from an academic phrase into a bristling fact. The notes of difference of the Florentine palace by Copley Square—more delicately elegant, in truth, if less sublimely rugged, than most Florentine palaces—resolve themselves, like so many such notes everywhere, into our impression here, once more, that every one is " in " everything, whereas in Europe so comparatively few persons are in anything (even as yet in " society," more and more the common refuge or retreat of the masses).

The Boston institution then is a great and complete institution, with this reserve of its striking the restored absentee as practically without *penetralia*. A library without *penetralia* may affect him but as a temple without altars ; it will at any rate exemplify the distinction between a benefit given and a benefit taken, a borrowed, a lent, and an owned, an appropriated convenience. The

British Museum, the Louvre, the Bibliothèque Nationale, the treasures of South Kensington, are assuredly, under forms, at the disposal of the people ; but it is to be observed, I think, that the people walk there more or less under the shadow of the right waited for and conceded. It remains as difficult as it is always interesting, however, to trace the detail (much of it obvious enough, but much more indefinable) of the personal port of a democracy that, unlike the English, is social as well as political. One of these denotements is that social democracies are unfriendly to the preservation of *penetralia ;* so that when *penetralia* are of the essence, as in a place of study and meditation, they inevitably go to the wall. The main staircase, in Boston, has, with its amplitude of wing and its splendour of tawny marble, a high and luxurious beauty—bribing the restored absentee to emotion, moreover, by expanding, monumentally, at one of its rests, into admirable commemoration of the Civil War service of the two great Massachusetts Volunteer regiments of *élite.* Such visions, such felicities, such couchant lions and recorded names and stirred memories as these, encountered in the early autumn twilight, *colour* an impression—even though to say so be the limit of breach of the silence in which, for persons of the generation of the author of these pages, appreciation of them can best take refuge : the refuge to which I felt myself anon reduced, for instance, opposite the State House, in presence of Saint-Gaudens's noble and exquisite monument to Robert Gould Shaw and the Fifty-fourth Massachusetts. There are works of memorial art that may suddenly place themselves, by their operation in a given case, outside articulate criticism—which was what happened, I found, in respect to the main feature, the rich staircase of the Library. Another way in which the bribe, as I have called it, of that masterpiece worked on the spot was by prompting one to immediate charmed perception of the character of the deep court and inner arcade of the palace, where a wealth of science and taste has gone to producing a sense, when the afternoon light sadly slants, of one of the myriad gold-coloured courts of the Vatican.

These are the refinements of the present Boston—keeping company as they can with the healthy animation, as it struck me, of the rest of the building, the multitudinous bustle, the coming and going, as in a railway-station, of persons with carpet-bags and other luggage, the simplicity of plan, the open doors and immediate accesses, admirable *for* a railway-station, the ubiquitous children, *most* irrepressible little democrats of the democracy, the vain quest, above all, of the deeper depths aforesaid, some part that should be sufficiently *within* some other part, sufficiently withdrawn and consecrated, not to constitute a thoroughfare. Perhaps I didn't adequately explore; but there was always the visible scale and scheme of the building. It was a shock to find the so brave decorative designs of Puvis de Chavannes, of Sargent and Abbey and John Elliott, hanging over mere chambers of familiarity and resonance; and then, I must quickly add, it was a shock still greater perhaps to find one had no good reason for defending them against such freedoms. What was sauce for the goose was sauce for the gander : had one not in other words, in the public places and under the great loggias of Italy, acclaimed it as just the charm and dignity of these resorts that, in their pictured and embroidered state, they still serve for the graceful common life? It was true that one had not been imprisoned in that consistency in the Laurentian, in the Ambrosian Library—and at any rate one was here on the edge of abysses. Was it not splendid, for example, to see, in Boston, such large provision made for the amusement of children on rainy afternoons?—so many little heads bent over their story-books that the edifice took on at moments the appearance worn, one was to observe later on, by most other American edifices of the same character, that of a lively distributing-house of the new fiction for the young. The note was bewildering— yet would one, snatching the bread-and-molasses from their lips, cruelly deprive the young of rights in which they have been installed with a majesty nowhere else approaching that of their American installation? I am not wrong, probably, at all events, in qualifying such a question as that as abysmal, and I remember how, more than once, I took refuge from it in craven flight, straight across the Square, to the already so interesting, the so rapidly-expanding Art Museum.

There, for some reason, questions exquisitely dropped ; perhaps only for the reason that things sifted and selected have, very visibly, the effect of challenging the confidence even of the rash. It is of the nature of objects doomed to show distinction that they virtually make a desert round them, and peace reigned unbroken, I usually noted, in the two or three Museum rooms that harbour a small but deeply-interesting and steadily-growing collection of fragments of the antique. Here the restless analyst found work to his hand—only too much ; and indeed in presence of the gem of the series, of the perhaps just too conscious grace of a certain little wasted and dim-eyed head of Aphrodite, he felt that his function should simply give way, in common decency, to that of the sonneteer. For it is an impression by itself, and I think quite worth the Atlantic voyage, to catch in the American light the very fact of the genius of Greece. There are things we don't know, feelings not to be foretold, till we have had that experience—which I commend to the *raffiné* of almost any other clime. I should say to him that he has not *seen* a fine Greek thing till he has seen it in America. It is of course on the face of it the most merciless case of transplanting—the mere moral of which, none the less, for application, becomes by no means flagrant. The little Aphrodite, with her connections, her antecedents and references exhibiting the maximum of breakage, is no doubt as *lonely* a jewel as ever strayed out of its setting; yet what does one quickly recognize but that the intrinsic lustre will have, so far as that may be possible, doubled? She has lost her background, the divine creature—has lost her company, and is keeping, in a manner, the strangest; but so far from having lost an iota of her power, she has gained unspeakably more, since what she essentially stands for she here stands for alone, rising ineffably to the occasion. She has in short, by her single presence, as yet, annexed an empire, and there are strange glimmers of moments when, as I have spoken of her consciousness, the very knowledge of this seems to lurk in the depth of her beauty. Where was she ever more, where was she ever so much, a goddess—and who knows but that, being thus divine, she foresees the time when, as she has "moved over," the place of her actual where-abouts will have become one of her shrines? Objects doomed to distinction make round them a desert, I have said; but that is only for any gross confidence in other matters. For confidence in *them* they make a garden, and that is why I felt this quarter of the Boston Art Museum bloom, under the indescribable dim eyes, with delicate flowers. The impression swallowed up every other; the place, whatever it was, was supremely justified, and I was left cold by learning that a much bigger and grander and richer place is presently to overtop it.

The present establishment "dates back," back almost to the good Boston of the middle years, and is full of all sorts of accumulated and concentrated pleasantness; which fact precisely gives the signal, by the terrible American law, for its coming to an end and giving a chance to the untried. It is a consistent application of the rotary system—the untried always awaiting its turn, and quite perceptibly stamping and snorting while it waits; all heedless as it is, poor innocent untried, of the certain hour of the impatiences before which it too will have to retreat. It is not indeed that the American laws, so operating, have not almost always their own queer interest; founded as they are, all together, on one of the strongest of the native impulses. We see this characteristic again and again at play, see it in especial wherever we see (which is more than frequently enough) a university or a college "started" or amplified. This process almost always takes the form, primarily, of more lands and houses and halls and rooms, more swimming-baths and football-fields and gymnasia, a greater luxury of brick and mortar, a greater ingenuity, the most artful conceivable, of accommodation and installation. Such is the magic, such the presences, that tend, more than any other, to figure *as* the Institution, thereby perverting not a little, as need scarce be remarked, the finer collegiate idea: the theory being, doubtless, and again most characteristically, that with all the wrought stone and oak and painted glass, the immense provision, the multiplied marbles and tiles and cloisters and acres, "people will come," that is, individuals of value will, and in some manner work some miracle. In the early American time, doubtless, individuals of value had to wait too much for things; but that is now made up by the way things are waiting for individuals of value. To which I must immediately add, however—and it is the ground of my allusion of a moment ago—that no impression of the "new" Boston can feel itself hang together without remembrance of what it owes to that rare exhibition of the living spirit lately achieved, in the interest of the fine arts, and of all that is noblest in them, by the unaided and quite heroic genius of a private citizen. To attempt to tell the story of the wonderfully-gathered and splendidly-lodged Gardner Collection would be to displace a little the line that separates private from public property ; and yet to find no discreet word for it is to appear to fail of feeling for the complexity of conditions amid which so undaunted a devotion to a great idea (undaunted by the battle to fight, losing, alas, with State Protection of native art, and with other scarce less uncanny things) has been able consummately to flower. It is in presence of the results magnificently attained, the energy triumphant over everything, that one feels the fine old disinterested tradition of Boston least broken.

8

Concord and Salem

I FELT myself, on the spot, cast about a little for the right expression of it, and then lost any hesitation to say that, putting the three or four biggest cities aside, Concord, Massachusetts, had an identity more palpable to the mind, had nestled in other words more successfully beneath her narrow fold of the mantle of history, than any other American town. " Compare me with places of my size, you know," one seemed to hear her plead, with the modesty that, under the mild autumn sun, so well became her russet beauty ; and this exactly it was that prompted the emphasis of one's reply, or, as it may even be called, of one's declaration.

"Ah, my dear, it isn't a question of places of your 'size,' since among places of your size you're too obviously and easily first : it's a question of places, so many of them, of fifty times your size, and which yet don't begin to have a fraction of your weight, or your character, or your intensity of presence and sweetness of tone, or your moral charm, or your pleasant appreciability, or, in short, of anything that is yours. Your ' size '? Why, you're the biggest little place in America—with only New York and Boston and Chicago, by what I make out, to surpass you ; and the country is lucky indeed to have you, in your sole and single felicity, for if it hadn't, where in the world should we go, inane and unappeased, for the particular communication of which you have the secret? The country is colossal, and you but a microscopic speck on the hem of its garment; yet there's nothing else like you, take you all round, for we *see* you complacently, with the naked eye, whereas there are vast sprawling, bristling areas, great grey 'centres of population' that spread, on the map, like irremediable grease-spots, which fail utterly of any appeal to our vision or any control of it, leaving it to pass them by as if they were not. If you are so thoroughly the opposite of one of these I don't say it's all your superlative merit; it's rather, as I have put it, your felicity, your good fortune, the result of the half-dozen happy turns of the wheel in your favour. Half-a-dozen such turns, you see, are, for any mortal career, a handsome allowance; and your merit is that, recognizing this, you have not fallen below your estate. But it's your fortune, above all, that's your charm. One doesn't want to be patronizing, but you didn't, thank goodness, make yours. That's what the other places, the big ones that are as nothing to you, are trying to do, the country over—to make theirs; and, from the point of view of these remarks, all in vain. Your luck is that you didn't have to; yours had been, just as it shows in you to-day, made *for* you, and you at the most but gratefully submitted to it. It must be said for you, however, that you keep it; and it isn't every place that would have been capable—— ! You keep the look, you keep the feeling, you keep the air. Your great trees arch over these possessions more protectingly, covering them in as a cherished presence; and you have settled to your tone and your type as to treasures that can now never be taken. Show me the other places in America (of the few that have *had* anything) from which the best hasn't mainly been taken, or isn't in imminent danger of being. There is old Salem, there is old Newport, which I am on my way to see again, and which, if you will, are, by what I hear, still comparatively intact ; but their having was never a having like yours, and they adorn, precisely, my little tale of your supremacy. No, I don't want to be patronizing, but your only fault is your tendency to improve—I mean just by your duration as you *are ;* which indeed is the only sort of improvement that is not questionable."

Such was the drift of the warm flood of appreciation, of reflection, that Concord revisited could set rolling over the field of a prepared sensibility ; and I feel as if I had quite made my point, such as it is, in asking what other American village could have done anything of the sort. I should have been at fault perhaps only in speaking of the interest in question as visible, on that large scale, to the "naked eye"; the truth being perhaps that one wouldn't have been so met half-way by one's impression unless one had rather particularly *known*, and that knowledge, in such a case, amounts to a pair of magnifying spectacles. I remember indeed putting it to myself on the November Sunday morning, tepid and bright and perfect for its use, through which I walked from the station under the constant archway of the elms, as yet but indulgently thinned : would one know, for one's self, what had formerly been the matter here, if one hadn't happened to be able to get round behind, in the past, as it were, and more or less understand ? Would the operative elements of the past—little old Concord Fight, essentially, and Emerson and Hawthorne and Thoreau, with the rest of the historic animation and the rest of the figured and shifting "transcendental" company, to its last and loosest ramifications—would even these handsome quantities have so lingered to one's intelligent after-sense, if one had not brought with one some sign by which they too would know; dim, shy spectralities as, for themselves, they must, at the best, have become ? Idle, however, such questions when, by the chance of the admirable day, everything, in its own way and order, unmistakably came *out*—every string sounded as if, for all the world, the loose New England town (and I apply the expression but to the relations of objects and places), were a lyre swept by the hand of Apollo. Apollo was the spirit of antique piety, looking about, pausing, remembering, as he moved to his music ; and there were glimpses and reminders that of course kept him much longer than others.

Seated there at its ease, as if placidly familiar with pilgrims and quite taking their homage for granted, the place had the very aspect of some grave, refined New England matron of the "old school," the widow of a high celebrity, living on and on in possession of all his relics and properties, and, though not personally addicted to gossip or to journalism, having become, where the great company kept by her in the past is concerned, quite cheerful and modern and responsive. From her position, her high-backed chair by the window that commands most of the coming and going, she looks up intelligently, over her knitting, with no vision of any limit on her part as yet, to this attitude, and with nothing indeed to suggest the possibility of a limit save a hint of that loss of temporal perspective in which we recognize the mental effect of a great weight of years. I had formerly the acquaintance of a very interesting lady, of extreme age, whose early friends, in "literary circles," are now regarded as classics, and who, toward the end of her life, always said, "You know Charles Lamb has produced a play at Drury Lane," or "You know William Hazlitt has fallen in love with such a very odd woman." Her facts were perfectly correct ; only death had beautifully passed out of her world—since I don't remember her mentioning to me the demise, which she might have made so contemporary, either of Byron or of Scott. When people were ill she admirably forebore to ask about them—she disapproved wholly of such conditions ; and there were interesting invalids round about her, near to her, whose existence she for long years consummately ignored.   It is some such quiet backward stride as those of my friend that I seem to hear the voice of old Concord take in reference to her annals, and it is not too much to say that where her soil is most sacred, I fairly caught, on the breeze, the mitigated perfect tense.   " You know there has been a fight between our men and the King's " —one wouldn't have been surprised, that crystalline Sunday noon, where so little had changed, where the stream and the bridge, and all nature, and the *feeling*, above all, still so directly testify, at any fresh-sounding form of such an announcement.

I had forgotten, in all the years, with what thrilling clearness that supreme site speaks—though anciently, while so much of the course of the century was still to run, the distinctness might have seemed even greater. But to stand there again was to take home this fore-shortened view, the gained nearness, to one's sensibility ; to look straight over the heads of the " American Weimar " company at the inestimable hour that had so handsomely set up for them their background.   The Fight had been the hinge—so one saw it—on which the large revolving future was to turn ; or it had been better, perhaps, the large firm nail, ringingly driven in, from which the beautiful portrait-group, as we see it to-day, was to hang.   Beautiful exceedingly the local Emerson and Thoreau and Hawthorne and (in a fainter way) *tutti quanti ;* but beautiful largely because the fine old incident down in the valley had so seriously prepared their effect. That seriousness gave once for all the pitch, and it was verily as if, under such a value, even with the seed of a " literary circle " so freely scattered by an intervening hand, the vulgar note would in that air never be possible. As I had inevitably, in long absence, let the value, for immediate perception, rather waste itself, so, on the spot, it came back most instantly with the extraordinary sweetness of the river, which, under the autumn sun, like all the American rivers one had seen or was to see, straightway took the whole case straightway into its hands. "Oh, you shall tell me of your impression when you have felt what *I* can do for it : so hang over me well!" —that's what they all seem to say.

I hung over Concord River then as long as I could, and recalled how Thoreau, Hawthorne, Emerson himself, have expressed with due sympathy the sense of this full, slow, sleepy, meadowy flood, which sets its pace and takes its twists like some large obese benevolent person, scarce so frankly unsociable as to pass you at all. It had watched the Fight, it even now confesses, without a quickening of its current, and it draws along the woods and the orchards and the fields with the purr of a mild domesticated cat who rubs against the family and the furniture. Not to be recorded, at best, however, I think, never to emerge from the state of the inexpressible, in respect to the spot, by the bridge, where one most lingers, is the sharpest suggestion of the whole scene—the power diffused in it which makes it, after all these years, or perhaps indeed by reason of their number, so irresistibly touching. All the commemorative objects, the stone marking the burial-place of the three English soldiers, the animated image of the young belted American yeoman by Mr. Daniel French, the intimately associated element in the presence, not far off, of the old manse, interesting theme of Hawthorne's pen, speak to the spirit, no doubt, in one of the subtlest tones of which official history is capable, and yet somehow leave the exquisite melancholy of everything unuttered. It lies too deep, as it always so lies where the ground has borne the weight of the short, simple act, intense and unconscious, that was to determine the event, determine the future in the way we call immortally. For we read into the scene too little of what we may, unless this muffled touch in it somehow reaches us so that we feel the pity and the irony of the *precluded* relation on the part of the fallen defenders. The sense that was theirs and that moved them we know, but we seem to know better still the sense that wasn't and that couldn't, and that forms our luxurious heritage as our eyes, across the gulf, seek to meet their eyes; so that we are almost ashamed of taking so much, such colossal quantity and value, as the equivalent of their dimly-seeing offer. The huge bargain they made for us, in a word, made by the gift of the little all they had—to the modesty of which amount the homely rural facts grouped there together have appeared to go on testifying—this brilliant advantage strikes the imagination that yearns over them as unfairly enjoyed at their cost. Was it delicate, was it decent—that is *would* it have been—to ask the embattled farmers, simple-minded, unwitting folk, to make us so inordinate a present with so little of the conscious credit of it? Which all comes indeed, perhaps, simply to the most poignant of all those effects of disinterested sacrifice that the toil and trouble of our forefathers produce for us. The minute-men at the bridge were of course interested intensely, as they believed—but such, too, was the artful manner in which we see *our* latent, lurking, waiting interest like, a Jew in a dusky back-shop, providentially bait the trap.

Beyond even such broodings as these, and to another purpose, moreover, the communicated spell falls, in its degree, into that pathetic oddity of the small aspect, and the rude and the lowly, the reduced and humiliated above all, that sits on so many nooks and corners, objects and appurtenances, old contemporary things—contemporary with the doings of our race; simplifying our antecedents, our annals, to within an inch of their life, making us ask, in presence of the rude relics even of greatness, mean retreats and receptacles, constructionally so poor, from what barbarians or from what pigmies we have sprung. There are certain rough black mementos of the early monarchy, in England and Scotland, there are glimpses of the original humble homes of other greatness as well, that strike in perfection this grim little note ; which has the interest of our being free to take it, for curiosity, for luxury of thought, as that of the real or that of the romantic, and with which, again, the deep Concord rusticity, momentary medium of our national drama, essentially consorts. We remember the small hard facts of the Shakespeare house at Stratford ; we remember the rude closet, in Edinburgh Castle, in which James VI of Scotland was born, or the other little black hole, at Holyrood, in which Mary Stuart "sat" and in which Rizzio was murdered. These, I confess, are odd memories at Concord ; although the manse, near the spot where we last paused, and against the edge of whose acre or two the loitering river seeks friction in the manner I have mentioned, would now seem to have shaken itself a trifle disconcertingly free of the ornamental mosses scattered by Hawthorne's light hand ; it stands there, beyond its gate, with every due similitude to the shrunken historic site in general. To which I must hasten to add, however, that I was much more struck with the way these particular places of visitation resist their pressure of reference than with their affecting us as below their fortune. Intrinsically they are as naught—deeply depressing, in fact, to any impulse to reconstitute, the house in which Hawthorne spent what remained to him of life after his return from the Italy of his Donatello and his Miriam. Yet, in common with everything else, this mild monument benefits by that something in the air which makes us tender, keeps us respectful; meets, in the general interest, waving it vaguely away, any closer assault of criticism.

It is odd, and it is also exquisite, that these witnessing ways should be the last ground on which we feel moved to ponderation of the "Concord school"—to use, I admit, a futile expression; or rather, I should doubtless say, it *would* be odd if there were not inevitably something absolute in the fact of Emerson's all but lifelong connection with them. We may smile a little as we "drag in" Weimar, but I confess myself, for my part, much more satisfied than not by our happy equivalent, "in American money," for Goethe and Schiller. The money is a potful in the second case as in the first, and if Goethe, in the one, represents the gold and Schiller the silver, I find (and quite putting aside any bimetallic prejudice) the same good relation in the other between Emerson and Thoreau. I open Emerson for the same benefit for which I open Goethe, the sense of moving in large intellectual space, and that of the gush, here and there, out of the rock, of the crystalline cupful, in wisdom and poetry, in Wahrheit and Dichtung; and whatever I open Thoreau for (I needn't take space here for the good reasons) I open him oftener than I open Schiller. Which comes back to our feeling that the rarity of Emerson's genius, which has made him so, for the attentive peoples, the first, and the one really rare, American spirit in letters, couldn't have spent his career in a charming woody, watery place, for so long socially and typically and, above all, interestingly homogeneous, without an effect as of the communication to it of something ineffaceable. It was during his long span his immediate concrete, sufficient world; it gave him his nearest vision of life, and he drew half his images, we recognize, from the revolution of its seasons and the play of its manners. I don't speak of the other half, which he drew from elsewhere. It is admirably, to-day, as if we were still seeing these things *in* those images, which stir the air like birds, dim in the eventide, coming home to nest. If one had reached a " time of life " one had thereby at least heard him lecture ; and not a russet leaf fell for me, while I was there, but fell with an Emersonian drop.

II

It never failed that if in moving about I made, under stress, an inquiry, I should prove to have made it of a flagrant foreigner. It never happened that, addressing a fellow-citizen, in the street, on one of those hazards of possible communion with the indigenous spirit, I should not draw a blank. So, inevitably, at Salem, when, wandering perhaps astray, I asked my way to the House of the Seven Gables, the young man I had overtaken was true to his nature ; he stared at me as a remorseless Italian—as remorseless, at least, as six months of Salem could leave him. On that spot, in that air, I confess, it was a particular shock to me to be once more, with my so good general intention, so "put off"; though, if my young man but glared frank ignorance of the monument I named, he left me at least with the interest of wondering how the native estimate of it as a romantic ruin might strike a taste formed for such features by the landscape of Italy. I will not profess that by the vibration of this note the edifice of my fond fancy—I mean Hawthorne's Salem, and the witches', and that of other eminent historic figures—was not rather essentially shaken ; since what had the intention of my pilgrimage been, in all good faith, in artless sympathy and piety, but a search again, precisely, for the New England homogeneous—for the renewal of that impression of it which had lingered with me from a vision snatched too briefly, in a midsummer gloaming, long years ago. I had been staying near, at that far-away time, and, the railroad helping, had got myself dropped there for an hour at just the right moment of the waning day. This memory had been, from far back, a kept felicity altogether; a picture of goodly Colonial habitations, quite the high-water mark of that type of state and ancientry, seen in the clear dusk, and of almost nothing else but a pleasant harbour-side vacancy, the sense of dead marine industries, that finally looked out at me, for a climax, over a grass-grown interval, from the blank windows of the old Customs House of the Introduction to *The Scarlet Letter.*

I could on that occasion have seen, with my eye on my return-train, nothing else; but the image of these things I had not lost, wrapped up as it even was, for the fancy, in some figment of the very patch of old embroidered cloth that Hawthorne's charming prefatory pages unfold for us—pages in which the words are as finely "taken" as the silk and gold stitches of poor Hester Prynne's compunctious needle. It had hung, all the years, closely together, and had served—oh, so conveniently!—as the term of comparison, the rather rich frame, for any suggested vision of New England life unalloyed. The case now was the more marked that, already, on emerging from the station and not knowing quite where to look again for my goodly Georgian and neo-Georgian houses, I had had to permit myself to be directed to them by a civil Englishman, accosted by the way, who, all kindness and sympathy, immediately mentioned that they formed the Grosvenor Square, as might be said, of Salem. We conversed for the moment, and settled, as he told me, in the town, he was most sustaining; but when, a little later on, I stood there in admiration of the noble quarter, I could only feel, even while doing it every justice, that the place was not quite what my imagination had counted on. It was possibly even better, for the famous houses, almost without exception ample and charming, seemed to me to show a grace even beyond my recollection; the only thing was that I had never bargained for looking at them through a polyglot air. Look at them none the less, and at the fine old liberal scale, and felt symmetry, and simple dignity, and solid sincerity of them, I gratefully did, with due speculation as to their actual chances and changes, as to what they represent to-day as social "values," and with a lively impression, above all, of their preserved and unsophisticated state. That was a social value—which I found myself comparing, for instance, with similar aspects, frequent and excellent, in old English towns.

The Salem houses, the best, were all of the old English family, and, from picture to picture, all the parts would have matched; but the moral, the social, the political climate, even more than the breath of nature, had had in each case a different action, had begotten on either side a different consciousness. Or was it nearer even to say that these things had on one side begotten a consciousness, and had on the other begotten comparatively none? The approximation would have been the more interesting as each arrayed group might pass for a supreme expression of respectability. It would be the tone and weight, the quantity and quality, of the respectability that make the difference; massive and square-shouldered, yet rather battered and mottled, chipped and frayed, at last rather sceptical and cynical, in fine, in the English figure—thin and clear, consistently sharp, boldly unspotted, blankly serene, in the American. It was more amusing at any rate to spin such fancies, in reaction from the alien snub, than simply to see one's antitheses reduced to a mere question of the effect of climate. There would be yet more to say for the Salem picture, many of the "bits" of which remain, as Ruskin might have put it, entirely delightful; but their desperate clean freshness was what was more to abide with me after the polyglot air had cleared a little. The spacious, courteous doorways of the houses, expansively columned, fluted, framed; their large honest windows, in ample tiers, only here and there dishonoured by the modern pane; their high bland foreheads, in short, with no musty secrets in the eaves—yes, not one, in spite of the "speciality," in this respect, of the Seven Gables, to which I am coming —clarify too much perhaps the expressive mask, the look of experience, depress the balance toward the type of the expensive toy, shown on its shelf, but too good to be humanly used. It's as if the old witches had been suffered to live again, penally, as public housemaids, using nocturnally, for purposes of almost viciously-thorough purification, the famous broomsticks they used wantonly to ride.

Was it a sacred terror, after this, that stayed me from crossing the threshold of the Witch House?—in spite of the quite definite sturdy stamp of this attraction. I think it was an almost sacred tenderness rather, the instinct of not pressing too hard on my privilege and of not draining the offered cup to the lees. It is always interesting, in America, to see any object, some builded thing in particular, look as old as it possibly can; for the sight of which effort we sometimes hold our breath as if to watch, over the course of the backward years, the straight "track" of the past, the course of some hero of the foot-race on whom we have staked our hopes. How long will he hold out, how far back will he run, and where, heroically blown, will he have to drop? Our suspense is great in proportion to our hope, and if we are nervously constituted we may very well, at the last, turn away for anxiety. It was really in some such manner I was affected, I think, before the Salem Witch House, in presence of the mystery of antiquity. It is a modest wooden structure, consciously primitive, standing, if I remember rightly, in some effective relation to a street-corner and putting no little purpose into its archaism. The pity is, however, that unrelieved wooden houses never very curiously testify—as I was presently to learn, to my cost, from the dreadful anti-climax of the Seven Gables. They look brief and provisional at the best—look, above all, incorrigibly and witlessly innocent. The quite sufficiently sturdy little timbered mass by the Salem street, none the less, with a sidelong crook or twist that we may take as symbolizing ancient perversity, runs the backward race as long-windedly as we may anywhere, over the land, see it run. Had I gone in, as a frank placard invited me, I might have better measured the exploit ; yet, on the other hand, fearing frank placards, in general, in these cases, fearing nothing so much as reconstituted antiquity, I might have lost a part of my good little impression—which otherwise, as a small pale flower plucked from a withered tree, I could fold away, intact, between the leaves of my romantic herbarium.

I wanted, moreover, to be honest, not to fail, within the hour, of two other urgent matters, my train away (my sense of Salem was too destined to be train-haunted) and a due visitation of the Seven Gables and of the birth-house of their chronicler. It was in the course of this errand that I was made to feel myself, as I have mentioned, living, rather witlessly, in a world unknown to the active Salemite of to-day—a world embodied, I seemed to make out, in the large untidy industrial quarter that had sprung up since my early visit. Did I quite escape from this impression before alighting at last happily upon the small stale structure that had sheltered the romancer's entrance into life and that now appears, according to the preference of fancy, either a strange recipient of the romantic germ or the very spot to cause it, in protest and desperation, to develop? I took the neighbourhood, at all events, for the small original Hawthornesque world, keeping the other, the smoky modernism, at a distance, keeping everything, in fact, at a distance—on so spare and bare and lean and mean a face did the bright hard sky strike me as looking down. The way to think of it evidently was in some frank rural light of the past, that of all the ancient New England simplicities, with the lap of wide waters and the stillness of rocky pastures never far off (they seem still indeed close at hand), and with any number of our present worryings and pamperings of the "literary temperament" too little in question to be missed. It kept at a distance, in fact, so far as my perception was concerned, everything but a little boy, a dear little harsh, intelligent, sympathetic American boy, who dropped straight from the hard sky for my benefit (I hadn't seen him emerge from elsewhere) and turned up at my side with absolute confidence and with the most knowing tips. He might have been a Weimar tout or a Stratford amateur—only he so beautifully wasn't. That is what I mean by my having alighted happily; the little boy was so completely master of his subject, and we formed, on the spot, so close an alliance. He made up to me for my crude Italian—the way they *become* crude over here!—he made up to me a little even for my civil Englishman; he was exactly what I wanted—a presence (and he was the only thing far or near) old enough, native and intimate enough, to reach back and to understand.

He showed me the window of the room in which Hawthorne had been born; wild horses, as the phrase is, wouldn't have dragged me into it, but *he* might have done so if he hadn't, as I say, understood. But he understood everything, and knew when to insist and

when not to; knew, for instance, exactly why I said
" Dear, dear, are you very sure?" after he had brought
me to sight of an object at the end of a lane, by a
vague waterside, I think, and looking across to Marble-
head, that he invited me to take, if I could, for the
Seven Gables. I couldn't take it in the least, as happens,
and though he was perfectly sure, our reasons, on either
side, were equally clear to him—so that in short I think
of him as the very genius of the place, feeding his small
shrillness on the cold scraps of Hawthorne's leaving and
with the making of his acquaintance alone worth the
journey. Yet the fact that, the Seven Gables being in
question, the shapeless object by the waterside wouldn't
do at all, not the least little bit, troubled us only till we
had thrown off together, with a quick, competent gesture
and at the breaking of light, the poor illusion of a
necessity of relation between the accomplished thing, for
poetry, for art, and those other quite equivocal things
that we inflate our ignorance with seeing it suggested
by. The weak, vague domiciliary presence at the end
of the lane may have " been " (in our poor parlance) the
idea of the admirable book—though even here we take
a leap into dense darkness; but the idea that is the
inner force of the admirable book so vividly forgets,
before our eyes, any such origin or reference, " cutting "
it dead as a low acquaintance and outsoaring the shadow
of its night, that the connection has turned a somersault
into space, repudiated like a ladder kicked back from the
top of a wall. Hawthorne's ladder at Salem, in fine,
has now quite gone, and we but tread the air if we
attempt to set our critical feet on its steps and its rounds,
learning thus as we do, and with infinite interest as I
think, how merely "subjective" in us are our discoveries
about genius. Endless are its ways of besetting and
eluding, of meeting and mocking us. When there are

appearances that might have nourished it we see it as swallowing them all; yet we see it as equally gorged when there are no appearances at all—*then* most of all, sometimes, quite insolently bloated; and we recognize ruefully that we are forever condemned to know it only after the fact.

9

Philadelphia

To be at all critically, or as we have been fond of calling it, analytically, minded—over and beyond an inherent love of the general many-coloured picture of things—is to be subject to the superstition that objects and places, coherently grouped, disposed for human use and addressed to it, must have a sense of their own, a mystic meaning proper to themselves to give out : to give out, that is, to the participant at once so interested and so detached as to be moved to a report of the matter. That perverse person is obliged to take it for a working theory that the essence of almost any settled aspect of anything may be extracted by the chemistry of criticism, and may give us its right name, its formula, for convenient use. From the moment the critic finds himself sighing, to save trouble in a difficult case, that the cluster of appearances can *have* no sense, from that moment he begins, and quite consciously, to go to pieces ; it being the prime business and the high honour of the painter of life always to *make* a sense—and to make it most in proportion as the immediate aspects are loose or confused. The last thing decently permitted him is to recognize incoherence—to recognize it, that is, as baffling ; though of course he may present and portray it, in all richness, *for* incoherence. That, I think, was what I had been mainly occupied with in New York ;

and I quitted so qualified a joy, under extreme stress of winter, with a certain confidence that I should not have moved even a little of the way southward without practical relief: relief which came in fact ever so promptly, at Philadelphia, on my feeling, unmistakably, the change of half the furniture of consciousness. This change put on, immediately, the friendliest, the handsomest aspect—supplied my intelligence on the spot with the clear, the salient note. I mean by this, not that the happy definition or synthesis instantly came—came with the perception that character and sense were there, only waiting to be disengaged; but that the note, as I say, was already, within an hour, the germ of these things, and that the whole flower, assuredly, wouldn't fail to bloom. I was in fact sniffing up its fragrance after I had looked out for three minutes from one of the windows of a particularly wide-fronted house and seen the large residential square that lay before me shine in its native light. This light, remarkably tender, I thought, for that of a winter afternoon, matched with none other I had ever seen, and announced straight off fifty new circumstances—an enormous number, in America, for any prospect to promise you in contradistinction from any other. It was not simply that, beyond a doubt, the outlook was more *méridional;* a still deeper impression had begun to work, and, as I felt it more and more glimmer upon me, I caught myself about to jump, with a single leap, to my synthesis. I of course stayed myself in the act, for there would be too much, really, yet to come; but the perception left me, I even then felt, in possession of half the ground on which later experience would proceed. It was not too much to say, as I afterwards saw, that I had in those few illumined moments put the gist of the matter into my pocket.

Philadelphia, incontestably then, was the American

city of the large type, that didn't *bristle*—just as I was afterwards to recognize in St. Louis the nearest approach to companionship with her in this respect; and to recognize in Chicago, I may parenthetically add, the most complete divergence. It was not only, moreover, at the ample, tranquil window there, that Philadelphia *didn't* "bristle" (by the record of my moment) but that she essentially couldn't and wouldn't ever; that no movement or process could be thought of, in fine, as more foreign to her genius. I do not just now go into the question of what the business of bristling, in an American city, may be estimated as consisting of; so infallibly is one aware when the thousand possible quills *are* erect, and when, haply, they are not—such a test does the restored absentee find, at least, in his pricked sensibility. A place may abound in its own sense, as the phrase is, without bristling in the least—it is liable indeed to bristle most, I think, when not too securely possessed of any settled sense to abound in. An imperfect grasp of such a luxury is not the weakness of Philadelphia—just as that admirable comprehensive flatness in her which precludes the image of the porcupine figured to me from the first, precisely, as her positive source of strength. The absence of the note of the perpetual perpendicular, the New York, the Chicago note—and I allude here to the material, the constructional exhibition of it—seemed to symbolize exactly the principle of indefinite level extension and to offer refreshingly, a challenge to horizontal, to lateral, to more or less tangental, to rotary, or, better still, to absolute centrifugal motion. If it was to befall me, during my brief but various acquaintance with the place, not to find myself more than two or three times hoisted or lowered by machinery, my prime illumination had been an absolute forecast of that immunity—a virtue of general premonition in it at which I have already glanced. I should in fact, I repeat, most truly or most artfully repaint my little picture by mixing my colours with the felt amenity of that small crisis, and by showing how this, that and the other impression to come had had, while it lasted, quite the definite prefigurement that the chapters of a book find in its table of contents. The afternoon blandness, for a fugitive from Madison Avenue in January snow, didn't mean nothing; the little marble steps and lintels and cornices and copings, all the so clear, so placed accents in the good prose text of the mildly purple houses across the Square, which seemed to wear them, as all the others did, up and down the streets, in the manner of nice white stockings, neckties, collars, cuffs, didn't mean nothing; and this was somehow an assurance that joined on to the vibration of the view produced, a few hours before, by so merely convenient a circumstance as my taking my place, at Jersey City, in the Pennsylvania train.

I had occasion, repeatedly, to find the Pennsylvania Railroad a beguiling and predisposing influence—in relation to various objectives; and indeed I quite lost myself in the singularity of this effect, which existed for me, certainly, only in that connection, touching me with a strange and most agreeable sense that the great line in question, an institution with a style and *allure* of its own, is not, even the world over, as other railroads are. It absolutely, with a little frequentation, affected me as better and higher than its office or function, and almost as supplying one with a mode of life intrinsically superior; as if it ought really to be on its way to much grander and more charming places than any that happen to mark its course—as if indeed, should one persistently keep one's seat, not getting out anywhere, it would in the end carry one to some such ideal city. One might under this extravagant spell, which always began to work for me at Twenty-third Street, and on the constantly-adorable Ferry, have fancied the train, disvulgarized of passengers, steaming away, in disinterested empty form, to some terminus too noble to be marked in *our* poor schedules. The consciousness of this devotion would have been thus like that of living, all sublimely, up in a balloon.   It was not, however—I recover myself—that if I had been put off at Philadelphia I was not, for the hour, contented; finding so immediately, as I have noted, more interest to my hand than I knew at first what to do with.   There was the quick light of explanation, following on everything else I have mentioned—the light in which I had only to turn round again and see where I was, and how it was, in order to feel everything "come out" under the large friendliness, the ordered charm and perfect peace of the Club, housing me with that *whole* protection the bestowal of which on occasion is the finest grace of the hospitality of American clubs.   Philadelphia, manifestly, was beyond any other American city, a *society*, and was going to show as such, as a thoroughly confirmed and settled one—which fact became the key, precisely, to its extension on one plane, and to its having no pretext for bristling.   Human groups that discriminate in their own favour do, one remembers, in general, bristle; but that is only when they have not been really successful, when they have not been able to discriminate enough, when they are not, like Philadelphia, settled and confirmed and content.   It would clearly be impossible not to regard the place before me as possessed of this secret of serenity to a degree elsewhere—at least among ourselves—unrivalled.   The basis of the advantage, the terms of the secret, would be still to make out—which was precisely the high interest; and I was afterwards to be justified of my conviction by the multiplication of my lights.

New York, in that sense, had appeared to me then not a society at all, and it was rudimentary that Chicago would be one still less; neither of them, as a human group, having been able to discriminate in its own favour with anything like such success. The proof of that would be, obviously, in one's so easily imputing to them alteration, extension, development; a change somehow unimaginable in the case of Philadelphia, which was a fixed quantity and had filled to the brim, one felt—and wasn't that really to be part of the charm?—the measure of her possibility. Boston even was thinkable as subject to mutation; had I not in fact just seemed to myself to catch her in the almost uncanny inconsequence of change? There had been for Boston the old epigram that she wasn't a place, but a state of mind; and that might remain, since we know how frequently states of mind alter. Philadelphia then wasn't a place, but a state of consanguinity, which is an absolute final condition. She had arrived at it, with nothing in the world left to bristle for, or against; whereas New York, and above all Chicago, were only, and most precariously, on the way to it, and indeed, having started too late, would probably never arrive. There were, for them, interferences and complications; they knew, and would yet know, other conditions, perhaps other beatitudes; only the beatitude I speak of—that of being, in the composed sense, a society—was lost to them forever. Philadelphia, without complications or interferences, enjoyed it in particular through having begun to invoke it in time. And now she had nothing more to invoke; she had everything; her *cadres* were all full; her imagination was at peace. This, exactly again, would be the reason of the bristling of the other places: the *cadres* of New York, Chicago, Boston, being as to a third of them empty and as to another third objectionably filled—with much consequent straining, reaching, heaving, both to attain and to eject. What makes a society was thus, more than anything else, the number of organic social relations it represents; by which logic Philadelphia would represent nothing *but* organic social relations. The degrees of consanguinity were the *cadres*; every one of them was full; it was a society in which every individual was as many times over cousin, uncle, aunt, niece, and so on through the list, as poor human nature is susceptible of being. These degrees are, when one reflects, the only really organic social relations, and when they are all there for every one the scheme of security, in a community, has been worked out. Philadelphia, in other words, would not only be a family, she would be a "happy" one, and a probable proof that the happiness comes as a matter of course if the family but be large enough. Consanguinity provides the marks and features, the type and tone and ease, the common knowledge and the common consciousness, but number would be required to make these things social. Number, accordingly, for her perfection, was what Philadelphia would have—it having been clear to me still, in my charming Club and at my illuminating window, that she couldn't *not* be perfect. She would be, of all goodly villages, the very goodliest, probably, in the world; the very largest, and flattest, and smoothest, the most rounded and complete.

II

The simplest account of such success as I was to have in putting my vision to the test will be, I think, to say that the place never for a moment belied to me that forecast of its animated intimacy. Yet it might be just here that a report of my experience would find itself hampered—this learning the lesson, from one vivid page of the picture-book to another, of how perfectly "intimate" Philadelphia is. Such an exhibition would be, prohibitively, the exhibition of private things, of private things only, and of a charmed contact with them, were it not for the great circumstance which, when what I have said has been fully said, remains to be taken into account. The state of infinite cousinship colours the scene, makes the predominant tone ; but you get a light upon it that is worth all others from the moment you see it as, ever so savingly, historic. This perception moreover promptly operates ; I found it stirred, as soon as I went out or began to circulate, by all immediate aspects and signs. The place "went back"; or, in other words, the social equilibrium, forestalling so that of the other cities, had begun early, had had plenty of time on its side, and thus had its history behind it—the past that looms through it, not at all luridly, but so squarely and substantially, to-day, and gives it, by a mercy, an extension other than the lateral. This, frankly, was required, it struck me, for the full comfort of one's impression—for a certain desirable and imputable richness. The backward extension, in short, is the very making of Philadelphia ; one is so uncertain of the value one would attach to her being as she is, if she hadn't been so by prescription and for a couple of centuries. This has established her right and her competence ; the fact is the parent, so to speak, of her consistency and serenity; it has made the very law under which her parts and pieces have held so closely together. To walk her streets is to note with all promptness that William Penn *must* have laid them out—no one else could possibly have done it so ill. It was his best, though, with our larger sense for a street, it is far from ours ; we at any rate no more complain of them, nor suggest that they might have been more liberally conceived, than we so express ourselves about the form of the chairs in sitting through a morning call.

I found myself liking them, then, as I moved among them, just in proportion as they conformed, in detail, to the early pattern—the figure, for each house, of the red-faced old gentleman whose thick eyebrows and moustache have turned to white; and I found myself detesting them in any instance of a new front or a new fashion. They were narrow, with this aspect as of a double file of grizzled veterans, or they were nothing; the narrowness had been positively the channel or conduit of continuity of character: it made the long pipe on which the tune of the place was played. From the moment it was in any way corrected the special charm broke—the charm, a rare civic possession, as of some immense old ruled and neatly-inked chart, not less carefully than benightedly flattened out, stretching its tough parchment under the very feet of all comings and goings. This was an image with which, as it furthermore seemed to me, everything else consorted—above all the soothing truth that Philadelphia was, yes, beyond cavil, solely and singly Philadelphian. There was an interference absent, or one that I at least never met: that sharp note of the outlandish, in the strict sense of the word, which I had already found almost everywhere so disconcerting. I pretend here of course neither to estimate the numbers in which the grosser aliens may actually have settled on these bland banks of the Delaware, nor to put my finger on the principle of the shock I had felt it, and was still to feel it, in their general power to administer; for I am not now concerned so much with the impression made by one's almost everywhere meeting them, as with the impression made by one's here and there failing of it. They may have been gathered, in their hordes, in some vast quarter unknown to me and of which I was to have no glimpse; but what would this have denoted, exactly, but some virtue in the air for reducing their presence, or their effect, to naught? There precisely was the difference from New York—that they themselves had been in that place half the virtue, or the vice, of the air, and that there were few of its agitations to which they had not something to say.

The logic of the case had been visible to me, for that matter, on my very first drive from the train—from that precious "Pennsylvania" station of Philadelphia which was to strike me as making a nearer approach than elsewhere to the arts of ingratiation. There was an object or two, windowed and chimneyed, in the central sky—but nothing to speak of: I then and there, in a word, took in the admirable flatness. And if it seemed so spacious, by the same token, this was because it was neither eager, nor grasping, nor pushing. It drew its breath at its ease, clearly—never sounding the charge, the awful "Step lively!" of New York. The fury of the pavement had dropped, in fine, as I was to see it drop, later on, between Chicago and St. Louis. This affected me on the spot of symbolic, and I was to have no glimpse of anything that gainsaid the symbol. It was somehow, too, the very note of the homogeneous; though this indeed is not, oddly enough, the head under which at St. Louis my impression was to range itself. I at all events here gave myself up to the vision—that of the vast, firm chess-board, the immeasurable spread of little squares, covered *all* over by perfect Philadelphians. It was an image, in face of some of the other features of the view, dissimilar to any by which one had ever in one's life been assaulted; and this elimination of the foreign element has been what was required to make it consummate. Nothing is more notable, through the States at large, than that hazard of what one may happen, or may not happen, to see; but the only use to be made of either accident is, clearly, to let it stand and to let it serve. This intensity and ubiquity of the local tone, that of the illimitable *town*, serves so successfully for my sense of Philadelphia that I should feel as if a little masterpiece of the creative imagination had been destroyed by the least correction. And there is, further, the point to make that if I knew, all the while, that there was something more, and different, and less beatific, under and behind the happy appearance I grasped, I knew it by no glimmer of direct perception, and should never in the world have guessed it if some sound of it had not, by a discordant voice, been, all superfluously, rather tactlessly, dropped into my ear.

It was not, however, disconcerting at the time, this presentation, as in a flash, of the other side of the medal —the other side being, in a word, as was mentioned to me, one of the most lurid pages in the annals of political corruption. The place, by this revelation, was two distinct things—a Society, from far back, the society I had divined, the most genial and delightful one could think of, and then, parallel to this, and not within it, nor quite altogether above it, but beside it and beneath it, behind it and before it, enclosing it as in a frame of fire in which it still had the secret of keeping cool, a proportionate City, the most incredible that ever was, organized all for plunder and rapine, the gross satisfaction of official appetite, organized for eternal iniquity and impunity. Such were the conditions, it had been hinted to me—from the moment the medal spun round ; but I even understate, I think, in speaking of the knowledge as only not disconcerting. It was better than that, for it positively added the last touch of colour to my framed and suspended picture. Here, strikingly then, was an American *case*, and presumably one of the best ; one of the best, that is, for some study of the wondrous problem, admiration and amazement of the nations, who yearn over it from far off : the way in which sane Society and pestilent City, in the United States, successfully cohabit, each keeping it up with so little of fear or flutter from the other. The thing presents itself, in its prime unlikelihood, as a thorough good neighbouring of the Happy Family and the Infernal Machine—the machine so rooted as to continue to defy removal, and the family still so indifferent, while it carries on the family business of buying and selling, of chattering and dancing, to the danger of being blown up. It is all puzzled out, from afar, as a matter of the exchange, and in a large decree of the observance, from side to side, of guarantees, and the interesting thing to get at, for the student of manners, will ever be just this mystery of the terms of the bargain. I must add, none the less, that, though one was one's self, inevitably and always and everywhere, that student, my attention happened to be, or rather was obliged to be, confined to one view of the agreement. The arrangement is, obviously, between the great municipalities and the great populations, on the grand scale, and I lacked opportunity to look at it all round. I had but my glimpse of the apparently wide social acceptance of it—that is I saw but the face of the medal most directly turned to the light of day, and could note that nowhere so much as in Philadelphia was any carking care, in the social mind, any uncomfortable consciousness, as of a skeleton at the banquet of life, so gracefully veiled.

This struck me (on my looking back afterwards with more knowledge) as admirable, as heroic, in its way, and as falling in altogether with inherent habits of sociability, gaiety, gallantry, with that felt presence of a "temperament" with which the original Quaker drab seems to flush—giving it, as one might say for the sake of the figure, something of the iridescence of the breast of a well-fed dove. The original Quaker drab is still there, and, ideally, for the picture, up and down the uniform streets, one should see a bland, broad-brimmed, square-toed gentleman, or a bonneted, kerchiefed, mittened lady, on every little flight of white steps; but the very note of the place has been the "worldly" overscoring, for most of the senses, of the primitive monotone, the bestitching of the drab with pink and green and silver. The mixture has been, for a social effect, admirably successful, thanks, one seems to see, to the subtle, the charming absence of pedantry in the Quaker purity. It flushes gracefully, that temperate prejudice (with its predisposition to the universal *tutoiement*), turning first but to the prettiest pink; so that we never quite know where the drab has ended and the colour of the world has begun. The "disfrocked" Catholic is too strange, the paganized Puritan too angular; it is the accommodating Friend who has most the secret of a *modus vivendi*. And if it be asked, I may add, whether, in this case of social Philadelphia, the genius for life, and what I have called the gallantry of it above all, wouldn't have been better shown by a scorn of *any* compromise to which the nefarious City could invite it, I can only reply that, as a lover, always of romantic phenomena, and an inveterate seeker for them, I should have been deprived, by the action of that particular virtue, of the thrilled sense of a society dancing, all consciously, on the thin crust of a volcano. It is the thinness of the crust that makes, in such examples, the wild fantasy, the gay bravery, of the dance—just as I admit that a preliminary, an original extinction of the volcano would have illustrated another kind of virtue. The crust, for the social tread, would in this case have been firm, but the spectator's imagination would have responded less freely, I think, to the appeal of the scene. If I may indeed speak my whole thought for him he would so have had to drop again, to his regret, the treasure of a small analogy picked up on its very threshold.

How shall he confess at once boldly and shyly enough that the situation had at the end of a very short time

begun to strike him, for all its immeasurably reduced
and simplified form, as a much nearer approach to
the representation of an " old order," an *ancien régime*,
socially speaking, than any the field of American manners
had seemed likely to regale him with ?   Grotesque the
comparison if pushed ; yet how had he encountered
the similitude if it hadn't been hanging about ? From the
moment he adopted it, at any rate, he found it taking on
touch after touch.   The essence of old orders, as history
lights them, is just that innocent beatitude of consanguinity, of the multiplication of the assured felicities, to
which I have already alluded. From this, in Philadelphia,
didn't the rest follow ?—the sense, for every one, of being
in the same boat with every one else, a closed circle that
would find itself happy enough if only it could remain
closed enough.   The boat might considerably pitch, but
its occupants would either float merrily together or
(almost as merrily) go down together, and meanwhile the
risk, the vague danger, the jokes to be made about it, the
general quickened sociability and intimacy, were the very
music of the excursion.   There are even yet to be
observed about the world fragments and ghosts of old
social orders, thin survivals of final cataclysms, and it
was not less positive than beguiling that the common
marks by which these companies are known, and which
we still distinguish through their bedimmed condition,
cropped up for me in the high American light, making
good my odd parallel at almost every point.   Yet if these
signs of a slightly congested, but still practically self-
sufficing, little world were all there, they were perhaps
there most, to my ear, in the fact of the little world's
proper intimate idiom and accent : a dialect as much its
very own, even in drawing-rooms and libraries, as the
Venetian is that of Venice or the Neapolitan is that of
Naples—representing the common things of association,
the things easily understood and felt, and charged as no

other vehicle could be with the fund of local reference.
There is always the difference, of course, that at Venice
and at Naples, "in society," an alternative, either that
of French or of the classic, the more or less academic
Italian, is offered to the uninitiated stranger, whereas in
Philadelphia he is candidly, consistently, sometimes
almost contagiously entertained in the free vernacular.
The latter may easily become, in fact, under its wealth
of idiosyncrasy and if he have the favouring turn of mind,
a tempting object of linguistic study; with the bridge
built for him, moreover, that, unlike the Venetian, the
Neapolitan and most other local languages, it contains,
itself, colloquially, a notable element of the academic
and the classic. It struck me even, truly, as, with
a certain hardness in it, *constituting* the society that
employed it—very much as the egg is made oval by its
shell; and really, if I may say all, as taking its stand a
bit consciously sometimes, if not a bit defiantly, on its
own proved genius. I remember the visible dismay of a
gentleman, a pilgrim from afar, in a drawing-room, at the
comment of a lady, a lady of one of the new generations
indeed, and mistress of the tone by which I had here and
there occasion to observe that such ornaments of the new
generation might be known. "Listen to the creature :
he speaks English!"—it was the very opposite of the
indulgence or encouragement with which, in a Venetian
drawing-room (I catch my analogies as I can) the sound
of French or of Italian might have been greeted. The
poor "creature's" dismay was so visible, clearly, for the
reason that such things have only to be said with a certain
confidence to create a certain confusion—the momentary
consciousness of some such misdeed, from the point of
view of manners, as the speaking of Russian at Warsaw.
I have said that Philadelphia didn't bristle, but the heroine
of my anecdote caused the so genial city to resemble,
for the minute, linguistically, an unreconciled Poland.

III

But why do I talk of the new generations, or at any rate of the abyss in them that may seem here and there beyond one's shallow sounding, when, all the while, at the back of my head, hovers the image in the guise of which antiquity in Philadelphia looks most seated and most interesting? Nowhere throughout the country, I think, unless it be perchance at Mount Vernon, does our historic past so enjoy the felicity of an "important" concrete illustration. It survives there in visible form as it nowhere else survives, and one can doubtless scarce think too largely of what its mere felicity of presence, in these conditions, has done, and continues, and will continue, to do for the place at large. It may seem witless enough, at this time of day, to arrive from Pennsylvania with "news" of the old State House, and my news, I can only recognize, began but with being news for myself—in which character it quite shamelessly pretended both to freshness and to brilliancy. Why *shouldn't* it have been charming, the high roof under which the Declaration of Independence had been signed?—that was of course a question that might from the first have been asked of me, and with no better answer in wait for it than that, after all, it might just have happened, in the particular conditions, not to be ; or else that, in general, one is allowed a margin, on the spot, for the direct sense of consecrated air, for that communication of its spirit which, in proportion as the spirit has been great, withholds itself, shyly and nobly, from any mere forecast. This it is exactly that, by good fortune, keeps up the sanctity of shrines and the lessons of history, to say nothing of the freshness of individual sensibility and the general continuity of things. There is positively nothing of Independence Hall, of its fine old Georgian amplitude and decency, its large serenity and symmetry of pink and drab, and its actual emphasis of detachment from the vulgar brush of things, that is *not* charming; and there is nothing, the city through, that doesn't receive a mild sidelight, that of a reflected interest, from its neighbourhood.

This element of the reflected interest, and more particularly of the reflected distinction, is for the most part, on the American scene, the missed interest—despite the ingenuities of wealth and industry and "energy" that strain so touchingly often, and even to grimace and contortion, somehow to supply it. One finds one's self, when it *has* happened to intervene, weighing its action to the last grain of gold. One even puts to one's self fantastic cases, such as the question, for instance, of what might, what might *not* have happened if poor dear reckless New York had been so distinguished or so blest—with the bad conscience she is too intelligent not to have, her power to be now and then ashamed of her "form," lodged, after all, somewhere in her interminable boots. One has of course to suppress there the prompt conviction that the blessing—that of the possession of an historical monument of the first order—would long since have been replaced by the higher advantage of a row of sky-scrapers yielding rents; yet the imagination none the less dallies with the fond vision of some respect somehow instilled, some deference somehow suggested, some revelation of the possibilities of a public *tenue* somehow effected. Fascinating in fact to speculate a little as to what a New York held in respect by something or other, some power not of the purse, might have become. It is bad, ever, for lusty youth, especially with a command of means, to grow up without knowing at least one "nice family"—if the family be not priggish; and this is the danger that the young Philadelphia, with its eyes on the superior connection I am speaking of, was enabled to escape. The charming old pink and drab heritage of the great time was to be the superior connection, playing, for the education of the place, the part of the nice family. Socially, morally, even æsthetically, the place was to be thus more or less inevitably built round it; but for which good fortune who knows if even Philadelphia too might have not been vulgar? One meets throughout the land enough instances of the opposite luck—the situation of immense and "successful" communities that have lacked, originally, anything "first-rate," as they might themselves put it, to be built round; anything better, that is, than some profitable hole in the earth, some confluence of rivers or command of lakes or railroads: and one sees how, though this deficiency may not have made itself felt at first, it has inexorably loomed larger and larger, the drawback of it growing all the while with the growth of the place. Our sense of such predicaments, for the gatherings of men, comes back, I think, and with an intensity of interest, to our sense of the way the human imagination absolutely declines everywhere to go to sleep without some apology at least for a supper. The collective consciousness, in however empty an air, gasps for a relation, as intimate as possible, to something superior, something as central as possible, from which it may more or less have proceeded and round which its life may revolve—and its dim desire is always, I think, to do it justice, that this object or presence shall have had as much as possible an heroic or romantic association. But the difficulty is that in these later times, among such aggregations, the heroic and romantic elements, even under the earliest rude stress, have been all too tragically obscure, belonged to smothered, unwritten, almost unconscious private history: so that the central something, the social *point de repère*, has had to be extemporized rather pitifully after the fact, and made to consist of the biggest hotel or the biggest common school, the biggest factory, the biggest newspaper office, or, for climax of desperation, the house of

the biggest billionaire. These are the values resorted to
in default of higher, for with *some* coloured rag or other
the general imagination, snatching its chance, must dress
its doll.

As a real, a moral value, to the general mind, at all
events, and not as a trumped-up one, I saw the lucky
legacy of the past, at Philadelphia, operate ; though I
admit that these are, at best, for the mooning observer,
matters of appreciation, mysteries of his own sensibility.
Such an observer has early to perceive, and to conclude
on it once for all, that there will be little for him in the
American scene unless he be ready, anywhere, everywhere, to read "into" it as much as he reads out. It is
at its best for him when most open to that friendly
penetration, and not at its best, I judge, when practically
most closed to it. And yet how can I pretend to be
able to say, under this discrimination, what was better
and what was worse in Independence Hall?—to say
how far the charming facts struck me as going of themselves, or where the imagination (perhaps on this sole
patch of ground, by exception, a meddler "not wanted
anyhow") took them up to carry them further. I am
reduced doubtless to the comparative sophism of making
my better sense here consist but of my sense of the fine
interior of the building. One sees them immediately as
"good," delightfully good, on architectural and scenic
lines, these large, high, wainscoted chambers, as good
as any could thinkably have been at the time ; embracing
what was to be done in them with such a noble congruity
(which in all the conditions they might readily have
failed of, though they were no mere tent pitched for the
purpose) that the historic imagination, reascending the
centuries, almost catches them in the act of directly
suggesting the celebrated *coup*. One fancies, under the
high spring of the ceiling and before the great embrasured window-sashes of the principal room, some

clever man of the period, after a long look round, taking the hint. "*What* an admirable place for a Declaration of something! What could one here—what *couldn't* one really declare?" And then after a moment: "I say, why not our Independence?—capital thing always to declare, and before any one gets in with anything tactless. You'll see that the fortune of the place will be made." It really takes some such frivolous fancy as that to represent with proper extravagance the reflection irresistibly rising there and that it yet would seem pedantic to express with solemnity : the sense, namely, of our beautiful escape in not having had to "declare" in any way meanly, of our good fortune in having found half the occasion made to our hand.

High occasions consist of many things, and it was extraordinary luck for our great date that not one of these, even as to surface and appearance, should have been wanting. There might easily have been traps laid for us by some of the inferior places, but I am convinced (and more completely than of anything else in the whole connection) that the genius of historic decency would have kept us enslaved rather than have seen us committed to one of those. In that light, for the intelligent pilgrim, the Philadelphia monument becomes, under his tread, under the touch of his hand and the echo of his voice, the very prize, the sacred thing itself, contended for and gained ; so that its quality, in fine, is irresistible and its dignity not to be uttered. I was so conscious, for myself, I confess, of the intensity of this perception, that I dip deep into the whole remembrance without touching bottom ; by which I mean that I grope, reminiscentially, in the full basin of the general experience of the spot without bringing up a detail. Distinct to me only the way its character, so clear yet so ample, everywhere hangs together and keeps itself up ; distinct to me only the large sense, in halls and spreading staircase and long-drawn upper gallery, of one of those rare precincts of the past against which the present has kept beating in vain. The present comes in and stamps about and very stertorously breathes, but its sounds are as naught the next moment; it is as if one felt there that the grandparent, reserved, irresponsive now, and having spoken his word, in his finest manner, once for all, must have long ago had enough of the exuberance of the young grandson's modernity. But of course the great impression is that of the persistent actuality of the so auspicious room in which the Signers saw their tossing ship into port. The lapse of time here, extraordinarily, has sprung no leak in the effect; it remains so robust that everything lives again, the interval drops out and we mingle in the business: the old ghosts, to our inward sensibility, still make the benches creak as they free their full coat-skirts for sitting down; still make the temperature rise, the pens scratch, the papers flutter, the dust float in the large sun-shafts; we place them as they sit, watch them as they move, hear them as they speak, pity them as they ponder, know them, in fine, from the arch of their eyebrows to the shuffle of their shoes.

I am not sure indeed that, for mere archaic insolence, the little old Hall of the Guild of Carpenters, my vision of which jostles my memory of the State House, does not carry it even with a higher hand—in spite of a bedizenment of restoration, within, which leads us to rejoice that the retouchings of the greater monument expose themselves comparatively so little. The situation of this elegant structure—of dimensions and form that scarce differ, as I recall them, from those of delicate little Holden Chapel, of the so floridly-overlaid gable, most articulate single word, in College Yard, of the small builded sense of old Harvard—comes nearer to representing an odd town-nook than any other corner of American life that I remember; American life having been organized, *ab ovo*, with an hostility to the town-nook which has left no scrap of provision for eyes needing on occasion a refuge from the general glare. The general glare seemed to me, at the end of something like a passage, in the shade of something like a court, and in the presence of something like a relic, to have mercifully intermitted, on that fine Philadelphia morning; I won't answer for the exact correspondence of the conditions with my figure of them, since the shade I speak of may have been but the shade of "tall" buildings, the vulgarest of new accidents. Yet I let my impression stand, if only as a note of the relief certain always to lurk, at any turn of the American scene, in the appearance of any individual thing within, or behind, or at the end, or in the depth, of any other individual thing. It makes for the sense of complexity, relieves the eternal impression of things all in a row and of a single thickness, an impression which the usual unprecedented length of the American alignment (always its source of pride) does by itself little to mitigate. Nothing in the array is "behind" anything else—an odd result, I admit, of the fact that so many things affirm themselves as preponderantly before. Little Carpenters' Hall *was*, delightfully, somewhere behind; so much behind, as I perhaps thus fantastically see it, that I dare say I should not be able to find my way to it again if I were to try. Nothing, for that matter, would induce me to revisit in fact, I feel, the object I so fondly evoke. It might have been, for this beautiful posteriority, somewhere in the City of London.

IV

I can but continue to lose myself, for these connections, in my *whole* sense of the intermission, as I have called it, of the glare. The mellower light prevailed, somehow, *all* that fine Philadelphia morning, as well as on two or three other occasions—and I cannot, after all, pretend I don't now see why. It was because one's experience of the place had become immediately an intimate thing—intimate with that intimacy that I had tasted, from the first, in the local air ; so that, inevitably, thus, there was no keeping of distinct accounts for public and private items. An ancient church or two, of aspect as Anglican still as you please, and taking, for another case, from the indifferent bustle round it, quite the look of Wren's mere steepled survivals in the backwaters of London churchyards ; Franklin's grave itself, in its own backwater of muffled undulations, close to the indifferent bustle ; Franklin's admirable portrait by Duplessis in the council-room of an ancient, opulent Trust, a conservative Company, vague and awful to my shy sense, that was housed after the fashion of some exclusive, madeira-drinking old gentleman with obsequious heirs : these and other matters, wholly thrilling at the time, float back to me as on the current of talk and as in the flood, so to speak, of hospitality. If Philadelphia had, in opposition to so many other matters, struck me as coherent, there would be surely no point of one's contact at which this might so have come home as in those mysterious chambers and before the most interesting of the many far-scattered portraits of Franklin—the portrait working as some sudden glimpse of the fine old incised seal, kept in its glass cabinet, that had originally stamped all over, for identification, the comparatively soft local wax. One thinks of Franklin's reputation, of his authority—and however much they may have been locally contested at the time—as marking the material about him much as his name might have marked his underclothing or his pocket-books. Small surprise one had the impression of a Society, with such a figure as that to start conversation. He seemed to preside over it all while one lingered there, as if he had been seated, at the mahogany, relentingly enough, near his glass of madeira; seemed to be "in" it even more freely than by the so interesting fact of his still having, in Philadelphia, in New York, in Boston, through his daughter, so numerous a posterity. The sense of life, life the most positive, most human and most miscellaneous, expressed in his aged, crumpled, canny face, where the smile wittily profits, for fineness, by the comparative collapse of the mouth, represents a suggestion which succeeding generations may well have found it all they could do to work out. It is impossible, in the place, after seeing that portrait, not to feel him still with them, with the genial generations—even though to-day, in the larger, more mixed cup, the force of his example may have suffered some dilution.

It was a savour of which, at any rate, for one's own draught, one could but make the most; and I went so far, on this occasion, as fairly to taste it there in the very quality of my company—in that of the distinguished guidance and protection I was enjoying, which could only make me ask myself in what finer modern form one would have wished to see Franklin's humanity and sagacity, his variety and ingenuity, his wealth of ideas and his tireless application of them, embodied. There was verily nothing to do, after this, but to play over the general picture that light of his assumption of the general ease of things—of things at any rate thereabouts; so that I now see each reminiscence, whatever the time or the place, happily governed and coloured by it. Times and places, in such an experience, ranged themselves, after a space, like valued objects in one of the assorted rooms of a "collection." Keep them a little, tenderly handled, wrapped up, stowed away, and they then come forth, into the room swept and garnished, susceptible of almost any pleasing arrangement. The only thing is that you shall scarce know, at a given moment, amid your abundance, which of them to take up first; there being always in them, moreover, at best, the drawback of value from mere association, that keepsake element of objects in a reliquary. Is not this, however, the drawback for exhibition of almost any item of American experience that may not pretend to deal with the mere monstrosities?—the immensities of size and space, of trade and traffic, of organisation, political, educational, economic. From the moment one's record is not, in fine, a loud statistical shout, it falls into the order of those shy things that speak, at the most (when one is one's self incapable even of the merest statistical whisper), but of the personal adventure—in other words but of one's luck and of one's sensibility. There are incidents, there are passages, that flush, in this fashion, to the backward eye, under the torch. But what solemn statement is one to make of the "importance," for example, of such a matter as the Academy soirée (as they say in London) of the Philadelphia winter, the festive commemoration of some long span of life achieved by the Pennsylvania Academy of Fine Arts? We may have been thrilled, positively, by the occasion, by the interesting encounters and discoveries, artistic and personal, to which it ministered; we may have moved from one charmed recognition to another, noting Sargents and Whistlers by the dozen, and old forgotten French friends, foreign friends in general, older and younger; noting young native upstarts, creatures of yesterday and to-morrow, who invite, with all success, a stand and a stare; but no after-sense of such vibrations, however lively, presumes to take itself as communicable.

One would regret, on the other hand, failing to sound some echo of a message everywhere in the United States so audible; that of the clamorous signs of a hungry social growth, the very pulses, making all their noise, of the engine that works night and day for a theory of civilization. There are moments at which it may well seem that, putting the sense of the spectacle even at its lowest, there is no such amusement as this anywhere supplied; the air through which everything shows is so transparent, with steps and stages and processes as distinct in it as the appearance, from a street-corner, of a crowd rushing on an alarm to a fire. The gregarious crowd "tells," in the street, and the indications I speak of tell, like chalk-marks, on the demonstrative American blackboard—an impression perhaps never so much brought home to me as by a wondrous Sunday morning at the edge of a vast vacant Philadelphia street, a street not of Penn's creation and vacant of everything but an immeasurable bourgeois blankness. I had turned from that scene into a friendly house that was given over, from top to toe, to a dazzling collection of pictures, amid which I felt myself catch in the very act one of the great ingurgitations of the hungry machine, and recognize as well how perfect were all the conditions for making it a case. What could have testified less, on the face of it, than the candour of the street's insignificance?—a pair of huge parted lips protesting almost to pathos their innocence of anything to say: which was exactly, none the less, where appetite had broken out and was feeding itself to satiety. Large and liberal the hospitality, remarkably rich the store of acquisition, in the light of which the whole energy of the keen collector showed: the knowledge, the acuteness, the audacity, the incessant watch for opportunity. These abrupt and multiplied encounters, intensities, ever so

various, of individual curiosity, sound the æsthetic note
sometimes with unprecedented shrillness and then again
with the most muffled discretion. Was the note muffled
or shrill, meanwhile, as I listened to it—under a fascination
I fully recognized—during an hour spent in the clustered
palæstra of the University of Pennsylvania? Here the
winter afternoon seemed to throw itself artfully back,
across the centuries, the climates, the seasons, the very
faiths and codes, into the air of old Greece and the age of
gymnastic glory: artfully, I rather insist, because I scarce
know what fine emphasis of modernism hung about it too.
I put that question, however, only to deny myself the
present luxury of answering it; so thickly do the visitor's
University impressions, over the land, tend to gather, and
so markedly they suggest their being reported of together.
I note my palæstral hour, therefore, but because it fell
through what it seemed to show me, straight into what
I had conceived of the Philadelphia scheme, the happy
family given up, though quite on "family" lines, to all
the immediate beguilements and activities ; the art in
particular of cultivating, with such gaiety as might be,
a brave civic blindness.

I became conscious of but one excrescence on this
large smooth surface; it is true indeed that the excrescence was huge and affected me as demanding in some
way to be dealt with. The Pennsylvania Penitentiary
rears its ancient grimness, its grey towers and defensive
moats (masses at least that uncertain memory so figures
for me) in an outlying quarter which struck me as
borrowing from them a vague likeness to some more or
less blighted minor city of Italy or France, black Angers
or dead Ferrara—yet seated on its basis of renown and
wrapped in its legend of having, as the first flourishing
example of the strictly cellular system, the complete
sequestration of the individual prisoner, thought wonderful in its day, moved Charles Dickens to the passionate

protest recorded in his *American Notes.* Of such substance was the story of these battlements; yet it was unmistakable that when one had crossed the drawbridge and passed under the portcullis the air seemed thick enough with the breath of the generations. A prison has, at the worst, the massive majesty, the sinister peace of a prison ; but this huge house of sorrow affected me as, uncannily, of the City itself, the City of all the cynicisms and impunities against which my friends had, from far back, kept plating, as with the old silver of their sideboards, the armour of their social consciousness. It made the whole place, with some of its oddly antique aspects and its oddly modern freedoms, look doubly cut off from the world of light and ease. The suggestions here were vast, however ; too many of them swarm, and my imagination must defend itself as it can. What I was most concerned to note was the complete turn of the wheel of fortune in respect to the measure of mere incarceration suffered, from which the worst of the rigour had visibly been drawn. Parts of the place suggested a sunny Club at a languid hour, with members vaguely lounging and chatting, with open doors and comparatively cheerful vistas, and plenty of rocking-chairs and magazines. The only thing was that, under this analogy, one found one's self speculating much on the implied requisites for membership. It was impossible not to wonder, from face to face, what these would have been, and not to ask what one would have taken them to be if the appearance of a Club had been a little more complete. I almost blush, I fear, for the crude comfort of my prompt conclusion. One would have taken them to consist, without exception, of full-blown basenesses ; one couldn't, from member to member, from type to type, from one pair of eyes to another, take them for anything less. Where was the victim of circumstances, where the creature merely misled or betrayed ? He fitted no type, he suffered in no face, he yearned in no history, and one felt, the more one took in his absence, that the numerous substitutes for him were good enough for each other.

The great interest was in this sight of the number and variety of ways of looking morally mean ; and perhaps also in the question of how much the effect came from its being proved upon them, of how little it might have come if they had still been out in the world. Considered as criminals the moral meanness here was their explication. Considered as morally mean, therefore, would possible criminality, out in the world, have been in the same degree their sole sense ? Was the fact of prison *all* the mere fact of opportunity, and the fact of freedom all the mere fact of the absence of it ? One inclined to believe that—the simplification was at any rate so great for one's feeling : the cases presented became thus, consistently, cases of the vocation, and from the moment this was clear the place took on, in its way, almost the harmony of a convent. I talked for a long time with a charming reprieved murderer whom I half expected, at any moment, to see ring for coffee and cigars : he explained with all urbanity, and with perfect lucidity, the real sense of the appearance against him, but I none the less felt sure that his merit was largely in the refinement wrought in him by so many years of easy club life. He was as natural a subject for commutation as for conviction, and had had to have the latter in order to have the former—in the enjoyment, and indeed in the subtle criticism, of which, *as* simple commutation he was at his best. They were there, all those of his companions, I was able to note, unmistakably at their best. One could, as I say, suffi-ciently rest in it, and to do that kept, in a manner, the excrescence, as I have called it, on the general scene, within bounds. I was moreover luckily to see the general scene definitely cleared again, cleared of everything save its own social character and its practical philosophy—and at no moment with these features so brightly presented as during a few days' rage of winter round an old country-house. The house was virtually distant from town, and the conditions could but strike any visitor who stood whenever he might with his back to the fire, where the logs were piled high, as made to press on all the reserves and traditions of the general temperament; those of gallantry, hilarity, social disposability, crowned with the grace of the sporting instinct. What was it confusedly, almost romantically, like, what "old order" commemorated in fiction and anecdote? I had groped for this, as I have shown, before, but I found myself at it again. Wasn't it, for freedom of movement, for jingle of sleigh-bells, for breasting of the elements, for cross-country drives in the small hours, for *crânerie* of fine young men and high wintry colour of muffled nymphs, wasn't it, brogue and all, like some audible echo of close-packing, chancing Irish society of the classic time, seen and heard through a roaring blizzard? That at least, with his back to the fire, was where the restless analyst was landed.

10

Baltimore

It had doubtless not been merely absurd, as the wild winter proceeded, to find one's self so enamoured of the very name of the South that one was ready to take it in any small atmospheric instalment and to feel the echo of its voice in the yell of any engine that happened not to drag one either directly North or directly West. One tended at least, on these terms, in some degree, toward the land where the citron blooms, and that was something to go on with, a handful of small change accepted for the time as a pledge of great gold pieces to come. It is astonishing, along the Atlantic coast, how, from the moment the North ceases to insist, the South may begin to presume; ever so little, no doubt, at first, yet with protrusive feelers that tell how she only wants the right sensibility, the true waiting victim, to play upon. It is a question certainly of where, on the so frequently torpid stretch of shore I speak of, the North does cease to insist; or perhaps I should more correctly say a question of when it does. It appeared incapable of this fine tact almost anywhere, I confess, at the season, the first supposedly relenting weeks, of my facing in earnest to Florida; and the interest indeed of that slightly grim adventure was to be in the way it ministered to the coincidence, for me, of two quite opposed strains of reflection. On the one hand nothing could "say" more to the subject long expatriated, condemned by the terms of his exile to a chronic consciousness of grey northern seas, than to feel how, from New York, or even from Boston, he had but to sit still in his portentous car, had but to exercise a due concentrated patience, in order to become aware, without personal effort or suffered transfer, of that most charming of all watchable processes, the gradual soft, the distinctively demoralized, conversion of the soul of Nature. This conversion, if I may so put it without profanity, has always struck me, on any south-ward course, as a return, on the part of that soul, from a comparatively grim Theistic faith to the ineradicable principle of Paganism ; a conscious casting-off of the dread theological abstraction—an abstraction still, even with all Puritan stiffening—in the interest of multiplied, lurking, familiar powers ; divinities, graces, presences as unseen but as inherent as the scents clinging to the folds of Nature's robe. It would be on such occasions the fault of the divine familiars themselves if their haunts and shrines were empty, for earth and air and day and night, as we go, still affect us as moods of their sympathy, still vibrate to the breath of their passage ; so that our progress, under the expanding sun, resembles a little less a journey through space than a retracing of the course of the ages.

These are fine fancies, however, and what is more to my point is that the theory (so agreeable to entertain at Jersey City) of a direct connection between the snow-banks and the orange-groves is a thing of sweetness only so long as practically unshaken. There is continuity, goodness knows, always in America—it is the last thing that is ever broken : the question for the particular case is but continuity of what ? The basis of my individual hope had been that of the reign of the orange-grove ; but what it proved, at the crisis I name, was positively that of the usurpation of the snow-bank. It was possible, indubitably, in such conditions, to go to Charleston on sledges—which made in fact, after all, for directness of connection.   It made moreover, by the same token, for a certain sinister light on the general truth of our grand territorial unity.   It was as if the winter, at the end of February, abroad for a walk, had marched as promptly and inevitably from the Arctic Circle to the Gulf as it might have proceeded, with pride in its huge clear course, from the top of Broadway to the Battery.   This brought home again, as I myself went, I remember, one of those three or four main ideas, suggested by the recurrent conditions, which become as obsessions for the traveller in the States—if he have a mind, that is, so indecently exposed to ideas : the sense, constantly fed, and from a hundred sources, that, as Nature abhors a vacuum, so it is of the genius of the American land and the American people to abhor, whenever may be, a discrimination. They are reduced, together, under stress, to making discriminations, but they make them, I think, as lightly and scantily as possible.   With the lively insistence of that impression, even though it quite undermined my fond view of a loose and overreaching citronic belt, I found my actually monotonous way beguiled.   Practically, till I reached Charleston, this way, disclaiming every invidious intent, refused to be dissociated from anything else in the world : it was only another case of the painting with a big brush, a brush steeped in crude universal white, and of the colossal size this implement was capable of assuming.   Gradations, transitions, differences of any sort, temporal, material, social, whether in man or in his environment, shrank somehow, under its sweep, to negligible items ; and one had perhaps never yet seemed so to move through a vast simplified scheme.   The illustration was oncemore, in fine, of the small inherent, the small accumulated resistance, in American air, to any force that does simplify.   One found the signs of such resistance as little in the prospect enjoyed from the car-window as one distinguished them in the vain images of the interior; those human documents, deciphered from one's seat in the Pullman, which yet do always, in *their* way, for the traveller, constitute precious evidence. The spread of this single great wash of winter from latitude to latitude struck me in fact as having its analogy in the vast vogue of some infinitely-selling novel, one of those happy volumes of which the circulation roars, periodic-ally, from Atlantic to Pacific and from great windy State to State, in the manner, as I have heard it vividly put, of a blazing prairie fire; with as little possibility of arrest from "criticism" in the one case as from the bleating of lost sheep in the other. Everything, so to speak, was monotonized, and the whole social order might have had its nose, for the time, buried, by one levelling doom, in the pages that, after the break of the spell, it would never know itself to mention again. Of course, one remembered meanwhile, there were spells and spells, and the free field—the particular freedom of which is the point of my remark—would on occasion be just as open to the far-exhaled breath of the South. That in fact is what I was to find it—though I thought all delightfully—later in the season, when the freedom of the field struck me as pure benefit. I was not, at the end of February, really to meet it (as I had looked for it) before crossing the Florida line; but toward the middle of June I was to meet it, enchantingly, at Baltimore, and this, then, as I had not stopped there in my previous course, was, even beyond the wondrous February Florida, to reveal to me, grateful for any such favour, the South in her freshness. The freshness was in part, no doubt—and even perhaps to extravagance—mine; I testify at all events first for Baltimore.

It would probably be again the freshness, of this con-fessedly subjective sort, it would probably be again the

state of alert response to any favour of the class just
hinted at ; but the immediate effect of the Maryland
capital was to place it, to my troubled vision, and quite
at the head of its group, in a category of images and
memories small at the best and the charm of which casts
a shadow, none the less, even as the rose wears a thorn.
I refer indeed in this slightly portentous figure to the
mere familiar truth that if representative values and the
traceable or the imaginable connections of things happen
to have, on occasion, for your eyes and your intelligence,
an existence of any intensity, your case, as a traveller, an
observer, a reporter, is " bound " from the first, under
the stirred impression, to loom for you in some distressful
shape. These representative values and constructive
connections, the whole of the latent vividness of things,
not only remain, under expression, subject to no definite
chemical test, no mathematical proof whatever, but
almost turn their charming backs and toss their wilful
heads at one's poor little array of terms and equivalents.
There thus immediately rises for the lone visionary,
betrayed and arrested in the very act of vision, that
spectre of impotence which dogs the footsteps of perception and whose presence is like some poison-drop in the
silver cup. Baltimore put on for me, from the first
glance, the form of the silver cup filled with the mildest,
sweetest decoction ; but I had no sooner begun to taste
of it than I began to taste also of the infused bitter. It
had, in its way, during that first early hour or two of the
summer evening, a perfect felicity : which meant, for the
touched intelligence, that it was full of pleasantly-playing
reference and reflection, that it exhaled on the spot, as
the word goes, an atmosphere ; that it wore, to contemplation, in fine, a character as marked with mild
accents as some faded old uniform is marked with
tarnished buttons and braid—albeit these sources of
interest were too closely of the texture to be snipped off,

in the guise of patterns or relics, by any mere sharp shears of journalism.

I arrived late in the day, and the day had been lovely; I alighted at a large fresh peaceful hostelry, imposingly modern yet quietly affable, and, having recognized the deep, soft general note, even from my windows, as that of a kind of mollified vivacity, I sought the streets with as many tacit questions as I judged they would tolerate, or as the waning day would allow me to put. It took but that hour, as I strolled in the early eventide, to give me the sense of the predicament I have glanced at; that of finding myself committed to the view of Baltimore as quite insidiously " sympathetic," quite inordinately amiable —which amounted, in other words, to the momentous proposition that she was interesting—and still of wondering, by the same stroke, how I was to make any such statement plausible. Character is founded on elements and features, so many particular parts which conduce to an expression. So I walked about the dear little city looking for the particular parts—all with the singular effect of rather failing to find them and with my impression of felicity at the same time persistently growing. The felicity was certainly not that of a mere blank; there must accordingly have been items and objects, signs and tokens, there must have been causes of so charming a consequence; there must have been the little numbers (not necessarily big, if only a tall enough column) for the careful sum on my slate. What happened then, remarkably, was that while I mechanically so argued my impression was fixing itself by a wild logic of its own, and that I was presently to see how it would, when once settled to a certain intensity, snap its fingers at warrants and documents. If it was a question of a slate the slate was used, at school, I remembered, for more than one purpose; so that mine, by my walk's end, instead of a show of neat ciphering, exhibited simply a bold drawn image—which had the merit moreover of not being in the least a caricature. The moral of this was precious— that of the fine impunity with which, if one but had sensibility, the ciphering could be neglected and in fact almost contemned : always, that is (and only) *with* one's finer wits about one. Without them one was at best, really, nowhere—even with "items" by the thousand ; so that the place became, quite adorably, a lesson in the use of that resource. It would be "no good" to a journalist—for *he* is nowhere, ever, without his items ; but it would be everything, always, to the mere restless analyst. He might by its aid stand against all comers ; and this alike in pleasure and in pain, in the bruised or in the soothed condition. That was the real way to work things out, and to feel it so brought home would by itself sufficiently crown this particular small pilgrimage.

II

If my sensibility yielded so completely to Baltimore, however, I should add, this was no doubt partly because the air seemed from the first to breathe upon it a pledge of no bruises. I mounted, in the golden June light, the neatest, amplest, emptiest street-vista, the builded side of a steepish hill, and, having come in due course to a spacious summit, laid out with monumental elegance and completely void, for the time, of the human footstep, I saw that to suffer in any fibre I should have positively, somewhere, to hurl myself upon the spears. Not a point protruded then or afterwards ; and the cunning of the restless analyst is essentially such that, with friction long enough in abeyance to leave him a start, he is already astride of his happier thesis, seated firm, having "elected" to be undismountable, and riding it as hard as it will go.

The absence of friction, on my monumental hilltop and in the prospects it overhung, constituted, I was to find, an absolute circus-ring for this exercise; and it is much to be able to say, while performing in the circus (even if but mainly to the public of one's own conscience), that one has never had the sense of a safer hour. The safety of Baltimore, I should indeed mention, consisted perhaps a little overmuch, during that first flush, in its apparently vacant condition: it affected me as a sort of perversely cheerful little city of the dead; and from the dead, naturally, comes no friction. Was it cheerful, that is, or was it only resigned and discreet?—with the manner of the good breeding that doesn't publicly prate of family troubles. I found myself handling, in imagination, these large quantities only because, as I suppose, it was impossible not to remember on that spot of what native generation one had come. It took no greater intensity of the South than Baltimore could easily give to figure again, however fadedly, and all as a ghostly presence, the huge shadow of the War, and to reproduce that particular bloodstained patch of it which, in the very first days, the now so irresponsible and absent community about me had flung across the path of the North. This one echo of old Time made the connections, for the instant, all vibrate, and the scene before me, somehow, as it stood, had to account for the great revolution. It was as if *that*, for the restless analyst, had to be disposed of before anything else: whereby, precisely, didn't the amenity of his impression partly spring from the descent there, on the spot, in a quick white flash, of the most august of the Muses? It was History in person that hovered, just long enough for me to recognize her and to read, in her strange deep eyes, *her* intelligence at least of everything. It might have been there fairly as re-assurance. "Yes, they have lived with *me*, and it has done them good, and we have buried together all their past—about which, wise creature as I am, I allow them, of course, all piety. But this—what you make out around us—is their real collective self, which I am delighted to commend to you. I've found Baltimore a charming patient." That was, in ten minutes, what it had come to ; as if the brush of the sublime garment had by itself cleared the air. If there was a fine warm hush everywhere it was indeed partly that of this historic peace.

But for the rest it only meant that the world was at such a season out of town. Houses were everywhere closed, and the neat perspectives, all domiciliary and all, as I have hinted, tending mildly to a vague elegance, were the more neat and more elegant, though doubtless also the more mild and the more vague, for their being so inanimate. A certain vividness of high decency seemed in spite of it to possess them, and this suggestion of the real southern glow, yet with no southern loose-ness, was clearly something by itself—all special and local and all, or almost all, expressed in repeated vistas of little brick-faced and protrusively door-stepped houses, which, overhung by tall, regular umbrage, suggested rows of quiet old ladies seated, with their toes tucked-up on uniform footstools, under the shaded candlesticks of old-fashioned tea-parties. The little ladylike squares, though below any tide-mark of fashion, were particularly frequent ; in which case it was as if the virtuous dames had drawn together round a large green table, albeit to no more riotous end than that each should sit before her individual game of patience. One sounds inevitably the note of the " virtue "—so little, in general, can any picture of American town-appearance hang together without it. It amounts, everywhere, to something intenser than the implied absence of " vice " ; it amounts to a sort of registered absence of the conception or the imagination of it, and still more of the provision for it ;

though, all the while, as one goes and comes, one feels that no community can really be as purged of peccant humours as the typical American has for the most part found itself foredoomed to look. It has been caught in the mechanism of that consistency—to an effect of convenience, doubtless, much more than to any other ; and has thus, in the whole vast connection, a relation to appearances that is all its own. The " European " scene, at a thousand points, looks all its sophistications straight out at us—or looks, in other words, at least as perverse as it practically is. The American, on the other hand, expressing physiognomically no sophistications at all— though plenty of quite common candours, crudities and vulgarities—makes one ask if the cash-register, the ice-cream freezer, the lightning-elevator, the "boys' paper," and other such overflows, do truly represent the sum of its passions. Incontestably, at all events, this immensely ingenuous aspect counts, for any country and any scheme of life, as a great force, just as the appearance of the stale and the congested residing in the comparatively battered mask of experience counts as a weakness : to conceive which the mind's eye has only to fix a little the colossal American face grimacing with anything of a subtler consciousness. That image, if actually presented, would become, as we feel, appalling. The inexorable fate of the countenance in question may be so to learn to grimace in time, but though few processes are slow, in the United States, and few exhibitions not contagious, any such transition, assuredly, will not be rapid, any more than any such tendency will easily predominate.

All of which would have carried me far from the simple sweetness of Baltimore, were it not that, for the restless analyst, there is no such thing as an unrelated fact, no such thing as a break in the chain of relations. Many a perceived American aspect, for that matter, would by itself have little to give; the student of manners, in other words, to make it presentable—by which I understand to make it *sufficiently* interesting— must first discover connections for it and then borrow from these, if possible, the elements of a wardrobe. And though it should sound a little monstrous, moreover, one had somehow not been prepared for so delicate an effect of propriety; since there are cases too, indubitably, in which propriety can show for almost as coarse as anything else. It couldn't have been, either, that one had expected any positive air of licence; but the fact was, I suppose, that, for a constitutional story-seeker, a certain still, small shock, a prompt need of readjustment of view, was involved in one's finding the element of the bourgeois crop up, so inveterately, in latitudes generally associated, so far as one knew them elsewhere, with some perceptible sacrifice to the sway of the senses. I had already, at this date, as I have noted, dipped deep into our own uttermost South, and had there had to reckon with that first slight disconcertment awaiting the observer whose southern categories happen to have been wholly European. His simplest expression for the anomaly he meets is that he sees the citronic belt all incongruously Protestantized: that big word (for so small a bewilderment perhaps) sticks to him and worries him—almost as absurdly, I grant, as if he had expected Charleston and Savannah to betray the moral accent of Naples or Seville. He had not, assuredly, done this; but he had as little allowed, in imagination, for the hyperborean note. A South without church-fronts and church-interiors had been superficially as strange, in its way, as a Methodism of the sub-tropic night, a Methodism of the orange and the palm. Such were the treacheries of association; though what indeed would observation be, for interest, if it were not, just by these armed surprises, constantly touched with adventure? The beauty of Baltimore was, all this time, that one could feel it as potentially harmonizing; the citronic belt would

not embrace here more Methodism than might consort
with it, nor the Methodism pretend to cultivate with any
success the hibiscus and the pomegranate.

That I could entertain so many incoherent ideas in
half-an-hour was in any case a proof that I felt, for the
occasion, left in possession; quite as the visitor as yet
unintroduced may feel during some long preliminary wait
in a drawing-room. He looks at the furniture, pictures,
books; he studies in these objects the character of the
house and of his hosts, and if there be some domestic
treasure visibly more important and conspicuous than the
others, it engages his attention as either with a fatal or
an engaging force. The top of the central eminence,
with its air of an ample plan and of sweeping the rest
of the circle, figured the documentary parlour and my
enjoyed leave to touch and examine; so that when
it was a question, in particular, of the monument to
Washington, the high column, in the middle, with its
surmounting figure and its spreading architectural base,
this presence was, for all the world, like that of some
vast and stately old-fashioned clock, a decorative "piece,"
an heirloom from generations now respectably remote,
occupying an inordinate space in proportion to the other
conveniences. The ornamental, the "important" clock
is apt to be in especial, at such a crisis, a telltale object;
its range of testimony, of possible treachery, is immense,
and cases are not unknown, I gather, in which it has put
the doubting visitor to flight. The greater the felicity,
thereby, for the overtopping Baltimore timepiece, which
hung about in mild reassurance, promptly aware that it
wasn't a bit vulgar, but, on the contrary, of a pleasant
jejune academic pomp that suggested to the fancy some
melancholy, some spectral, man-at-arms mounting guard
at the angles, in due military form, over suspected
treasures of Style. One could imagine, somehow, under
the summer stars, the mystic vigil of these mild heroes;

and one could above all catch again the interesting hint of the terms on which, in the United States, the consecration of time may be found operating. It has a trick there all of its own, thanks to which the effect of duration is produced very much as, before the footlights, the prestidigitator produces the effect of extracting a live fowl from a hat. This is a law under which, the material permitting, the decades count as centuries and the centuries as æons. The misfortune is that too often the material, futile and treacherous, doesn't permit. Yet the law is in the happiest cases none the less strikingly vindicated. There, for instance—to pursue undiscouraged my figure of the guest in the empty parlour—were the best houses, the older, the ampler, the more blandly quadrilateral; which in spite of their still faces met one's arrest, at their commodious corners and other places of vantage, with an unmistakable *manner*. The quiet assurance of a position in the world—the world, the only one, with which they were concerned—testified again, in an interesting way, to the simple source of their impressiveness, showing how almost any modern interval could have been long enough to make them nobly antique if such interval might only have been vulgar enough. The age of "brown stone" was to have found no difficulty in *that;* the prolongation of its rage for a quarter of a century amply sufficed to dignify every antecedent thing it had spared (as the survivors of reigns of Terror grow by mere survival distinguished); while, steeped in dishonour up to the eyebrows, that is up to its false cornices of painted and sanded wood and iron, it was never to enjoy, for itself, the advantage it elsewhere conferred. Nothing has ever been vulgar enough to rehabilitate the odd ugliness, so distinct, yet after all so undemonstrable, of this luckless material; the way one shuddered, in particular, at the touch, on balustrade and elsewhere, of the sanded iron! It has been followed by other rages and other errors, but even the grace of the American time-measure can do nothing for it.

III

It was of course the fact that the "values" here were all such, and such alone, as might be reflected from the social conditions and the state of manners, even if reflected, for the hour, almost into empty space—it was this that gave weight to each perceived appearance and permitted none to show as trivial enough to project me, in reaction or in inanition, upon the comparative obviousness of the "burnt district." There is almost always a burnt district to eke out the interest of an American city —it is the pride of the citizen and the resource of the visitor when all else fails ; and I can scarce, I think, praise Baltimore so liberally as to note that this was the last of her beauties I was conscious of. She had lost by fire, a few months before, the greater part of her business quarter, which she was now rapidly and artfully calling back to existence ; but the entertainment she offered me was guiltless, ever so gracefully and gallantly guiltless, as it struck me, of reference, even indirect, to the majesty either of ruin or of remedy. One was, on further acquaintance, thoroughly beguiled, but the burnt district had so little to do with it that the days came and went without my so much as discovering its whereabouts. Wonderful little Baltimore, in which, whether when perched on a noble eminence or passing from one seat of the humanities, one seat of hospitality, to another—a process mainly consisting indeed, as it seemed to me, of prompt drives through romantic parks and woodlands that were all suburban yet all Arcadian—I caught no glimpse of traffic, however mild, nor spied anything "tall" at the end of any vista. This was in itself really a benediction, since I had nowhere, from the first, been infatuated with tallness ; I was infatuated only with the question of manners, in their largest sense—to the finer essence of which tallness had already defined itself to me as positively abhorrent. What occurred betimes, and ever so happily, was simply that the delicate blank of those first hours flushed into animation, and that with this indeed the embroidery of the fine canvas turned thick and rich. It came back again, no doubt, in the inveterate way, to the University presence, and to the eagerness with which, on the American scene, as I tire not, you see, of repeating, the visiting spirit, on such occasions, throws itself straight into sanctuary. It breaks in at any cost, this distracted appetite, and, recomposing the elements to their greater distinction, if need be, and with a high imaginative hand, makes of the combination obtained the only firm standpoint for the rest of the view. It has even in this connection an occasional sharp chill ; air-borne rumours reach it of perversities and treacheries, conspiracies possibly hatching in the very bosom of the temple and against its very faith. One hears of the University idea threatened in more than one of the great institutions—reduced to some pettifogging conception of a short brisk term and a simplified culture ; a lively thrifty training for " business-competition." This is a blow to the collective fond fancies set humming, at once, in almost any scholastic shade—under the effect of which one can but give one's own scant scholar's hood, while one winces, a further protesting pull over abashed brows. It would have been a question, very much, of what I call breaking-in (into the Johns Hopkins) at this moment, had I not here been indulged, in all liberality, with an impression the more charming, in a manner, for the fact of halls and courts brooding in vacation stillness. Perversely adorable always—and I scarce know why—the late afternoon light in deserted haunts of study ; with the secret of supreme dignity lurking, above all, in high, dusky, wainscoted chambers where the sound of one's footfall lingers, to one's pleasure, like a caress, and where portraits of the appurtenant worthies, the heroes and patrons, grow vague in the twilight. It is a tribute to the forces of idealism lurking again and again, over the country, in the amenity of the general Collegiate appearance, that the last thing these conditions overtly suggest, or seem to accept as their imputed virtue, is this precipitation of the young intelligence into the mere vociferous market.

I scarcely know why, however, I should have appeared, even by waving it away, to make room at our banquet for the possible skeleton of the false, the barbarizing, note; since the natural pitch of Baltimore, the pictorial, so to speak, as well as the social, struck me, once a certain contact established, as that of disinterested sensibility, the passion of which her University is the highest and clearest example. There was on the splendid Sunday in particular a warm, soft fusion of aspects—a *con*fusion, in fact, while I now gather it in—which seems to defy, though all unconsciously, the sharper edge of discrimination and to offer itself, insistently, as a general wash of brave Southern shade, the play of a liquid brush of which the North knows nothing. The episodes melt together, yet they also, under a little pressure, come happily apart, and over the large sun-chequered picture the generous boughs hang heavy. Admirable I found them, the Maryland boughs, and so immediately disposed about the fortunate town, by parkside and lonely lane, by trackless hillside and tangled copse, that the depth of rural effect becomes at once bewildering. You wonder at the absent transitions, you look in vain for the shabby fringes—or at least, under my spell, I did; you have never seen, on the lap of nature, so large a burden so neatly accommodated. Baltimore sits there as some quite robust but almost unnaturally good child might sit on the green apron of its nurse, with no concomitant crease or crumple, no uncontrollable "mess," by the nursery term, to betray its temper. It was with something like that figure before me that I kept communing, as I say, with the bland presence. Even a morning hour or two at the great University Hospital—for one's experience of the higher tone, one's irrepressible pursuit of charm, in America, has, to its great enrichment, these odd sequences—even that beginning of the day did nothing to obtrude the ugly or to overemphasize the real ; it simply contributed, under some perversion that I can neither explain nor defend, to the general grace of the picture. Why should the great Hospital, with its endless chambers of woe, its whole air as of *most* directly and advisedly facing, as the hospitals of the world go, the question of the immensities of pain—why should such an impression actually have turned, under the spell, to fine poetry, to a mere shining vision of the conditions, the high beauty of applied science ? The conditions, positively, as I think of them after the interval, make the poetry—the large art, above all, by which, in a place bristling with its terrible tale, everything was made to seem fair, and fairest even while it most intimately concurred in the work. In short if the Hospital was fundamentally Universitarian—as of the domain of the great Medical Faculty—so it partook for me, in its own way, of the University glamour, and so the tempered morning, and the shaded splendour, and the passive rows, the grim human alignments that became, in their cool vistas, delicate "symphonies in white," and, more even than anything else, the pair of gallant young Doctors who ruled, for me, so gently, the whole still concert, abide with me, collectively, as agents of the higher tone.

No example could speak more of that enlargement of function, for constituting some picture of life, which many an American element or object, many an institution, has to be felt as practising—usually with high success. It comes back, one notes for the thousandth time, to that redistribution and reconsecration of values, of representative weight, which it is *the* interesting thing, over the land, to see take effect—to see in special take all the effect of which it is capable. There are a thousand " European " values that are absent, and, whether as a consequence or not of that, there are innumerable felt solutions of the social continuity. The instinct of missing—by which I mean not at all either the consciousness or the confession of lacking—keeps up, however, its own activity ; for the theory at least of the native spirit is to consent wittingly to no privation. It has a genius, the native spirit, for desiring things of the existence, and even of the possibility of which it is actually unaware, and it views the totality of nature and the general life of man, I think, as more than anything else commissioned and privileged to wait on these awakenings. Thus new values arise as expansion proceeds ; the marked character of which, for comparative sociology, is that they are not at all as other values. What they " count " for is the particular required American quantity ; and we see again and again how large a quantity symbol and figure have to represent. The interesting thing is that, on the spot, the representation does practically cover the ground : it covers elements that in communities employing a different scale require for their expression (and perhaps sometimes to an effect of waste) a much greater number of terms. Hence the constant impression of elasticity, and that of those pressures of necessity under which value and virtue, character and quantity, greatness and glory even, to a considerable extent, are imputed and projected. There has to be a facility for the working of any social form—facility of comparison and selection in some communities, facility of rapid conversion in others

That is where the American material is elastic, where it affects one, as a whole, in the manner of some huge india-rubber cloth fashioned for " field " use and warranted to bear inordinate stretching.

One becomes aware thus wherever one turns, both of the tension and of the resistance ; everything and every one, all objects and elements, all systems, arrangements, institutions, functions, persons, reputations, give the sense of their pulling hard at the india-rubber : almost always, wonderfully, without breaking it off, yet never quite with the effect of causing it to lie thick. The matter of interest, however, is just this fact that its thinness should so generally—in some cases, to all intents and purposes, so richly—suffice ; suffice, that is, for producing unaided, impressions of a sort that make their way to us in " Europe " through superimposed densities, a thousand thicknesses of tradition. Which is what one means, again, by the differing "values" ; the thinness doing perforce, on the one side, much of the work done by the thickness on the other : the work, in particular, of the appeal to the fond observer. He is by his very nature committed everywhere to his impression—which means essentially, I think, that he is foredoomed, in one place as in another, to " put in " a certain quantity of emotion and reflection. The turn his sensibility takes depends of course on what is before him ; but when is it ever not in some manner exposed and alert ? If it be anything really of a touch-stone it is more disposed, I hold, to easy bargains than to hard ones ; it only wants to be *somehow* interested, and is not without the knowledge that an emotion is after all, at the best or the worst, but an emotion. All of which is a voluminous commentary, I admit, on the modest text that I perhaps made the University Hospital stand for too many things. That establishes at all events my contention—that the living fact, in the United States, *will* stand, other facts not preventing, for almost anything you may ask of it. Other facts, at Baltimore, didn't prevent—there being none, outside the University circle, of any perceptibly public, any majestic or impressive or competitive order. So it was as if this particular experience had been (as the visitation of cities goes) that of *all* present art and organization, that of all antiquity, history, piety, sociability, that of the rich real and the rich romantic, in fine, at a stroke. Had there been more to see and to feel I should possibly have seen and felt more ; yet what was absent, with this sense of feeling and seeing so much ?

IV

There *were* other facts, in abundance, I hasten to add ; only they were not, as I say, competitive, not of the public or majestic order—so that they the less imposed, for appreciation, any rearrangement of values. They were a matter still of the famous, the felicitous Sunday—into which as into an armful of the biggest and bravest June roses I seemed to find my perceptions cluster. Foremost among these meanwhile was that of the plentiful presence, freshly recognized, of absolute values too—which offer themselves, in the midst of the others, with a sharpness of their own, and which owe nothing, for interest, to any question of the general scale. The Country Club, for instance, as I have already had occasion to note, is everywhere a clear American felicity ; a *complete* product of the social soil and air which alone have made it possible, and wearing whenever met that assured face of the full-blown flower and the proved proposition. These institutions speak so of American life as a success that they affected me at moments as crying aloud to be commemorated—since it is on American life only that they are founded, and since they

render it, to my mind, the good office of making it keep
all its graces and of having caused it to shed, by the
same stroke, the elements that are contrary to these.
Nothing is more suggestive than to recognize, each time,
on the premises, the thing that "wouldn't do in Europe"
—for a judgment of the reasons of its doing so well in
the one hemisphere and so ill in the other promptly
becomes illuminating.   The illumination is one at which,
had I space, I should have liked to light here a candle or
two—partaking indeed by that character of a like baffled
virtue in many another group of social phenomena.   The
Country Club testifies, in short, and gives its evidence,
from the box, with the inimitable, invaluable accent of
American authority.   It becomes, for the restless analyst,
one of the great garden-lamps in which the flame of
Democracy burns whitest and steadiest and most floods
the subject; taking its place thus on the positive side of
a line which has its other side overscored with negatives.
I may seem too much to brood upon it, but the interest
of the American scene being, beyond any other, the show,
on so immense a scale, of what Democracy, pushing and
breaking the ice like an Arctic explorer, is making of
things, any scrap that contributes to it wears a part of its
dignity.   To have been beforehand with the experiments,
with several rather risky ones at least, and to have got
on with these so beautifully while other rueful nations
prowl, in the dusk, inquisitive but apprehensive, round
the red windows of the laboratory, peeping, for the last
news, between each other's shoulders—all this is, for the
democratic force, to have stolen a march over no little of
the ground, and to have gained time on such a scale as
perhaps to make the belated of the earth, the critical
group at the windows, still live to think of themselves as
having too much wasted it.

There had been one—I mean a blest Country Club—
in the neighbourhood of Boston (where indeed I believe

there were a dozen, at least as exemplary, out of my range) ; there had been another, quite marvellous, on the Hudson—one of a numerous array, probably, within an hour's run of New York ; there had been a supreme specimen, supreme for a documentary worth, even at Charleston (I reserve to myself to explain in due course, and ah, in such an exquisite sense, my "even"). This had made for me, if you will, a short list, but it had made a long admonition, to which the embowered institution near Baltimore was to add a wonderful emphasis. An admonition of what? it will meanwhile be asked : to which the answer may perhaps, for the moment, not be more precipitate than by one's saying that with any feeling for American life you soon enough see. You see its most complete attestation of its believing in itself unlimitedly, and also of its being right about itself at more points than it is wrong. You see it apply its general theory of its nature and strength—much of this doubtless quite an unconscious one—with a completeness and a consistency that will strike you also (or that ought to) as constituting an unconscious heroism. You will see it accept in detail, with a sublime serenity, certain large social consequences—the consequences of the straight application, in the most delicate conditions, of the prime democratic idea. As this idea is that of an universal eligibility, so you see it, under the application, beautifully resist the strain. So you see, in a word, everything staked on the conception of the young Family as a clear social unit—which, when all is said and done, remains, roundabout you, the ubiquitous fact. The conception of the Family is, goodness knows, "European" enough ; but the difference resides in its working on one side of the world in the vertical and on the other in the horizontal sense. If its identity in "Europe," that is, resides more especially in its perpendicular, its backward and forward extension, its ascent and descent of the long ladder of time, so it develops in the United States mainly by its lateral spread, as one may say ; expressing itself thus rather by number than by name, and yet taking itself for granted, when one comes to compare, with an intensity to which mere virtue of name elsewhere scarce helps it. American manners, as they stand, register therefore the apotheosis of the Family—a truth for which they have by no means received due credit ; and it is in the light of Country Clubs that all this becomes vivid. These organizations accept the Family as the social unit—accept its extension, its *whole* extension, through social space, and accept it as many times over as the question comes up : which is what one means by their sublime and successful consistency. No, if I may still insist, nothing anywhere accepts anything as the American Country Club accepts these whole extensions.

That is why I speak of it as accepting the universal eligibility. With no palpable result does the democratic idea, in the States, more bristle than with the view that the younger are " as good " as the elder ; family life is in fact, as from child to parent, from sister to brother, from wife to husband, from employed to employer, the eminent field of the democratic demonstration. This then is the unit that, with its latent multiplications, the Country Club takes over—and it is easy to see how such units must multiply. This is the material to which it addresses, with such effect, the secret of its power. I may of course be asked what I mean by an eligibility that is "universal"; but it seems needless to remark that even the most inclusive social scheme must in a large community always stop somewhere   Distinctly diverting, often, to Americans, the bewilderment of the " European " mind on the subject of "differences" and of the practicability of precautions for maintaining these ; so beset is that mind, to the American view, with this theory, this habit or need of precautions, and so disposed apparently to fear, in its anxiety, that without the precautions the differences—dreadful thought—may cease. The American theory is, I think, but vague, and the inevitable consciousness of differences reduced to a matter of practice—a matter which, on the whole, very much takes care of itself. Glimpses and revelations come to it, across the sea, on the great wave of modern publicity—images of a social order in which the precautions, as from above to below, are more striking than the differences and thereby out of proportion to them : an appearance that reads a lesson, of a sort, as to leaving precautions alone. It is true, at any rate, that no application of the aristocratic, none of the democratic, idea is ever practically complete ; discriminations are produced by the mere working of the machine, and they so engage alike almost every one's interest, meet alike almost every one's convenience. Nature and industry keep producing differences as fast as constitutions keep proclaiming equality, and there are always, at the best, in any really liberal scheme or human view, more conscious inaptitudes to convince of their privilege than conscious possibilities to remind of their limits. All of which reflections, however, I agree, would probably have remained a little dim even for the restless analyst, had not the most shining of his examples bathed the subject, to his eyes, in radiance. This could only be, as I have intimated, that of the bright institution on the Hudson, as half-an-hour's vision of it, one splendid Sunday of the May-time put it before me—all in terms so eloquent that I would fain have translated them on the spot.

For there, to every appearance, was the high perfection of the type—the ample, spreading, galleried house, hanging over the great river, with its beautiful largeness of provision for associated pleasures. The American note was *there*—in the intensity and continuity of the association, and the interest of the case was in its thus enjoying, for the effect, all the advantages that experience, chastening experience, and taste, "real" taste, could heap upon it. Somewhere in one's mind, doubtless, lurked the apprehension that such a "proposition" might, in that emphatic form, have betrayed a thousand flaws— whereas all one *could* say face to face with it, treading its great verandahs and conversation-rooms, its halls of refreshment, repose and exercise, its kitchens and its courts and its baths and its gardens, its wondrous inside and outside palæstra, was that it positively revealed new forms of felicity. It was thus a new and original thing— rare phenomenon—and actually an "important" one; for what did it represent (all discriminations made and recognized) but the active Family, as a final social fact, or in other words the sovereign People, as a pervasive and penetrative mass, "doing" themselves on unprecedented lines? They had invoked, certainly, high and congruous countenance; but vain I thought the objection made when I exclaimed to a friend on these marvels. "It depends upon whom I call the People? Of course it depends: so I call them, exactly, the groups and figures we see, here before us, enjoying, and enjoying both so expertly and so discreetly, these conveniences and luxuries. That's their interest—that they *are* the people; for what interest, under the sun, would they have if they weren't? They are the people 'arrived,' and, what is more, disembarked: that's all the difference. It seems a difference because elsewhere (in 'Europe,' say again), though we see them begin, at the very most, to arrive, socially, we yet practically see them still on the ship—we have never yet seen them disembark thus *en masse*. This is the effect they have when, all impediments and objections on the dock removed, they do *that*." And later on, at the afternoon's end, on the platform of the large agreeable riverside station which spread there, close at hand, as the appanage of the club itself, I could but call attention to the manner in which every impression reinforced my moral. The Families, the parties, the groups and couples (the element of the Individual, as distinguished from that of the Family, being remarkably absent) had gathered in the soft eventide for the return to New York, and it was impossible not to read each sign of the show in the vivid "popular" light. Only one did so—and this was the great point—with a positive uplifting of the spirit. Everything hung together and every one was charming. It was my explanatory word therefore to my companion. "That's what the People *are* when they've disembarked."

Having said so much—and with the sense, strange as it may appear, that there would still be much to say—I must add that I suddenly seem to see consternation in the charming face of the establishment, deep in the Baltimore countryside, my impression of which was to lay a train for these reflections: so that with a conscience less clear I might take the image as a warning against the vice of reading too much meaning into simple intentions. Therefore let me admit that the conscious purpose of this house of hospitality didn't look beyond the immediate effect of luncheon or dinner on one of its deep southern verandahs, with great trees, close at hand, flinging their shade, with the old garden of the old country home that the Club had inherited forming one prospect, and with a deep woodland valley, stream-haunted if I am not mistaken, giving breadth of style to another. The Maryland boughs, for that matter, creating in the upper air great classic serenities of shade, give breadth of style ; and the restless analyst, all grateful, and truly for the nonce at rest, could but ruefully note how little they had borrowed from any Northern, and least of all from any New England, model their almost academic grace. They might have borrowed it straight from far-away Claudes and Turners ; yet one made no point of that either—their interest was so sufficiently their own. Distances of view have often in the North the large elegance, but nearnesses almost never ; these are at their worst constitutionally coarse and at their best merely well-meaning. I was to find food all day for that observation ; I was to remain under a charm of which breadth of style was the key. Earth and air, between them, had taken it in hand—so that one was always moving, somehow, under arches that were "triumphal" or sitting in bowers that made one think of temples. It was not that man, or that art, had done much, though indeed they had incurred no shame and had even been capable of a masterpiece, seen in the waning light, of which I shall presently speak. It was the diffused, mitigated glow, the happy medium itself that continued to be meanwhile half the picture. I wandered through it from one impression to another, and I keep, with intensity, that of the admirable outlying Park, treasure of the town, through which I had already three or four times driven, but the holiday life of which, on the warm Sunday night, humming, languidly, under the stars, as with spent voices of the homeward-bound, attested more than ever its valuable function.

That must have been, in the whole pleasant incoherence, on my way back from the sweet old Carroll house, climax of an afternoon drive, yet before another, an ultimate visit, which was the climax of everything. I have sufficiently noted already the charming law under which, in the States, any approach to really ripe architectural charm —for the real ripeness is indispensable—enjoys advantages, those of mystery and sanctity, that are achieved in "Europe" but on greatly harder terms. The observed practice of this art, at times singularly subtle, is in fact half the reward of one's attention, puzzled though the latter may none the less be to see how the trick is played. So much at any rate one remembers; yet where, after all, would the sweet old Carroll house, nestling under its wood in the late June afternoon, and with something vaguely haunted in its lonely refinement, not have made an insidious appeal? There are sweet old Carroll houses, I believe, on several other sites—the luckiest form perhaps in which a flourishing family may have been moved to write its annals. The intimation of "annals" hangs about the place, and again we try to capture, under the charming pillared portico, before the mild red brick and the pale pediment and facings, in the series of high chambers, quite instinct with style (small far-off cousins of such "apartments," say, as those of Kensington Palace, though they cover, bungalow-fashion, scarce more than one floor), some lingering, living accents of such a profession of history. We capture verily, I think, nothing; we merely project a little, from one room and from one mild aspect of the void to another, our old habit of suppositions. Bred of other historic contacts, it instinctively puts forth feelers; but the feelers drop, after a little, like hands that meet nothing; our suppositions themselves, as I have called them, and which but return to us like toy ships that won't sail, are all they find tangible. There is satisfaction of a sort, however, even in such arrested questions, when, as before this delicate faintly-resonant shell, each other element also helping, they have been vividly enough suggested. Later on, for the real crown of my day, no wonderments were checked and no satisfactions imperfect. Attained, for the high finish of the evening, by another plunge, behind vaguely-playing carriage-lamps, into the bosky, odorous, quite ridiculously-romantic suburban night, this was the case of an ancient home without lapses or breaks, where the past and the present were in friendliest fusion, so that the waiting future evidently slumbered with confidence ; and where, above the easy open-air "Southern" hospitality, an impression now of shafts of mild candle-light across overlaced outer galleries and of throbs of nature's voice in the dark vaster circle, the Maryland boughs, at their best, presided in the unforgettable grand manner.

11

Washington

I was twice in Washington, the first time for a winter visit, the second to meet the wonderful advance of summer, to which, in that climate of many charms, the first days of May open wide the gates. This latter impression was perforce much the more briefly taken; yet, though I had gathered also from other past occasions, far-away years now, something of the sense of the place at the earlier season, I find everything washed over, at the mention of the name, by the rare light, half green, half golden, of the lovely leafy moment. I see all the rest, till I make the effort to break the spell, through that voluminous veil; which operates, for memory, quite as the explosion of spring works, even to the near vision, in respect to the American scene at large—dressing it up as if for company, preparing it for social, for human intercourse, making it in fine publicly presentable, with an energy of renewal and an effect of redemption not often to be noted, I imagine, on other continents. Nowhere, truly, can summer have such work cut out for it as here —nowhere has it to take upon itself to repaint the picture so completely. In the "European." landscape, in general, some, at least, of the elements and objects remain upon the canvas; here, on the other hand, one seems to see intending Nature, the great artist of the season, decline to touch that surface unless it be first swept clean—decline, at any rate, to deal with it save by ignoring all its perceived pretensions. Vernal Nature, in England, in France, in Italy, has still a use, often a charmed or amused indulgence, for the material in hand, the furniture of the foreground, the near and middle distances, the heterogeneous human features of the face of the land. She looks at her subject much as the portrait-painter looks at the personal properties, this or that household object, the official uniform, the badges and ornaments, the favourite dress, of his sitter—with an "Oh, yes, I can bring them in; they're just what I want, and I see how they will help me out." But I try in vain to recall a case in which, either during the New England May and June, or during those of the Middle States (since these groups of weeks have in the two regions a differing identity and value), the genius in question struck me as adopting with any frankness, as doing more than passively, helplessly accept, the supplied paraphernalia, the signs of existing life. The business is clearly to get rid of them as far as may be, to cover and smother them; dissimulating with the biggest, freest brush their impertinence and their ugliness.

I must ask myself, I meanwhile recognize, none the less, why I should have found Mount Vernon exquisite, the first of May, if the interest had all to be accounted for in the light of nature. The light of nature was there, splendid and serene; the Potomac opened out in its grandest manner; the bluff above the river, before the sweep of its horizon, raised its head for the historic crown. But it was not for a moment to be said that this was the whole story; the human interest and the human charm lay in wait and held one fast—so that, if one had been making light, elsewhere, of their suggestion and office, one had at least this case seriously to reckon with. I speak straightway, thus, of Mount Vernon, though it be but an outlying feature of Washington, and at the best a minor impression ; the image of the particular occasion is seated so softly in my path. There was a glamour, in fine, for the excursion—that of an extraordinarily gracious hospitality ; and the glamour would still have been great even if I had not, on my return to the shadow of the Capitol, found the whole place transfigured. The season was over, the President away, the two Houses up, the shutters closed, the visitor rare ; and one lost one's way in the great green vistas of the avenues quite as one might have lost it in a "sylvan solitude"—that is in the empty alleys of a park. The emptiness was qualified at the most, here and there, by some encounter with a stray diplomatic agent, wreathed for the most part in sincerer smiles than we are wont to attribute to his class. "This" —it was the meaning of these inflections—"was the *real* Washington, a place of enchantment; so that if the enchantment were never less who could ever bring himself to go away ?" The enchantment had been so much less in January—one could easily understand ; yet the recognition seemed truly the voice of the hour, and one picked it up with a patriotic flutter not diminished by the fact that the speaker would probably be going away, and with delight, on the morrow.

The memory of some of the smiles and inflections comes back in that light; Washington being the one place in America, I think, where those qualities are the values and vehicles, the medium of exchange. No small part of the interest of the social scene there consists, inevitably, for any restless analyst, in wonder about the "real" sentiments of appointed foreign participants, the delegates of Powers and pledged alike to penetration and to discretion, before phenomena which, whatever they may be, differ more from the phenomena of other capitals and other societies than they resemble them. This interest is susceptible, on occasion, of becoming intense ; all the more that curiosity must, for the most part, pursue its object (that of truly looking over the alien shoulder and of seeing, judging, building, fearing, reporting with the alien sense) by subtle and tortuous ways. This represents, first and last, even for a watcher abjectly irresponsible, a good deal of speculative tension ; so that one's case is refreshing in presence of the clear candour of such a proposition as that the national capital *is* charming in proportion as you don't see it. For that is what it came to, in the bowery condition ; the as yet unsurmounted bourgeois character of the whole was screened and disguised ; the dressing-up, in other words, was complete, and the great park-aspect gained, and became nobly artificial, by the very complexity of the plan of the place—the perpetual perspectives, the converging, radiating avenues, the frequent circles and crossways, where all that was wanted for full illusion was that the bronze generals and admirals, on their named pedestals, should have been great garden-gods, mossy mythological marble. This would have been the perfect note ; the long vistas yearned for it, and the golden chequers scattered through the gaps of the high arches waited for some bending nymph or some armless Hermes to pick them up. The power of the scene to evoke such visions sufficiently shows, I think, what had become, under the mercy of nature, of the hard facts, as one must everywhere call them ; and yet though I could, diplomatically, patriotically pretend, at the right moment, that such a Washington *was* the "real" one, my assent had all the while a still finer meaning for myself.

I am hanging back, however, as with a sacred terror, from Mount Vernon, where indeed I may not much linger, or only enough to appear not to have shirked the responsibility incurred at the opening of these remarks. There, in ample possession, was masking, dissimulating summer, the envelope and disguise to which I have hinted that the American picture owes, on its human side, *all* its best presentability ; and at the same time, unmistakably, there was the spell, as quite a distinct matter, of the hard little facts in themselves. How came it that if they could throw a spell they were yet so abject and so negligible? How came it that if they had no intrinsic sweetness, no visible dignity, they could yet play their part in so unforgettable an impression? The answer to this can only be, I think, that we happen here to "strike," as they say, one of the rarest of cases, a spot on which all sorts of sensibilities are touched and on which a lively emotion, and one yet other than the æsthetic, makes us its prey. The old high-placed house, unquestionably, is charming, and the felicity of the whole scene, on such a day as that of my impression, scarce to be uttered. The little hard facts, facts of form, of substance, of scale, facts of essential humility and exiguity, none the less, look us straight in the face, present themselves literally to be counted over—and reduce us thereby to the recognition of our supreme example of the rich interference of association. Association does, at Mount Vernon, simply what it likes with us—it is of so beautiful and noble a sort ; and to this end it begins by making us unfit to say whether or no we would in its absence have noticed the house for any material grace at all. We scarce care more for its being proved picturesque, the house, than for its being proved plain ; its architectural interest and architectural nullity become one and the same thing for us. If asked what we should think of it if it hadn't been, or if we hadn't known it for, Washington's, we retort that the inquiry is inane, since it is not the possessive case, but the straight, serene nominative, that we are dealing with. The whole thing *is* Washington—not his invention and his property, but his presence and his person ; with discriminations (as distinguished from enthusiasms) as invidious and unthinkable as if they were addressed to his very ears.

The great soft fact, as opposed to the little hard ones, is the beauty of the site itself; that is definitely, if ever so delicately, sublime, but it fails to rank among the artificial items that I began by speaking of, those of so generally compromising an effect in the American picture. Everything else is *communicated* importance, and the magic so wrought for the American sensibility—by which I mean the degree of the importance and the sustained high pitch of the charm—place it, doubtless, the world over, among the few supreme triumphs of such communication. The beauty of the site, meanwhile, as we stand there, becomes but the final aspect of the man; under which everything conduces to a single great representative image, under which every feature of the scene, every object in the house, however trivial, borrows from it and profits by it. The image is the largest, clearest possible of the resting, as distinguished from the restless, consciousness of public service consummately rendered. The terms we commonly use for that condition—peace with honour, well-earned repose, enjoyment of homage, recognition of facts—render but dimly the luminous stillness in which, on its commanding eminence, we see our image bathed. It hangs together with the whole bright immensity of air and view. It becomes truly the great white, decent page on which the whole sense of the place is written. It does more things even besides; attends us while we move about and goes with us from room to room; mounts with us the narrow stairs, to stand with us in these small chambers and look out of the low windows; takes up for us, to turn them over with spiritual hands, the objects from which we respectfully forbear, and places an accent, in short, through the rambling old phrase, wherever an accent is required. Thus we arrive at the full meaning, as it were—thus we know, at least, why we are so moved.

It is for the same reason for which we are always

inordinately moved, on American ground, I think, when the unconscious minor scale of the little old demonstrations to which we owe everything is made visible to us, when their disproportionate modesty is proved upon them. The reason worked at Mount Vernon, for the restless analyst, quite as it had worked a few months before, on the small and simple scene of Concord Fight: the slight, pale, bleeding Past, in a patched homespun suit, stands there taking the thanks of the bloated Present—having woundedly rescued from thieves and brought to his door the fat, locked pocket-book of which that personage appears the owner. The pocket-book contains, "unbeknown" to the honest youth, bank-notes of incredible figure, and what breaks our heart, if we be cursed with the historic imagination, is the grateful, wan smile with which the great guerdon of sixpence is received. I risk, floridly, the assertion that half the intensity of the impression of Mount Vernon, for many a visitor, will ever be in this vision there of Washington *only* (so far as consciously) so rewarded. Such fantastications, I indeed admit, are refinements of response to any impression, but the ground had been cleared for them, and it ministered to luxury of thought, for instance, that we were a small party at our ease there, with no other circulation—with the prowling ghosts of fellow-pilgrims, too harshly present on my previous occasion, all conveniently laid. This alone represented privilege and power, and they in turn, with their pomp and circumstance of a charming Government launch, under official attendance, at the Navy-Yard steps, amid those large, clean, protecting and protected properties of the State which always make one think much of the State, whatever its actual infirmities—these things, to say nothing of other rich enhancements, above all those that I may least specify, flung over the day I scarce know what iridescent reflection of the star-spangled banner itself, in the folds of which I had never come so near the sense of being positively wrapped. That consciousness, so un-familiar, was, under the test, irresistible; it pressed the spring, absolutely, of intellectual exaltation—with the consequent loud resonance that my account of my impressions doubtless sufficiently translates.

II

Washington itself meanwhile—the Washington always, I premise, of the rank outsider—had struck me from the first as presenting two distinct faces; the more obvious of which was the public and official, the monumental, with features all more or less majestically playing the great administrative, or, as we nowadays put it, Imperial part. This clustered, yet at the same time oddly scattered, city, a general impression of high granite steps, of light grey corniced colonnades, rather harmoniously low, con-tending for effect with slaty mansard roofs and masses of iron excrescence, a general impression of somewhat vague, empty, sketchy, fundamentals, however expectant, however spacious, overweighted by a single Dome and overaccented by a single Shaft—this loose congregation of values seemed, strangely, a matter disconnected and remote, though remaining in its way portentous and bristling all incoherently at the back of the scene. The back of the scene, indeed, to one's quite primary sense, might have been but an immense painted, yet unfinished cloth, hung there to a confessedly provisional end and marked with the queerness, among many queernesses, of looking always the same; painted once for all in clear, bright, fresh tones, but never emerging from its flatness, after the fashion of other capitals, into the truly, the variously, modelled and rounded state. (It appeared provisional therefore because looking as if it might have been unhooked and removed as a whole; because any one object in it so treated would have made the rest also come off.) The foreground was a different thing, a thing that, ever so quaintly, seemed to represent the force really in possession; though consisting but of a small company of people engaged perpetually in conversation and (always, I repeat, for the rank outsider) singularly destitute of conspicuous marks or badges. This little society easily became, .for the detached visitor, the city itself, *the* national capital and the greater part of the story; and that, ever, in spite of the comparatively scant intensity of its political permeation. The political echo was of course to be heard in it, and the public character, in his higher forms, to be encountered—though only in "single spies," not in battalions; but there was something that made it much more individual than any mere predominance of political or administrative colour would have made it; leaving it in that case to do no more than resemble the best society in London, or that in best possession of the field in Paris.

Two sharp signs my remoter remembrance had shown me the then Washington world, and the first met, as putting forth; one of these the fact of its being extraordinarily easy and pleasant, and the other that of one's appearing to make out in it not more than half-a-dozen members of the Lower House and not more than a dozen of the Upper. This kept down the political permeation, and was bewildering, if one was able to compare, in the light of the different London condition, the fact of the social ubiquity there of the acceptable M.P. and that of the social frequency even of his more equivocal hereditary colleague. A London nestling under the towers of Westminster, yet practically void of members of the House of Commons, and with the note of official life far from exclusively sounding, that might have been in those days the odd image of Washington, had not the picture been stamped with other variations still. These were a whole cluster, not instantly to be made out, but constituting the unity of the place as soon as perceived; representing that finer extract or essence which the self-respecting observer is never easy till he be able to shake up and down in bottled form. The charming company of the foreground then, which referred itself so little to the sketchy back-scene, the monstrous Dome and Shaft, figments of the upper air, the pale colonnades and mere myriad-windowed Buildings, was the second of the two faces, and the more one lived with it the more, up to a certain point, one lived away from the first. In time, and after perceiving *how* it was what it so agreeably was, came the recognition of common ground; the recognition that, in spite of strange passages of the national life, liable possibly to recur, during which the President himself was scarce thought to be in society, the particular precious character that one had apprehended could never have ripened without a general consensus. One had put one's finger on it when one had seen disengage itself from many anomalies, from not a few drolleries, the superior, the quite majestic fact of the City of Conversation pure and simple, and positively of the only specimen, of any such intensity, in the world.

That had remained for me, from the other time, the properest name of Washington, and nothing could so interest me, on a renewal of acquaintance, too long postponed and then too woefully brief, as to find my description wholly justified. If the emphasis added by " pure and simple " be invariably retained, the description will continue, I think, to embrace and exhaust the spectacle, while yet leaving it every inch of its value. Clearly quite immeasurable, on American ground, the value of such an assertion of a town-type directly opposed to the unvarying American, and quite unique, on any ground, so organized a social indifference to the vulgar vociferous Market. Washington may of course *know* more than she confesses—no community could perhaps really be as ignorant as Washington used at any rate to look, and to like to look, of this particular thing, of "goods" and shares and rises and falls and all such sordidities; but she knows assuredly still the very least she can get off with, and nothing even yet pleases her more than to forget what she does know. She unlearns, she turns her back, while London, Paris, Berlin, Rome, in their character of political centres, strike us as, on the contrary, feverishly learning, trying more and more to do the exact opposite. (I speak, naturally, as to Washington, of knowing actively and interestedly, in the spirit of gain—not merely of the enjoyed lights of political and administrative science, doubtless as abundant there as anywhere else.) It might fairly have been, I used to think, that the charming place—charming in the particular connection I speak of—had on its conscience to make one forget for an hour the colossal greed of New York. Nothing, in fact, added more to its charm than its appearing virtually to invite one to impute to it some such vicarious compunction.

If I be reminded, indeed, that the distinction I here glance at is negative, and be asked what then (if she knew nothing of the great American interest) Washington did socially know, my answer, I recognize, has at once to narrow itself, and becomes perhaps truly the least bit difficult to utter. It none the less remains distinct enough that, the City of Conversation being only in question, and a general subject of all the conversation having thereby to be predicated, our responsibility is met as soon as we are able to say what Washington mainly talks, and appears always to go mainly talking, about. Washington talks about herself, and about almost nothing else ; falling superficially indeed, on that ground, but into line with the other capitals. London, Paris, Berlin, Rome, goodness knows, talk about themselves : that is each member of this sisterhood talks, sufficiently or inordinately, of the great number of divided and differing selves that form together her controlling identity. London, for instance, talks of everything in the world without thereby for a moment, as it were, ceasing to be egotistical. It has taken everything in the world to make London up, so that she is in consequence simply doomed never to get away from herself. Her conversation is largely, I think, the very effort to do that ; but she inevitably figures in it but as some big buzzing insect which keeps bumping against a treacherous mirror. It is in positive quest of an identity of some sort, much rather—an identity other than merely functional and technical—that Washington goes forth, encumbered with no ideal of avoidance or escape : it is about herself *as* the City of Conversation precisely that she incessantly converses ; adorning the topic, moreover, with endless ingenuity and humour. But that, absolutely, remains the case ; which thus becomes one of the most thorough, even if probably one of the most natural and of the happiest, cases of collective self-consciousness that one knows. The spectacle, as it at first met my senses, was that of a numerous community in ardent pursuit of some workable conception of its social self, and trying meanwhile intelligently to talk itself, and even this very embarrassment, into a *subject* for conversation. Such a picture might not seem purely pleasing, on the side of variety of appeal, and I admit one may have had one's reserves about it ; reserves sometimes reflected, for example, in dim inward speculation—one of the effects of the Washington air I have already glanced at—as to the amount of response it might evoke in the diplomatic body. It may have been on my part a morbid obsession, but the diplomatic body was liable to strike one there as more characteristically "abysmal" than elsewhere, more impenetrably bland and inscrutably blank; and it was obvious, certainly, that their concern to help the place intellectually to find itself was not to be expected to approach in intensity the concern even of a repatriated absentee. You were concerned only if you had, by your sensibility, a stake in the game; which was the last thing a foreign representative would wish to confess to, this being directly opposed to all his enjoined duties. It is no part of the office of such personages to assist the societies to which they are accredited to find themselves—it is much more their mission to leave all such vaguely and, so far as may be, grotesquely groping: so apt are societies, in finding themselves, to find other things too. This detachment from the whole mild convulsion of effort, the considerate pretence of not being too aware of it, combined with latent probabilities of alarm about it no less than of amusement, represented, to the unquiet fancy, much more the spirit of the old-time Legations.

What *was*, at all events, better fun, of the finer sort, than having one's self a stake in the outcome?—what helped the time (so much of it as there was!) more to pass than just to join in the so fresh experiment of constitutive, creative talk? The boon, it should always be mentioned, meanwhile went on not in the least in the tone of solemnity. That would have been fatal, because probably irritating, and it was where the good star of Washington intervened. The tone was, so to speak, of *conscious* self-consciousness, and the highest genius for conversation doubtless dwelt in the fact that the ironic spirit was ready always to give its very self away, fifty times over, for the love, or for any quickening, of the theme. The foundation for the whole happy predicament remained, moreover, of the firmest, and the essence of the case was to be as easily stated as the great social fact is, in America, whether through exceptions or aggravations, everywhere to be stated. Nobody was in "business"—that was the sum and substance of it; and for the one large human assemblage on the continent of which this was true the difference made was huge. Nothing could strike one more than that it was the only way in which, over the land, a difference *could* be made, and than how, in our vast commercial democracy, almost any difference—by which I mean almost any exception—promptly acquires prodigious relief. The value here was at once that the place could offer to view a society, the only one in the country, in which Men existed, and that that rich little fact became the key to everything. Superficially taken, I recognize, the circumstance fails to look portentous; but it looms large immediately, gains the widest bearing, in the light of any direct or extended acquaintance with American conditions. From the moment it is adequately borne in mind that the business-man, in the United States, may, with no matter what dim struggles, gropings, yearnings, never hope to be anything *but* a business-man, the size of the field he so abdicates is measured, as well as the fact of the other care to which his abdication hands it over. It lies there waiting, pleading from all its pores, to be occupied—the lonely waste, the boundless gaping void of "society"; which is but a rough name for all the *other* so numerous relations with the world he lives in that are imputable to the civilized being. Here it is then that the world he lives in accepts its doom and becomes, by his default, subject and plastic to his mate; his default having made, all around him, the unexampled opportunity of the woman—which she would have been an incredible fool not to pounce upon. It needs little contact with American life to perceive how she *has* pounced, and how, outside business, she has made it over in her image.

She has been, up to now, on the vast residual tract, in peerless possession, and is occupied in developing and extending her wonderful conquest, which she appreciates to the last inch of its extent.

III

She has meanwhile probably her hours of amazement at the size of her windfall; she cannot quite live without wonder at the oddity of her so "sleeping" partner, the strange creature, by her side, with his values and his voids, but who is best known to her as having yielded what she would have clutched to the death. Yet these are mere mystic, inscrutable possibilities—dreams, for us, of her hushed, shrouded hours: the face she shows, on all the facts, is that of mere unwinking tribute to the matter of course. The effect of these high signs of assurance in her has been—and it is really her master-stroke—to represent the situation as perfectly normal. Her companion's attitude, totally destitute of high signs, does everything it can to further this feat; so that, as disposed together in the American picture, they testify, extraordinarily, to the *successful* rupture of a universal law, the sight is at first, for observation, most mystifying. Then the impunity of the whole thing gains upon us; the equilibrium strikes us, however strangely, as at least provisionally stable; we see that a society in many respects workable would seem to have been arrived at, and that we shall in any case have time to study it. The phenomenon may easily become, for a spectator, the sentence written largest in the American sky: when he is in search of the characteristic, what else so plays the part? The woman is two-thirds of the apparent life —which means that she is absolutely all of the social; and, as this is nowhere else the case, the occasion is unique for seeing what such a situation may make of her. The result elsewhere, in Europe generally, of conditions in which men have actively participated and to which, throughout, they personally contribute, she has only the old story to tell, and keeps telling it after her fashion. The woman produced by a women-made society alone has obviously quite a new story—to which it is not for a moment to be gainsaid that the world at large has, for the last thirty years in particular, found itself lending an attentive, at times even a charmed, ear. The extent and variety of this attention have been the specious measure of the personal success of the type in question, and are always referred to when its value happens to be challenged. "The American woman?—why, she has beguiled, she has conquered, the globe : look at her fortune everywhere and fail to accept her if you can."

She has been, accordingly, about the globe, beyond all doubt, a huge success of curiosity ; she has at her best—and far beyond any consciousness and intention of her own, lively as these for the most part usually are—infinitely amused the nations. It has been found among them that, for more reasons than we can now go into, her manner of embodying and representing her sex has fairly made of her a new human convenience, not unlike fifty of the others, of a slightly different order, the ingenious mechanical appliances, stoves, refrigerators, sewing-machines, type-writers, cash-registers, that have done so much, in the household and the place of business, for the American name. By which I am of course far from meaning that the revelation has been of her utility as a domestic drudge ; it has been much rather in the fact that the advantages attached to her being a woman at all have been so happily combined with the absence of the drawbacks, for persons intimately dealing with her, traditionally suggested by that condition. The cor-

responding advantages, in the light of almost any old
order, have always seemed inevitably paid for by the
drawbacks ; but here, unmistakably, was a case in
which—as at first appeared, certainly—they were to
be enjoyed very nearly for nothing. What it came to,
evidently, was that she had been grown in an air in
which a hundred of the " European" complications and
dangers didn't exist, and in which also she had had
to take upon herself a certain training for freedom. It
was not that she had had, in the vulgar sense, to " look
out " for herself, inasmuch as it was of the very essence
of her position not to be threatened or waylaid ; but
that she could develop her audacity on the basis of her
security, just as she could develop her "powers" in a
medium from which criticism was consistently absent.
Thus she arrived, full-blown, on the general scene, the
least criticized object, in proportion to her importance,
that had ever adorned it. It would take long to say
why her situation, under this retrospect, may affect the
inner fibre of the critic himself as one of the most
touching on record ; he may merely note his perception
that she was to have been after all but the sport of fate.
For why need she originally, he wonders, have embraced
so confidently, so gleefully, yet so unguardedly, the terms
offered her to an end practically so perfidious ? Why
need she, unless in the interest of her eventual discipline,
have turned away with so light a heart after watching
the Man, the deep American man, retire into his tent
and let down the flap ? She had her "paper" from him,
their agreement signed and sealed ; but would she not,
in some other air and under some other sky, have been
visited by a saving instinct ? Would she not have said
" No, this is too unnatural ; there must be a trap in
it somewhere—it's addressed really, in the long run, to
making a fool of me ? " It is impossible, of course, to
tell ; and her case, as it stands for us, at any rate, is

that she showed no doubts. It is not on the American scene and in the presence of mere American phenomena that she is even yet to be observed as showing them; but does not my digression find itself meanwhile justified by the almost clear certainty that the first symptoms of the revulsion—of the *con*vulsion, I am tempted to say—must break out in Washington?

For here—and it is what I have been so long in coming to—here alone in the American world, do we catch the other sex not observing the agreement. I have described this anomaly, at Washington, as that of Man's socially "existing"; since we have seen that his fidelity to his compact throughout the country in general has involved his not doing so. What has happened, obviously, has been that his reasons, at a stroke, have dropped, and that he finds himself, without them, a different creature. He has discovered that he *can* exist in other connections than that of the Market, and that all he has therefore to settle is the question of whether he may. The most delicate interest of Washington is the fact that it is quite practically *being* settled there—in the practical way which is yet also the dramatic. *Solvitur ambulando;* it is being settled—that is the charm—as it goes, settled without discussion. It would be awkward and gross to say that Man has dealt any conscious blow at the monopoly of his companion, or that her prestige, as mistress of the situation, has suffered in any manner a noted abatement. Yet none the less, as he has there, in a degree, socially found himself and, allured by the new sense, is evidently destined to seek much further still, the sensible effect, the change of impression on one's coming from other places, is of the most marked. Man is solidly, vividly present, and the presence of Woman has consequently, for the proposed intensity, to reckon with it. The omens on behalf of the former appearance are just now strikingly enhanced, as happens, by the accident of the rare quality, as it were, of the particular male presence supremely presiding there; and it would certainly be strange that this idea of the re-committal to masculine hands of some share at least in the interests of civilization, some part of the social property and social office, should not, from so high an example, have received a new impulse and a new consecration. Easily enough, if we had space here to consider it, might come up the whole picture of the new indications thus afforded, the question of the degree in which a sex capable, in the American air, of having so despoiled itself may really be capable of retracing its steps and repairing its mistake. It would appear inevitable to ask whether such a mistake on such a scale *can* prove effectively reparable—whether ground so lost can be effectively recovered. Has not the American woman, with such a start, gained such an irreducible advance, on the whole high plane of the amenities, that her companion will never catch up with her? This last is an inquiry that I must, alas, brush aside, though feeling it, as I have already noted, *the* most oddly interesting that the American spectacle proposes to us; only saying, provisionally, that the aspect of manners through the nation at large offers no warrant whatever for any prompt " No " to it.

It is not, however, of the nation at large I here speak; the case is of the extremely small, though important and significant, fraction of the whole represented by the Washington group—which thus shows us the Expropriated Half in the very act of itself pondering that issue. Is the man "up to it," up to the major heritage, the man who *could*, originally, so inconceivably, and for a mere mess of pottage if there ever was one, let it go? "Are we up to it, really, at this time of day, and what on earth will awfully become of us if the question, once put to the test, shall have to be decided against us?" I think it not merely fanciful to say that some dim, distressful interrogative sound of that sort frequently reached, in the Washington air, the restless analyst—though not to any quickening of his own fear. With a perfect consciousness that it was still early to say, that the data are as yet insufficient and that the missing quantity must absolutely be found before it can be weighed and valued, he was none the less struck with the felicity of many symptoms and would fairly have been able to believe at moments that the character hitherto so effaced has but to show the confidence of taking itself for granted. That act of itself reveals, restores, reinstates and completes this character. Is it not, for that matter, essentially implied in our recognition of the place as the City of Conversation? The victim of effacement, the outcast at the door, has, all the while we have been talking of him, *talked himself* back ; and if anything could add to this happy portent it would be another that had scarcely less bearing. Nowhere more than in Washington, positively, were the women to have struck me as naturally and harmoniously in the social picture—as happily, soothingly, proportionately, and no more than proportionately, participant and ministrant. Hence the irresistible conclusion that with the way really shown them they would only ask to take it ; the way being their assent to the truth that the abdication of the Man proves ever (after the first flush of their triumph) as bad really for their function as for his. Hence, in fine, the appearance that, with the proportions re-established, they will come to recognize their past world as a fools' paradise, and their present, and still more their future, as much more made to endure. They could not, one reasoned, have been, in general, so perfectly agreeable unless they had been pleased, and they could not have been pleased without the prospect of gaining, by the readjusted relation,

more, on the whole, than they were to lose ; without
the prospect even again perhaps of truly and insidiously
gaining more than the other beneficiary. That *would*
be, I think, the feminine conception of a readministered
justice. Washington, at such a rate, in any case, might
become to them as good as " Europe," and a Europe
of their own would obviously be better than a Europe
of other people's. There are, after all, other women on
the other continents.

IV

One might have been sure in advance that the character of a democracy would nowhere more sharply mark
itself than in the democratic substitute for a court city,
and Washington is cast in the mould that expresses most
the absence of salient social landmarks and constituted
features. Here it is that conversation, as the only invoked presence, betrays a little its inadequacy to the
furnishing forth, all by itself, of an outward view. It
tells us it must be there, since in all the wide empty
vistas nothing else is, and the general elimination *can*
but have left it. A pleading, touching effect, indeed,
lurks in this sense of it as seated, at receipt of custom,
by any decent door of any decent domicile and watching
the vacancy for reminder and appeal. It is left to conversation alone to people the scene with accents ; putting
aside two or three objects to be specified, there is *never*
an accent in it, up and down, far and wide, save such as
fall rather on the ear of the mind : those projected by
the social spirit starved for the sense of an occasional
emphasis. The White House is an accent—one of the
lightest, sharpest possible ; and the Capitol, of course,
immensely, another ; though the latter falls on the exclusively political page, as to which I have been waiting

to say a word. It should meanwhile be mentioned that we are promised these enhancements, these illustrations, of the great general text, on the most magnificent scale ; a splendid projected and announced Washington of the future, with approaches even now grandly outlined and massively marked ; in face of which one should perhaps confess to the futility of any current estimate. If I speak thus of the Capitol, however, let me not merely brush past the White House to get to it—any more than feel free to pass into it without some preliminary stare at that wondrous Library of Congress which glitters in fresh and almost unmannerly emulation, almost frivolous irrelevance of form, in the neighbourhood of the greater building. About the ingenuities and splendours of this last costly structure, a riot of rare material and rich ornament, there would doubtless be much to say—did not one everywhere, on all such ground, meet the open eye of criticism simply to establish with it a private intelligence, simply to respond to it by a deprecating wink. The guardian of that altar, I think, is but too willing, on such a hint, to let one pass without the sacrifice.

It is a case again here, as on fifty other occasions, of the tribute instantly paid by the revisiting spirit ; but paid, all without question, to the general *kind* of presence for which the noisy air, over the land, feels so sensibly an inward ache—the presence that corresponds there, no matter how loosely, to that of the housing and harbouring European Church in the ages of great disorder. The Universities and the greater Libraries (the smaller, for a hundred good democratic reasons, are another question), repeat, in their manner, to the imagination, East and West, the note of the old thick-walled convents and quiet cloisters : they are large and charitable, they are sturdy, often proud and often rich, and they have the incalculable value that they represent the only intermission to inordinate rapacious traffic that the scene offers to view. With this suggestion of sacred ground they play even upon the most restless of analysts as they will, making him face about, with ecstasy, any way they seem to point; so that he feels it his business much less to count over their shortcomings than to proclaim them places of enchantment. They are better at their worst than anything else at its best, and the comparatively sweet sounds that stir their theoretic stillness are for him as echoes of the lyre of Apollo. The Congressional Library is magnificent, and would become thus a supreme sanctuary even were it ten times more so: there would seem to be nothing then but to pronounce it a delight and have done with it—or let the appalled imagination, in other words, slink into it and stay there. But here is pressed precisely, with particular force, the spring of the question that takes but a touch to sound: is the case of this remarkable creation, by exception, a case in which the violent waving of the pecuniary wand *has* incontinently produced interest? The answer can only be, I feel, a shy assent—though shy indeed only till the logic of the matter is apparent. This logic is that, though money alone can gather in on such a scale the treasures of knowledge, these treasures, in the form of books and documents, themselves organize and furnish their world. They appoint and settle the proportions, they thicken the air, they people the space, they create and consecrate all their relations, and no one shall say that, where they scatter life, which they themselves in fact *are*, history does not promptly attend. Emphatically yes, therefore, the great domed and tiered, galleried and statued central hall of the Congressional, the last word of current constructional science and artistic resource, already crowns itself with that grace.

The graceful thing in Washington beyond any other, none the less, is the so happily placed and featured White House, the late excellent extensions and em-

The White House 355

bellishments of which have of course represented expenditure—but only of the refined sort imposed by some mature portionless gentlewoman on relatives who have accepted the principle of making her, at a time of life, more honourably comfortable. The whole ample precinct and margin formed by the virtual continuity of its grounds with those expanses in which the effect of the fine Washington Obelisk rather spends or wastes itself (not a little as if some loud monosyllable had been uttered, in a preoccupied company, without a due production of sympathy or sense)—the fortunate isolation of the White House, I say, intensifies its power to appeal to that musing and mooning visitor whose perceptions alone, in all the conditions, I hold worthy of account. Hereabouts, beyond doubt, history had from of old seemed to me insistently seated, and I remember a short spring-time of years ago when Lafayette Square itself, contiguous to the Executive Mansion, could create a rich sense of the past by the use of scarce other witchcraft than its command of that pleasant perspective and its possession of the most prodigious of all Presidential effigies, Andrew Jackson, as archaic as a Ninevite king, prancing and rocking through the ages. If that atmosphere, moreover, in the fragrance of the Washington April, was even a quarter of a century since as a liquor of bitter-sweet taste, overflowing its cup, what was the ineffable mixture now, with all the elements further distilled, all the life further sacrificed, to make it potent? One circled about the place as for meeting the ghosts, and one paused, under the same impulse, before the high palings of the White House drive, as if wondering at haunted ground. There the ghosts stood in their public array, spectral enough and clarified; yet scarce making it easier to "place" the strange, incongruous blood-drops, as one looked through the rails, on that revised and freshened page. But one fortunately has one's choice, in all these connections, as one turns away; the mixture, as I have called it, is really here so fine. General Jackson, in the centre of the Square, still rocks his hobby and the earth; but the fruit of the interval, to my actual eyes, hangs nowhere brighter than in the brilliant memorials lately erected to Lafayette and to Rochambeau. Artful, genial, expressive, the tribute of French talent, these happy images supply, on the spot, the note without which even the most fantasticating sense of our national past would feel itself rub forever against mere brown homespun. Everything else gives way, for me, I confess, as I again stand before them; everything, whether as historic fact, or present *agrément*, or future possibility, yields to this one high luxury of our old friendship with France.

The "artistic" Federal city already announced spreads itself then before us, in plans elaborated even to the finer details, a city of palaces and monuments and gardens, symmetries and circles and far radiations, with the big Potomac for water-power and water-effect and the recurrent Maryland spring, so prompt and so full-handed, for a perpetual benediction. This imagery has, above all, the value, for the considering mind, that it presents itself as under the wide-spread wings of the general Government, which fairly make it figure to the rapt vision as the object caught up in eagle claws and lifted into fields of air that even the high brows of the municipal boss fail to sweep. The wide-spread wings affect us, in the prospect, as great fans that, by their mere tremor, will blow the work, at all steps and stages, clean and clear, disinfect it quite ideally of any germ of the job, and prepare thereby for the American voter, on the spot and in the pride of possession, quite a new kind of civic consciousness. The scheme looms largest, surely, as a demonstration of the possibilities of that service to him, and nothing about it will be more interesting than to measure—though

this may take time—the nature and degree of his allevia-
tion. Will the new pride I speak of sufficiently inflame
him? Will the taste of the new consciousness, finding
him so fresh to it, prove the right medicine? One can
only regret that we must still rather indefinitely wait to
see—and regret it all the more that there is always, in
America, yet another lively source of interest involved in
the execution of such designs, and closely involved just
in proportion as the high intention, the formal majesty,
of the thing seems assured. It comes back to what we
constantly feel, throughout the country, to what the
American scene everywhere depends on for half its
appeal or its effect; to the fact that the social conditions,
the material, pressing and pervasive, make the particular
experiment or demonstration, whatever it may pretend
to, practically a new and incalculable thing. This general
Americanism is often the one tag of character attaching
to the case after every other appears to have abandoned
it. The thing is happening, or will have to happen, in
the American way—that American way which is more
different from all other native ways, taking country with
country, than any of these latter are different from each
other; and the question is of how, each time, the American
way will see it through.

The element of suspense—beguilement, ever, of the
sincere observer—is provided for by the fact that, though
this American way never fails to come up, he has to
recognize as by no means equally true that it never fails
to succeed. It is inveterately applied, but with consequences bewilderingly various; which means, however,
for our present moral, but that the certainty of the
determined American effect is an element to attend quite
especially such a case as the employment of the arts of
design, on an unprecedented scale, for public uses, the
adoption on this scale of the whole æsthetic law. Encountered in America, phenomena of this order strike us

mostly as occurring in the historic void, as having to present themselves in the hard light of that desert, and as needing to extort from it, so far as they can, something of the shading of their interest. Encountered in older countries, they show, on the contrary, as taking up the references, as consenting perforce to the relations, of which the air is already full, and as having thereby much rather to get themselves expressive by charm than to get themselves expressive by weight. The danger "in Europe" is of their having too many things to say, and too many others to distinguish these from; the danger in the States is of their not having things enough—with enough tone and resonance furthermore to give them. What therefore will the multitudinous and elaborate forms of the Washington to come have to " say," and what, above all, besides gold and silver, stone and marble and trees and flowers, will they be able to say it *with*? That is one of the questions in the mere phrasing of which the restless analyst finds a thrill. There is a thing called interest that has to be produced for him—positively as if he were a rabid usurer with a clutch of his imperilled bond. He has seen again and again how the most expensive effort often fails to lead up to interest, and he has seen how it may bloom in soil of no more worth than so many layers of dust and ashes. He has learnt in fact—he learns greatly in America—to mistrust any plea for it *directly* made by money, which operates too often as the great puffing motor-car framed for whirling him, in his dismay, quite away from it. And he has inevitably noted, at the same time, from how comparatively few other sources this rewarding dividend on his invested attention may be drawn. He thinks of these sources as few, that is, because he sees the same ones, which are the references by which interest is fed, used again and again, with a desperate economy; sees the same ones, even as the human heroes, celebrities, extemporized lions or scapegoats, required social and educational figure-heads and "values," having to serve in *all* the connections and adorn all the tales. That is one of the liveliest of his American impressions. He has at moments his sense that, in presence of such vast populations and instilled, emulous demands, there is not, outside the mere economic, enough native history, recorded or current, to go round.

V

It seemed to me on the spot, moreover, that such reflections were rather more than less pertinent in face of the fact that I was again to find the Capitol, whenever I approached, and above all whenever I entered it, a vast and many-voiced creation. The thing depends of course somewhat on the visitor, who will be the more responsive, I think, the further back into the "origins" of the whole American spectacle his personal vision shall carry him ; but this hugest, as I suppose it, of all the homes of debate only asks to put forth, on opportunity, an incongruous, a various, an inexhaustible charm. I may as well say at once that I had found myself from the first adoring the Capitol, though I may not pretend here to dot all the i's of all my reasons—since some of these might appear below the dignity of the subject and others alien to its simplicity. The ark of the American covenant may strike one thus, at any rate, as a compendium of all the national ideals, a museum, crammed full, even to overflowing, of all the national terms and standards, weights and measures and emblems of greatness and glory, and indeed as a builded record of half the collective vibrations of a people ; their conscious spirit, their public faith, their bewildered taste, their ceaseless curiosity, their arduous and interrupted education. Such were to my vision at least some of its aspects, but the place had a hundred sides, and if I had had time to look for others still I felt I should have found them. What it comes to—whereby the "pull," in America, is of the greatest—is that association really reigns there, and in the richest, and even again and again in the drollest, forms; it is thick and vivid and almost gross, it assaults the wondering mind. The labyrinthine pile becomes thus inordinately *amusing*—taking the term in its finer modern sense. The analogy may seem forced, but it affected me as playing in Washington life very much the part that St. Peter's, of old, had seemed to me to play in Roman : it offered afternoon entertainment, at the end of a longish walk, to any spirit in the humour for the uplifted and flattered vision—and this without suggesting that the sublimities in the two cases, even as measured by the profanest mind, tend at all to be equal. The Washington dome is indeed capable, in the Washington air, of admirable, of sublime, effects ; and there are cases in which, seen at a distance above its yellow Potomac, it varies but by a shade from the sense—yes, absolutely the divine campagna-sense—of St. Peter's and the like-coloured Tiber.

But the question is positively of the impressiveness of the great terraced Capitol hill, with its stages and slopes, staircases and fountains, its general presentation of its charge. And if the whole mass and prospect "amuse," as I say, from the moment they are embraced, the visitor curious of the *democratic assimilation* of the greater dignities and majesties will least miss the general logic. That is the light in which the whole thing is supremely interesting ; the light of the fact, illustrated at every turn, that the populations maintaining it deal with it so directly and intimately, so sociably and humorously. We promptly take in that, if ever we are to commune in a concentrated way with the sovereign people, and see their exercised power raise a side-wind of irony for forms and arrangements other than theirs, the occasion here will amply serve. Indubitably, moreover, at a hundred points, the irony operates, and all the more markedly under such possible interference; the interference of the monumental spittoons, that of the immense amount of vulgar, of barbaric, decoration, that of the terrible artistic tributes from, and scarce less to, the different States—the unassorted marble mannikins in particular, each a portrayal by one of the commonwealths of her highest worthy, which make the great Rotunda, the intended Valhalla, resemble a stonecutter's collection of priced sorts and sizes. Discretion exists, throughout, only as a flower of the very first or of these very latest years; the large middle time, corresponding, and even that unequally, with the English Victorian, of sinister memory, was unacquainted with the name, and waits there now, in its fruits, but for a huge sacrificial fire, some far-flaring act-of-faith of the future: a tribute to the æsthetic law which one already feels stirring the air, so that it may arrive, I think, with an unexampled stride. Nothing will have been more interesting, surely, than so public a wiping-over of the æsthetic slate, with all the involved collective compunctions and repudiations, the general exhibition of a colossal conscience, a conscience proportionate to the size and wealth of the country. To such grand gestures does the American scene lend itself!

The elements in question are meanwhile there, in any case, just as the sovereign people are there, "going over" their property; but we are aware none the less of impressions—that of the ponderous proud Senate, for instance, so sensibly massive; that of the Supreme Court, so simply, one almost says so chastely, yet, while it breathes supremacy, so elegantly, so all intellectually, in session—under which the view, taking one extravagance with another, recurs rather ruefully to glimpses elsewhere caught, glimpses of authority emblazoned, bewigged, bemantled, bemarshalled, in almost direct defeat of its intention of gravity. For the reinstated absentee, in these presences, the mere recovery of native privilege was at all events a balm—after too many challenged appeals and abused patiences, too many hushed circuitous creepings, among the downtrodden, in other and more bristling halls of state. The sense of a certain large, final benignity in the Capitol comes then, I think, from this impression that the national relation to it is that of a huge flourishing Family to the place of business, the estate-office, where, in a myriad open ledgers, which offer no obscurity to the hereditary head for figures, the account of their colossal revenue is kept. They meet there in safe sociability, as all equally initiated and interested—not as in a temple or a citadel, but by the warm domestic hearth of Columbia herself; a motherly, chatty, clear-spectacled Columbia, who reads all the newspapers, knows, to the last man, every one of her sons by name, and, to the last boy, even her grandsons, and is fenced off, at the worst, but by concentric circles of rocking-chairs. It is impossible, as I say, not to be fondly conscious of her welcome—unless again, and yet again, I read into the general air, confusedly, too much of the happy accident of the basis of my introduction. But if my sensibility responds with intensity to this, so much the better; for what were such felt personal aids and influences, after all, but cases and examples, embodied expressions of character, type, distinction, products of the *working* of the whole thing?—specimens, indeed, highly concentrated and refined, and made thereby, I admit, more charming and insidious.

It must also be admitted that to exchange the inner aspects of the vast monument for the outer is to be reminded with some sharpness of a Washington in which half the sides that have held our attention drop, as if rather abashed, out of sight. Not its pleasant brightness as of a winter watering-place, not its connections, however indirect, with the older, but those with the newer, the newest, civilization, seem matter of recognition for its various marble fronts ; it rakes the prospect, it rakes the continent, to a much more sweeping purpose, and is visibly concerned but in immeasurable schemes of which it can consciously remain the centre. Here, in the vast spaces—mere empty light and air, though such pleasant air and such pretty light as yet—the great Federal future seems, under vague bright forms, to hover and to stalk, making the horizon recede to take it in, making the terraces too, below the long colonnades, the admirable standpoints, the sheltering porches, of political philosophy. The comparatively new wings of the building filled me, whenever I walked here, with thanksgiving for their large and perfect elegance : so, in Paris, might the wide mated fronts that are of such a noble effect on either side of the Rue Royale shine in multiplied majesty and recovered youth over an infinite Place de la Concorde. These parts of the Capitol, on their Acropolis height, are ideally constructed for "raking," and for this suggestion of their dominating the American scene in playhouse gallery fashion. You are somehow possessed of it *all* while you tread them—their marble embrace appears so the complement of the vast democratic lap. Though I had them in general, for contemplation, quite to myself, I met one morning a trio of Indian braves, braves dispossessed of forest and prairie, but as free of the builded labyrinth as they had ever been of these ; also arrayed in neat pot-hats, shoddy suits and light overcoats, with their pockets, I am sure, full of photographs and cigarettes : circumstances all that quickened their resemblance, on the much bigger scale, to Japanese celebrities, or to specimens, on show, of what the Government can do with people with whom it is supposed able to do nothing.   They seemed just then and there, for a mind fed betimes on the Leatherstocking Tales, to project as in a flash an image in itself immense, but foreshortened and simplified—reducing to a single smooth stride the bloody footsteps of time.   One rubbed one's eyes, but there, at its highest polish, shining in the beautiful day, was the brazen face of history, and there, all about one, immaculate, the printless pavements of the State.

12

Richmond

IT was, toward the end of the winter, fairly romantic to
feel one's self "going South"—in verification of the
pleasant probability that, since one's mild adventure had
appeared beforehand, and as a whole, to promise that
complexion, there would now be aspects and occasions
more particularly and deeply dyed with it. The inevitability of his being romantically affected—being so more
often than not—had been taken for granted by the restless analyst from the first; his feeling that he might
count upon it having indeed, in respect to his visit, the
force of a strong appeal. The case had come to strike
him as perfectly clear—the case for the singular history,
the odd evolution of this confidence, which might appear
superficially to take some explaining. It was "Europe"
that had, in very ancient days, held out to the yearning
young American some likelihood of impressions more
numerous and various and of a higher intensity than those
he might gather on the native scene; and it was doubtless in conformity with some such desire more finely and
more frequently to vibrate that he had originally begun
to consult the European oracle. This had led, in the
event, to his settling to live for long years in the very
precincts, as it were, of the temple; so that the voice of
the divinity was finally to become, in his ears, of all
sounds the most familiar. It was quite to lose its primal

note of mystery, to cease little by little to be strange, impressive and august—in the degree, at any rate, in which it had once enjoyed that character. The consultation of the oracle, in a word, the invocation of the possible thrill, was gradually to feel its romantic essence enfeebled, shrunken and spent. The European complexity, working clearer to one's vision, had grown usual and calculable—presenting itself, to the discouragement of wasteful emotion and of "intensity" in general, as the very stuff, the common texture, of the real world. Romance and mystery—in other words the *amusement* of interest—would have therefore at last to provide for themselves elsewhere ; and what curiously befell, in time, was that the native, the forsaken scene, now passing, as continual rumour had it, through a thousand stages and changes, and offering a perfect iridescence of fresh aspects, seemed more and more to appeal to the faculty of wonder. It was American civilization that had begun to spread itself thick and pile itself high, in short, in proportion as the other, the foreign exhibition had taken to writing itself plain ; and to a world so amended and enriched, accordingly, the expatriated observer, with his relaxed curiosity reviving and his limp imagination once more on the stretch, couldn't fail again to address himself. Nothing could be of a simpler and straighter logic : Europe had been romantic years before, because she was different from America ; wherefore America would now be romantic because she was different from Europe. It was for this small syllogism then to meet, practically, the test of one's repatriation ; and as the palpitating pilgrim disembarked, in truth, he had felt it, like the rifle of a keen sportsman, carried across his shoulder and ready for instant use.

What employment it was thus to find, what game it was actually to bring down, this directed and aimed appetite for sharp impressions, is a question to which these pages may appear in a manner to testify—constituting to that extent the "proof" of my fond calculation. It was in respect to the South, meanwhile, at any rate, that the calculation had really been fondest—on such a stored, such a waiting provision of vivid images, mainly beautiful and sad, might one surely there depend. The sense of these things would represent for the restless analyst, more than that of any others, intensity of impression ; so that his only prime discomfiture was in his having had helplessly to see his allowance of time cut short, reduced to the smallest compass in which the establishment of a relation to any group of aspects might be held conceivable. This last soreness, however—and the point is one to be made —was not slow, I noted, to find itself healingly breathed upon. More promptly in America than elsewhere does the relation to the group of aspects begin to work— whatever the group, and I think I may add whatever the relation, may be. Few elements of the picture are shy or lurking elements—tangled among others or hidden behind them, packed close by time and taking time to come out. They stand there in their row like the letters of an alphabet, and this is why, in spite of the vast surface exposed, any item, encountered or selected, con- tributes to the spelling of the word, becomes on the spot generally informing and characteristic. The word so recognized stands thus, immediately, for a multitude of others and constitutes, to expert observation, an all- sufficient specimen. " Here, evidently, more quickly than in Europe," the visitor says to himself, " one knows what there is and what there isn't : whence there is the less need, for one's impression, of a multiplication of cases." A single case speaks for many—since it is again and again, as he catches himself repeating, a question not of clustered meanings that fall like over-ripe fruit into his lap, but of the picking out of the few formed features, signs of character mature enough and firm enough to promise a savour or to suffer handling. These scant handfuls illustrate and typify, and, luckily, they are (as the evidence of manners and conditions, over the world, goes) quickly gathered; so that an impression founded on them is not an undue simplification. And I make out, I think, the reflection with which our anxious explorer tacitly concludes. " It's a bad country to be stupid in—none on the whole so bad. If one doesn't know *how* to look and to see, one should keep out of it altogether. But if one does, if one *can* see straight, one takes in the whole piece at a series of points that are after all comparatively few. One may neglect, by interspacing the points, a little of the accessory matter, but one neglects none of the essential. And if one has not at last learned to separate with due sharpness, pen in hand, the essential *from* the accessory, one has only, at best, to muffle one's head for shame and await deserved extinction."

II

It was in conformity with some such induction as the foregoing that I had to feel myself, at Richmond, in the midst of abnormal wintry rigours, take in at every pore a Southern impression; just as it was also there, before a picture charmless at the best, I seemed to apprehend, and not redeemed now by mistimed snow and ice, that I was to recognize how much I had staked on my theory of the latent poetry of the South. This theory, during a couple of rather dark, vain days, constituted my one solace or support, and I was most of all occupied with my sense of the importance of carrying it off again unimpaired. I remember asking myself at the end of an hour or two what I had then expected—expected of the interesting Richmond; and thereupon, whether or no I mustered, on this first challenge, an adequate answer, trying to supply the original basis of expectation. By that effort, as happened, my dim perambulation was lighted, and I hasten to add that I felt the second branch of my question easy enough to meet. How was the sight of Richmond not to be a potent idea ; how was the place not, presumably, to be interesting, to a restless analyst who had become conscious of the charge involved in that title as long ago as at the outbreak of the Civil War, if not even still more promptly ; and to whose young imagination the Confederate capital had grown lurid, fuliginous, vividly tragic—especially under the process through which its fate was to close round it and overwhelm it, invest it with one of the great reverberating historic names ? They hang together on the dreadful page, the cities of the supreme holocaust, the final massacres, the blood, the flames, the tears ; they are chalked with the sinister red mark at sight of which the sensitive nerve of association forever winces. If the mere shadow had that penetrative power, what affecting virtue might accordingly not reside in the substances, the place itself, the haunted scene, as one might figure it, of the old, the vast intensity of drama ? One thing at least was certain—that, however the sense of actual aspects was to disengage itself, I could not possibly have drawn near with an intelligence more respectfully and liberally prepared for hospitality to it. So, conformably with all this, how could it further not strike me, in presence of the presented appearances, that the needful perceptions were in fact at play ?

I recall the shock of that question after a single interrogative stroll, a mere vague mile of which had thrown me back wondering and a trifle mystified. One had had brutally to put it to one's self after a conscientious stare about : " This then the tragic ghost-haunted city, this the centre of the vast blood-drenched circle, one of the *most* blood-drenched, for miles and miles around, in the dire catalogue aforesaid ? " One had counted on a sort of registered consciousness of the past, and the truth was that there appeared, for the moment, on the face of the scene, no discernible consciousness, registered or unregistered, of anything. Richmond, in a word, looked to me simply blank and void—whereby it was, precisely, however, that the great emotion was to come. One could never consent merely to *taking* it for that : intolerable the discredit so cast on one's perceptive resources. The great modern hotel, superfluously vast, was excellent ; but it enjoyed as a feature, as a " value," an uncontested priority. It was a huge well-pitched tent, the latest thing in tents, proclaiming in the desert the name of a new industry. The desert, I have mentioned, was more or less muffled in snow—that furthered, I admit, the blankness ; the wind was harsh, the sky sullen, the houses scarce emphasized at all as houses ; the "Southern character," in fine, was nowhere. I should doubtless have been embarrassed to say in what specific items I had imagined it would naturally reside— save in so far as I had attached some mystic virtue to the very name of Virginia : this instinctive imputation constituting by itself, for that matter, a symptom of a certain significance. I watched and waited, giving the virtue a chance to come out ; I wandered far and wide— as far, that is, as weather and season permitted ; they quite forbade, to my regret, the long drives involved in a visitation of the old battlefields. The shallow vistas, the loose perspectives, were as sadly simple as the faces of the blind. Was it practically but a question then, deplorable thought, of a poor Northern city ?—with the bare difference that a Northern city of such extent would, however stricken, have succeeded, by some Northern art in pretending to resources. Where, otherwise, were the " old Southern mansions " on the wide verandahs and in

the rank, sweet gardens of which Northern resources had
once been held so cheap?

Well, I scarce remember at what point of my peregrination, at what quite vague, senseless street-corner
it was that I felt my inquiry—up to that moment rather
embarrassing—turn to clearness and the whole picture
place itself in a light in which contemplation might for
the time find a warrant and a clue.   I at any rate almost
like to live over the few minutes in question—for the
sake of their relief and their felicity.   So retracing
them, I see that the spring had been pressed for them
by the positive force of one's first dismay; a sort of
intellectual bankruptcy, this latter, that one felt one
really couldn't afford.   There were no *references*—that
had been the trouble; but the reaction came with the
sense that the large, sad poorness·was in itself a reference, and one by which a hundred grand historic
connections were on the spot, and quite thrillingly,
re-established.   What was I tasting of, at that time
of day, and with intensity, but the far consequences
of things, made absolutely majestic by their weight and
duration?   I was tasting, mystically, of the very essence
of the old Southern idea—the hugest fallacy, as it
hovered there to one's backward, one's ranging vision,
for which hundreds of thousands of men had ever laid
down their lives.   I was tasting of the very bitterness
of the immense, grotesque, defeated project—the project,
extravagant, fantastic, and to-day pathetic in its folly,
of a vast Slave State (as the old term ran) artfully,
savingly isolated in the world that was to contain it
and trade with it.   This was what everything round
me meant — that that absurdity had once flourished
there; and nothing, immediately, could have been
more interesting than the lesson that such may remain,
for long years, the tell-tale face of things where such
absurdities *have* flourished.   Thus, by a turn of my

hand, or of my head, interest was evoked; so that from this moment I had never to let go of it. It was to serve again, it was to serve elsewhere, and in much the same manner; all aspects straightway were altered by it, and the pious pilgrim came round again into his own. He had wanted, his scheme had fairly required, this particular part of the country to be beautiful; he had really needed it to be, he couldn't afford, in due deference to the intellectual economy imposed on him, its not being. When things were grandly sad, accordingly—sad on the great scale and with a certain nobleness of ruin—an element of beauty seemed always secured, even if one could scarce say why: which truth, clearly, would operate fortunately for the compromised South.

It came back again—it was always, after this fashion, coming back, as if to make me extravagantly repeat myself—to the quantity to be "read into" the American view, in general, before it gives out an interest. The observer, like a fond investor, must spend on it, boldly, ingeniously, to make it pay; and it may often thus remind one of the wonderful soil of California, which is nothing when left to itself and the fine weather, but becomes everything conceivable under the rainfall. What would many an American prospect be for him, the visitor bent on appreciation frequently wonders, without his preliminary discharge upon it of some brisk shower of general ideas? The arid sand has, in a remarkable degree, the fine property of absorbing these latter and then giving them back to the air in proportionate signs of life. There be blooming gardens, on the other hand, I take it, where the foliage of Time is positively too dense for the general idea to penetrate or to perch—as if too many ideas had already been concerned and involved and there were nothing to do but to accept the complete demonstration. It was not to this order, at any rate, that my decipherable South was to belong; but Richmond at least began to repay my outlay, from point to point, as soon as the outlay had been made. The place was *weak*—"adorably" weak: that was the word into which the whole impression flowered, that was the idea, evidently, that all the rest of the way as well, would be most brought home. That was the form, in short, that the interest would take; the charm—immense, almost august—being in the long, unbroken connections of the case. Here, obviously, would be the prime source of the beauty; since if to be sad was to be the reverse of blatant, what was the sadness, taken all round, but the incurable after-taste of the original vanity and fatuity, with the memories and penalties of which the very air seemed still charged? I had recently been studying, a little, the record, reading, with other things, the volume of his admirable History in which Mr. James Ford Rhoades recounts the long preliminaries of the War and shows us, all lucidly and humanely, the Southern mind of the mid-century in the very convulsions of its perversity—the conception that, almost comic in itself, was yet so tragically to fail to work, that of a world rearranged, a State solidly and comfortably seated and tucked-in, in the interest of slave-produced Cotton.

The solidity and the comfort were to involve not only the wide extension, but the complete intellectual, moral and economic reconsecration of slavery, an enlarged and glorified, quite beatified, application of its principle. The light of experience, round about, and every finger-post of history, of political and spiritual science with which the scene of civilization seemed to bristle, had, when questioned, but one warning to give, and appeared to give it with an effect of huge derision: whereby was laid on the Southern genius the necessity of getting rid of these discords and substituting for the ironic face of the world an entirely new harmony, or in other words a different scheme of criticism. Since nothing in the Slave-scheme could be said to conform—conform, that is, to the reality of things—it was the plan of Christendom and the wisdom of the ages that would have to be altered.   History, the history of everything, would be rewritten *ad usum Delphini*—the Dauphin being in this case the budding Southern mind. This meant a general and a permanent quarantine ; meant the eternal bowdlerization of books and journals ; meant in fine all literature and all art on an expurgatory index.   It meant, still further, an active and ardent propaganda ; the reorganization of the school, the college, the university, in the interest of the new criticism.   The testimony to that thesis offered by the documents of the time, by State legislation, local eloquence, political speeches, the "tone of the press," strikes us to-day as beyond measure queer and quaint and benighted—innocent above all ; stamped with the inalienable Southern sign, the inimitable *rococo* note. We talk of the provincial, but the provinciality projected by the Confederate dream, and in which it proposed to steep the whole helpless social mass, looks to our present eyes as artlessly perverse, as untouched by any intellectual tradition of beauty or wit, as some exhibited array of the odd utensils or divinities of lone and primitive islanders.   It came over one that they *were* there, in the air they had breathed, precisely, lone—even the very best of the old Southerners ; and, looking at them over the threshold of approach that poor Richmond seemed to form, the real key to one's sense of their native scene was in that very idea of their solitude and their isolation.   Thus they affected one as such passive, such pathetic victims of fate, as so played upon and betrayed, so beaten and bruised, by the old burden of their condition, that I found myself conscious, on their behalf, of a sort of ingenuity of tenderness.

Their condition was to have waked up from far back to this thumping legacy of the intimate presence of the negro, and one saw them not much less imprisoned in it and overdarkened by it to-day than they had been in the time of their so fallacious presumption. The haunting consciousness thus produced is the prison of the Southern spirit; and how was one to say, as a pilgrim from afar, that with an equal exposure to the embarrassing fact one would have been more at one's ease? I had found my own threatened, I remember— my ease of contemplation of the subject, which was all there could be question of—during some ten minutes spent, a few days before, in consideration of an African type or two encountered in Washington. I was waiting, in a cab, at the railway-station, for the delivery of my luggage after my arrival, while a group of tatterdemalion darkies lounged and sunned themselves within range. To take in with any attention two or three of these figures had surely been to feel one's self introduced at a bound to the formidable question, which rose suddenly like some beast that had sprung from the jungle. These were its far outposts; they represented the Southern black as we knew him not, and had not within the memory of man known him, at the North; and to see him there, ragged and rudimentary, yet all portentous and "in possession of his rights as a man," was to be not a little discomposed, was to be in fact very much admonished. One understood at a glance how he must loom, how he must count, in a community in which, in spite of the ground it might cover, there were comparatively so few other things. The admonition accordingly remained, and no further appeal was required, I felt, to disabuse a tactful mind of the urgency of preaching, southward, a sweet reasonableness about him. Nothing was less contestable, of course, than that such a sweet reasonableness might play, in the whole situation, a beautiful part; but nothing, also, was on reflection more obvious than that the counsel of perfection, in such a case, would never prove oil upon the waters. The lips of the non-resident were, at all events, not the lips to utter this wisdom; the non-resident might well feel themselves indeed, after a little, appointed to silence, and, with any delicacy, see their duty quite elsewhere.

It came to one, soon enough, by all the voices of the air, that the negro had always been, and could absolutely not fail to be, intensely "on the nerves" of the South, and that as, in the other time, the observer from without had always, as a tribute to this truth, to tread the scene on tiptoe, so even yet, in presence of the immitigable fact, a like discretion is imposed on him. He might depart from the discretion of old, if he were so moved, intrusively, fanatically, even heroically, and he would depart from it to-day, one quite recognized, with the same effect of importunity, but not with the same effect of gallantry. The moral of all of which fairly became, to my sense, a soft inward dirge over the eternal "false position" of the afflicted South—condemned as she was to institutions, condemned to a state of temper, of exasperation and depression, a horrid heritage she had never consciously invited, that bound up her life with a hundred mistakes and make-believes, suppressions and prevarications, things that really all named themselves in the noted provincialism. None of them would have lived in the air of the greater world—which was the world that the North, with whatever abatements, had comparatively been, and had conquered by being; so that if the actual visitor was conscious now, as I say, of the appeal to his tenderness, it was by this sight of a society still shut up in a world smaller than what one might suppose its true desire, to say nothing of its true desert. I can doubtless not sufficiently tell why, but there was something in my whole sense of the South that projected at moments a vivid and painful image—that of a figure somehow blighted or stricken, discomfortably, impossibly seated in an invalid-chair, and yet fixing one with strange eyes that were half a defiance and half a deprecation of one's noticing, and much more of one's referring to, any abnormal sign. The deprecation, in the Southern eyes, is much greater to-day, I think, than the old lurid challenge; but my haunting similitude was an image of the keeping-up of appearances, and above all of the maintenance of a tone, the historic "high" tone, in an excruciating posture. There was food for sympathy—and the restless analyst must repeat that when he had but tasted of it he could but make of it his full meal. Which brings him back, by a long way round, to the grim street-corner at Richmond where he last left himself.

III

He could look down from it, I remember, over roofs and chimneys, through some sordid gap, at an abased prospect that quite failed to beckon—that of the James River embanked in snow and attended by waterside industries that, in the brown haze of the weather, were dingy and vague. There had been an indistinct sign for him—"somewhere there" had stood the Libby prison; an indication that flung over the long years ever so dreary a bridge. He lingered to take it in—from so far away it came, the strange apparition in the dress of another day; and with the interest of noting at the same time how little it mattered for any sort of intensity (whether of regret or of relief) that the structure itself, so sinister to the mind's eye, should have materially vanished. It was still there enough to parade its poor ghosts, but the value of the ghosts, precisely, was that they consented, all alike, on either side, to the grand epic dimness. I recognize, moreover, with the lapse of time, the positive felicity of my not having to connect them with the ruin of a particular squalid tobacco-house. The concrete, none the less, did, in the name of history, await me, and I indeed recollect pursuing it with pertinacity, for conscience' sake, all the way down a wide, steep street, a place of traffic, of shops and offices and altogether shabby Virginia vehicles, these last in charge of black teamsters who now emphasized for me with every degree of violence that already-apprehended note of the negro really at home. It fades, it melts away, with a promptitude of its own almost, any random reflection of the American picture ; and though the restless analyst has arts of *his* own for fixing and saving it—as he at least on occasion fondly flatters himself—he is too often reduced to wondering what it can have consisted of in a given case save exactly that projected light of his conscience. Richmond—*there* at least was a definite fact—is a city of more or less nobly-precipitous hills, and he recalls, of his visit to the avenue aforesaid, no intellectual consequence whatever but the after-sense of having remounted it again on the opposite side.

It was in succession to this, doubtless, that he found himself consulting the obscure oracle of the old State House or Capitol, seat of the Confederate legislature, strange intellectual centre of the general enterprise. I scarce know in what manner I had expected it to regale either my outward or my inward sense ; one had vaguely heard that it was "fine" and at the height, or in the key, of the old Virginian dignity. The approach to it had been adorned, from far back, moreover, as one remembered, with Crawford's celebrated monument to Washington

attended by famous Virginians—which work indeed, I
promptly perceived, answered to its reputation, with a
high elegance that was quite of the mid-century, and
yet that, indescribably archaic, made the mid-century
seem remote and quaint and queer, as disconnected from
us as the prolific age of Cyprus or of Crete. It is
positive that of the "old" American sculpture, about the
Union, a rich study might be made. What shall I say
of this spot at large, and of the objects it presented to
view, if not that here, where all the elements of life had
been most in fiery fusion, everything was somehow
almost abjectly frigid and thin? The small shapeless
Square, ancient acropolitan seat, ill placed on its
eminence, showed, I recollect, but a single figure in
motion—that of a gentleman to whom I presently put a
question and who explained to me that the Capitol,
masked all round in dense scaffolding, though without a
labourer visible, had been "very bad," a mere breakable
shell, and was now, from top to bottom, in course of
reconstruction. The shell, one could see, was empty
and work suspended; and I had never, truly, it seemed
to me, seen a human institution so coldly and logically
brought low as this memorial mass, anything rewritten
so mercilessly small as this poor passage of a great
historic text. The effect was as of a page of some
dishonoured author—printed "on grey paper with blunt
type," and when I had learned from my informant that
a fairly ample white house, a pleasant, honest structure
in the taste of sixty or eighty years since, had been
Jefferson Davis's official residence during part of the
War, every source of interest had been invoked and had
in its measure responded. The impression obeys, I
repeat, a rigorous law—it irremediably fades, it melts
away; but was there not, further, as a feature of the
scene, one of those decent and dumb American churches
which are so strangely possessed of the secret of mini-

mizing, to the casual eye, the general pretension of churches?

The extent to which the American air affects one as a non-conductor of such pretensions is, in the presence of these heterogeneous objects, a constant lively lesson. Looking for the most part no more established or seated than a stopped omnibus, they are reduced to the inveterate bourgeois level (that of private, accommodated pretensions merely) and fatally despoiled of the fine old ecclesiastical arrogance. This, the richest attribute they elsewhere enjoy, keeps clear of them only to betray them, so that they remind one everywhere of organisms trying to breathe in the void, or of those creatures of the deep sea who change colour and shrink, as one has heard, when astray in fresh water. The fresh water makes them indeed pullulate, but to the loss of "importance," and nothing could more have fallen in with that generalization, for the restless analyst, than the very moral of the matter, as he judged, lately put before him at the national capital. Washington already bristles, for the considering eye, with national affirmations—big builded forms of confidence and energy; but when you have embraced them all, with the implication of all the others still to come, you will find yourself wondering what it is you so oddly miss. Numberless things are represented, and one interest after the other counts itself in; the great Congressional Library crowns the hill beside the Capitol, the Departments and Institutes cover their acres and square their shoulders, the obelisk to the memory of Washington climbs still higher; but something is absent more even than these masses are present—till it at last occurs to you that the existence of a religious faith on the part of the people is not even remotely suggested. Not a Federal dome, not a spire nor a cornice pretends to any such symbolism, and though your attention is thus concerned with a mere negative, the negative presently becomes its sharp obsession. You reach out perhaps in vain for something to which you may familiarly compare your unsatisfied sense. You liken it perhaps not so much to a meal made savourless by the failure of some usual, some central dish, as to a picture, nominally finished, say, where the canvas shows, in the very middle, with all originality, a fine blank space.

For it is most, doubtless, the æsthetic appetite in you —long richly fed elsewhere—that goes unassuaged; it is your sense of the comprehensive picture *as* a comprehensive picture that winces, for recognition of loss, like a touched nerve. What is the picture, collectively seen, you ask, but the portrait, more or less elaborated, of a multitudinous People, of a social and political order? —so that the effect is, for all the world, as if, with the body and the limbs, the hands and feet and coat and trousers, all the accessories of the figure showily painted, the neat white oval of the face itself were innocent of the brush. You marvel at the personage, you admire even the painting—which you are largely reduced, however, to admiring in the hands and the boots, in the texture of accompanying table-cloth, inkstand, newspaper (introduced with a careless grace) and other paraphernalia. You wonder how he would look if the face *had* been done; though you have compensation, meanwhile, I must certainly add, in your consciousness of assisting, as you apprehensively stand there, at something new under the sun. The size of the gap, the intensity of the omission, in the Washington prospect, where so much else is representative, dots with the last sharpness the distinct *i*, as it were, of one of the promptest generalizations of the repatriated absentee. The field of American life is as bare of the Church as a billiard-table of a centre-piece; a truth that the myriad little structures " attended " on Sundays and on the " off " evenings of their " sociables "

proclaim as with the audible sound of the roaring of a
million mice.   Or that analogy reinsists—of the difference
between the deep sea of the older sphere of spiritual
passion and the shallow tide in which the inhabiting
particles float perforce near the surface.   And however
one indicates one's impression of the clearance, the clearance itself, in its completeness, with the innumerable odd
connected circumstances that bring it home, represents,
in the history of manners and morals, a deviation in the
mere measurement of which hereafter may well reside
a certain critical thrill.   I say hereafter because it is a
question of one of those many measurements that would
as yet, in the United States, be premature.   Of all the
solemn conclusions one feels as "barred," the list is quite
headed, in the States, I think, by this particular abeyance
of judgment.   When an ancient treasure of precious
vessels, overscored with glowing gems and wrought,
artistically, into wondrous shapes, has, by a prodigious
process, been converted, through a vast community, into
the small change, the simple circulating medium of dollars
and "nickels," we can only say that the consequent permeation will be of values of a new order.   Of *what* order
we must wait to see.

All of which remarks would constitute a long excursion,
I admit, from the sacred edifice by the Richmond street,
were it not for that saving law, the enrichment of each
hour on the American scene, that wings almost any
observed object with a power to suggest, a possible social
portée, soaring superior to its plain face.   And I seem to
recover the sense of a pretext for incurable mooning, then
and there, in my introduction, but little delayed, to the
next in the scant group of local lions, the usual place of
worship, as I understood, of the Confederate leader,
from his proper pew in which Jefferson Davis was called,
on that fine Sunday morning of the spring-time of 1865,
by the news of Lee's surrender.   The news had been

big, but the place of worship was small, and, linger in it as one would, fraternize as one would with the mild old Confederate soldier, survivor of the epic age, who made, by his account, so lean a living of his office of sexton, one could but moodily resent, again, its trivialization of history—a process one scarce knows how to name—its inaccessibility to legend. Perhaps, after all, it represented, in its comfortable " denominational " commonness, the right scene of concentration for the promoters of so barren a polity, that idea of the perpetual Southern quarantine ; but no leaders of a great movement, a movement acclaimed by a whole nation and paid for with every sacrifice, ever took such pains, alas, to make themselves not interesting.   It was positively as if legend would have nothing to say to them ; as if, on the spot there, I had seen it turn its back on them and walk out of the place.   This is the horse, ever, that one may take to the water, but that drinks not against his will.   That was at least what it came back to—for the musing moralist : if the question is of legend we dig for it in the deposit of history, but the deposit must be thick to have given it a cover and let it accumulate.   It was on the battle-fields and in all the blood-drenched radius that it would be thick ; here, decidedly, in the streets of melancholy Richmond, it was thin.   Just so, since it was the planners and plotters who had bidden unsuccessfully for our interest, it was for the sacrificed multitude, the unsophisticated, irresponsible agents, the obscure and the eminent alike, that distinction might be pleaded. *They* were buried, if one would, in the " deposit "—where the restless analyst might scratch, all tenderly, to find them.

He had fortunately at this moment his impression as to where, under such an impulse, he had best look ; and he turned his steps, as with an appetite for some savour in his repast still too much withheld to that Museum of the relics of the Confederacy installed some years since in the eventual White House of Richmond, the "executive mansion" of the latter half of the War. Here, positively, the spirit descended—and yet all the more directly, it seemed to me, strange to say, by reason of the very nudity and crudity, the historic, the pathetic poverty of the exhibition.   It fills the whole large house, each of the leagued States enjoying an allotted space; and one assuredly feels, in passing from room to room, that, up and down the South, no equal area can so offer itself as sacred ground.   Tragically, indescribably sanctified, these documentary chambers that contained, so far as I remember, not a single object of beauty, scarce one in fact that was not altogether ugly (so void they were of intrinsic charm), and that spoke only of the absence of means and of taste, of communication and resource.   In these rude accents they phrased their interest—which the unappeased visitor, from the moment of his crossing the general threshold, had recognized in fact as intense.   He was at his old trick : he had made out, on the spot, in other words, that here was a pale page into which he might read what he liked.   He had not exchanged ten words of civility with a little old lady, a person soft-voiced, gracious, mellifluous, perfect for her function, who, seated by her fire in a sort of official ante-room, received him as at the gate of some grandly bankrupt plantation—he had not surrendered to this exquisite contact before he felt himself up to his neck in a delightful, soothing, tepid medium, the social tone of the South that *had* been.   It was but the matter of a step over—he was afloat on other waters, and had remounted the stream of Time.   I said just now that nothing in the Museum had beauty ; but the little old lady had it, with her thoroughly "sectional" good manners, and that punctuality and felicity, that inimitability, one must again say, of the South in her, in the patriotic unction of her reference to

the sorry objects about, which transported me as no
enchanted carpet could have done. No little old lady
of the North could, for the high tone and the right
manner, have touched her, and poor benumbed Richmond might now be as dreary as it liked : with that
small observation made my pilgrimage couldn't be a
failure.

The sorry objects about were old Confederate documents, already sallow with time, framed letters, orders,
autographs, extracts, tatters of a paper-currency in the
last stages of vitiation ; together with faded portraits of
faded worthies, primitive products of the camera, the
crayon, the brush ; of all of which she did the honours
with a gentle florid reverence that opened wide, for the
musing visitor, as he lingered and strolled, the portals,
as it were, of a singularly interesting " case." It was the
case of the beautiful, the attaching oddity of the general
Southern state of mind, or stage of feeling, in relation to
that heritage of woe and of glory of which the mementos
surrounded me. These mementos were the sorry
objects, and as I pursued them from one ugly room to
another—the whole place wearing the air thus, cumulatively, of some dim, dusty collection of specimens, prehistoric, paleolithic, scientific, and making one grope for
some verbal rendering of the grey effect—the queer
elements at play wrote themselves as large as I could
have desired. On every side, I imagine, from Virginia
to Texas, the visitor must become aware of them—the
visitor, that is, who, by exception, becomes aware of
anything : was I not, for instance, presently to recognize
them, at their finest, for an almost comic ambiguity, in
the passionate flare of the little frontal inscription behind
which the Daughters of the Confederacy of the Charleston section nurse the old wrongs and the old wounds ?
These afflictions are still, thus, admirably ventilated, and
what is wonderful, in the air, to-day, is the comfort and

cheer of this theory of an undying rancour. Every facility is enjoyed for the publication of it, but as the generation that immediately suffered and paid has almost wholly passed away, the flame-coloured *idea* has flowered out of the fact, and the interest, the "psychologic" interest, is to see it so disengage itself, as legend, as valuable, enriching, inspiring, romantic legend, and settle down to play its permanent part. Practically, and most conveniently, one feels, the South is reconciled, but theoretically, ideally, and above all for the new generation and the amiable ladies, the ladies amiable like the charming curatrix of the Richmond Museum, it burns with a smothered flame. As we meanwhile look about us there, over a scene as sad, throughout, as some raw spring eventide, we feel how something of the sort must, in all the blankness, respond morally and socially to a want.

The collapse of the old order, the humiliation of defeat, the bereavement and bankruptcy involved, represented, with its obscure miseries and tragedies, the social revolution the most unrecorded and undepicted, in proportion to its magnitude, that ever was ; so that this reversion of the starved spirit to the things of the heroic age, the four epic years, is a definite soothing salve—a sentiment which has, moreover, in the South, to cultivate, itself, intellectually, from season to season, the field over which it ranges, and to sow with its own hands such crops as it may harvest. The sorry objects, at Richmond, brought it home—so low the æsthetic level : it was impossible, from room to room, to imagine a community, of equal size, more disinherited of art or of letters. These about one were the only echoes—daubs of portraiture, scrawls of memoranda, old vulgar newspapers, old rude uniforms, old unutterable "mid-Victorian" odds and ends of furniture, all ghosts as of things noted at a country fair. The illiteracy seemed to hover like a queer smell ; the social revolution had begotten neither song nor story—only, for literature, two or three biographies of soldiers, written in other countries, and only, for music, the weird chants of the emancipated blacks. Only for art, I was an hour later to add, the monument to General Lee by M. Mercié of Paris ; but to that, in its suburban corner, and to the strange eloquence of its isolation, I shall presently come. The moral of the show seemed to me meanwhile the touching inevitability, in such conditions, of what I have called the nursing attitude. " What on earth—nurse of a rich heroic past, nurse of a fierce avenging future, nurse of any connection that would make for *any* brood of visions about one's knee—wouldn't one have to become," I found myself inwardly exclaiming, " if one had this great melancholy void to garnish and to people ! " It was not, under this reflection, the actual innocent flare of the altar of memory that was matter for surprise, but that such altars should strike one, rather, as few and faint. They would have been none too many for countenance and cheer had they blazed on every hilltop.

The Richmond halls, at any rate, appeared, through the chill of the season, scantly trodden, and I met in them no fellow-visitor but a young man of stalwart and ingenuous aspect who struck me so forcibly, after a little, as exhaling a natural piety that, as we happened at last to be rapt in contemplation of the same sad glass case, I took advantage of the occasion to ask him if he were a Southerner. His affirmative was almost eager, and he proved—for all the world like the hero of a famous novel—a gallant and nameless, as well as a very handsome, young Virginian. A farmer by occupation, he had come up on business from the interior to the capital, and, having a part of his morning on his hands, was spending it in this visitation —made, as I gathered, by no means for the first time, but which he still found absorbing. As a son of the new South he presented a lively interest of type—linguistically not least (since where doesn't the restless analyst grope for light?)—and this interest, the ground of my here recalling him, was promptly to arrive at a climax.   He pointed out to me, amid an array of antique regimentals, certain objects identical with relics preserved in his own family and that had belonged to his father, who, enrolled at the earliest age, had fought to the end of the War.   The old implements before us bore the number of the Virginia regiment in which this veteran had first seen service, and a question or two showed me how well my friend was acquainted with his parent's exploits.   Enjoying, apparently—for he was intelligent and humorous and highly conversable—the opportunity to talk of such things (they being, as it were, so advantageously present there with a vague Northerner), he related, felicitously, some paternal adventure of which I have forgotten the particulars, but which comprised a desperate evasion of capture, or worse, by the lucky smashing of the skull of a Union soldier.   I complimented him on his exact knowledge of these old, unhappy, far-off things, and it was his candid response that was charmingly suggestive.   "Oh, I should be ready to do them all over again myself!"   And then, smiling serenely, but as if it behoved even the least blatant of Northerners to understand : "That's the kind of Southerner *I* am!"   I allowed that he was a capital kind of Southerner, and we afterwards walked together to the Public Library, where, on our finally parting, I could but thank him again for being so much the kind of Southerner I had wanted.   He was a fine contemporary young American, incapable, so to speak, of hurting a Northern fly—*as* Northern; but whose consciousness would have been poor and unfurnished without this cool platonic passion.   With what other pattern, personal views apart, *could* he have adorned its bare walls?   So I wondered till it came to me that, though he wouldn't have hurt a Northern fly, there were things (ah, we had touched on some of these!) that, all fair, engaging, smiling, as he stood there, he would have done to a Southern negro.

IV

The Public Libraries in the United States are, like the Universities, a challenge to fond fancy; by which I mean that, if, taken together, they bathe the scene with a strange hard light of their own, the individual institution may often affect the strained pilgrim as a blessedly restful perch.   It constitutes, in its degree, wherever met, a more explicit plea for the amenities, or at least a fuller exhibition of them, than the place is otherwise likely to contain; and I remember comparing them, inwardly, after periods of stress and dearth, after long, vacant stretches, to the mast-heads on which spent birds sometimes alight in the expanses of ocean.   Their function for the student of manners is by no means exhausted with that attribute—they project, through the use made of them, twenty interesting sidelights; but it was by that especial restorative, that almost romantic character I have just glanced at, that I found myself most solicited.   It is to the inordinate value, in the picture, of the non-commercial, non-industrial, non-financial note that they owe their rich relief; being, with the Universities, as one never wearied of noting, charged with the *whole* expression of that part of the national energy that is not calculable in terms of mere arithmetic.   They appeared to express it, at times, I admit, the strange national energy, in terms of mere subjection to the spell of the last "seller"—the new novel, epidemically swift, the ubiquity of which so mirrors the great continental conditions of unity, equality and prosperity; but this view itself was compatible with one's sense of their practical bid for the effect of distinction. There are a hundred applications of the idea of civilization which, in a given place, outside its Library, would be all wrong, if conceivably attempted, and yet that immediately become right, incur in fact the highest sanction, on passing that threshold. They often more or less fail of course, they sometimes completely fail, to assert themselves even within the precinct ; but one at least feels that the precinct attends on them, waits and confessedly yearns for them, consents indeed to *be* a precinct only on the understanding that they shall not be forever delayed. I wondered, everywhere, under stress of this perception, at the general associations of the word that best describes them and that remains so quaintly and admirably *their* word even when their supreme right in it is most vulgarly and loudly disputed. They are the *rich* presences, even in the " rich " places, among the sky - scrapers, the newspaper - offices, the highly-rented pews and the billionaires, and they assert, with a blest imperturbable serenity, not only that everything would be poor without them, but that even with them much is as yet deplorably poor. They in fact so inexorably establish this truth that when they are in question they leave little to choose, I think, round about them, between the seats of wealth and the seats of comparative penury : they are intrinsically so much more interesting than either.

Was it then because Richmond at large, the " old " Richmond, seemed to lie there in its icy shroud with the very dim smile of modesty, the invalid gentleness, of a patient who has been freely bled—was it through profit of this impression that the town Library struck me as flushing with colour and resource, with confidence and temperament ? The beauty of the matter is that these *penetralia*, to carry it off as they do, call to their aid, of necessity, no great store of possessions—play their trick, if they must, with the mildest rarities. It sufficed, really, at Richmond, that the solid structure—ample and detached indeed, and keeping, where it stood, the best company the place could afford—should make the affirmation furthest removed from the vain vaunt of the other time, the pretence of a social order founded on delusions and exclusions. Everything else was somehow, however indirectly, the bequest of that sad age and partook more or less of its nature ; this thing alone either had nothing to do with it or had to do with it by an appealing, a quite affecting lapse of logic—his half-hour's appreciation of which had for the restless analyst a positive melancholy sweetness. The place had of course to be in its way a temple to the Confederate cause, but the charm, in the spacious, " handsome," convenient upper room, among books of value and pictures of innocence, and glass cases of memorabilia more refined than those of the collection I had previously visited, among gentle readers, transported and oblivious, and the still gentler specimens, if I rightly recollect, of the pale sisterhood of the appointed and attendant fair who predominantly, throughout the States, minister to intellectual appetite and perform the intellectual service, directing and controlling them and, as would appear, triumphantly minimizing their scope, feminizing their too possible male grossnesses—the charm, I say, was now in the beautiful openness to the world-relation, in the felt balm, really, of the disprovincializing breath. Once such a summer air as that had begun softly to stir, even the drearier little documents might flutter in it as confederately as they liked. The terrible framed canvases, portraits of soldiers and statesmen, strange images, on the whole, of the sectional great, might seem to shake, faintly, on the wall, as in vague protest at a possible doom. Disinherited of art one could indeed, in presence of such objects, but feel that the old South had been ; and might not this thin tremor, on the part of several of those who had had so little care for it, represent some sense of what the more liberal day—so announced there on the spot—might mean for their meagre memories?

This was a question, however, that it naturally concerned me not to put to the old mutilated Confederate soldier who, trafficking in photographs in a corner of the room, rejoiced to proclaim the originals of the portraits. Nothing could have been a happier link than the old Confederate soldier—a link as from past to present and future, I mean, even when individually addicted to "voicing" some of the more questionable claims of the past. What will they be, at all events, the Southern shrines of memory, on the day the last old Confederate soldier shall have been gathered to his fate? Never, thanks to a low horizon, had the human figure endowed with almost anything at all in the nature of a presence or a silhouette such a chance to stand out; never had the pictorial accident, on a vast grey canvas, such a chance to tell. But a different matter from these, at Richmond, in fact the greatest matter of all, is the statue of General Lee, which stands, high aloft and extraordinarily by itself, at the far end of the main residential street—a street with no imputable "character" but that of leading to it. Faithful, experimentally, to a desperate practice, I yet had to renounce here—in the main residential street—the subtle effort to "read" a sense into the senseless appearances about me. This ranked, I scarce know why, as a disappointment: I had presumed with a fond extravagance, I have hinted, that they would give out here and there some unmistakable backward reference, show, from the old overclambered but dispeopled double galleries that I might liken to desecrated cloisters, some wan, faded face of shrunken gentility. Frankly, however, with the best will in the world—really too good a will, which found itself again and again quite grimly snubbed—frankly I could do nothing: everything was there but the material. The disposition had been a tribute to old Virginia, but old Virginia quite unceremoniously washed her hands of me. I have spoken of scratching, scratching for romance, and all tenderly, in the deposit of history ; but, plainly, no deposit would show, and I tried to remember, for fairness, that Richmond had been after all but a modern and upstart capital. Indistinct there, below the hill, was the James River, and away in the mists of time "romantic" Jamestown, the creation of a Stuart king. That would have to do, though it also, in its way, was nothing; for meanwhile in truth, just here—here above all and in presence of the monument completing the vista —were other things to remember, provoked reflections that took on their own intensity.

The equestrian statue of the Southern hero, made to order in far-away uninterested Paris, is the work of a master and has an artistic interest—a refinement of style, in fact, under the impression of which we seem to see it, in its situation, as some precious pearl of ocean washed up on a rude bare strand. The very high florid pedestal is of the last French elegance, and the great soldier, sitting his horse with a kind of melancholy nobleness, raises his handsome head as he looks off into desolate space. He does well, we feel, to sit as high as he may, and to appear, in his lone survival, to see as far, and to overlook as many things ; for the irony of fate, crowning the picture, is surely stamped in all sharpness on the scene about him. The place is the mere vague centre of two or three crossways, without form and void, with a circle half sketched by three or four groups of small, new, mean houses. It is somehow empty in spite of being ugly, and yet expressive in spite of being empty. "Desolate," one has called the air ; and the effect is, strangely, of some smug "up-to-date specimen or pattern of desolation. So long as one stands there the high figure, which ends for all the world by suggesting to the admirer a quite conscious, subjective, even a quite sublime, effort to ignore, to sit, as it were, superior and indifferent, enjoys the fact of company and thereby, in a manner, of sympathy—so that the vast association of the futile for the moment drops away from it.   But to turn one's back, one feels, is to leave it again alone, communing, at its altitude, which represents thus some prodigious exemplary perched position, some everlasting high stool of penitence, with the very heaven of futility. So at least I felt brought round again to meeting my first surprise, to solving the riddle of the historic poverty of Richmond.   It is the poverty that *is*, exactly, historic: once take it for that and it puts on vividness. The condition attested is the condition—or, as may be, one of the later, fainter, weaker stages—of having worshipped false gods.   As I looked back, before leaving it, at Lee's stranded, bereft image, which time and fortune have so cheated of half the significance, and so, I think, of half the dignity, of great memorials, I recognized something more than the melancholy of a lost cause.   The whole infelicity speaks of a cause that could never have been gained.

13

Charleston

To arrive at Charleston early in the chill morning was to appear to have come quite adventurously far, and yet to be not quite clear about the grounds of the appearance. Did it rest on impressions gathered by the way, on the number of things one had been, since leaving Richmond, aware of?—or was it rather explained by the long succession of hours, the nights and days, consumed as mere tasteless time and without the attending relish of excited interest? What, definitely, could I say I had seen, that my journey should already presume to give itself airs, to seat itself there as a chapter of experience? To consider of this question was really, I think, after a little, to renew one's appreciation of the mystery and the marvel of experience. That accretion may amount to an enormous sum, often, when the figures on the slate are too few and too paltry to mention. It may count for enrichment without one's knowing why; and so again, on occasion, with a long column of items, it may count for nothing at all. I reached Charleston ever so much (as it seemed to me) the wiser—the wiser, that is, for the impression of scarce distinguishable things. One made them out, with no great brilliancy, as just Southern; but one would have missed the point, I hasten to add, in failing to see what an application and what a value they derived from that name. One was already beginning—that was the truth

—one's convenient induction as to the nature of the South; and, once that account was opened, how could everything, great or small, positive or negative, not become straightway a contribution to it? The large negatives, in America, have, as well as other matters, their meaning and their truth: so what if my charged consciousness of the long way from Richmond were that of a negative modified by small discomforts?

The discomforts indeed were as nothing, for importance—compared, candidly, with the importance of the rest of the impression. The process, certainly, however one qualified it, had been interrupted by one of the most positive passages of one's life—which may not figure here, alas, unfortunately, as of the essence of my journey. Vast brackets, applied, as it were, to the very face of nature, enclosed and rounded this felicity; which was no more of the texture of the general Southern stuff than a patch of old brocade would be of the woof of the native homespun. I had, by a deviation, spent a week in a castle of enchantment; but if this modern miracle, of which the mountains of North Carolina happened to be the scene, would have been almost anywhere miraculous, I could at least take it as testifying, all relevantly, all directly, for the presence, as distinguished from the absence, of feature. One felt how, in this light, the extent and the splendour of such a place was but a detail; these things were accidents, without which the great effect, the element that, in the beautiful empty air, made all the difference, would still have prevailed. What was this element but just the affirmation of resources?— made with great emphasis indeed, but in a clear and exemplary way; so that if large wealth represented some of them, an idea, a fine cluster of ideas, a will, a purpose, a patience, an intelligence, a store of knowledge, immediately workable things, represented the others. What it thus came to, on behalf of this vast parenthetic

Carolinian demonstration, was that somebody had *cared* enough—and that happily there had been somebody *to* care; which struck me at once as marking the difference for the rest of the text. My view of the melancholy of it had been conveniently expressed, from hour to hour, by the fond reflection, through the dreary land, that nobody cared—cared really for *it* or for anything. That fairly *made* it dreary, as the crazy timber viaducts, where the train crawled, and sometimes nervously stopped, spanned the deep gorges and the admirable nameless and more or less torrential streams; as the sense of landscape in mere quantity became, once more, the vehicle of effect; and as we pulled up at the small stations where the social scene might be sufficiently penetrated, no doubt, from the car window.

The social scene, shabby and sordid, and lost in the scale of space as the quotable line is lost in a dull epic or the needed name in an ageing memory, would have been as interesting, probably, as a "short story" in one of the slangy dialects promoted by the illustrated monthly magazines; but it affected me above all, and almost each time, I seem to remember, as speaking of the number of things not cared for. There were some presumably, though not at all discernibly, that *were*—enough to beget the loose human cohesion, the scant consistency of parts and pieces, to which the array by the railway platform testified; but questions came up, plentifully, in respect to the whole picture, and if the mass of interests that were absent was so remarkably large, this would be certainly because such interests were ruled out. The grimness with which, as by a hard inexorable fate, so many things were ruled out, fixed itself most perhaps as the impression of the spectator enjoying from his supreme seat of ease his extraordinary, his awful modern privilege of this detached yet concentrated stare at the misery of subject populations. (Subject, I mean, to this

superiority of his bought convenience—subject even as
never, of old, to the sway of satraps or proconsuls.)   If
the subject populations on the road to Charleston, seemingly weak indeed in numbers and in energy, had to be
viewed, at all events, so vividly, as not "caring," one
made out quite with eagerness that it was because they
naturally couldn't.   The negroes were more numerous
than the whites, but still there *were* whites—of aspect
so forlorn and depressed for the most part as to depre-
cate, though not cynically, only quite tragically, any
imputation of value.   It was a monstrous thing, doubtless, to sit there in a cushioned and kitchened Pullman
and deny to so many groups of one's fellow-creatures
any claim to a "personality"; but this was in truth what
one was perpetually doing.   The negroes, though superficially and doubtless not at all intendingly sinister, were
the lustier race; but how could they care (to insist on
my point) for such equivocal embodiments of the right
complexion?   Yet these were, practically, within the
picture the only affirmations of life except themselves;
and they obviously, they notoriously, didn't care for
themselves.   The moral of all of which was that really,
through the more and more southward hours, the wondering stops and the blank renewals, it was only the restless
analyst himself who cared—and enough, after all, he
finally felt, to make up for other deficiencies.

He cared even when, in the watches of the night, he
was roused, under the bewilderment that was rarely to
leave him, in America, at any stage of any transaction
to which the cars and their sparse stern functionaries
formed a party, for unpremeditated transfer to a dark
and friendless void where, with what grace he could, he
awaited the February dawn.   The general American
theory is that railway-travel within the confines of the
Republic is a matter of majestic simplicity and facility—
qualified at the worst by inordinate luxury; I should

need therefore an excursion here forbidden me to present another and perhaps a too highly subjective view of it. There are lights in which the majesty, if the question be of that, may strike the freshly repatriated, or in other words the unwarned and inexpert, as quite grimly formidable ; lights, however, that must be left to shine for us in some other connection. Let it none the less glimmer out of them for the moment that this implication of the penalty of imperfect expertness is really a clue to the essence of the matter ; a core packed, in relation to the whole subject of expertness, with fruitful suggestion. No single admonition, in the States, I think, is more constant and vivid than the general mass of intimation of what may happen to you, in transit, unless you have had special and confirmed practice. You may have been without it in " Europe," for moving about, and yet not perish ; but to be inexpert in the American battle would be, it struck me, much more quickly to go down. Your luggage, in America, is " looked after," but you are not, save so far as you receive on occasion a sharp order or a sharper shove : by sufferance of which discipline, moreover, you by no means always purchase a prompt delivery of your effects. This indeed is but a translation of the general truth that it is the country in the world in which you must do most things for yourself. It may be " better " for you to have thus to do for yourself the secondary as well as the primary things— but that is not here the question. It begins to strike you, at all events, as soon as you begin to circulate, that your fellow-travellers are for the most part, as to the complex act itself, professional ; whereas you may perform it all in " Europe " successfully enough as an amateur. Whether to your glory or your shame you must of course yourself decide ; but impunity, nay more, success, may at least attend your empiricism.

If it was not success, however, for the strayed amateur

to have found himself stranded in the small hours of
morning by the vast vague wayside, he still nevertheless remembers how quickly even this interlude took
on an interest. The gloom was scarce penetrable, but
a light glimmered here and there, and formless sheds and
shanties, dim, discomfortable things, straggled about and
lost themselves. Indistinguishable engines hooted, before
and behind, where red fires also flared and vanished;
indistinguishable too, from each other, while one sought
a place of temporary deposit for the impedimenta that
attested one's absurd want of rehearsal, were the cold
steel of the rails, the vague composition of the platform,
and the kinder, the safer breast of earth. The place was
apparently a junction, and it was but a question of waiting—of selecting as the wisest course, among the hoots
and the flares, to stand huddled just where one was.
That almost completely unservanted state which is so
the mark, in general, of the American station, was here
the sole distinctness. I had succeeded in artlessly becoming a perfectly isolated traveller, with nobody to
warn or comfort me, with nobody even to command.
But it was precisely in this situation that I felt again,
as by the click of a spring, that my adventure had, in
spite of everything, or perhaps indeed just because of
everything, a charm all its own—and a charm, moreover,
which I was to have from that moment, for any connection, no difficulty whatever in recognizing. It must
have broken out more particularly, then and there, in
the breath of the night, which was verily now the bland
air of the South—mild, benignant, a benediction in itself
as it hung about me, and with that blest quality in it
of its appearing a medium through which almost any
good might come. It was the air of the open gates—
not, like that of the North, of the closed; and one
inhaled it, in short, on the spot, as the very boon of
one's quest.

A couple of hours later, in the right train, which had at last arrived, I had so settled to submission to this spell that it had wrought for me, I think, all its magic— ministered absolutely to the maximum of suggestion, which became thus, for my introduction to Charleston, the presiding influence.   What had happened may doubtless show for no great matter in a bare verbal statement; yet it was to make all the difference, I felt, for impressions (happy and harsh alike) still to come.   It couldn't have happened without one's beginning to wander; but the lively interest was that the further one wandered the more the suggestion spoke.   The sense of the size of the Margin, that was the name of it—the Margin by which the total of American life, huge as it already appears, is still so surrounded as to represent, for the mind's eye on a general view, but a scant central flotilla huddled as for very fear of the fathomless depth of water, the too formidable future, on the so much vaster lake of the materially possible.   Once that torch is at all vividly lighted it flares, for any pair of open eyes, over every scene, and with a presence that helps to explain their owner's inevitable failure to conclude.   He feels it in all his uncertainties, and he never just escapes concluding without the sense that this so fallacious neatness would more or less absurdly have neglected or sacrificed it. Not by any means that the Margin always affects him as standing for the vision of a possible greater good than what he sees in the given case—any more than as standing for a possible greater evil; these differences are submerged in the immense fluidity; they lurk confused, disengaged, in the mere looming mass of the *more*, the more and more to come.   And as yet nothing makes definite the probable preponderance of particular forms of the more.   The one all positive appearance is of the perpetual increase of everything, the growth of the immeasurable muchness that shall constitute the deep sea into which the seeker for conclusions must cast his nets. The fact that, with so many things present, so few of them are not on the way to become quite other, and possibly altogether different, things, conduces to the peculiar interest and, one often feels tempted to add, to the peculiar irritation of the country.

II

Charleston early in the morning, on my driving from the station, was, it had to be admitted, no very finished picture, but at least, already, it was different—ever so different in aspect and "feeling," and above all for intimation and suggestion, from any passage of the American scene as yet deciphered; and such became on the spot one's appetite for local colour that one was fairly grateful to a friend who, by having promised to arrive from the interior of the State the night before, gave one a pretext for seeking him up and down. My quest, for the moment, proved vain; but the intimations and suggestions, while I proceeded from door to door in the sweet blank freshness of the day, of the climate, of the streets, began to swarm at such a rate that I had the sense of gathering my harvest with almost too eager a thrift. It was like standing steeped at the bookstall itself in the volume picked up and opened—though I may add that when I had presently retreated upon the hotel, to which I should in the first instance have addressed myself, it was quite, for a turning of pages, as if I had gone on with the "set." Thus, before breakfast, I entered upon my brief residence with the right vibrations already determined and unable really to say which of a couple of contacts just enjoyed would have most ministered to them. I had roused, guilelessly, through an easy misunderstanding, two more or less sleeping households ; but if I had still missed my clue to my friend I had yet put myself into possession of much of whatever else I had wanted. What had I most wanted, I could easily ask myself, but some small inkling (a mere specimen-scrap would do) of the sense, as I have to keep forever calling my wanton synthesis, of "the South before the War"?—an air-bubble only to be blown, in any case, through some odd fragment of a pipe. My pair of early Charleston impressions were thus a pair of thin prismatic bubbles—which could have floated before me moreover but for a few seconds, collapsing even while I stood there.

Prismatically, none the less, they had shown me the "old" South ; in one case by the mere magic of the manner in which a small, scared, starved person of colour, of very light colour, an elderly mulattress in an improvised wrapper, just barely held open for me a door through which I felt I might have looked straight and far back into the past. The past, that of the vanished order, was hanging on there behind her—as much of it as the scant place would accommodate ; and she knew this, and that I had so quickly guessed it ; which led her, in fine, before I could see more, and that I might not sound the secret of shy misfortune, of faded pretension, to shut the door in my face. So, it seemed to me, had I been confronted, in Italy, under quite such a morning air and light, quite the same touch of a tepid, odorous medium, with the ancient sallow crones who guard the locked portals and the fallen pride of provincial *palazzini*. That was all, in the one instance ; there had been no more of it than of the little flare of a struck match—which lasted long enough, however, to light the sedative cigarette, smoked and thrown away, that renews itself forever between the picture-seeker's lips. The small historic whiff I had momentarily inhaled required the correction, I should add, of the sweeter breath of my commentary. Fresh altogether was the air behind the garden wall that next gave way to my pursuit; there being a thrill, for that matter, in the fact that here at last again, if nowhere else over the land, rose the real walls that alone make real gardens and that admit to the same by real doors. Close such a door behind you, and you are at once *within* —a local relation, a possibility of retreat, in favour of which the custom of the North has so completely ceased to discriminate. One sacrificed the North, with its mere hard conceit of virtuously meeting exhibition—much as if a house were just a metallic machine, number so-and-so in a catalogue—one sacrificed it on the spot to this finer feeling for the enclosure.

That had really sufficed, no doubt, for my second initiation; since I remember withdrawing, after my fruitless question, as on the completion of a mystic process. Initiation into *what* I perhaps couldn't have said; only, at the most, into the knowledge that what such Southern walls generally shut in proves exactly what one would have wished. I was to see this loose quantity afterwards in greater profusion; but for the moment the effect was as right as that of privacy for the habit of the siesta. The details escape me, or rather I tenderly withhold them. For the siesta there—what would it have been most like but some deep doze, or call it frankly some final sleep, of the idea of "success"? And how could one better have described the privacy, with the mild street shut off and with the deep gallery, where resignation might sit in the shade or swing without motion in a hammock, shut in, than as some dim dream that things were still as they had been—still pleasant behind garden walls—before the great folly? I was to find myself liking, in the South and in the most monstrous fashion, it appeared, those aspects in which the consequences of the great folly were, for extent and gravity, still traceable; I was cold-bloodedly to prefer them, that is, to the aspects, occasionally to be met, from which the traces had been removed. And this, I need hardly say, from a point of view having so little in common with the vindictive as to be quite directly opposed to it. For what in the world was one candidly to do? It is the manner of the purged and renovated, the disconnected element, anywhere, after great trials, to express itself in forms comparatively vulgar; whereas those parts of the organism that, having been through the fire, still have kept the scorches and scars, resemble for tone, for colour and value, the products of the potter's oven; when the potter, I mean, or when, in other words, history, has been the right great artist. They at least are not cheerful rawnesses—they have been baked beautiful and hard.

I even tried, I fear, when once installed there, to look at my hotel in that light; availing myself, to this end, of its appearance of "dating," with its fine old neo-classic front and of a certain romantic grandeur of scale, the scale positively of "Latin" construction, in my vast saloon-like apartment, which opened to a high colonnade. The great canopied and curtained bed was really in the grand manner, and the ghost of a rococo tradition, the tradition of the transatlantic South, memory of other lands, glimmered generally in the decoration. When once I had—though almost exclusively under the charm of these particular faded graces, I admit—again privately protested that the place might have been a "palace," my peace was made with Charleston: I was ripe for the last platitude of appreciation. Let me say indeed that this consciousness had from the first to struggle with another—the immediate sense of the degree in which the American scene is lighted, on occasion, to the critical eye, by the testimony of the hotel. As had been the case for me already at Richmond, so here again the note of that truth was sounded; the visitor interested in manners was too clearly not to escape it, and I scarce know under what slightly sinister warning he braced himself to the fact.

He had not, as yet, for repatriation, been thrown much upon the hotel; but this was the high sense of looking further and seeing more, this present promise of that adventure. One is thrown upon it, in America, as straight upon the general painted scene over which the footlights of publicity play with their large crudity, and against the freely-brushed texture and grain of which you thus rub your nose more directly, and with less of ceremony, than elsewhere. There are endless things in "Europe," to your vision, behind and beyond the hotel, a multitudinous complicated life; in the States, on the other hand, you see the hotel as itself that life, as constituting for vast numbers of people the richest form of existence. You have to go no distance for this to come over you—twenty appearances so vividly speak of it. It is not so much, no doubt, that "every one" lives at hotels, according to the witless belief of "Europe," but that you so quickly seem to measure the very limited extent to which those who people them, the populations they appeal to in general, may be conceived as "living" out of them. I remember how often, in moving about, the observation that most remained with me appeared to be this note of the hotel, and of the hotel-like chain of Pullman cars, as the supreme social expression. For the Pullmans too, in their way, were eloquent; they affected me ever, by the end of twenty-four hours, as carrying, if not Cæsar and his fortune, at least almost *all* the facts of American life. There were some of course that didn't fit into them, but so many others did, and these fitted somehow so perfectly and with such a congruity.

What it comes back to is that in such conditions the elements of the situation show with all possible, though quite unnoted, intensity; they tell you all about it (about the situation) in a few remarkably plain and distinct words; they make you feel in short how its significance is written upon it. It is as if the figures before you and

all round you, less different from each other, less different
too, I think, from the objects about them, whatever these
in any case may be, than any equal mass of appearances
under the sun—it is as if every one and everything said
to you straight : " Yes, this is how we are ; this is what
it is to enjoy our advantages ; this moreover is all there
is of us ; we give it all out.   Make what you can of it ! "
The restless analyst would have had indeed an unusual
fit of languor if he had not begun from the first to make
of it what he could, divided even though he was between
his sense of this largely-written significance and his
wonderment, none the less, as to its value and bearing :
which constituted, after all, a shade of perplexity as to
its meaning.   " Yes, I see how you are, God knows "—
he was ready with his reply ; " for nothing in the world
is easier to see, even in all the particulars.   But what
does it *mean* to be as you are ?—since I suppose it
means something ; something more than your mere one
universal type, with its small deflections but never a
departure ; something more than your way of sitting in
silence together at table, than your extraordinary, your
enormous passivity, than your apparent absence of
criticism or judgment of anything that is put before you
or that happens to you (beyond occasionally remarking
that it's 'fine!') than, in a word, the fact of what you
eat and the fact of how you eat it.   You are not final,
complacently as you appear so much of the time to
assume it—your mere inevitable shaking about in the
Margin must more or less take care of that ; since you
can't be so inordinately passive (everywhere, one infers,
but in your particular wary niche of your 'business-
block') without being in *some* degree plastic.   Distinct
as you are, you are not even definite, and it would be
terrible not to be able to suppose that you are as yet but
an instalment, a current number, like that of the morning
paper, a specimen of a type in course of serialization—

like the hero of the magazine novel, by the highly-successful author, the climax of which is still far off. Thus, as you are perpetually provisional, the hotels and the Pullmans—the Pullmans that are like rushing hotels and the hotels that are like stationary Pullmans—represent the stages and forms of your evolution, and are not a bit, in themselves, more final than you are. The particulars still to be added either to you or to them form an insoluble question; and meanwhile, clearly, your actual stage will not be short." So much as that, I recall, had hummed about my ears at Richmond, where the strong vertical light of a fine domed and glazed cortile, the spacious and agreeable dining-hall of the inn, had rested on the human scene as with an effect of mechanical pressure. If the scene constituted evidence, the evidence might have been in course of being pressed out, in this shining form, by the application of a weight and the turn of a screw. There it was, accordingly; there was the social, the readable page, with its more or less complete report of the conditions. The report was to be fuller as to some of these at Charleston; but I had at least grasped its general value. And I shall come back to the Charleston report.

It would have been a sorry business here, however, if this had been mainly the source of my impressions—which was so far from the case that I had but to go forth, after breakfast, to find insidious charm, the appeal of the outer, the larger aspect, await me at every turn. The day announced itself as warm and radiant, and, keeping its promise to the end, squared itself there as the golden frame of an interesting picture—interesting above all from the moment one desired with any intensity to find it so. The vision persists, with its charming, touching features; yet when I look back and ask myself what can have made my impression, all round, so positive, I am at a loss for elements to refer it to. Elements there were, certainly ; in especial the fact that during these first bland hours, charged with the splendour of spring, I caught the wide-eyed smile of the South, that expression of a temperamental felicity in which shades of character, questions of real feature, other marks and meanings, tend always to lose themselves. But a deficiency was clear, which was neither more nor less than the deficiency of life ; without life, all gracefully, the picture managed to compose itself. Even while one felt it do so one missed the precious presence ; so that there at least was food for wonderment, for admiration of the art at play. To what, all the while, as one went, could one compare the mystification?—to what if not to the image of some handsome pale person, a beauty (to call her so) of other days, who, besides confessing to the inanimate state from closed eyes and motionless lips, from the arrest of respiration and gesture, was to leave one, by the day's end, with the sense of a figure prepared for romantic interment, stretched in a fair winding-sheet, covered with admirable flowers, surrounded with shining tapers. *That*, one reasoned, would be something to have seen ; and yet one's interest was not so limited. Ruins, to be interesting, have to be massive ; and poor bittersweet Charleston suffered, for the observer, by the merciless law of the thinness, making too much for transparency, for the effect of paucity, still inherent in American groupings ; a law under which the attempt to subject them to portraiture, to see them as " composing," resembles the attempt to play whist with an imperfect pack of cards. If one had already, at the North, divined the general complexion as probably thin, in this sense, everywhere—thin, that is, for all note-taking but the statistical, under which it might of course show as portentously thick—it wouldn't turn dense or rich of a sudden, even in an air that could so drench it with benignity. Therefore if the scene, as one might say, was but the historic Desert without the historic Mausoleum, how was one's impression to give out, as it clearly would, the after-taste of experience ?

To let this small problem worry me no longer than it might, I sought an answer, and quickly found one, in the fortunate fact of my not having failed, after all, of the admirably suggestive society of my distinguished and competent friend. He *had* arrived over-night, according to my hope, and had only happened to lodge himself momentarily out of my ken ; so that as soon as I had his company to profit by I felt the "analytic" burden of my own blessedly lifted. I took over his analysis, infinitely better adjusted to the case and which clearly would suffice for everything—if only it should itself escape disintegration. Let me say at once that it quite averted —whether consciously or unconsciously, whether as too formidably bristling or as too perfectly pacific—that menace ; which success was to provide for us both, I think, a rounded felicity. My companion, a Northerner of Southern descent (as well as still more immediately, on another side, of English), knew his South in general and his Carolina of that ilk in particular, with an intimacy that was like a grab-bag into which, for illustration, he might always dip his hand (a movement that, had the grab-bag been "European," I should describe rather as a plunge of his arm : so that it comes back again to the shallowness of the American grab-bag, as yet, for illustrations other than the statistical). He held up for me his bright critical candle, which even in the intrinsic Charleston vividness made its gay flicker, and it was under this aid that, to my extreme convenience, I was able to "feel" the place. My fortune had indeed an odd sequel—which I mention for its appreciatory value ; the mishaps and accidents of appreciation being ever, in their way, I think, as contributive to judgment as the felicities. I was to challenge, too recklessly, the chances of a second day; having by the end of the first, and by the taking of example, quite learned to treat the scene as a grab-bag for my own hand. I went over it again, in an evil hour—whereupon I met afresh the admonition, already repeatedly received, that where, in the States, the interest, where the pleasure of contemplation is concerned, discretion is the better part of valour and insistence too often a betrayal. It is not so much that the hostile fact crops up as that the friendly fact breaks down. If you have luckily *seen*, you have seen; carry off your prize, in this case, instantly and at any risk. Try it again and you don't, you won't, see; for there is in all contemplation, there is even in any clear appreciation, an element of the cruel. These things demand that your exposed object shall, first of all, exist; and to exist for exposure is to be at the best impaled on the naturalist's pin. It takes superpositions, at any rate, to defy sufficiently this sort of attention; it takes either the stoutnesses of history or the rarest rarities of nature to resist fatal penetration. That was to come home to me presently in Florida—through the touched sense of the truth that Florida, ever so amiably, is weak. You may live there serenely, no doubt—as in a void furnished at the most with velvet air; you may in fact live there with an idea, if you are content that your idea shall consist of grapefruit and oranges. Oranges, grapefruit and velvet air constitute, in a manner, I admit, a feast; but press upon the board with any greater weight and it quite gives way—its three or four props treacherously forsake it. That is what I mean by the impression, in the great empty peninsula, of weakness; which I was to feel still clearer about on being able to compare it afterwards with the impression of California. California was to have—if I may decently be premature about it— her own treachery; but she was to wind one up much higher before she let one down. I was to find her,

especially at the first flush, unlike sweet frustrated
Florida, ever so amiably strong : which came from the
art with which she makes the stoutnesses, as I have
called them, of natural beauty stand you in temporary
stead of the leannesses of everything else (everything
that might be of an order equally interesting).   This she
is on a short acquaintance quite insolently able to do,
thanks to her belonging so completely to the " handsome" side of the continent, of which she is the finest
expression.   The aspect of natural objects, up and down
the Pacific coast, is as " aristocratic " as the comprehensive American condition permits anything to be : it
indeed appears to the ingenious mind to represent an
instinct on the part of Nature, a sort of shuddering,
bristling need, to brace herself in advance against the
assault of a society so much less marked with distinction
than herself.   If I was to conceive therefore under these
later lights, that her spirit had put forth nowhere on the
sub-tropical Atlantic shore anything to approach this
conscious pride, so, doubtless, the Carolinian effect, even
at its sweetest, was to strike me as related to it very
much as a tinkle is related to a boom.

III

To stray but for an instant into such an out-of-the-way
corner of one's notes, however, is to give the lie to the
tenderness that asserted itself so promptly as the very
medium of one's perception.   There was literally no
single object that, from morn to nightfall, it was not
more possible to consider with tenderness, a rich consistency of tenderness, than to consider without it : *such*
was the subtle trick that Charleston could still play.
There echoed for me as I looked out from the Battery
the recent speech of a friend which had had at the time

a depressing weight; the Battery of the long, curved sea-front, of the waterside public garden furnished with sad old historic guns, with live-oaks draped in trailing moss, with palmettos that, as if still mindful of their State symbolism, seem to try everywhere, though with a melancholy sceptical droop, to repeat the old escutcheon; with its large, thrilling view in particular—thrilling to a Northerner who stands there for the first time. "Filled as I am, in general, while there," my friend had said, " with the sadness and sorrow of the South, I never, at Charleston, look out to the old betrayed Forts without feeling my heart harden again to steel." One remembered that, on the spot, and one waited a little—to see what was happening to one's heart. I found this to take time indeed; everything differed, somehow, from one's old conceived image—or if I had anciently grasped the remoteness of Fort Sumter, near the mouth of the Bay, and of its companion, at the point of the shore forming the other side of the passage, this lucidity had so left me, in the course of the years, that the far-away dimness of the consecrated objects was almost a shock. It was a blow even to one's faded vision of Charleston viciously firing on the Flag; the Flag would have been, from the Battery, such a mere speck in space that the vice of the act lost somehow, with the distance, to say nothing of the forty years, a part of its grossness. The smitten face, however flushed and scarred, was out of sight, though the intention of smiting and the force of the insult were of course still the same. This reflection one made, but the old fancied perspective and proportions were altered; and then the whole picture, at that hour, exhaled an innocence. It was as blank as the face of a child under mention of his naughtiness and his punishment of week before last. The Forts, faintly blue on the twinkling sea, looked like vague marine flowers; innocence, pleasantness ruled the prospect: it was as if the compromised slate, sponged clean of all the wicked words and hung up on the wall for better use, dangled there so vacantly as almost to look foolish. Ah, there again was the word : the air still just tasted of the antique folly ; so that in presence of a lesson so sharp and so prolonged, of the general *sterilized* state, of the brightly-lighted, delicate dreariness recording the folly, harshness was conjured away. There was that in the impression which affected me after a little as one of those refinements of irony that wait on deep expiations : one could scarce conceive at this time of day that such a place had ever been dangerously moved. It was the *bled* condition, and mostly the depleted cerebral condition, that was thus attested—as I had recognized it at Richmond ; and I asked myself, on the Battery, what more one's sternest justice could have desired. If my heart wasn't to harden to steel, in short, access to it by the right influence had found perhaps too many other forms of sensibility in ambush.

To justify hardness, moreover, one would have had to meet something hard ; and if my peregrination, after this, had been a search for such an element, I should have to describe it as made all in vain. Up and down and in and out, with my companion, I strolled from hour to hour ; but more and more under the impression of the consistency of softness. One could have expressed the softness in a word, and the picture so offered would be infinitely touching. It was a city of gardens and absolutely of no men—or of so few that, save for the general sweetness, the War might still have been raging and all the manhood at the front. The gardens were matter for the women ; though even of the women there were few, and that small company—rare, discreet, flitting figures that brushed the garden walls with noiseless skirts in the little melancholy streets of interspaced, over-tangled abodes—were clad in a rigour of mourning that

was like the garb of a conspiracy. The effect was
superficially prim, but so far as it savoured of malice
prepense, of the Southern, the sentimental *parti-pris*, it
was delightful. What was it all most like, the incoherent jumble of suggestions?—the suggestion of a
social shrinkage and an economic blight unrepaired,
irreparable; the suggestion of by-ways of some odd far
East infected with triumphant women's rights, some
perspective of builded, plastered lanes over the enclosures
of which the flowering almond drops its petals into sharp
deep bands of shade or of sun. It is not the muffled
ladies who walk about predominantly in the East; but
that is a detail. The likeness was perhaps greater to
some little old-world quarter of quiet convents where
only priests and nuns steal forth—the priests mistakable
at a distance, say, for the nuns. It was indeed thoroughly
mystifying, the whole picture—since I was to get, in
the freshness of that morning, from the very background of the scene, my quite triumphant little impression of the "old South." I remember feeling with
intensity at two or three points in particular that I should
never get a better one, that even this was precarious—
might melt at any moment, by a wrong touch or a false
note, in my grasp—and that I must therefore make the
most of it. The rest of my time, I may profess, was
spent in so doing. I made the most of it in several
successive spots: under the south wall of St. Michael's
Church, the sweetest corner of Charleston, and of which
there is more to say; out in the old Cemetery on the
edge of the lagoon, where the distillation of the past
was perhaps clearest and the bribe to tenderness most
effective; and even not a little on ground thereunto
almost adjacent, that of a kindly Country-Club installed
in a fine old semi-sinister mansion, and holding an
afternoon revel at which I was privileged briefly to
assist. The wrong touch and the false note were

doubtless just sensible in this last connection, where the
question, probed a little, would apparently have been of
some new South that has not yet quite found the effective
way romantically, or at least insidiously, to appeal. The
South that is cultivating country-clubs is a South presumably, in many connections, quite in the right; whereas
the one we were invidiously "after" was the one that
had been so utterly in the wrong. Even there, none the
less, in presence of more than a single marked sign of
the rude Northern contagion, I disengaged, socially
speaking, a faint residuum which I mention for proof of
the intensity of my quest and of my appreciation.

There were two other places, I may add, where one
could but work the impression for all it was, in the
modern phrase, "worth," and where I had, I may venture
to say, the sense of making as much of it as was likely
ever to be made again. Meanings without end were
to be read, under tuition, into one of these, which was
neither more nor less than a slightly shy, yet after all
quite serene place of refection, a luncheon-room or tea-
house, denominated for quaint reasons an " Exchange"
—*the* very Exchange in fact lately commemorated in a
penetrating study, already much known to fame, of the
little that is left of the local society. My tuition, at the
hands of my ingenious comrade, was the very best it
was possible to have. Nothing, usually, is more wonderful than the quantity of significant character that, with
such an example set, the imagination may recognize
in the scantest group of features, objects, persons. I
fantastically feasted here, at my luncheon-table, not only,
as the genius of the place demanded, on hot chocolate,
sandwiches and " Lady Baltimore" cake (this last a
most delectable compound), but on the exact *nuance* of
oddity, of bravery, of reduced gentility, of irreducible
superiority, to which the opening of such an establishment, without derogation, by the proud daughters of

war-wasted families, could exquisitely testify. They hovered, the proud impoverished daughters, singly or in couples, behind the counter—a counter, again, delectably charged; they waited, inscrutably, irreproachably, yet with all that peculiarly chaste *bonhomie* of the Southern tone, on the customers' wants, even coming to ascertain these at the little thrifty tables; and if the drama and its adjusted theatre really contained all the elements of history, tragedy, comedy, irony, that a pair of expert romancers, closely associated for the hour, were eager to evoke, the scene would have been, I can only say, supreme of its kind. That desire of the artist to linger where the breath of a "subject," faintly stirring the air, reaches his vigilant sense, would here stay my steps—as this very influence was in fact, to his great good fortune, to stay those of my companion. The charm I speak of, the charm to cherish, however, was most exhaled for me in other conditions—conditions that scarce permit of any direct reference to their full suggestiveness. If I alluded above to the vivid Charleston background, where its "mystification" most scenically persists, the image is all rounded and complete, for memory, in this connection at which—as the case is of an admirably mature and preserved interior—I can only glance as I pass. The puzzlement elsewhere is in the sense that though the elements of earth and air, the colour, the tone, the light, the sweetness in fine, linger on, the "old South" could have had no such unmitigated mildness, could never have seen itself as subject to such strange feminization. The feminization is there just to promote for us some eloquent antithesis; just to make us say that whereas the ancient order was masculine, fierce and moustachioed, the present is at the most a sort of sick lioness who has so visibly parted with her teeth and claws that we may patronizingly walk all round her.

This image really gives us the best word for the

general effect of Charleston—that of the practically
vacant cage which used in the other time to emit sounds,
even to those of the portentous shaking of bars, audible
as far away as in the listening North. It is the vacancy
that is a thing by itself, a thing that makes us endlessly
wonder. How, in an at all complex, a "great political,"
society, can *everything* so have gone?—assuming indeed
that, under this ægis, very much ever had come. How
can everything so have gone that the only "Southern"
book of any distinction published for many a year is
The Souls of Black Folk, by that most accomplished
of members of the negro race, Mr. W. E. B. Du Bois?
Had the *only* focus of life then been Slavery?—from the
point onward that Slavery had reached a quarter of a
century before the War, so that with the extinction of
that interest none other of any sort was left. To say
"yes" seems the only way to account for the degree of the
vacancy, and yet even as I form that word I meet as a
reproach the face of the beautiful old house I just mentioned, whose ample spaces had so unmistakably echoed to
the higher amenities that one seemed to feel the accumulated traces and tokens gradually come out of their corners
like blest objects taken one by one from a reliquary
worn with much handling. The note of such haunted
chambers as these—haunted structurally, above all, quite
as by the ghost of the grand style—was not, certainly, a
thinness of reverberation; so that I had to take refuge
here in the fact that everything appeared thoroughly to
antedate, to refer itself to the larger, the less vitiated
past that had closed a quarter of a century or so before
the War, before the fatal time when the South, mono-
maniacal at the parting of the ways, "elected" for
extension and conquest. The admirable old house of
the stately hall and staircase, of the charming coved and
vaulted drawing-room, of the precious mahogany doors,
the tall unsophisticated portraits, the delicate dignity of

welcome, owed nothing of its noble identity, nothing at all appreciable, to the monomania. However that might be, moreover, I kept finding the mere melancholy charm reassert itself where it could—the charm, I mean, of the flower-crowned waste that was, by my measure, what the monomania had most prepared itself to bequeathe. In the old Cemetery by the lagoon, to which I have already alluded, this influence distils an irresistible poetry —as one has courage to say even in remembering how disproportionately, almost anywhere on the American scene, the general place of interment is apt to be invited to testify for the presence of charm. The golden afternoon, the low, silvery, seaward horizon, as of wide, sleepy, game-haunted inlets and reed-smothered banks, possible site of some Venice that had never mustered, the luxury, in the mild air, of shrub and plant and blossom that the pale North can but distantly envy; something that I scarce know how to express but as the proud humility of the whole idle, easy loveliness, made even the restless analyst, for the hour, among the pious inscriptions that scarce ever belie the magniloquent clime or the inimitable tradition, feel himself really capable of the highest Carolinian pitch.

To what height did he rise, on the other hand, on being introduced another day, at no great distance from this point, and where the silvery seaward outlook still prevails, to the lapsed and readministered residence, also already named, that was to give him his one glimpse of any local modernism? This was the nearest approach for him to any reanimation of the flower-crowned waste, and he has still in memory, for symbol of the modernism, a vision of the great living, blazing fire of logs round which, as the afternoon had turned wet and chill, this contribution to his view of a possible new society, a possible youthful tone, a possible Southern future in short, had disposed itself. There were men here, in the picture—a few, and young ones : that odd other sense as of a becraped, feminized world was accordingly for the moment in abeyance. For the moment, I say advisedly —for the moment only ; since what aspect of the social scene anywhere in the States strikes any second glance as exempt from that condition ? It is overwhelmingly feminized or it *is* not—that is the formula with which its claim to existence pierces the ear. Lest, however, the recognition again of this truth should lead me too far, I content myself with noting a matter perhaps more relevant just here—one's inevitable consciousness, in presence of the "new" manifestations, that the South is in the predicament of having to be tragic, as it were, in order to beguile. It was very hard, I said to myself, and very cruel and very perverse, and above all very strange ; but what "use" had the restless analyst here for a lively and oblivious type ? Was there not something in the lively and oblivious that, given the materials employed for it and the effect produced by it, threw one back with renewed relish on the unforgetting and the devoted, on the resentful and even, if need might be, the vindictive ? These things would represent certainly a bad *état d'âme* —and was one thus cold-bloodedly, critically, to wish such a condition perpetuated? The answer to that seemed to be, monstrously enough, "Well, yes—for these people ; since it appears the only way by which they can be interesting. See when they try other ways ! Their sadness and sorrow, as my friend called it, has at least for it that it has been expensively produced. Everything else, on the other hand, anything that may pretend to be better—oh, so cheaply ! "

One had already, in moving about, winced often enough at sight of where one was, intellectually, to " land," under these last consistencies of observation and reflection ; so I may put it here that I *didn't*, after all, land, but recoiled rather and forbore, making my skiff

fast to no conclusion whatever, only pushing out again
and letting it, for a supreme impression and to prepare
in the aftertime the best remembrance, drift where it
would. So, accordingly, the aftertime having a little
arrived, it touches now once more of its own motion,
carries me back and puts me ashore on the one spot
where the impression had been perfectly felicitous. I
have already named the place—under the mild, the
bright south wall of St. Michael's Church, where the
whole precinct offered the full-blown Southern spring,
that morning, the finest of all canvases to embroider.
The canvas here, yes, was of the best; not only did
Charleston show me none other so good, but I was
doubtless to have met, South or North, none of an
equal happy grain and form. The high, complicated,
inflated spire of the church has the sincerity, approved of
time, that is so rare, over the land, in the work of man's
hands, laden though these be with the millions he offers
as a vain bribe to it; and in the sweet old churchyard
ancient authority seemed to me, on the occasion of my
visit, to sit, among the sun-warmed tombs and the inter-
related slabs and the extravagant flowers, as on the sole
cushion the general American bareness in such connections had left it. There was more still of association
and impression; I found, under this charm, I confess,
character in every feature. Even in the much-main-
tained interior revolutions and renovations have respected
its sturdy, rather sombre essence: the place feels itself,
in the fine old dusky archaic way, the constituted temple
of a faith—achieves, in a word, the air of reality that one
had seen in every other such case, from town to town and
from village to village, missed with an unconsciousness
that had to do duty for success.

14

Florida

It is the penalty of the state of receiving too many impressions of too many things that when the question arises of giving some account of these a small sharp anguish attends the act of selection and the necessity of omission. They have so hung together, have so almost equally contributed, for the fond critic, to the total image, the chapter of experience, whatever such may have been, that to detach and reject is like mutilation or falsification ; the history of any given impression residing often largely in others that have led to it or accompanied it. This I find the case, again and again, with my American memories ; there was something of a hundred of those I may not note in each of those I may, and I feel myself, amid the swarm, pluck but a fruit or two from any branch. When I think of Florida, for instance, I think of twenty matters involved in the start and the approach ; I think of the moist, the slightly harsh, Sunday morning under the portico of the Charleston Hotel ; I think of the inauspicious drizzle about the yellow omnibus, archaic and "provincial," that awaited the departing guests—remembering how these antique vehicles, repudiated, rickety "stages" of the age ignorant of trolleys, affected me here and there as the quaintest, most immemorial of American things, the persistent use of which surely represented the very superstition of the past.   I think of the gentleman, in the watchful knot, who, while our luggage emerged, was moved to say to me, for some reason, " I guess we manage our travelling here better than in *your* country ! " —whereby he so easily triumphed, blank as I had to remain as to the country he imputed to me.   I think of the inimitable detachment with which, at the very moment he spoke, the negro porter engaged at the door of the conveyance put straight down into the mud of the road the dressing-bag I was obliged, a few minutes later, in our close-pressed company, to nurse on my knees ; and I go so far, even, as almost to lose myself in the sense of other occasions evoked by that reminiscence ; this marked anomaly, the apparently deep-seated inaptitude of the negro race at large for any alertness of personal service, having been throughout a lively surprise.

One had counted, with some eagerness, in moving southward, on the virtual opposite—on finding this deficiency, encountered right and left at the North, beautifully corrected ; one had remembered the old Southern tradition, the house alive with the scramble of young darkies for the honour of fetching and carrying ; and one was to recognize, no doubt, at the worst, its melancholy ghost.   Its very ghost, however, by my impression, had ceased to walk ; or, if this be not the case, the old planters, the cotton gentry, were the people in the world the worst ministered to.   I could have shed tears for them at moments, reflecting that it was for *this* they had fought and fallen.   The negro waiter at the hotel is in general, by an oddity of his disposition, so zealous to break for you two or three eggs into a tumbler, or to drop for you three or four lumps of sugar into a coffee-cup, that he scarce waits, in either case, for your leave ; but these struck me everywhere as the limit of his accomplishment.   He lends himself sufficiently to the rough, gregarious bustle of crowded feeding-places, but seemed to fall below the occasion on any appeal to his individual promptitude. Which reflections, doubtless, exactly illustrate my profession of a moment ago as to the insidious continuity, the close inter-relation, of observed phenomena. I might with a little audacity insist still further on that—which was in fact what I had originally quite promised myself to do. I certainly should have been half heart-broken at the hour itself, for example, had I *then* had to estimate as pure waste my state of sensibility to the style and stamp of my companions ; aspects and sounds burned into my memory, as I find, but none the less overstraining, I am obliged to feel, the frame of these remarks. So vivid on the spot was the sense of these particular human and "sectional" appearances, and of certain others of the same cluster, that they remained for me afterwards beautifully *placed*—placed in this connection of the pilgrimage to Palm Beach, and not the less relevant for being incidental. I was to find the obvious "bagman," the lusty "drummer" of the Southern trains and inns (if there be not, as yet unrevealed to me, some later fond diminutive of designation for the ubiquitous commercial traveller)—I was to find, I say, this personage promptly insist on a category of his own, a category which, at the moments I here recall, loomed so large as to threaten to block out of view almost every other object.

Was I the victim of grave mischance ? was my infelicity exceptional ?—or was the type with which the scene so abounded, were the specimens I was thus to treasure, all of the common class and the usual frequency ? I was to treasure them as specimens of something I had surely never yet so *undisputedly* encountered. They went, all by themselves, as it were, so far—were, as to facial character, vocal tone, primal rawness of speech, general accent and attitude, extraordinarily base and vulgar ; and it was interesting to make out why this fact took on, for my edification, so unwonted an intensity. The fact of the influence, on the whole man, of a sordid and ravenous habit, was naturally no new thing; one had met him enough about the world, the brawny peddler more or less gorged with the fruits of misrepresentation and blatant and brazen in the key of his "special line of goods" and the measure of his need. But if the figure was immemorial, why did it now usurp a value out of proportion to other values? What, for instance, were its remorseless reasons for treating the restless analyst, at the breakfast-hour perhaps above all, to so lurid a vision of its triumph? He had positively come to associate the breakfast-hour, from hotel to dining-car and from dining-car to hotel, with the perfect security of this exhibition, the sight of the type in completely unchallenged possession. I scarce know why my sensibility, at the juncture in question, so utterly gave way to it; why I appealed in vain from one of these so solemnly-feeding presences to another. They refused to the wondering mind any form of relief; they insisted, as I say, with the strange crudity of their air of commercial truculence, on being exactly as "low" as they liked. And the affirmation was made, in the setting of the great greasy inelegant room, as quietly as possible, and without the least intention of offence: there were ladies and children all about—though indeed there may have been sometimes *but* the lone breakfasting child to reckon with; the little pale, carnivorous, coffee-drinking ogre or ogress who prowls down in advance of its elders, engages a table—dread vision!—and has the "run" of the bill of fare.

The great blank decency, at all events, was no more broken than, on the general American scene, it ever is; yet the apprehension of marks and signs, the trick of speculation, declined none the less to drop. Whom were they constructed, such specimens, to talk with, to talk over, or to talk under, and what form of address or of intercourse, what uttered, what intelligible terms of introduction, of persuasion, of menace, what developed, what specific human process of any sort, was it possible to impute to them? What reciprocities did they imply, what presumptions did they, could they, create? what happened, inconceivably, when such Greeks met such Greeks, such faces looked into such faces, and such sounds, in especial, were exchanged with such sounds? What women did they live with, what women, living with them, could yet leave them as they were? What wives, daughters, sisters, did they in fine make credible; and what, in especial, was the speech, what the manners, what the general dietary, what most the monstrous morning meal, of ladies receiving at such hands the law or the licence of life? Questions, these latter, some of which, all the while, were not imperceptibly answered—save that the vainest, no doubt, was that baffled inquiry as to the thinkable ground, amid such relations, of preliminary confidence. What *was* preliminary confidence, where it had to reckon so with the minimum of any finished appearance? How, when people were like that, did any one trust any one enough to begin, or understand any one enough to go on, or keep the peace with any one enough to survive? Wasn't it, however, at last, none the less, the sign of a fallacy somewhere in my impression that the peace *was* kept, precisely, while I so luxuriously wondered?—the consciousness of which presently led me round to something that was at the least a temporary, a working answer. My friends the drummers bore me company thus, in the smoking-car, through the deepening, sweetening South (where the rain soon gave way to a refinement of mildness) all the way to Savannah; at the end of which time, under the enchantment of the spreading scene, I had more or less issued from my maze.

It was not, probably, that, inflated though they might

be, after early refreshment, with the inward conflict of a greater number of strange sacrifices to appetite than I had ever before seen perpetrated at once, they were really more gruesome examples of a class at best disquieting than might elsewhere have been discovered; it was only that, by so sad a law of their situation, they were at once more exposed and less susceptible of bearing exposure. They so became, to my imagination, and by a mere turn of the hand of that precious faculty, something like victims and martyrs, creatures touchingly, tragically doomed. For they hadn't *asked,* when one reflected, to be almost the only figures in the social landscape—hadn't wanted the fierce light to beat *all* on themselves. They hadn't actively usurped the appearance of carrying on life without aid of any sort from other *kinds* of persons, other types, presences, classes. If these others were absent it wasn't *their* fault; and though they devoured, at a matutinal sitting, thirty little saucers of insane, of delirious food, this was yet a law which, over much of the land, appeared to recognize no difference of application for age, sex, condition or constitution, and it had not in short been their pretension to take over the whole social case. It would have been so different, this case, and the general effect, for the human scene, would have been so different, with a due proportion of other presences, other figures and characters, members of other professions, representatives of other interests, exemplars of other possibilities in man than the mere possibility of getting the better of his fellow-man over a "trade." Wondrous always to note is this sterility of aspect and this blight of vulgarity, humanly speaking, where a single type has had the game, as one may say, all in its hands. Character is developed to visible fineness only by friction and discipline on a large scale, only by its having to reckon with a complexity of forces—a process which results, at the worst, in a certain amount of social training.

No kind of person—that was the admonition—is a very good kind, and still less a very pleasing kind, when its education has not been made to some extent by contact with other kinds, by a sense of the existence of other kinds, and, to that degree, by a certain relation with them. This education may easily, at a hundred points, transcend the teaching of the big brick school-house, for all the latter's claim to universality. The last dose ever administered by the great wooden spoon so actively plied *there* is the precious bitter-sweet of a sense of proportion ; yet to miss that taste, ever, at the table of civilization is to feel ourselves seated surely too much below the salt. We miss it when the social effect of it fails—when, all so dismally or so monstrously, every one strikes us as "after" but one thing, and as thus not only unaware of the absent importances and values, but condemned and restricted, as a direct conse-quence of it, to the mere raw stage of their own particular connection. I so worked out, in a word, that what was the matter with my friends was not at all that they were viciously full-blown, as one might say, were the ultimate sort of monstrosity they had at first appeared ; but that they were, on the contrary, just unformed, undeveloped, unrelated above all—unrelated to any merciful modifying terms of the great social proposition. They were not in their place—not relegated, shaded, embowered, protected ; and, dreadful though this might be to a stray observer of the fact, it was much more dreadful for themselves. They had the helpless weakness and, I think even, some-where in dim depths, deeper down still than the awful breakfast-habit, the vaguely troubled sense of it. They would fall into their place at a touch, were the social proposition, as I have called it, completed ; they would then help, quite subordinately assist, the long sentence to read—relieved of their ridiculous charge of supplying all its clauses. I positively at last thought of them as appealing from this embarrassment; in which sublime patience I was floated, as I say, to Savannah.

II

After that it was plain sailing; in the sense, I mean, of the respite—temporary at least—of speculation; of feeling impressions file in and seat themselves as quietly as decorous worshippers (say mild old ladies with neat prayer-books) taking possession of some long-drawn family pew. It was absurd what I made of Savannah—which consisted for me but of a quarter of an hour's pause of the train under the wide arch of the station, where, in the now quite confirmed blandness of the Sunday noon, a bright, brief morning party appeared of a sudden to have organized itself. Where was the charm?—if it wasn't already, supremely, in the air, the latitude, the season, as well as in the imagination of the pilgrim capable not only of squeezing a sense from the important city on these easy terms and with that desperate economy, but of reading heaven knows what instalment of romance into a mere railroad matter. It is a mere railroad matter, in the States, that a station should appear at a given moment to yield to the invasion of a dozen or so of bare-headed and vociferous young women in the company of young men to match, and that they should all treat the place, in the public eye, that of the crowded contem-plative cars, quite as familiar, domestic, intimate ground, set apart, it might be, for the discussion and regulation of their little interests and affairs, and for that so oddly, so innocently immodest ventilation of their puerile privacies at which the moralizing visitor so frequently gasps. I recall my fleeting instants of Savannah as the taste of a cup charged to the brim; I recall the swarming, the hatless, pretty girls, with their big-bowed cues, their romping swains, their inveterate suggestion of their having more to say about American manners than any other single class; I recall the thrill produced by the hawkers of scented Southern things, sprigs and specimens of flower and fruit that mightn't as yet be of the last exoticism, but that were native and fresh and over-priced, and so all that the traveller could ask.

But most of all, I think, I recall the quite lively resolve not to give way, under the assault of the be-ribboned and "shirt-waisted" fair, to the provocation of *their* suggestiveness—even as I had fallen, reflectively speaking, straight into the trap set for me by the Charleston bagmen; a resolve taken, I blush to say, as a base economic precaution only, and not because the spectacle before me failed to make reflections swarm. They fairly hummed, my suppressed reflections, in the manner of bees about a flower-bed, and burying their noses as deep in the *corollæ* of the subject. Had I allowed myself time before the train resumed its direction, I should have thus found myself regarding the youths and the maidens—but especially, for many reasons, the maidens—quite in the light of my so earnestly-considered drummers, quite as creatures extraordinarily disconcerting, at first, as to the whole matter of their public behaviour, but covered a little by the mantle of charity as soon as it became clear that what, like the poor drummers, they suffer from, is the tragedy of their social, their cruel exposure, that treachery of fate which has kept them so out of their place. It was a case, I more than ever saw, like the case of the bagmen; the case of the bagmen lighted it here, in the most interesting way, by propinquity and coincidence. If the bagmen had seemed monstrous, in their occupancy of the scene, by their disproportioned possession of it, so was not the hint sufficient that this also explains much of the effect of the American girl as encountered in the great glare of her publicity, her uncorrected, unrelated state? There had been moments, as I moved about the country, when she had seemed to me, for affirmation of presence, for immunity from competition, fairly to share the field but with the bagman, and fairly to speak as my inward ear had at last heard him speak.

" Ah, once *place* me and you'll see—I shall be different, I shall be better; for since I am, with my preposterous 'position,' falsely beguiled, pitilessly forsaken, thrust forth in my ignorance and folly, what do I know, helpless chit as I can but be, about manners or tone, about proportion or perspective, about modesty or mystery, about a condition of things that involves, for the interest and the grace of life, other forms of existence than this poor little mine—pathetically broken reed as it is, just to find itself waving all alone in the wind? How can I do *all* the grace, *all* the interest, as I'm expected to?—yes, literally all the interest that isn't the mere interest on the money. I'm expected to supply it all— while I wander and stray in the desert. Was there ever such a conspiracy, on the part of a whole social order, toward the exposure of incompetence? Were ever crude youth and crude presumption left so unadmonished as to their danger of giving themselves away? Who, at any turn, for an hour, ever pityingly overshadows or dispossesses me? By what combination of other presences ever am I disburdened, ever relegated and reduced, ever restored, in a word, to my right relation to the whole? All I want—that is all I need, for there is perhaps a difference—is, to put it simply, that my parents and my brothers and my male cousins should consent to exist otherwise than occultly, undiscoverably, or, as I suppose you'd call it, irresponsibly. That's a trouble, yes—but *we* take it, so why shouldn't they? The rest—don't you make it out for me?—would come of itself. Haven't I, however, as it is, been too long abandoned and too *much* betrayed? Isn't it too late, and am I not, don't you think, practically lost?" Faintly and from far away, as through dense interpositions, this questioning wail of the maiden's ultimate distressed consciousness seemed to reach me; but I had steeled my sense, as I have said, against taking it in, and I did no more, at the moment, than all pensively suffer it again to show me the American social order in the guise of a great blank unnatural mother, a compound of all the recreant individuals misfitted with the name, whose ear the mystic plaint seemed never to penetrate, and whose large unseeing complacency suggested some massive monument covered still with the thick cloth that precedes a public unveiling. We wonder at the hidden marble or bronze; we suppose, under the cloth, some attitude or expression appropriate to the image; but as the removal of the cloth is perpetually postponed the character never emerges. The American mother, enshrouded in her brown holland, has, by this analogy, never emerged; only the daughter is meanwhile seated, for the inspection of the world, at the base of the pedestal, hypothetically supporting some weight, some mass or other, and we may each impute to her, for this posture, the aspect we judge best to beseem her.

My point here, at any rate, is that I had quite forgotten her by the time I was seated, after dinner that evening, on a bench in the small public garden that formed a prospect for my hotel at Jacksonville. The air was divinely soft—it was such a Southern night as I had dreamed of; and the only oddity was that we had come to it by so simple a process. We had travelled indeed all day, but the process seemed simple when there was nothing of it, nothing to speak of, to remember, nothing that succeeded in getting over the footlights, as the phrase goes, of the great moving proscenium of the Pullman. I seemed to think of it, the wayside imagery, as something that had been there, no doubt, as the action or the dialogue are presumably there in some untoward drama that spends itself at the back of the stage, that goes off, in a passion, at side doors, and perhaps even bursts back, incoherently, through windows; but that doesn't reach the stall in which you sit, never quickens to acuteness your sense of what is going on. So, as if the chair in the Pullman had been my stall, my sense had been all day but of intervening heads and tuning fiddles, of queer refreshments, such as only the theatre and the Pullman know, offered, with vociferation, straight through the performance. I was a little uncertain, afterwards, as to when I had become distinctively aware of Florida; but the scenery of the State, up to the point of my first pause for the night, had not got over the footlights. I was promptly, however, to make good this loss; I felt myself doing so quite with intensity under the hot-looking stars at Jacksonville. I had come out to smoke for the evening's end, and it mattered not a scrap that the public garden was new and scant and crude, and that Jacksonville is not a name to conjure with; I still could sit there quite in the spirit, for the hour, of Byron's immortal question as to the verity of his Italian whereabouts: *was* this the Mincio, *were* those the distant turrets of Verona, and should I sup— well, if the train to Palm Beach, arriving there on the morrow in time, should happen to permit me? At Jacksonville I had, as I say, already supped, but I projected myself, for the time, after Byron's manner, into the exquisite sense of the dream come true.

I was not to sup at all, as it proved, at Palm Beach— by the operation of one of those odd, anomalous rigours that crop up even by the more flowery paths of American travel; but I was meanwhile able, I found, to be quite Byronically foolish about the St. John's River and the various structures, looming now through the darkness, that more or less adorned its banks. The river served for my Mincio—which it moreover so greatly surpassed in extent and beauty ; while the remoter buildings figured sufficiently any old city of the South. For that was the charm—that so preposterously, with the essential notes of the impression so happily struck, the velvet air, the extravagant plants, the palms, the oranges, the cacti, the architectural fountain, the florid local monument, the cheap and easy exoticism, the sense as of people feeding, off in the background, very much *al fresco*, that is on queer things and with flaring lights—one might almost have been in a corner of Naples or of Genoa. Everything is relative—this illuminating commonplace, the clue to any just perception of effects anywhere, came up for the thousandth time ; by the aid of which I easily made out that absolute and impeccable poetry of site and circumstance is far to seek, but that I was now immeasurably nearer to some poetic, or say even to some romantic, effect in things than I had hitherto been. And I had tried to think Washington relaxed, and Richmond itself romantic, and Charleston secretly ardent ! There always comes, to any traveller who doesn't depart and arrive with the mere security and punctuality of a registered letter, some moment for his beginning to feel within him—it happens under some particular touch—the finer vibration of a sense of the real thing. He thus knows it when it comes, and it has the great value that it never need fail. There is no situation, wherever he may turn, in which the note of that especial reality, the note of character, for bliss or bale, may not insist on emerging. The note of Florida emerged for me then on the vulgar little dusky— and dusty—Jacksonville *piazzetta*, where other vague persons sat about, amid those spikey sub-tropical things that show how the South can be stiff as nothing else is stiff ; while my rich sense of it incited me to resent the fact that my visit had been denounced, in advance, as of an ungenerous brevity. I had few days, deplorably few, no doubt, to spend; but it was afterwards positive to me that, with my image, as regards the essence of the matter, richly completed, I had virtually foretasted it all on my dusky Jacksonville bench and in my tepid Jacksonville stroll. Such reserves, in a complex of few interweavings, must impose themselves, I think, even upon foolish fondness, and Florida was quite remorselessly to appear to me a complex of few interweavings.

III

The next day, for instance, was all occupied with but one of these; the railway run from Jacksonville to Palm Beach begins early and ends late, yet I waited, the live-long time, for any other "faetor" than that of the dense cypress swamp to show so much as the tip of an ear. I had quite counted on being thrilled by this very intensity and monotony of the characteristic note; and I doubtless *was* thrilled—I invoked, I cultivated the thrill, as we went, by every itinerant art that experience had long since taught me; yet with a presentiment, all the while, of the large field, in the whole impression, that this simplicity would cover. Possible diversions doubtless occurred, had the attuned spirit been moved to avail itself; Ormond, for instance, off to our right, put in, toward the dim centre of the stretch, a claim as large as a hard white racing-beach, an expanse of firm sand thirty miles long, could make it. This, I recognized, might well be an appeal of the grand and simple order—the huge band of shining silver beside the huge band of sapphire sea; and I inquired a little as to what filled in the picture. "Oh, the motor-cars, the bicycles and the trotting-waggons, tearing up and down." And then, as one seemed perhaps to yearn for another touch : " Ah, the hotels of course—plenty of *them*, plenty of people ; very popular resort." It sounded charming, with its hint again of two or three great facts of composition—so definite that their paucity constituted somehow a mild majesty ; but it ministered none the less to a reflection I had already, on occasion, found myself perhaps a little perversely making. One was liable, in the States, on many a scene, to react, as it were, from the people, and to throw one's self passionately on the bosom of con-tiguous Nature, whatever surface it might happen to offer ; one was apt to be moved, in possibly almost invidious preference, or in deeper and sweeter confidence, to try what might be made of *that*. Yet, all unreasonably, when any source of interest did express itself in these mere rigorous terms, in these only—terms all of elimina-tion, just of sea and sky and river-breast and forest and beach (the "beaches" in especial were to acquire a trick of getting on one's nerves !) that produced in turn a wanton wonder about the "human side," and a due recurrence to the fact that the human side had been from the first one's affair.

So, therefore, one seemed destined a bit incoherently to proceed ; asking one's self again and again what the play would have been without the scenery, sometimes "even such" scenery, and then once more not quite seeing why such scenery (in especial) should propose to put one off with so little of a play. The thing, absolutely, everywhere, was to provide one's own play ; anything, everything made scenery for that, and the recurrence of such questions made scenery most of all. I remember no moment, over the land, when the mere Pullman itself didn't overarch my observations as a positive temple of the drama, and when the comedy and the tragedy of manners didn't, under its dome, hold me raptly attent. With which there were other resources—a rising tide that, before we got to Palm Beach, floated me back into remembered depths of youth. Why shouldn't I hold it not trivial that, as the day waned, and the evening gathered, and the heat increased, and my companions removed, one after the other, the articles of clothing that had consorted with our early start, I felt myself again beneath the spell of Mayne Reid, captain of the treasure-ship of romance and idol of my childhood? I might again have held in my very hand *The War Trail*, a work that had seemed matchless to my fourteenth year, for was not the train itself rumbling straight into *that* fantastic Florida, with its rank vegetation and its warm, heroic, amorous air ?—the Florida of the Seminoles and the Everglades, of the high old Spanish Dons and the passionate Creole beauties gracing the primal " society "; of Isolina de Vargas, whose voluptuous form was lashed Mazeppa-like, at the climax of her fortunes, to the fiery mustang of the wilderness, and so let loose adown the endless vista of our young suspense. We had thus food for the mind, I recall, if we were reduced to that ; and I remember that, as my buffet-car (there was none other) was hours late, the fond vision of the meal, crown of the endless day, awaiting me ultimately at the famous hotel, yielded all the inspiration necessary for not appealing again, great though the stress and strain, to the inde-scribable charity of the " buffet." The produce of the buffet, the procedure of the buffet, were alike (wherever resorted to) a sordid mockery of desire ; so I but suffered desire to accumulate till the final charming arrest, the platform of the famous hotel, amid generous lights and greetings, and excellent arrangements, and balmy Southern airs, and the breath of the near sea, and the vague crests of great palms, announced the fulfilment of every hope.

The question of whether one's hope was really fulfilled, or of whether one had, among all those items of ease, to go supperless to bed, would doubtless appear beneath the dignity of even such history as this, were it not for a single fact—which, then and there looming large to me, blocked out, on the spot, all others. It is difficult to render the intensity with which one felt the great sphere of the hotel close round one, covering one in as with high, shining crystal walls, stretching beneath one's feet an immeasurable polished level, revealing itself in short as, for the time, for the place, the very order of nature and the very form, the only one, of the habitable world. The effect was like nothing else of the sort one had ever known, and of surpassing interest, truly, as any supreme illustration of manners, any complete and organic projection of a "social" case is apt to be. The whole picture presented itself as fresh and luminous—as was natural to phenomena shown in the splendid Florida light and off there at the end of a huge peninsula especially appointed to them, and kept clear, in their interest, as it struck me, of any shadow of anything but themselves. One had been aware enough, certainly, for long years, of that range of American aspects, that diffusion of the American example, to which one had given, from far back, for convenience, the name of hotel-civilization; why, accordingly, was this renewed impression so hugely to impose itself; why was it, to the eye of the restless analyst, to stand for so much more than ever yet? Why was it, above all, so to succeed in making, with insistence, its appeal?—an appeal if not to the finer essence of interest, yet to several of the fond critic's livelier sensibilities. Wasn't, for that matter, his asking of such questions as these the very state of being interested?—and all the more that the general reply to them was not easy to throw off.

The vision framed, the reflections suggested, corresponded closely with those to which, in New York, some weeks before, on its harsh winter afternoon, the Waldorf-Astoria had prescribed such a revel; but it was wondrous that if I had there supposed the apogee of the impression (or, better still, of the *ex*pression) reached, I was here to see the whole effect written lucidly larger. The difference was doubtless that of the crowded air and encumbered ground in the great Northern city—in the fact that the demonstration is made in Florida as in a vast clean void expressly prepared for it. It has nothing either in nature or in man to reckon with—it carries everything before it; meaning, when I say "it," in this momentarily indefinite way, the perfect, the exquisite adjustability of the "national" life to the sublime hotel-spirit. The whole appearance operates as by an economy so thorough that no element of either party to the arrangement is discoverably sacrificed; neither is mutilated, docked in any degree of its identity, its amplitude of type; nothing is left unexpressed in either through its relation with the other. The relation would in fact seem to stimulate each to a view of the highest expression as yet open to it. The advantage—in the sense of the "upper hand"—may indeed be, at a few points, most with the hotel-spirit, as the more concentrated of the two; there being so much that is comparatively undeveloped and passive in the social organism to which it looks for response, and the former agency, by its very nature full-blown and expert, "trying it on" the latter much more than the latter is ever perceptibly moved to try it on the former. The hotel-spirit is an omniscient genius, while the character of the tributary nation is still but struggling into relatively dim self-knowledge. An illustration of this met me, precisely, at the very hour of my alighting: one had entered, toward ten o'clock in the evening, the hotel-world; it had become the all in all and made and imposed its law.

This took the form, for me, at that hungry climax, at the end of the long ordeal of the buffet-car, of a refusal of all food that night; a rigour so inexorable that, had it not been for the charity of admirable friends, able to provide me from a private store, I should have had to go, amid all the suggestions of everything, fasting and faint to bed. There one seemed to get the hotel-spirit *taking* the advantage—taking it unfairly; for whereas it struck me in general as educative, distinctly, in respect to the society it deals with, keeping for the most part well in advance of it, and leading it on to a larger view of the social interest and opportunity than might otherwise accrue, here, surely, it was false to its mission, it fell behind its pretension, its general pretension not only of meeting all American ideals, but of creating (the Waldorf-Astoria being in this sense, for example, a perfect riot of creation) new and superior ones. Its basis, in those high developments, is not that it merely gratifies them as soon as they peep out, but that it lies in wait for them, anticipates and plucks them forth even before they dawn, setting them up almost prematurely and turning their face in the right direction. Thus the great national ignorance of many things is artfully and benevolently practised upon; thus it is converted into extraordinary appetites, such as can be but expensively sated. The belated traveller's appetite for the long-deferred "bite" could scarce be described as *too* extraordinary; but the great collective, plastic public, so vague yet about many things, didn't *know* that it couldn't, didn't know that, in communities more knowing, the great glittering, costly caravansery, where the scale of charges is an implication of a high refinement of service, grave lapses are not condoned.

One appears ridiculously to be regretting that unsupplied mouthful, but the restless analyst had in truth quickly enough left it behind, feeling in his hand, already, as a clue, the long concatenation of interlinked appearances. Things short in themselves might yet have such large dimensions of meaning. The revelation, practically dazzling to the uninformed many, was constantly proving, right and left, if one gave it time, a trick played on the informed few; and there was no quarter of the field, either the material or the "social," in which that didn't sooner or later come out. The fact that the individual, with his preferences, differences, habits, accidents, might still fare imperfectly even where the crowd could be noted as rejoicing before the Lord more ingenuously than on any other human scene, added but another touch to one's impression, already so strong, of the success with which, throughout the land, even in conditions which might appear likely, on certain sides, to beget reserves about it, the all-gregarious and generalized life suffices to every need. I by no means say that it is not touching, the so largely witless confidence with which the universal impulse hurls its victims into the abyss of the hotel-spirit, trusting it so blandly and inviting it to throw up, round and about them and far and wide, the habitable, the practicable, the agreeable sphere toward which other arts of construction fail. There were lights in which this was to strike me as one of the most affecting of all social exhibitions; lights, positively, in which I seemed to see again (as, once more, at the universal Waldorf-Astoria) the whole housed populace move as in mild and consenting suspicion of its captured and governed state, its having to consent to inordinate fusion as the price of what it seemed pleased to regard as inordinate luxury. Beguiled and caged, positively thankful, in its vast vacancy, for the sense and the definite horizon of a cage, were there yet not moments, were there yet not cases and connections, in which it still dimly made out that its condition was the result of a compromise into the detail of which there might some day be an alarm in entering? The detail of the compromise exacted of the individual, throughout American life, affects the observer as a great cumulative sum, growing and growing while he awaits time and opportunity to go into it; and I asked myself again and again if I couldn't imagine the shadow of that quantity by no means oppressively felt, yet already vaguely perceived, and reflected a bit portentously in certain aspects of the native consciousness.

The jealous cultivation of the common mean, the common mean only, the reduction of everything to an average of decent suitability, the gospel of precaution against the dangerous tendency latent in many things to become too good for their context, so that persons partaking of them may become too good for their company—the idealized form of all this glimmered for me, as an admonition or a betrayal, through the charming Florida radiance, constituting really the greatest interest of the lesson one had travelled so far to learn. It might superficially seem absurd, it might savour almost of blasphemy, to put upon the "romantic" peninsula the affront of that particular prosaic meaning; but I profess that none of its so sensibly thin sources of romance—thin because everywhere asking more of the imagination than they could be detected in giving it— appealed to me with any such force or testified in any such quantity. Definitely, one had made one's pilgrimage but to find the hotel-spirit in sole *articulate* possession, and, call this truth for the mind an anti-climax if one would, none of the various climaxes, the minor effects— those of Nature, for instance, since thereabouts, far and wide, was no hinted history—struck me as for a moment dispossessing it of supremacy. So little availed, comparatively, those of the jungle, the air, the sea, the sky, the sunset, the orange, the pineapple, the palm; so little such a one, amid all the garden climaxes, as that of the divine bougainvillæa which, here and there, at Palm Beach, smothers whole " homes " in its purple splendour.

For the light of the hotel-spirit really beat upon every-thing ; it was the only torch held up for the view or the sense of anything else. The case, therefore, was perfect, for what did this mean but that its conscience, so to speak, its view of its responsibility, would be of the highest, and that, given the whole golden frame of the picture, the appearances could be nowhere else so grandly in its favour ? That prevision was to be in fact afterwards confirmed to me.

IV

On a strip of sand between the sea and the jungle in one quarter, between the sea and the Lake in another, the clustered hotels, the superior Pair in especial, stand and exhale their genius. One of them, the larger, the more portentously brave, of the Pair, is a marvel indeed, proclaiming itself of course, with all the eloquence of an interminable towered and pinnacled and gabled and ban-nered sky-line, the biggest thing of its sort in the world. Such is the responsive geniality begotten by its apparently perfect adequacy to this pretension, or to any other it might care to put forth, that one took it easily as leaving far behind mere figures of speech and forms of advertise-ment ; to stand off and see it rear its incoherent crest above its gardens was to remember—and quite with relief—nothing but the processional outline of Windsor Castle that could appear to march with it. I say with relief because the value of the whole affirmation, which was but the scale otherwise expressed, seemed thereby assured : no world *but* an hotel-world could flourish in such a shadow. Every step, for a mile or two round, conduced but to show how it did flourish ; every aspect of everything for which our reclaimed patch, our liberal square between sea and jungle, yielded space, was a demonstration of that. The gardens and groves, the vistas and avenues between the alignments of palms, the fostered insolence of flame-coloured flower and golden fruit, were perhaps the rarest attestation of all ; so recent a conquest did this seem to me of ground formerly abandoned, in the States, to the general indifference. There came back to me from other years a vision of the rude and sordid margins, the untended approaches surrounding, at " resorts," the crowded caravansery of the earlier time—and marking even now, I inferred, those of the type that still survive ; and I caught verily at play that best virtue of the potent presence. The hotel was leading again, not following—imposing the standard, not submitting to it ; teaching the affluent class how to " garden," how, in fact, to tidy up its "yard "— since affluence alone was supposable there ; not receiving at other hands the lesson. It was doing more than this —discriminating in favour of the beautiful, and above all in favour of the "refined," with an energy that again, in the most interesting way, seemed to cause the general question of the future of beauty in America to heave in its unrest.

Fifty times, already, I had felt myself catching this vibration, received some vivid impression of the growing quantity of force available for that conquest—of all the latent powers of freedom of space, of wealth, of faith and knowledge and curiosity, verily perhaps even of sustained passion, potentially at its service. These possibilities glimmer before one at times, in presence of some artistic effect expensively yet intelligently, yet even charmingly produced, with the result of your earnestly saying : " Why not more and more then, why not an immense exploration, an immense exhibition, of such possibilities ? What is wanting for it, after all, in the way of—— ? " Just there it is indeed that you pull yourself up—ah, in the way of what ? You are conscious that what you recognize in especial is not so much the positive as the negative strength of the case. What you see is the space and the freedom—which at every turn, in America, make one yearn to take other things for granted. The ground is so clear of preoccupation, the air so clear of prejudgment and doubt, that you wonder why the chance shouldn't be as great for the æsthetic revel as for the political and economic, why some great undaunted adventure of the arts, meeting in its path none of the aged lions of prescription, of proscription, of merely jealous tradition, should not take place in conditions unexampled. From the moment it is but a question of some one's, of every one's caring, where was the conceivable quantity of care, where were the means and chances of application, ever so great? And the precedent, the analogy, of the universal organizing passion, the native aptitude for putting affairs "through," indubitably haunts you : you are so aware of the acuteness and the courage that you fall but a little short of figuring them as æsthetically contributive. But you do fall short ; you remember in time that great creations of taste and faith never express themselves *primarily* in terms of mere convenience and zeal, and that all the waiting money and all the general fury have, at the most, the sole value of being destined to be good for beauty *when it shall appear.* They have it in them so little, by themselves, to make it appear, that your unfinished question arrives easily enough, in that light, at its end.

"What is wanting in the way of taste?" is the right form of the inquiry—that small circumstance alone being *positively* contributive. The others, the boundless field, the endless gold, the habit of great enterprises, are, you feel, at most, simple negations of difficulty. They affect you none the less, however, as a rank of stalwart soldiers and servants who, as they stand at attention, plead from wistful eyes to be enrolled and used ; so that before any embodied symptom of the precious principle they are there in the background of your thought. These lingering instants spent in the presence of such symptoms, these brief moments of æsthetic arrest—liable to occur in the most diverse connections—have an interest that quite picks them, I think, from the heap of one's American hours. And the interest is always fine, throwing one back as, by a further turn, it usually does, on the question of the trick possibly played, for your appreciation, by mere negation of difficulty. To what extent may the absence of difficulty, to what extent may not facility of purchase and sweet simplicity of pride, surprise you into taking them momentarily for a demonstration of taste? You remain on your guard, very properly; but the interest, as I have called it, doesn't flag, none the less, since there is one mistake into which you never need fall, and one charming, one touching appearance that you may take as representing, wherever you meet it, a reality. When once you have interpreted the admonitory sign I have just named as the inordinate *desire for taste*, a desire breaking into a greater number of quaint and candid forms, probably, than have ever been known upon earth, the air is in a manner clearer, and you know sufficiently where you are. Isn't it cleared, moreover, beyond doubt, to the positive increase of the interest, and doesn't the question then become, almost thrillingly, that of the degree to which this pathos of desire may be condemned to remain a mere heartbreak to the historic muse? *Is* that to be, possibly, the American future—so far as, over such a mystery of mysteries, glibness may be permitted? The fascination grows while you wonder—as, from the moment you have begun to go into the matter at all, wonder you certainly must. If with difficulties so conjured away by power, the clear vision, the creative freshness, the real thing in a word, *shall* have to continue to be represented, indefinitely, but by a gilded yearning, the inference is then irresistible that these blessings are indeed of their essence a sovereign rarity.   If with so many of the conditions they yet hang back, on what particular occult furtherance must they not incorruptibly depend? What are the other elements that make for them, and in what manner and at what points does the wrong combination of such elements, on the American scene, work for frustration? Entrancing speculation!—which has brought me back by a long circuit to the shining marble villa on the edge of Lake Worth.

I was about to allude to this wondrous creation as the supreme instance of missionary effort on the part of the hotel-spirit—by which I mean of the effort to illustrate and embody a group of its ideals, to give a splendid concrete example of its ability to flower, at will, into concentration, into conspicuous privacy, into a care for all the refinements.   The palace rears itself, behind its own high gates and gilded, transparent barriers, at a few minutes' walk from the great caravanseries; it sits there, in its admirable garden, amid its statues and fountains, the hugeness of its more or less antique vases and sarcophagi—costliest reproductions all—as if to put to shame those remembered villas of the Lake of Como, of the Borromean Islands, the type, the climate, the horticultural elegance, the contained curiosities, luxuries, treasures, of which it invokes only to surpass them at every point.   New with that consistency of newness which one sees only in the States, it seems to say, some-how, that to some such heaven, some such public exaltation of the Blest, those who have conformed with due earnestness to the hotel-spirit, and for a sufficiently long probation, may hope eventually to penetrate or perhaps actually retire.

It has sprung from the genius of the divine Pair, the Dioscuri themselves—as Castor and Pollux were the sons of Zeus; and has this, above all, of exemplary, that whereas one had in other climes and countries often seen the proprietor of estates construct an hotel, or hotels, on a piece of his property, and even, when rigid need was, in proximity to his "home," one had not elsewhere seen the home adjoined to the hotel, and placed, with such magnificence, under its protection and, as one might say, its star. In the former case—it was easy to reflect—there had been ever, at best, an effect of incoherence; while the beauty of logic, of the strictly consequent, was all on the side of the latter. So much as that one may say; but I should find it hard to express without some air of extravagance my sense of the beauty of the lesson read to the general Palm Beach consciousness from behind the gilded gates and between the large interstices of the enclosure. It had the immense merit that it was suited, admirably, to the "boarders"; it preached them the gospel of civilization all in their own terms and without the waste of an accent; it was in short the apotheosis, the ideal form of the final home that may pretend to crown a career of sufficiently expensive boarding. Anything less gorgeous wouldn't have been proportioned to so much expense, nor anything more sequestered in the key of such a mode of life. But I detach myself, with reluctance, from the view of this interesting creation— interesting in its sense of bathing the whole question of manners in a light. Anything that does that is a boon to the restless analyst; and I remember rejoicing that he should have been introduced promptly to the marble palace, which struck him as rewarding attention the more attention was privileged and the further it might penetrate. Such an experience was, all properly, pre-liminary to a view of the rest of the scene; since other-wise, frankly, in relation to what at all represented ideal were the boarders, in their vast multitude, to be viewed?

For the boarders, verily, were the great indicated

show, as I had gathered in advance, at Palm Beach; it
had been promised one, on all sides, that there, as nowhere else, in America, one would find Vanity Fair in
full blast—and Vanity Fair not scattered, not discriminated and parcelled out, as among the comparative
privacies and ancientries of Newport, but compressed
under one vast cover, enclosed in a single huge *vitrine*,
which there would be nothing to prevent one's flattening
one's nose against for days of delight. It was into
Vanity Fair, accordingly, that one embraced every
opportunity to press; it was the boarders, frankly, who
engaged one's attention in default of any great array of
other elements. The other elements, it must be confessed, strike the visitor as few; he has soon come
to the end of them, even though they consist of the
greater part of the rest of the sense of Florida. And he
seems to himself to pursue them, mainly, at the tail, and
in the constant track of the boarders; these latter are so
numerous, and the clearing in the jungle so comparatively
minute, that there is scant occasion for the wandering
apart which always forms, under the law of the herd, the
intenser joy. The velvet air, the colour of the sea, the
"royal" palms, clustered here and there, and, in their
nobleness of beauty, their single sublime distinction,
putting every other mark and sign to the blush, these are
the principal figures of the sum—these, with the custom
of the short dip into the jungle, at two or three points of
which, approached by charming, winding wood-ways, the
small but genial fruit-farm offers hospitality—offers it in
all the succulence of the admirable pale-skinned orange
and the huge sun-warmed grape-fruit, plucked from the
low bough, where it fairly bumps your cheek for solicitation, and partaken of, on the spot, as the immortal ladies
of Cranford partook of dessert—with a few steps aside,
the back turned and a betrayed ingurgitation. It is by
means of a light perambulator, of "adult size," but con-

structed of wicker-work, and pendent from a bicycle propelled by a robust negro, that the jungle is thus visited; the bicycle follows the serpentine track, the secluded ranch is swiftly reached, the peaceful retirement of the cultivators multitudinously admired, the perambulator promptly re-entered, the darkey restored to the saddle and his charge again to the hotel.

V

It is all most agreeable and diverting, it is almost, the boarders apart, romantic; but it is soon over, and there is not much more of it. The uncanny conception, the rank eccentricity of a walk encounters neither favour nor facility—but on the subject of the inveteracy with which the conditions, over the land, conspire against that sweet subterfuge there would be more to say than I may here deal with. One of these gentle ranches was approached by water, as Palm Beach has a front on its vast, fresh lake as well as seaward; a steam-launch puts you down at the garden foot, and the place is less infested by the boarders, less confessedly undefended, less artlessly ignorant in fine (thanks perhaps to the mere interposing water) of any possible right to occultation; the general absence of conception of that right, nowhere asserted, nowhere embodied, everywhere in fact quite sacrificially abrogated, qualifying at last your very sense of the American character—qualifying it very much as a pervading unsaltedness qualifies the taste of a dinner. This brief excursion remains with me, at any rate, as a delicate and exquisite impression; the neck of land that stretched from the languid lake to the anxious sea, the approach to real detachment, the gracious Northern hostess, just veiled, for the right felicity, in a thin nostalgic sadness, the precious recall in particular of having succeeded in straying a little, through groves of the pensive palm, down to the sandy, the vaguely-troubled shore. There was a certain concentration in the hour, a certain intensity in the note, a certain intimacy in the whole communion; I found myself loving, quite fraternally, the palms, which had struck me at first, for all their human-headed gravity, as merely dry and taciturn, but which became finally as sympathetic as so many rows of puzzled philosophers, dishevelled, shock-pated, with the riddle of the universe. This scantness and sweetness and sadness, this strange peninsular spell, *this*, I said, was sub-tropical Florida— and doubtless as permitted a glimpse as I should ever have of any such effect. The softness was divine—like something mixed, in a huge silver crucible, as an elixir, and then liquidly scattered. But the refinement of the experience would be the summer noon or the summer night—it would be then the breast of Nature would open; save only that, so lost in it and with such lubrication of surrender, how should one ever come back?

As it was, one came back soon enough, back to one's proper business : which appeared to be, urgently, strictly, severely, the pursuit of the boarders up and down the long corridors and round about the wide verandahs of their crowded career. I had been admirably provided for at the less egregious of the two hotels ; which was vast and cool and fair, friendly, breezy, shiny, swabbed and burnished like a royal yacht, really immaculate and delightful ; full of interesting lights and yet standing but on the edge of the whirlpool, the centre of which formed the heart of the adjacent colossus. One could plunge, by a short walk through a luxuriance of garden, into the deeper depths ; one could lose one's self, if so minded, in the labyrinth of the other show. There, if Vanity Fair was not encamped, it was not for want of booths ; the long corridors were streets of shops, dealing, naturally, in commodities almost beyond price—not the cheap gimcracks of the usual watering-place barrack, but solid (when not elaborately ethereal), formidable, incalculable values, of which it was of an admonitory economic interest to observe the triumphant appeal. They hadn't terrors, apparently, for the clustered boarders, these idols and monsters of the market—neither the wild fantastications of the milliner, the uncovered fires, disclosed secrets of the gem-merchant, the errant tapestries and *bahuts* of the antiquarian, nor, what I found most impressive and what has everywhere its picture-making force, those ordered dispositions and stretched lengths of old " point " in the midst of which a quiet lady in black, occupied with some small stitch of her own, is apt to raise at you, with expensive deliberation, a grave, white Flemish face. The interest of the general spectacle was supposed to be, I had gathered, that people from all parts of the country contributed to it; and the value of the testimony as to manners was that it brought to a focus so many elements of difference. The elements of difference, whatever they might latently have been, struck me as throughout forcibly simplified by the conditions of the place; this prompt reducibility of a thousand figures to a common denominator having been in fact, to my sense, the very moral of the picture. Individuality and variety is attributed to " types," in America, on easy terms, and the reputation for it enjoyed on terms not more difficult; so that what I was most conscious of, from aspect to aspect, from group to group, from sex to sex, from one presented boarder to another, was the continuity of the fusion, the dimness of the distinctions.

The distinction that was least absent, however, would have been, I judge, that of the comparative ability to spend and purchase; the ability to spend with freedom being, as one made out, a positive consistent with all sorts of negatives. That helped to make the whole thing documentary—that you had to be financially more or less at your ease to enjoy the privileges of the Royal Poinciana at all; enjoy them through their extended range of saloons and galleries, fields of high publicity all; pursue them from dining-halls to music-rooms, to ball-rooms, to card-rooms, to writing-rooms, to a succession of places of convenience and refreshment, not the least characteristic of which, no doubt, was the terrace appointed to mid-morning and mid-afternoon drinks— drinks, at the latter hour, that appeared, oddly, never to comprise tea, the only one appreciated in " Europe " at that time of day. (The quest of tea indeed, especially at the hour when it is most a blessing, struck me as attended, throughout the country, with difficulties, even with dangers; over ground where one's steps are beset, everywhere, with an infinite number of strange, sweet iced liquidities—many of these, I hasten to add, charmingly congruous, in their non-alcoholic ingenuity, with the heats of summer : a circumstance that doesn't prevent their flourishing equally in the rigour of cold.) The implication of " ease " was thus a light to assist inquiry; it is always a gained fact about people—as to "where" they are, if not as to who or what—that they are either in confirmed or in casual possession of money, and thereby, presumably, of all that money may, in this negotiable world, represent. Add to this that the company came, in its provided state, by common report, from "all over," that it converged upon Palm Beach from every prosperous corner of the land, and the case was clear for a compendious view of American society in the largest sense of the term. "Society," as we loosely use the word, is made up of the fortunate few, and, if that number be everywhere small at the best, it was yet the fortunate who, after their fashion, filled the frame. Every obligation lay upon me to "study' them as so gathered in, and I did my utmost, I remember, to render them that respect; yet when I now, after an interval, consult my notes, I find the page a blank, and when I knock at the door of memory I find it perversely closed. If it consents a little to open, rather, a countenance looks out—that of the inscrutable warden of the precinct—and seems to show me the ambiguous smile that accompanies on occasion the plea to be excused.

From which I infer that the form and pressure of the boarders, for all I had expected of the promised picture, failed somehow to affect me as a discussable quantity. It is of the nature of many American impressions, accepted at the time as a whole of the particular story, simply to cease to be, as soon as your back is turned—to fade, to pass away, to leave not a wreck behind. This happens not least when the image, whatever it may have been, has exacted the tribute of wonder or pleasure : it has displayed every virtue but the virtue of being able to remain with you. Its pressure and power have failed of some weight, some element of density or intensity, some property or quality in short that makes for the authority of a figure, for the complexity of a scene. The "European" vision, in general, of whatever consisting, and even when making less of an explicit appeal, has behind it a driving force—derived from sources into which I won't pretend here to enter—that make it, comparatively, "bite," as the plate of the etcher is bitten by aquafortis. That doubtless is the matter, in the States, with the vast peaceful and prosperous human show—in conditions, especially, in which its peace and prosperity most shine out : it registers itself on the plate with an incision too vague and, above all, too uniform. The paucity of one's notes is in itself, no doubt, a report of the consulted oracle ; it describes and reconstitutes for me the array of the boarders, this circumstance that I only grope for their features and seek in vain to discriminate between sorts and conditions. There were the two sexes, I think, and the range of age, but, once the one comprehensive type was embraced, no other signs of differentiation. How should there have been when the men were consistently, in all cases, thoroughly obvious products of the "business-block," the business-block unmitigated by any other influence definite enough to name, and the women were, under the same strictness, the indulged ladies of such lords? The business-block has perhaps, from the north-east to the south-west, its fine diversities, but any variety so introduced eluded even the most brooding of analysts.

And it was not of course that the marks of uniformity, among so many persons, were not on *their* side perfectly appreciable ; it was only that when one had noted them as marks of "success," no doubt, primarily, and then as those of great gregarious decency and sociability and good-humour, one had exhausted the list. It was the scant diversity of type that left me short, as a story-seeker or picture-maker ; contributive as this very fact might be to admiration of the costly processes, as they thus appear, that ensure, and that alone ensure, in other societies, the opposite of that scantness. With this, as the foredoomed observer may never escape from the dreadful faculty that rides him, the very simplifications had in the highest degree their illustrative value ; they gave all opportunity to anything or any one that might be salient. They gave it to the positive bourgeois propriety, serenely, imperturbably, massively seated, and against which any experimental deviation from the bourgeois would have dashed itself in vain. This neutrality of respectability might have been figured by a great grey wash of some charged moist brush causing colour and outline, on the pictured paper, effectually to run together. What resisted it best was the look of "business success" in some of the men ; when that success had been very great (and there were indicated cases of its prodigious greatness) the look was in its turn very great; when it had been small, on the other hand, there was doubtless no look at all—since there were no other conceivable sources of appearance. The people had not, and the women least of all, one felt, in general, been transferred from other backgrounds; the scene around them and behind them constituted as replete a medium as they could ever have been conscious of; the women in particular failed in an extraordinary degree to engage the imagination, to offer it, so to speak, references or openings: it faltered—doubtless respectfully enough—where they for the most part so substantially and prosaically sat, failing of any warrant to go an inch further. As for the younger persons, of whom there were many, as for the young girls in especial, they were as perfectly in their element as goldfish in a crystal jar: a form of exhibition suggesting but one question or mystery. Was it they who had invented it, or had it inscrutably invented *them*?

VI

The case of St. Augustine afterwards struck me as presenting, on another side, its analogy with the case at Palm Beach: if the "social interest" had in the latter place appeared but of a weak constitution, so the historic, at the former, was to work a spell of a simpler sort than one had been brought up, as it were, to look to. Hadn't one been brought up, from far back, on the article of that faith in St. Augustine, by periodical papers in the magazines, fond elucidations of its romantic character, accompanied by drawings that gave one quite proudly, quite patriotically, to think—that filled the cup of curiosity and yearning? The old town—for the essence of the faith had been that there *was* an "old town"—

receded into an all but untraceable past; it had been of all American towns the earliest planted, and it bristled still with every evidence of its Spanish antiquity. The illustrations in the magazines, wondrous vignettes of old street vistas, old architectural treasures, gateways and ramparts, odds and ends, nooks and corners, crowned with the sweetness of slow decay, conveyed the sense of these delights and renewed at frequent intervals their appeal. But oh, as I was to observe, the school of " black and white " trained up by the magazines has much, in the American air, to answer for: it points so vividly the homely moral that when you haven't what you like you must perforce like, and above all misrepresent, what you have. Its translation of these perfunctory passions into pictorial terms saddles it with a weight of responsibility that would be greater, one can only say, if there ever were a critic, some guardian of real values, to bring it to book. The guardians of real values struck me as, up and down, far to seek. The whole matter indeed would seem to come back, interestingly enough, to the general truth of the æsthetic need, in the country, for much greater values, of certain sorts, than the country and its manners, its aspects and arrangements, its past and present, and perhaps even future, really supply; whereby, as the æsthetic need is also intermixed with a patriotic yearning, a supply has somehow to be extemporized, by any pardonable form of pictorial "hankey-pankey"—has to be, as the expression goes, cleverly "faked." But it takes an inordinate amount of faking to meet the supposed intensity of appetite of a body of readers at once more numerous and less critical than any other in the world; so that, frankly, the desperate expedient is written large in much of the "artistic activity" of the country.

The results are of the oddest; they hang all traceably together; wonderful in short the general spectacle and lesson of the scale and variety of the faking. They renew again the frequent admonition that the pabulum provided for a great thriving democracy may derive most of its interest from the nature of its testimony to the thriving democratic demand. No long time is required, in the States, to make vivid for the visitor the truth that the nation is almost feverishly engaged in producing, with the greatest possible activity and expedition, an "intellectual" pabulum after its own heart, and that not only the arts and ingenuities of the draftsman (called upon to furnish the picturesque background and people it with the "aristocratic" figure where neither of these revelations ever meets his eye) pay their extravagant tribute, but that those of the journalist, the novelist, the dramatist, the genealogist, the historian, are pressed as well, for dear life, into the service. The illustrators of the magazines improvise, largely—that is when not labouring in the cause of the rural dialects—improvise the field of action, full of features at any price, and the characters who figure upon it, young gods and goddesses mostly, of superhuman stature and towering pride ; the novelists improvise, with the aid of the historians, a romantic local past of costume and compliment and sword-play and gallantry and passion ; the dramatists build up, of a thousand pieces, the airy fiction that the life of the people in the world among whom the elements of clash and contrast are simplest and most superficial abounds in the subjects and situations and effects of the theatre ; while the genealogists touch up the picture with their pleasant hint of the number, over the land, of families of royal blood. All this constitutes a vast home-grown provision for entertainment, rapidly superseding any that may be borrowed or imported, and that indeed already begins, not invisibly, to press for exportation. As to quantity, it looms immense, and resounds in proportion, yet with the property, all its own, of ceasing to be, of fading like the mist of dawn—that is of giving no account of itself whatever—as soon as one turns on it any intending eye of appreciation or of inquiry. It is the public these appearances collectively refer us to that becomes thus again the more attaching subject; the public so placidly uncritical that the whitest thread of the deceptive stitch never makes it blink, and sentimental at once with such inveteracy and such simplicity that, finding everything everywhere perfectly splendid, it fairly goes upon its knees to be humbuggingly humbugged. It proves ever, by the ironic measure, quite incalculably young.

That perhaps was all that had been the matter with it in presence of the immemorial legend of St. Augustine as a mine of romance; St. Augustine proving primarily, and of course quite legitimately, but an hotel, of the first magnitude—an hotel indeed so remarkable and so pleasant that I wondered what call there need ever have been upon it to prove anything else. The Ponce de Leon, for that matter, comes as near producing, all by itself, the illusion of romance as a highly modern, a most cleverly-constructed and smoothly-administered great modern caravansery can come; it is largely "in the Moorish style" (as the cities of Spain preserve the record of that manner); it breaks out, on every pretext, into circular arches and embroidered screens, into courts and cloisters, arcades and fountains, fantastic projections and lordly towers, and is, in all sorts of ways and in the highest sense of the word, the most "amusing" of hotels. It did for me, at St. Augustine, I was well aware, everything that an hotel could do—after which I could but appeal for further service to the old Spanish Fort, the empty, sunny, grassy shell by the low, pale shore; the mild, time-silvered quadrilateral that, under the care of a single exhibitory veteran and with the still milder remnant of a town-gate near it, preserves alone, to any effect of appreciable emphasis, the memory of the Spanish occupation. One wandered there for meditation —it is not congruous with the genius of Florida, I gathered, to permit you to wander very far; and it was there perhaps that, as nothing prompted, on the whole, to intenser musings, I suffered myself to be set moralizing, in the manner of which I have just given an example, over the too " thin" projection of legend, the too dry response of association. The Spanish occupation, shortest of ineffectual chapters, seemed the ghost of a ghost, and the burnt-out fire but such a pinch of ashes as one might properly fold between the leaves of one's *Baedeker*. Yet if I made this remark I made it without bitterness; since there was no doubt, under the influence of this last look, that Florida still had, in her ingenuous, not at all insidious way, the secret of pleasing, and that even round about me the vagueness was still an appeal. The vagueness was warm, the vagueness was bright, the vagueness was sweet, being scented and flowered and fruited; above all, the vagueness was somehow consciously and confessedly weak. I made out in it something of the look of the charming shy face that desires to communicate and that yet has just too little expression. What it would fain say was that it really knew itself unequal to any extravagance of demand upon it, but that (if it might so plead to one's tenderness) it would always do its gentle best. I found the plea, for myself, I may declare, exquisite and irresistible: the Florida of that particular tone was a Florida adorable.

VII

This last impression had indeed everything to gain from the sad rigour of steps retraced, an inevitable return to the North (in the interest of a directly subsequent, and thereby gracelessly roundabout, move Westward); and I confess to having felt on that occasion, before the dire backwardness of the Northern spring, as if I had, while travelling in the other sense, but blasphemed against the want of forwardness of the Southern. Every breath that one might still have drawn in the South—might if twenty other matters had been different—haunted me as the thought of a lost treasure, and I settled, at the eternal car window, to the mere sightless contemplation, the forlorn view, of an ugly—ah, such an ugly, wintering, waiting world. My eye had perhaps been jaundiced by the breach of a happy spell—inasmuch as on thus leaving the sad fragments there where they had fallen I tasted again the quite saccharine sweetness of my last experience of Palm Beach, and knew how I should wish to note for remembrance the passage, supremely charged with that quality, in which it had culminated. I asked myself what other expression I should find for the incident, the afternoon before I left the place, of one of those mild progresses to the head of Lake Worth which distil, for the good children of the Pair, the purest poetry of their cup. The poetic effect had braved the compromising aid of the highly-developed electric launch in which the pilgrim embarks, and braved as well the immitigable fact that his shrine, at the end of a couple of hours, is, in the vast and exquisite void, but an institution of yesterday, a wondrous floating tea-house or restaurant, inflated again with the hotel-spirit and exhaling modernity at every pore.

These associations are—so far as association goes—the only ones; but the whole impression, for simply sitting there in the softest lap the whole South had to offer, seemed to me to dispense with any aid but that of its own absolute felicity. It was, for the late return at least, the return in the divine dusk, with the flushed West at one's right, a concert of but two or three notes—the alignment, against the golden sky, of the individual black palms, a frieze of chiselled ebony, and the texture, for faintly-brushed cheek and brow, of an air of such silkiness of velvet, the very throne-robe of the star-crowned night, as one can scarce commemorate but in the language of the loom.   The shore of the sunset and the palms, what was that, meanwhile, like, and yet with what did it, at the moment one asked the question, refuse to have anything to do ?   It was like a myriad pictures of the Nile ; with much of the modern life of which it suggested more than one analogy.   These indeed all dropped, I found, before I had done—it would have been a Nile so simplified out of the various fine senses attachable.   One had to put the case, I mean, to *make* a fine sense, that here surely then was the greater antiquity of the two, the antiquity of the infinite *previous*, of the time, before Pharaohs and Pyramids, when everything was still to come. It was a Nile, in short, without the least little implication of a Sphinx or, still more if possible, of a Cleopatra. I had the foretaste of what I was presently to feel in California—when the general aspect of that wondrous realm kept suggesting to me a sort of prepared but unconscious and inexperienced Italy, the primitive *plate*, in perfect condition, but with the impression of History all yet to be made.

Of how grimly, meanwhile, under the annual rigour, the world, for the most part, waits to be less ugly again, less despoiled of interest, less abandoned to monotony, less forsaken of the presence that forms its only resource, of the one friend to whom it owes all it ever gets, of the pitying season that shall save it from its huge insignificance—of so much as this, no doubt, I sufficiently renewed my vision, and with plenty of the reviving ache of a question already familiar.   To what extent was hugeness, to what extent *could* it be, a ground for complacency of view, in any country not visited for the very love of wildness, for positive joy in barbarism ?

Where was the charm of boundless immensity as over-looked from a car-window ?—with the general pretension to charm, the general conquest of nature and space, affirmed, immediately round about you, by the general pretension of the Pullman, the great monotonous rumble of which seems forever to say to you : " See what I'm making of all this—see what I'm making, what I'm making ! " I was to become later on still more intimately aware of the spirit of one's possible reply to that, but even then my consciousness served, and the eloquence of my exasperation seems, in its rude accents, to come back to me.

" I see what you are *not* making, oh, what you are ever so vividly not ; and how can I help it if I am subject to that lucidity?—which appears never so welcome to you, for its measure of truth, as it ought to be ! How can I not be so subject, from the moment I don't just irre-flectively gape ? If I were one of the painted savages you have dispossessed, or even some tough reactionary trying to emulate him, what you are making would doubtless impress me more than what you are leaving unmade ; for in that case it wouldn't be to *you* I should be looking in any degree for beauty or for charm. Beauty and charm would be for me in the solitude you have ravaged, and I should owe you my grudge for every disfigurement and every violence, for every wound with which you have caused the face of the land to bleed. No, since I accept your ravage, what strikes me is the long list of the arrears of your undone ; and so constantly, right and left, that your pretended message of civilization is but a colossal recipe for the *creation* of arrears, and of such as can but remain forever out of hand. You touch the great lonely land—as one feels it still to be—only to plant upon it some ugliness about which, never dreaming of the grace of apology or contrition, you then proceed to brag with a cynicism all your own. You convert the large and noble sanities that I see around me, you convert them one after the other to crudities, to invalidities, hideous and unashamed ; and you so leave them to add to the number of the myriad aspects you simply spoil, of the myriad unanswerable questions that you scatter about as some monstrous unnatural mother might leave a family of unfathered infants on doorsteps or in waiting-rooms. This is the meaning surely of the inveterate rule that you shall multiply the perpetrations you call 'places'—by the sign of some name as senseless, mostly, as themselves—to the sole end of multiplying to the eye, as one approaches, every possible source of displeasure. When nobody cares or notices or suffers, by all one makes out, when no displeasure, by what one can see, is ever felt or ever registered, why shouldn't you, you may indeed ask, be as much in your right as you need? But in that fact itself, that fact of the vast general unconsciousness and indifference, looms, for any restless analyst who may come along, the accumulation, on your hands, of the unretrieved and the irretrievable !"

I remember how it was to come to me elsewhere, in such hours as those, that south of Pennsylvania, for instance, or beyond the radius of Washington, I had caught no glimpse of anything that was to be called, for more than a few miles and by a stretch of courtesy, the honour, the decency or dignity of a road—that most exemplary of all civil creations, and greater even as a note of morality, one often thinks, than as a note of facility ; and yet had nowhere heard these particular arrears spoken of as matters ever conceivably to be made up. I was doubtless aware that if I had been a beautiful red man with a tomahawk I should of course have rejoiced in the occasional sandy track, or in the occasional mud-channel, just in proportion as they fell so short of the type. Only in that case I shouldn't have been seated by the great square of plate-glass through which the missionary Pullman appeared to invite me to admire the achievements it proclaimed. It was in this respect the great symbolic agent; it seemed to stand for all the irresponsibility behind it; and I am not sure that I didn't continue, so long as I was in it, to "slang" it for relief of the o'erfraught heart. "You deal your wounds—that is the 'trouble,' as you say—in numbers so out of proportion to any hint of responsibility for them that you seem ever moved to take; which is the devil's dance, precisely, that your vast expanse of level floor leads you to caper through with more kinds of outward clumsiness—even if also with more kinds of inward impatience and avidity, more leaps and bounds of the spirit at any cost to grace—than have ever before been collectively displayed. The expanse of the floor, the material opportunity itself, has elsewhere failed; so that what is the positive effect of their inordinate presence but to make the lone observer, here and there, but measure with dismay the trap laid by the scale, if he be not tempted even to say by the superstition, of continuity? Is the germ of anything finely human, of anything agreeably or successfully social, supposably planted in conditions of such endless stretching and such boundless spreading as shall appear finally to minister but to the triumph of the superficial and the apotheosis of the raw? Oh for a split or a chasm, one groans beside your plate-glass, oh for an unbridgeable abyss or an insuperable mountain!"—and I could so indulge myself though still ignorant of how one was to groan later on, in particular, after taking yet further home the portentous truth that this same criminal continuity, scorning its grandest chance to break down, makes but a mouthful of the mighty Mississippi. That was to be in fact my very next "big" impression.

NOTES

BIBLIOGRAPHICAL NOTE

The American Scene was published in London by Chapman and Hall, Ltd., 30 January 1907, anticipating American publication by one week. In the United States it was published 7 February by Harper and Brothers. The book included four sections which had not been serialized, those on the Bowery in New York, Concord and Salem, and the sections on Charleston and Florida. Section VII of the essay on Florida, which appeared in the English edition, was omitted from the American edition. There was some revision, largely verbal and stylistic, throughout the book of the serialized material.

Serial publication of the various chapters of *The American Scene* was as follows:

"New England: An Autumn Impression." *North American Review*, CLXXX (April–June), 481–501, 641–60, 800–16.

"New York and the Hudson: A Spring Impression." *North American Review*, CLXXXI (December), 801–33.

"New York: Social Notes. I." *North American Review*, CLXXXII (January), 19–31; *Fortnightly Review*, LXXXV (February), 250–61.

"New York: Social Notes, II." *North American Review*, CLXXXII (February), 179–93.

"New York Revisited." *Harper's Magazine*, CXII (February–March, May), 400–406, 603–608, 900–907.

"Boston." *North American Review*, CLXXXII (March),

333–55; *Fortnightly Review*, LXXXV (March), 439–59.

"Philadelphia." *North American Review*, CLXXXII (April), 542–64; *Fortnightly Review*, LXXXV (April), 751–71.

"Washington." *North American Review*, CLXXXII (May–June), 660–75, 896–905.

"The Sense of Newport" (Illustrated by Jules Guerin, H. D. Nichols, and Marguerite Downing). *Harper's Magazine*, CXIII (August), 343–54.

"Baltimore." *North American Review*, CLXXXIII (August), 250–71.

"Richmond, Virginia." *Fortnightly Review*, LXXXV (November), 850–70.

NOTES ON CHAPTERS

Most of the unpublished material used in the writing of the introduction and in the notes to this edition is to be found in the manuscript collections at Harvard, Yale, the Library of Congress, and the Brotherton Library at Leeds in England, and I wish to thank these institutions for giving me access to this material. I would like at the same time to renew my thanks to the President and Fellows of Harvard College for continued access to the James papers in the Houghton Library and to its librarian, Dr. W. H. Bond, for many courtesies shown me during my researches. I have also received generous help from Mr. C. Waller Barrett and the Clifton Waller Barrett Library of the University of Virginia Library.

Henry James sailed from Southampton 24 August 1904 for the United States on the liner *Kaiser Wilhelm II*. He had last been in his homeland in 1883. Friends aboard included Clara Woolson Benedict, sister of his novelist friend Constance Fenimore Woolson, who had died in Venice in 1894, and Mrs. Benedict's daughter, Clare; also Frederick Sturges, brother of his friend and intimate, the young American *littérateur*, Jonathan Sturges.

Headline in the New York *Sun*, 31 August 1904: "Henry James Home at Last. Novelist Reaches America after 20 Years Absence." The reporters at the dock found James "vigorous at sixty."

Within a fortnight James's reaction to the first flush of recognition was beginning to set in, and a combined amazement, bewilderment, fondness, and horror was to continue to be reflected in his letters. To Mrs. George Hunter: "I have need of all your indulgence, feeling, as I do, like a poor helpless baby in the midst of monstrous things." To his agent J. B. Pinker (MS Yale) "I had an assault of interviewers and escaped them all for the time." One intrepid lady journalist, Florence Brooks of the New York *Herald*, pushed her way through to Chocorua with a letter from Scribner's, and James granted her one of his rare interviews. It appeared in the *Herald* on 2 October 1904.

Miss Brooks described Henry James as of middle height, slightly bald, his black hair turned iron grey at the sides. He wore a sack suit of dark gray. She found mingling traits of strength and mellowness, shyness and kindness. His eyes were blue-grey; and apparently his customary sharpness of vision was suspended for his interviewer–she wondered how "those opaque eyes could have seen such subtleties." He wasn't "formidable," but he was informal, "absolutely natural." He fenced with her. She asked him about "purpose" in his wrtings. Didn't he leave his readers with questions of moral purpose at the end? "Ah is not that the trick that life plays?" the interviewer quoted him. "Life leaves you with a question–it asks you questions."

On 3 September the New York *Times* in its Saturday review of books ran a lead editorial headed "Woolett Revisited," (an allusion to the New England town of Woolett in *The Ambassadors*), and said: "We have got well past the stage of caring what born foreigners say about us, but we shall quite seriously attend to what Mr. James says." While at Chocorua, where he remained until the end of September, Henry James read final proofs of his forthcoming novel *The Golden Bowl*. It was published by Scribner in November.

I NEW ENGLAND: AN AUTUMN IMPRESSION

Pages 4–5.   James spent thirty-six hours at the suburban home of one of his publishers, Colonel George Harvey, head of Harper and Brothers, at Deal Beach, New Jersey–where "poor dear old Mark Twain, who is here, beguiles the sessions on the deep piazza." (To William James, MS Harvard)

14–34. Henry James arrived at Chocorua, country home of his brother William (WJ) 3 September. In letters he described the White Mountain retreat as "a real New England Arcadia" where he led "a pure bucolic and Arcadian and wildly informal and unfrilled life."

36–38. HJ's visit to Cape Cod was paid during the last days of September. At Cotuit he was with his American friend, Howard O. Sturgis, who was also interrupting a long expatriation to visit the United States and who that year published his novel *Belchamber*. HJ also went to Jackson, New Hampshire, to spend a day with Katherine Prescott Wormeley, American biographer and translator of Balzac, and it was after this meeting that he probably decided to lecture in America on "The Lesson of Balzac." For details of his lecture tour which took him south and west, see "Henry James, Lecturer" by Marie P. Harris, *American Literature*, XXIII, No. 3 (November 1951), 302–22.

40. James went also to Salisbury, Connecticut in late September to visit his Emmet cousins, and to Concord to see his brother Robertson James.

49–51. In mid-October, James paid the first of his visits to Edith Wharton, at her home at Lenox, "The Mount," which he described to Howard Sturgis as "a delicate French chateau mirrored in a Massachusetts pond (repeat not this formula,) and a monument to the almost too impeccable taste of its so accomplished mistress." (MS Harvard) The motor trips here mentioned were probably in the company of Mrs. Wharton.

From The Mount, where HJ spent a fortnight, he wrote on 21 October to Colonel Harvey outlining his plans for *The Amer-*

ican Scene. "I am moved inwardly to believe that I shall be able not only to write the best book (of social and pictorial and, as it were, human observation,) ever devoted to this country, but one of the best—or why 'drag in' one *of*, why not say frankly *the* Best?—ever devoted to any country at all." (MS Congress) To his agent James wrote: "I can't knock off pages of prose like a war-correspondent, writing on his knee or his hat, and want to do a really artistic and valuable book." (MS Yale)

HJ to Jessie Allen, The Mount, 22 October 1904: "I came with a neat little project of paying no visits . . . whatever, and have carried it out, still more neatly, by having spent but two nights at an hotel, and done nothing but proceed from one irresistable hospitable house to another." He also wrote: "I am finding my native land indeed a most agreeable and absorbing adventure and this golden glorious American autumn (*such* weather, as of tinkling crystal, and *such* colours, as of molten topaz and ruby and amber!) a prolonged fairy-tale." He added: "This country is too terrifically big." (MS Harvard)

One of his hostesses during October was Isabella Stewart Gardner, in her new Venetian palace in the Fenway of Boston.

56.   HJ wrote to Edmund Gosse 27 October 1904 that he had greatly been struck with the way Harvard in a quarter of a century "has come to mass so much larger and to have gathered about her such a swarm of distinguished specialists and such a big organization of learning." (MS Brotherton Library, Leeds)

58.   The allusion to the "young modern" unconscious of HJ's reveries is to the novelist's nephew Henry James, eldest son of WJ.

59.   The "distinguished friend, all alone, belatedly working" in the new Law Library James recognized was the Royall professor of law, John C. Gray, who with HJ and Oliver Wendell Holmes Jr. (later Justice Holmes) in their youth had spent a memorable week-end in the White Mountains. For an account of this, see Leon Edel, *Henry James: The Untried Years* (New York and London, 1953), the chapter in Book Four, "Heroine of the Scene." Minny Temple's letters published in *Notes of a*

Son and Brother (1914) were addressed to John Gray. See also HJ's *Notebooks*, ed. Matthiessen and Murdock (1947), 324, in which James decides to allude to this glimpse of Gray and identifies him.

68–69. For a more intimate account of James's visit to the graves of his parents and sister at Cambridge Cemetery see his *Notebooks*, 320–21. The only surviving American notebook at Harvard contains a few vivid entries, one in Cambridge and a section written in California, recording eastern memories. James wrote his name "H. James Jr." on its cover, a curious return to the use of Junior, which he had discarded promptly after the death of his father in 1882.

69–71. In evoking the Cambridge of his memories, James signals two old friends by their initials, James Russell Lowell, dead for more than a decade, and William Dean Howells.

2 NEW YORK REVISITED

HJ was in and out of New York a number of times during his 1904–1905 visit to America. He returned briefly at the beginning of December to attend a dinner given in his honor by Colonel George Harvey. The head of Harper's had first wanted to stage a large public dinner. HJ replied he never went to dinners with a big "D," and that "if I should miraculously live to see one offered to myself" that would be the one "from which I should most be absent." The dinner finally given was a more modest affair at the Metropolitan Club, although James still found it full of ostentation, speaking in his letters of $500 worth of flowers on the table. He found the food very good but could not enjoy it, as he had had some strenuous dental sessions in Boston. Among those at the dinner were Mark Twain, Mrs. Schuyler Van Rensselaer, Mr. and Mrs. Cornelius Vanderbilt, Arthur Brisbane, Mr. and Mrs. Booth Tarkington, Hamlin Garland, G. W. Smalley, the future ambassador James W. Gerard, and Elizabeth Jordan of *Harper's Bazar*.

James remained in New York only a few days, staying with Mrs. Cadwalader Jones (Mrs. Frederic Rhinelander Jones),

Edith Wharton's sister-in-law. She was an old friend and James returned to stay at her home at 21 East 11th Street a number of times. However, he left Mrs. Jones on this occasion to stay with Mrs. Wharton for a few days at 884 Park Avenue where he found himself in "elegant though very gentle bondage." The apartment was "a *bonbonnière* of the last daintiness." From New York after a brief return to Boston he made his first foray to Philadelphia and Washington early in January 1905.

The Golden Bowl had been published 12 November and was being widely reviewed. To a friend in England (W. E. Norris, MS Yale) James wrote from Boston 15 December: "New York is appalling, fantastically charmless and elaborately dire; but Boston has quality and convenience, and now that one sees American life in the longer piece one profits by many of its great ingenuities." He said he enjoyed traveling by day and expatiated on "a marvel the perfect organisation of the universal telephone (with interviews and contacts that begin in two minutes and settle all things in them)." It was also "an exquisite curse when it isn't an exquisite blessing."

The winter proved extremely cold; there was much snow, great blizzards, and icy streets and James decided to travel south and then west. His fullest exploration of the city of his birth occurred in the spring at the end of April and in May, after much of his travel was over and he had completed most of his speaking engagements. In the spring, he stayed again with Mrs. Jones in West 11th Street and also in West 10th Street with his old friend, whom he had known as a boy, Lawrence Godkin. During his various visits to New York he met the young Witter Bynner who entertained him at the Players' Club. (See Witter Bynner, "A Word or Two with Henry James," *The Critic,* XLVI [February 1905], 146–48.) He greatly liked the young poet and the hours of quiet spent in the old club in the Gramercy section of the city. He also frequented the Century Club of which he had been briefly a member before his expatriation and where he had a guest membership through W. D. Howells.

89.   The area described here was later used by HJ to place the old New York house which figures as "The Jolly Corner" in the tale so named.

90.   These recollections are greatly amplified in *A Small Boy and Others* (1913).

91.   The original building of New York University had stood on the east side of the Square and was architecturally imitative of an Oxford College. It had been torn down, and also HJ's birthplace, which had been located beside it at 21 Washington Place. Today a plaque on the Brown'Building of New York University commemorates the birthplace.

93.   John La Farge, the painter, muralist, and worker in stained glass (1835–1910). Though older than HJ, he had taken an interest in the young writer when they had met at Newport before the Civil War. While they saw little of each other in later years and ceased to correspond, HJ cherished the memory of this friendship and continued to admire La Farge's work. See his tribute to him in *Notes of a Son and Brother* (1914), Chapter IV.

113.   An allusion to the Rhinelander mansion, demolished years later to make way for an apartment house.

3–5   NEW YORK

HJ's spring exploration of New York was leisurely and took him into the foreign sections and the slums. It was during this period that he paid the visits and made the inquiries into the life of the new Americans described in the introduction to this edition. James saw New York now within the perspective of his visit to the South; he had travelled as far as Florida and then westward to Los Angeles. He had lectured in Philadelphia, Chicago, Indianapolis, St. Louis, San Francisco, Los Angeles, and was to speak in Washington and at Northampton and Amherst as well as in New York City and at Harvard. He had a feeling, after the "rawness" of the rest of the land, of "meeting again a ripe old civilization" on returning to the east.

139.   HJ's reference to his drinking tea in the Tower of London alludes to his periodic visits there as guest of Angelina Milman, later Mrs. Edward Clarke, whose writings appeared in the *Yellow Book* and elsewhere. She was in charge of the "modernized and civilized" exhibition room at the Tower.

157. James's recollection of Washington Irving is told in *A Small Boy and Others* (1913), V.

6–7 NEWPORT, BOSTON

HJ revisited Newport, where he had spent his adolescent years before and during the Civil War, in November 1904 and again in June 1905, shortly before sailing for England. For details of his earlier Newport experiences see *The Untried Years*, "Newport Idyll," in Book Three.

227. Ashburton Place, near the State House, was a remembered place in James's life; in his father's house here he came of age and began to write. See *Notebooks*, 321–23; also *Untried Years*, "Ashburton Place," in Book Four.

243. Mount Vernon Street on Beacon Hill figured in HJ's life during the period of the death of his parents in 1881–1882. On the death of his mother, his father left Cambridge and settled in a house in Mount Vernon Street. After the father's death in 1882, HJ lived for several months here with his sister Alice.

244–45. James alludes here to the old "salon" of Mr. and Mrs. J. T. Fields at their home in 28 Charles Street where he had been made welcome when he was writing his earliest tales. His memories of this time were embodied in a late reminiscence shortly before his death, "Mr. and Mrs. Fields," published in the *Cornhill Magazine* and in the *Atlantic Monthly* in July 1915. It is interesting to note that James singled out Thackeray as one of the Fields's distinguished guests but omitted the much more publicized visit of Dickens.

251. HJ had taken an interest in the painting of the Abbey murals for the library and had seen the sketches for them in Abbey's studio in England. See E. V. Lucas, *Life and Work of Edwin Austin Abbey R.A.*, 2 vols. (1921).

254–55. Mrs. Gardner's *palazzo* in the Fenway had been officially opened two years earlier, in February 1903. HJ had known her for many years. For an account of their friendship see Leon Edel, *The Conquest of London* (New York and London, 1962), Book Seven.

8 CONCORD AND SALEM

HJ had visited Emerson in Concord in the early 1870s after his first trip to Europe. His younger brothers had gone to F. B. Sanborn's school there long before. He thus had a long retrospective view of the town. (See *Conquest of London*, Book One.) HJ revisited Concord several times during his ten months in America to see his youngest brother Robertson, who lived there.

259–60. The portrait of "the very interesting lady" here sketched is that of Mrs. Procter, friend of most of the leading writers in England from the time of the romantics to the 1890s. (See *Conquest of London*, Book Seven, the chapter entitled "Three Old Women.")

265–72. HJ's interest in Hawthorne remained constant during all of his life. He published his study of the novelist in 1879; he also wrote several essays and reviews on him at various times; and he had contributed a paper to the observance of the Hawthorne centenary the previous June. There are several pages devoted to Hawthorne in *Notes of a Son and Brother* (1914), XII.

9–10 PHILADELPHIA, BALTIMORE

HJ had visited Philadelphia in earlier years, during the lifetime of his friend Fanny Kemble when she had resided there in Germantown. There are allusions to this in his biographical portrait of her, in *Essays in London*, 1891. During the 1905 visit HJ journeyed to Philadelphia on 9 January to deliver for the first time his lecture on "The Lesson of Balzac" before the Contemporary Club, with Agnes Repplier, the essayist, presiding. On this occasion he met and became a friend of Dr. J. William White, the eminent American surgeon, a friend of the painter, John Singer Sargent. Later that month, and again in February, HJ visited Dr. White, staying with him at his home in Rittenhouse Square. (Agnes Repplier, *J. William White, M.D., A*

Biography [1919].) HJ also visited at Butler Place, home of Mrs. Wister, Fanny Kemble's daughter and a friend of his Roman days. She was the mother of the novelist, Owen Wister.

298–99. HJ's visit to the penitentiary and his talk with the murderers was arranged by Dr. S. Weir Mitchell, the eminent psychiatrist, who was also a novelist and a friend of Edith Wharton's.

303. HJ did not linger in Baltimore during his visit to Philadelphia and Washington in January and February; but he visited it in June, shortly before returning to England. He lectured in Baltimore on Saturday, 10 June and stayed over to visit the hospital, the country club, and Johns Hopkins. While here he wrote to Mrs. William James: "I find I spout, more and more, strangely, as one to the manner born." (MS Harvard) And to his literary agent he wrote at this time: "I move among complications and importunities (all of a most kind and cordial and even applausive sort) but they too much overwhelm and obstruct me." (MS Yale)

304. The passage describing HJ's feelings on journeying southward suggests the deepest meaning of his frequent journeys in earlier years to Italy–the casting off of the rigidities of Victorian England for the more expansive qualities "divinities, graces, presences as unseen but as inherent as the scents clinging to the folds of Nature's robe."

322. HJ's discussion of the Country Club as an institution has been taken perhaps much too literally by earlier critics. "I cannot share James's pleasure in that institution," Mr. Auden remarks; and F. O. Matthiessen read the passage as proclaiming the values of democracy against "European exclusiveness." A careful reading of these passages suggests that James may be talking of something else–he foresees what was later called "togetherness" in the family in American society, which he had always argued placed the young in a dominant position and short-circuited mature conversation and mature attitudes in the drawing-room.

11 WASHINGTON

HJ paid a rapid visit to Washington immediately after his first lecture in Philadelphia. His friend, John Hay, Secretary of State, invited him to join in the round of festivities marking the impending inaugural of Theodore Roosevelt's second term of office. James stayed with his old friend Henry Adams. He found in the capital his old friend, Jules Jusserand, whom he had known in London in the 1880s and '90s, now French ambassador to the United States. With friends in high places, HJ had easy access to official Washington. In 1881 he had chatted with President Chester Arthur in the home of Secretary of State James G. Blaine, and had enjoyed Washington gossip at the tea-table of "Clover" Adams, a few years before her untimely death. Now he was convoyed to the White House to dine with 100 guests after the annual diplomatic reception. Teddy Roosevelt, who would later call HJ a "snob," was cordiality itself, and placed the novelist at his own table (there were small tables of eight). Augustus Saint-Gaudens and HJ's friend John La Farge were also present that evening, and HJ's letters reflect large amusement at Roosevelt's trying to establish a "court." On the evening of 11 January HJ attended a dinner of the American Institute of Architects, representing "literature" at this occasion. John La Farge spoke, as did Jusserand, Elihu Root, and Justice Harlan. HJ felt that "the Eagle screamed in the speeches." He found the evening "quaint and queer." (MS Harvard) During HJ's stay in the capitol Senator Cabot Lodge took the novelist to visit the Senate.

HJ remained in Washington one week. He returned in late April for a further stay.

12–14 RICHMOND, CHARLESTON, FLORIDA

The cold spell in the North made HJ hasten his trip southward. He arrived in Richmond, 1 February 1905. The cold spell extended to the South, however, and he found the place under snow. He had never been in the South; and he came to it with little sense of the historical interval between his own Civil War youth and the four decades that had elapsed.

373.   James Ford Rhodes, American historian (1848–1927). HJ had been reading some of the volumes of his major work, *History of the U.S. From the Compromise of 1850*, six of its seven volumes having appeared at the time of HJ's American tour.

395.   HJ arrived in Charleston on 10 February and found balmier weather. He was met by Owen Wister, who wanted to "show" it to HJ, and the novelist did indeed have a pleasant visit. "I delighted in being with him," he said of his company. (MS Congress)

396.   The ambiguous passage on this page about HJ's stay in "a castle of enchantment" in the mountains of North Carolina refers to his visit, between his departure from Richmond and his arrival in Charleston, to the George Vanderbilt Biltmore House, at Biltmore, North Carolina. Here James spent six chilly days, detained by a sudden attack of gout. "I lately spent a week of all but polar rigour at the high-perched Biltmore, in North Carolina, the extraordinary colossal French château of George Vanderbilt in the said N. C. mountains–the house 2500 feet in air, and a thing of the high Rothschild manner, but of a size to contain two or three Mentmores and a Waddesdon, the *gageure* of an imperfectly aesthetic young billionaire." (HJ to Edmund Gosse, MS Congress).

403.   The friend alluded to here is Owen Wister.

410.   HJ's reference to the southern descent of his Northern companion is an allusion to the fact that Owen Wister's mother, Sarah Wister, was the daughter of the Southern slave owner Pierce Butler and of Fanny Kemble, the English actress who wrote *Journal of a Residence on a Georgia Plantation* (1863).

416.   HJ's mention of "Lady Baltimore" cake may be an oblique way of mentioning Owen Wister's romantic novel of life in Charleston, *Lady Baltimore*, published in 1906, a year before *The American Scene*.

419.   The reference to the Southern cemetery and the curious association of Venice may be a recall of HJ's old friend Con-

stance Fenimore Woolson (1840–1894), who had written one of the best-known stories about Civil War cemeteries in the South, "Rodman the Keeper," and who had died in Venice in 1894. Miss Woolson was one of the first American writers to picture the post-Civil-War world in her Southern sketches, and HJ had paid tribute to them in his essay on her work included in *Partial Portraits* (1888). See also the chapters devoted to the friendship between Miss Woolson and Henry James in *The Conquest of London* and *The Middle Years* (New York and London, 1962, 1963).

432–35. HJ went to Jacksonville from Charleston 12 February "straight into the real, though the as yet so dreary South." (To Mrs. WJ, MS Harvard) The next day he reached Palm Beach, where he stayed at The Breakers for five days, going thence to St. Augustine, where he was at the Hotel Ponce de Leon. He returned to Cambridge 24 February 1905. "Florida is a fearful fraud." (To Mrs. Jones, MS Harvard)

CHRONOLOGY AND ITINERARY OF
HENRY JAMES'S AMERICAN VISIT 1904–1905

1904

24 August	HJ sails on *Kaiser Wilhelm II* for New York.
30 August	Lands at Hoboken, New Jersey. Passes through New York and spends 36 hours at Deal Beach, New Jersey.
3–17 September	Arrives at Chocorua, New Hampshire, to stay with William James.
17 September–16 October	At 95 Irving Street, Cambridge; makes brief trip to Jackson, New Hampshire, Cotuit, Massachusetts, Salisbury, Connecticut, at end of September.
17–31 October	The Mount, Lenox, Massachusetts, visiting Edith Wharton.

1 November–4 December	In Cambridge. In mid-November visits Newport.
6–10 December	In New York at 21 East 11th Street, home of Mrs. Cadwalader Jones.
11–21 December	In Cambridge and Boston.

1905

21 December–9 January	In New York, 21 East 11th Street, and from 3 January to 9 January at Mrs. Wharton's, 884 Park Avenue.
9–10 January	In Philadelphia, lectures to Contemporary Club on Balzac.
11–18 January	In Washington, 1603 H Street. Henry Adams's.
19–30 January	Repeats lectures at Bryn Mawr and visits Mrs. Wister and Dr. White in Philadelphia.
1–3 February	Jefferson Hotel, Richmond, Virginia.
4–9 February	Biltmore House, Biltmore, North Carolina, residence of the George Vanderbilts.
10–12 February	Charleston Hotel, Charleston, South Carolina.
13–14 February	Jacksonville, Florida.
15–17 February	The Breakers, Palm Beach, Florida.
18–21 February	Hotel Ponce de Leon, St. Augustine, Florida.
22 February	In Philadelphia at Dr. J. W. White's, 1810 Rittenhouse Square.
23 February	New York, Manhattan Hotel.

24 February–5 March	95 Irving Street, Cambridge.
6–9 March	Washington Hotel, St. Louis. Lectures March 7 to Contemporary Club.
10–13 March	In Winnetka, Illinois, at home of the George Higginsons. Lectures in Chicago to 20th Century Club 10 March, and Fortnightly Club 11 March.
13–16 March	At University Club, Chicago. Lectures at Notre Dame 14 March in afternoon and at Catholic Convent School in evening.
17–18 March	Indianapolis for combined lecture to three clubs: Indiana Literary, Contemporary, and Irvington Athenaeum.
19–20 March	University Club, Chicago.
20–23 March	En route to Los Angeles.
24–28 March	Hotel Van Nuys, Los Angeles.
29 March–5 April	Hotel del Coronado, San Diego.
6 April	Lectures in Los Angeles.
10 April	Hotel del Monte, Monterey.
11–15 April	St. Dunstan's, San Francisco. Lectures at "Bohemian Club."
17 April	The Portland Hotel, Portland, Oregon.
18–20 April	University Club, Seattle.
24 April	Annex Hotel, Chicago.
27 April	New York, 21 East 11th Street, for lecture.
29 April	600 I Street, Washington, for lecture; goes thence to Smith College, Northampton, also for lecture.
4 May	Boston, Brunswick Hotel.
6–22 May	21 West 11th Street, New York.

23 May	Boston, Brunswick Hotel. Lectures in Sanders Theater, Harvard.
1–8 June	36 West 10th Street, New York, guest of Lawrence Godkin.
8 June	Speaks on "The Question of Our Speech" at Bryn Mawr commencement.
9 June	Hotel Chelsea, Atlantic City.
10–11 June	Lectures in Baltimore, staying at Hotel Belvedere.
14–15 June	Visits Mrs. Wister at Butler Place in Philadelphia.
17 June	Visits W. D. Howells at Kittery Point, Maine.
20 June	Revisits Newport.
25–29 June	95 Irving Street, Cambridge.
30 June–1 July	Revisits Mrs. Wharton at The Mount, Lenox; takes long motor drive, visiting at Ashfield, Massachusetts, his old friend Charles Eliot Norton.
2–4 July	95 Irving Street, Cambridge.
5 July	Sails on *Cunarder Ivernia* for England, arriving at Liverpool 13 July.

INDEX